D1529036

ATLANTIC STUDIES ON SOCIETY IN CHANGE

NO. 133

Editor-in-Chief, Béla K. Király

Associate Editor-in-Chief, Kenneth Murphy

Editor, László Veszprémy

HUNGARY IN THE AGE OF THE TWO WORLD WARS 1914–1945

Mária Ormos

WITHDRAWN

Translated by Brian McLean
Copyedited by Matthew Suff
Typeset by Andrea T. Kulcsár

Social Science Monographs, Boulder, Colorado
Atlantic Research and Publications, Inc.

Highland Lakes, New Jersey

Distributed by Columbia University Press, New York
2007

EAST EUROPEAN MONOGRAPHS, NO. DCCXXIII

Publication of the Hungarian Academy of Sciences

The publication of this volume was made possible by grants from the
National Cultural Found
and the Hungarian Institute of International Affairs

Nemzeti Kulturális Alap

Magyar Külügyi Intézet
Hungarian Institute of International Affairs

ISBN 978-0-88033-621-5
Library of Congress Catalog Card Number 2007933053

Printed in Hungary

Table of Contents

Preface to the Series

The present volume is a component of a series that is intended to present a comprehensive survey of the many aspects of East Central European society. The books in this series deal with peoples whose homelands lie between the Germans to the west, the Russians, Ukrainians and Belorussians to the east, and the Mediterranean and Adriatic seas to the south. They constitute a particular civilization, one that is at once an integral part of Europe, yet substantially different from the West. The area is characterized by a rich diversity of languages, religions and governments. The study of this complex area demands a multidisciplinary approach, and, accordingly, our contributors to the series represent several academic disciplines. They have been drawn from universities and other scholarly institutions in the United States and Western Europe, as well as East Central Europe.

The editor-in-chief is responsible for ensuring the comprehensiveness, cohesion, internal balance, and scholarly quality of the series he has launched. He cheerfully accept these responsibilities and intends this work to be neither justification nor condemnation of the policies, attitudes, and activities of any person involved. At the same time, because the contributors represent so many different disciplines, interpretations, and schools of thought, our policy in this, as in the past and future volumes, is to present their contributions without major modifications.

The author of the present volume is a distinguished historian, member of the Hungarian Academy of Sciences and head of the doctoral training program in the 19th and 20th century Hungarian and European history.

Budapest, June 4, 2007

Béla K. Király
Editor-in-Chief

INTRODUCTION

The two world wars and the worldwide economic crisis between them caused disruption in all parts of the world and brought great changes in people's lives. Both the successive massacres of those wars, costing millions of lives, and the long years of insecurity, hunger and destitution for millions during the Depression were indications that there was some grave disorder underlying the structures of European societies. Only by the use of force could the inherited system of state and political principles and tools still be applied; a chasm had opened up between reality and the way in which reality was interpreted.

Also upset after 1918 was the familiar power system in Europe and the balance of power that had applied there after a fashion. The eastern half of the continent experienced something of a power vacuum, with Russia in a quarantine that was partly imposed from outside and partly self-imposed. The state known as Austria-Hungary had vanished from the map. Russia's place on the scales should have gone to the various small states, new or transformed, that lay in a band stretching from the Baltic to the Balkans, but that was precluded by opposing interests, disputes and antagonisms. Meanwhile, the center of economic power moved overseas to the United States, which repeatedly intervened in European countries financially, and thereby economically, although it would be another two decades before Washington assumed any political responsibility beyond the Americas.

The weakening of the eastern part of Europe automatically enhanced the economic, political and military importance of Germany. The truth was quite the opposite of what the German public imagined: the pressure from Britain and France on the one

1

hand and Russian power on the other ceased after the war, leaving Germany a chance to extend its influence through an open gateway to the east. An exceptional part in that was played by the breakup of its old ally, Austria-Hungary, for the Dual Monarchy had been at the same time an ally and an obstacle—a state whose interests Germany had to respect, if to a diminishing extent. This was much less the case with the small successor states into which Austria-Hungary was divided, yet Germany failed to seize that historic opportunity. Its policy-making passed in 1933 to a system and a leader that attached no importance to economic influence and sought at any price to gain territory for the "superior" Germanic peoples by confining or wholly or partly exterminating others. That policy of territorial expansion set Europe ablaze again, and with it most of the world, and led to an altered world system that was to last for 45 years. The East rose again, in power terms. The swath of territory between East and West fell into the lap of the Soviet Union. Altogether, that area was prevented from acting as a separate factor in power politics for almost 70 years.

This book examines how Hungary fared in that stormy period. It explores the forces that propelled Hungarian history, amidst hope and despair, independence and enfeeblement, democracy and dictatorship, relative development and decline. To what degree did the Hungarians determine their own destiny? How far was Hungary's history decided by its geographical position and Great Power interests and policies in the region? How far did its defenselessness extend and where did it begin? Wherein lies the Hungarians' responsibility for their own history? The scholarly findings of Hungarian historians in the last 10–15 years seem to have allowed a summary to be written and indeed made it necessary to do so.

Nevertheless, what is offered in this book is simply a comprehensible review, addressed to all those interested, notably history teachers, and students at home and abroad. Although the subject of the book is history between the two world wars from the signing of the peace treaty, attention has also been paid to some of the antecedent events. For a proper understanding calls also for an outline of the events of World War I and a consideration of two attempts to break out: the People's Republic hallmarked by Mihály Károlyi, and the Hungarian Soviet Republic associated with Béla Kun.

1. AN ANCIENT EMPIRE IN A MODERN WAR

1. The Outbreak of War

Empires, scholars argue, are bound after a longer or shorter phase of splendor to vanish without trace. Sooner or later their radiance is dulled by internal conflicts that leave them powerless even against relatively weak external attack. Indeed, some empires are known to have started to break up without any real outside attack at all, as if they had simply outlived themselves. It is questionable even whether the Habsburg Empire had shone at any time, but it seems fairly certain that it was very weak internally by the time of the strong external attack that finally swept it away. In fact, what was supporting it by then was that very threat from outside. This section disregards the intricate decision-making structure of the Empire. The object is simply to know whether the Hungarian leading strata played a part in the fateful decision to go to war, and if so to what extent, and whether, by that time, Hungary had even a minimal chance of staying out of it.

The formula of "punishing Serbia" was not a reflex reaction. Francis Ferdinand, heir apparent, and his wife Sophia Chotek were murdered by the Bosnian Serb student Gavrilo Princip on June 28, 1914, but Vienna presented its ultimatum to Serbia only on July 23—four weeks later. There had been a good deal of hesitation before the fatal move was made. After the war, it was repeatedly claimed in the victorious camp that the delay came because the reactionary, imperialist Hungarian politicians needed time to coerce more temperate leaders of the Dual Monarchy into making that move. One persistent view was that Vienna had been goaded into war by István Tisza, the Hungarian prime minister. This was far

4

from the truth. The roles were actually the reverse of that: belligerent Austrian circles had needed time to dispel Tisza's objections and anxieties.

The leading political circles of Hungary were against expanding the Slav-inhabited territory of the Empire, which they feared might jeopardize the Dual system. Dualism had brought about a shared Austro-Hungarian hegemony within the Empire, and Hungary's political elite would have nothing to do with "Trialism" or with extending the rights of Slav peoples living within the Empire,[1] because there was obviously more cake available if it was cut two ways, not three ways or four. Despite the warnings from the mid-nineteenth century onwards, from figures such as Miklós Wesselényi, István Széchenyi and Ferenc Deák, the leading political group in the period of Dualism had put off any moves to assuage the desires for greater rights and autonomy among the other nations (Slovaks and Croats) and part-nations (Romanians and Germans) on Hungarian soil. Nothing had changed in that regard by the time that war broke out. Tisza and his government also feared that an attack on Serbia might prompt a move by the Romanian army, at a time when the Romanian–Hungarian border was not seen as militarily secure at all. So Tisza even kept up his opposition to war for some time after Germany had committed itself to supporting Austria-Hungary.

But quibbling by the prime minister was not the only reason why Hungary played a minimal part in fomenting the war. Its inaction also derived from the Dualist structure, which gave Hungary a strong, sometimes decisive, voice in the Empire's domestic affairs, but no such say in foreign or military policy. Hungary's political leadership was largely sovereign in domestic matters—able, for instance, to block the introduction of universal male franchise, which had reached the other half of the Empire in December 1906. That omission had strong repercussions in the autumn of 1918, after the revolutionary events, when the country found itself without a legislative body on which a new political elite could rely even temporarily for continuity or for the purposes of laying the foundations of independent statehood.

Although successes had been scored in Hungarian policy—when the independence coalition took power against the royal will, for instance, or extension of Bohemian and Moravian rights had been forestalled—the Hungarians had scant influence on foreign affairs or the views of the army General Staff. There was no separate Hungarian apparatus for foreign affairs: no ministry, no diplomatic or consular corps, and so no diplomatic relations. This deficiency was very damaging in 1918 and for many years thereafter. With the army, the omelet comparison made by the British historian C. A. Macartney is an apt one: from the omelet that was the mixed-nationality army of the Dual Monarchy, you could not simply extract the eggs again. The armed forces of Austria-Hungary consisted of the Common Army, the Navy, the Hungarian *Honvédség* (National Defense Force), the Austrian *Landwehr*, and the General Levy. Only the Common Army had any military value in terms of strength, scope or equipment, as the fleet was dwarfed by those of the great maritime powers,[2] and the other bodies, including the *Honvédség*, were designed only "for support of the Common Army and for domestic defense." The act establishing the *Honvédség*[3] stated that it was to "join the common defense force as an auxiliary part."

So most of the Hungarian military force had no organization of its own, and the *Honvédség* had no General Staff to deal with strategy or related operative matters, or intelligence or counter-intelligence organization.[4] It also says much that the Common Army General Staff contained not one Hungarian officer, and very few Hungarians of German extraction or "aulic" Austrianized Hungarians held high military posts, the one exception being Miklós Horthy, who commanded the fleet for a short while. This truncation and lack of self-reliance in Hungary's armed forces likewise created great difficulties after the country became independent in 1918.

There was a further requirement for independent action by Hungary that was lacking. It had no currency of its own and so no monetary or financial policy.

Each of these circumstances separately, let alone together, would have sufficed to prevent a separate Hungarian decision about the war being made in 1914. The only part that the Hungarians ultimately had in the ultimatum was the action (or inaction) of István Tisza, who refrained from protesting against it at the July 19 meeting of the Common Council of Ministers. He simply wished that the ultimatum would not be one that its recipient could never accept and that it would state concurrently that Austria-Hungary had no territorial claims. The latter he obtained, the former not. On July 23, the Dual Monarchy took the first step towards self-annihilation and on July 28 the second, when the reply from the Serbian prime minister, Nikola Pašić, was declared to be unsatisfactory and war was declared on Serbia.

At this point it makes sense to ask whether Hungary and its policy could have stayed the hand of Field Marshal Franz Conrad von Hötzendorf, the deciding voice in the strategy of the General Staff. Could it have swayed the Vienna *Camarilla* to such an extent as to prevent the war breaking out, or might Hungary have stayed out of the war, at the expense of domestic tensions and strife, of course? Hardly. Such eventualities were ruled out (apart from by the factors already mentioned) by the character of the war, by Hungary's geopolitical position, and by the ethnic composition of the Hungarian state. It is worth noting also that the entire population of Hungary, bar a few pacifists, went happily to war. There again, did other peoples everywhere in Europe not do just the same?

"Punishing Serbia" was no more than an excuse, in terms of the world war. The real reasons were a mixture of traditional continental aspirations to power (involving the Franco-German border, the Polish–Baltic zone and the Balkans) and criteria concerned with retaining, extending and obtaining a new type of influence on a new worldwide or almost worldwide scale. Austria-Hungary was not directly concerned in Anglo-Franco-German antagonisms and was indifferent to questions of great trade routes and overseas colonial empires as well. However, the aspirations of the Russian Empire and its allies, Romania and Serbia, affected the whole Dual state, its Austrian half and (especially) Hungary. If Russia were to move against Austria, it could be expected to invade the Carpathians and move into the Polish lands or Hungary too, while its allies could be expected to do likewise if they could, as most of their territorial demands were on Hungary. The "Destroy Austria" of the Czecho-slovak foreign minister Edvard Beneš meant politically the breakup of the Empire, but territorially the destruction of Hungary most of all. The champion of the idea was Russia, and the Italian state had similar aspirations, although Italy's territorial ambitions affected Hungary only in Croatia. Hungary's position in this constellation of circumstances was set by the way in which it impinged on one of the focuses of power struggle and by the fact that only 54.5 percent of its inhabitants were Hungarian,[5] and so the territorial demands on it were to no small degree justified in ethnic terms. The war could not avoid Hungary and Hungary could not avoid the war.

However, Austria-Hungary in 1914 still had to reckon only with Serbia and Russia. The Romanian question remained open, and further agreements and negotiations could still have decided what Italy would do, deeply interested though it was in the region. Taken in order of time, four fronts developed on which the Hungarian armed forces played a significant role. Hungarian troops fought against Serbia and Russia in 1914, while the Italian front opened in the spring of 1915 and the Romanian one in 1916. However, three of those conflicts—on the Serbian, Russian and Romanian fronts—were concluded while the war was still going on: the Austro-Hungarian forces overran Serbia in 1916 as the remaining Serbian forces fled, and the Russian Bolsheviks and the Romanian government concluded armistices in 1917. However, in 1918 the Western Allies set up the *Armée d'Orient*, with its High Command in Salonica (Thessaloniki), to which reorganized Serbian units were also attached, and so the Serbian front reopened in principle in 1918, although the Allied forces met with practically no resistance in their advance. On November 9, 1918, Romania declared that it was renewing hostilities with Germany, although that could not be done against Austria-Hungary, as the latter had already concluded an armistice on November 3.

So Hungary in late 1917 and throughout 1918 fought only on the Italian front. There were no separate Hungarian maneuvers during the four years of war, and outstanding Hungarian military action occurred only on isolated occasions. The entire human potential of the Hungarian people took part in the struggles, and sacrifices were proportional. The soldiery did their duty, fighting the enemy without loathing them. They were taken prisoner, wounded, maimed or killed, or returned home to find unprecedented, unfathomable upheaval. Yet despite its full commitment of its human resources, this was not Hungary's war. From the Hungarian point of view, the war was both fatal and incomprehensible. No Hungarian military objectives were formulated, but the defeat, the objectives that others had formulated, and the conceptual changes among the decision-makers in the Allied camp led to a peace treaty that questioned the very grounds for the country's existence. So the war, in Hungarian eyes, was not only alien and incomprehensible, but tragic. "We sentient people," wrote one thinking person, "felt that this war meant the death of free Hungary. For if we won, we would come under German influence, and if we lost? ... A ghastly alternative..."

While the soldiers were fighting an embittered struggle or squatting in trenches unfit for human habitation, people on the home front suffered from a scarcity of breadwinners, frozen stocks, war loans, capped prices, rationing, and mounting supply shortages. Official communiqués reported ever more dead and missing.

It soon became apparent to attentive observers that this war differed from those before it. There was no winning it in a few heroic attacks and decisive battles. The miraculous weapons from which both sides were expecting rapid victory instead changed the war into slaughter, to be lost by the side that ran out of men and materials first. Although the art of war and the role of generalship did not cease, they were pushed into the background. Decisive importance passed to logistical considerations such as the organization of supplies, or equipment of the forces with arms, ammunition and clothes, speed, reliability of communications, technical reliability of links, the numerical size of states and armies, and the level of industrial and technical development. Only the side that gained superiority in these could win, which meant that the relations of power changed as well.

Notes

1. Psychologically, Hungary's leaders can hardly have grieved too deeply for an heir apparent known to be a committed advocate of "Trialism."
2. In world terms, it stood eighth in size.
3. XL/1868.
4. The Common Army had a pre-war peacetime strength of 500,000 and the *Honvédség* of 30,000; the war-footing strengths were 1,500,000 and 200,000 respectively.
5. According to 1910 census returns, discounting Croatia.

2. Changes in Power Relations and Objectives

Power relations and relative weights of nations changed over time in terms of military superiority. There had already been changes in 1914–1916, as further countries joined in the war—Turkey and Bulgaria, for instance, on one side and Italy and Romania on the other, but those decisive to the war and the future of Europe took place in 1917–1918. The decisive changes included the collapse of Russia and the entry of the United States into the war. Germany's scope was increased by the armistice and subsequent Peace Treaty of Brest-Litovsk, which decisively affected Germany's military objectives. On the other hand, the appearance of the United States and President Wilson had far-reaching effects on the chances and principles of the Allied and Associated Powers.

Radically new opportunities began to appear before the German Command in the spring of 1917. On March 12, revolution broke out in Russia, the Tsar resigned, and a provisional government took measures to introduce a bourgeois democratic state. This enormous change was obviously precipitated by Russia's military and economic exhaustion. Mobilization of the urban and rural poor reinforced political groups dissatisfied with the operation of the Tsarist system, which had been talking about reforms for some time, but which were studiously ignored by Tsar Nicholas II. Then came rumors of Tsarist feelers towards a separate peace, which prompted action by pro-Entente military leaders who still believed in victory. The new government continued to support the Entente politically, although many feared that the Russian army was showing signs of disintegration that nobody would be able to control.

The situation produced by the Russian Revolution almost certainly had something to do with the fact that US President Thomas Woodrow Wilson brought up the question of war and peace and managed to bring the United States into the war on April 6, while the longstanding German U-boat campaign, revived at the beginning of

1917, was presumably far less of a factor, if not simply a pretext. The great danger was that with the eastern front weakened, the Central Powers might swiftly conclude the hostilities in that region, turn their full strength on the Americans' Western allies, and win the war. Any German hegemony of that kind on the continent of Europe was diametrically opposed to US interests.

At that point, the time factor began to play an important part in the war. If the German war leaders managed to knock out Russia fast—fast enough to redeploy their forces in the west before most of the fresh, well-equipped American forces had reached the war zone, the game was won. That was precisely the thinking of Paul von Hindenburg, the German supreme commander, and he developed his strategy accordingly, but not consistently enough. On the western front 1917 was a year of relative calm and preparation, but in the east it was one of victory and armistice.

Kerensky, the Russian minister of defense, in conjunction with Brusilov, the commander-in-chief, planned the great attack in the direction of Lemberg (Lviv). This was begun by the Russian army on July 2, after heavy artillery preparation, but after Russian successes in the first few days, the attack collapsed. The combined forces of the Central Powers occupied Bukovina, and Germans were already in the Baltic by September. This defeat made it even more questionable whether Russia could continue the war. In the end it could not. On November 7, power was seized in Petrograd by a small group of Bolsheviks headed by Lenin, who sought peace at any price and could hardly do otherwise in the light of earlier promises to the masses.

At the end of October, success also crowned the strenuous efforts on the southwestern front. The attack with German reinforcements began against the Italian forces in the Caporetto region on October 24, which was recorded as a black day in the annals of the Italian army. Although the troops were not prepared for giving chase to the enemy, a great victory was won, with about 300,000

Italian soldiers being taken prisoner. So things stood quite well for the Central Powers at the end of 1917.

But relations among the Central Powers had deteriorated. Emperor Francis Joseph I, who died on November 21, 1916, after a reign of almost 60 years, was succeeded by Charles I (Charles IV as King of Hungary),[1] who was suspect to the Germans from the outset. Charles had taken no part in the beginning of the war and did not believe in it. His consort, Zita of Bourbon-Parma, was expressly hostile to the Germans. Charles's two brothers, Xavier and Sixtus, had extensive Entente connections, especially among the Belgians and French. Charles managed in March 1917 to send a letter to the president of the French Republic through Sixtus, expressing a desire for peace and a willingness to recognize French claims to Alsace and Lorraine. (There was some justice in a later German quip about the Austrian Emperor ceding territories that did not belong to him in the first place.)

Although that letter and subsequent peace talks remained secret for the time being, Vienna and the Emperor caused mounting annoyance to the Germans. They became irreconcilable over the Polish question, where Germany sought full influence over a reunited Poland and Vienna would have liked to incorporate Poland and the Habsburg crown in some form. Germany and Austria-Hungary were also at loggerheads over the impending peace treaty with Romania. Again the Germans sought to exert primary influence and would not countenance the idea of the dynasty remaining on the throne there, having once sided with the Entente. Charles opposed Germany's plans vehemently and favored moderation towards Romania in other regards as well. An even more heated Austro-German dispute arose at the peace negotiations at Brest-Litovsk, with a Soviet delegation headed by Leon Trotsky. The Austrian delegation did not want to put the chance of peace at risk by advancing what they saw as inordinate German demands in the Baltic. When Trotsky decided to break off the talks after all and the

Germans advanced into Belorussian and Ukrainian territory, the Austro-Hungarian troops did not follow them. Nor did they do so when the Germans embarked on further military operations, after the peace was signed on March 3, 1918, and advanced as far as the Caucasus.

A bitter row broke out in March 1918, when the French government published the letter that Charles had written a year earlier. The reputation of Charles and Vienna in German eyes fell to an all-time low, and Vienna had to consider before every move whether it would expose the country to German occupation or not.

Meanwhile, the Germans had initiated negotiations designed to drive Austria-Hungary into an economic and military union in which Germany was clearly to be the decisive component. These negotiations took place over the heads of the Hungarian government, although when this or that leaked out, or some decision was made public, strong hostility was expressed in Budapest, from opposition and government parties alike. Yet the Austrian ministers could not resist the German pressure for long, and had to agree to both plans. Even they were unaware of the plans being made by the German military under von Hindenburg and Ludendorff[2] for a German sphere of influence to include not only Poland and Romania, but the Balkans, the Baltic and Ukraine, with military bases in Russia, even along its southern border. This was the new *Mitteleuropa* plan, defining the prospects for the Danube basin and Hungary should Germany win the war.

But revising war plans was not the sole prerogative of the Germans in late 1917 and early 1918. The Allied and Associated Powers also had to address the future of the territories between the German and Russian lines after the Bolsheviks took power and displayed plans for intervention and expansion. It was clear that Poland had to be supported, but debates on the future of Austria-Hungary continued for some time. Initially it had seemed as if British and French groups backing and hastening a complete breakup of the Empire would triumph, but at this point the process was temporarily stalled, as counterarguments were advanced in political and economic circles. Many considered that Austria-Hungary could play an important role in the European balance of power and in containing the Bolshevik ideas that were a threat from Russia, and would be better at doing it than any collection of small states succeeding it. Others emphasized the point that for this state to vanish would bring after it the collapse of an important economic unit, causing damage to its constituent parts and to the European economy as a whole.

At this point, US President Wilson presented his peace program of 14 Points, with goals that included transforming Austria-Hungary according to principles of internal autonomy. The president continued in subsequent statements to support national self-determination, an end to diplomatic secrecy, and recognition and observance of basic democratic principles. Around that time, the British prime minister, David Lloyd George, made a speech plainly stating that the Allied and Associated Powers had no demands to make against Austria-Hungary. In early 1918, the American Commission to Negotiate Peace devised proposals to transform the Dual Monarchy after the war into a federation of six autonomous territories with equal rights—quite favorable to Hungary compared with its situation at the time, and extremely favorable compared with what ultimately happened.

But events took a new turn in the spring of 1918. One reason was the fact that Austria-Hungary proved to be unable to leave its alliance. The "Sixtus Scandal" meant that Emperor Charles had to humble himself before the Germans, while the Czechs and South Slavs stepped up their propaganda, and the Italian government (with its direct interest in the fall of Austria) initiated a Congress of Oppressed Austrian Nationalities in Rome, where delegates proclaimed the right of self-determination for nations on April 8. At the end of May, the US secretary of state, Robert Lansing, arrived in

Europe to recommend to the British and French governments that they recognize the rights of the Polish, Czech and Slovak, and South Slav peoples to secede and combine.[3] It was almost certainly exiled Polish and Czech politicians who convinced the US president of the need for this. So the spring and summer of 1918 brought the first fruits of propaganda that had been conducted for some years, without any compensatory effort coming from the Austrian or Hungarian side. There was no Hungarian political group in exile, and Hungarian politicians had no access to the Allied governments, and so Hungarian arguments were not presented during the discussions that prepared for the end of the war, an omission that can certainly be blamed on leading circles in Hungary.

At the beginning of June, the representatives of the Great Powers unanimously agreed in Paris that the Poles and the Czechs and Slovaks had the right to secession and independence. A similar statement about the South Slavs was made only by the United States, due to objections by Italy. In fact, it became clear from the succession of statements by the British, French and Americans that Hungary would lose its northern and southern territories if the Central Powers were defeated, while the Romanian treaty with Germany meant that the secret agreement with Bucharest left the question of Transylvania open for the time being.

Notes

1. According to the numbering of Hungary's kings, Charles III had been the Holy Roman Emperor Charles VI, but the new King Charles IV was only the first Emperor of Austria of that name.
2. Erich Ludendorff was the chief of General Staff.
3. Romania was not mentioned in the discussions, as it had signed a peace treaty with the Central Powers on May 7, although it was later stressed in Bucharest that the document had never received the king's assent.

3. The Endgame

The German chiefs of staff proved to have been wrong in expecting 1918 to bring a victorious offensive on the western front. One factor against them was the entry of fresh US forces into the battle, and another the large, well-armed and intact German forces tied down in the vast occupation zones of the east. The Germans had won more than they could cope with in Russia, while the Austrian Command shrank from any attack because of the state that the army and hinterland were in. And only the Italian front remained as a possibility once the peace treaties with Russia and Romania had been signed and Serbia, Montenegro and Albania occupied by the Entente. In the end, Vienna yielded to German demands and agreed to a suicidal attack down a bare, steep hillside on better-equipped Italian forces backed by British and French troops. This attack on the 150-kilometer-long front on June 15 had collapsed by June 20. Another attempt, similarly unsuccessful, was followed on October 24 by an Italian offensive that ended all Austro-Hungarian resistance four days later. There were no further obstacles in the path of the Italian army. It is unclear why General Armando Diaz halted his troops instead of advancing onto Vienna, which he could have done.

The Entente Eastern Command, based in Salonica, also went into action on September 15, when the so-called Eastern Army of mainly French and Serbian troops under General Louis Franchet d'Espérey moved northwest, and British forces under General George Milne advanced against Bulgaria and Turkey, which rapidly signed cease-fire agreements, on September 29 and 30 respectively. This opened up the way to the Black Sea and Romania. The Franco-Serbian force, meanwhile, advanced more slowly, reaching Skopje at the end of September. The Eastern Army then divided, with French troops withdrawn from the command of Franchet d'Espérey being formed into a Danube Army under General Henri

17

Berthelot, to push forward through Bulgaria into Romania, bringing about a change of government in Bucharest and a declaration of
war on the Central Powers.[1]

By that time, the Austro-Hungarian army was already disinte-
grating. The symptoms included disproportionately frequent cases
of desertion, absence without leave, disobedience and mutiny.
Vienna had already written off the war by then and would have
liked to end it, but that did not prove to be simple to arrange. The
victors would not hear of a negotiated peace, and there was little
chance for the October 4 memorandum of Foreign Minister István
Burián, in which he called for negotiations based on Wilson's 14
Points, as Wilson, as seen already, had struck out the point covering the Dual Monarchy in May. On October 16, Emperor Charles
issued a manifesto announcing that the Austrian part of the Empire
would change into a federation based on far-reaching national
rights. This belated measure could not curb the secession movement, which had been organizing itself for some months, and did
not cover the Hungarian question at all. On the contrary, it accelerated the breakup, as did Wilson's reply on October 18 to Burián's
memorandum, informing him that the demand for autonomous
areas within the Empire no longer applied, as the Allied powers had
already recognized the right of the Slav people to statehood.

The first reactions to the two declarations came from German-
speaking members of the House of Deputies (*Abgeordnetenhaus*) in
Vienna. Meeting on October 21, they announced that the German-
speaking territories would secede from the Empire, and sought to
include the whole German-speaking area in the new state, including the Sudeten Germans of Bohemia. On the 27th, a new foreign
minister, Gyula Andrássy, sought a separate peace from the
Americans and recognized the rights of the Czechs, Slovaks and
South Slav peoples to self-determination. This statement also
proved to be belated, and to provide help to the political forces
seeking a break with the Dual Monarchy. On October 28–31 came
a rapid succession of events. The National Council in Prague

declared secession and the formation of an independent state, to which the Slovak National Council that had assembled in Túrócszentmárton (Martin) acceded. Secession was also declared by the Croatian and Slovenian deputies meeting in Zagreb. In Vienna, there were revolutionary stirrings and the German-speaking deputies declared themselves the provisional national assembly of German Austria. A revolution in Hungary brought the government of Count Mihály Károlyi to power.

The foundations of the new states began to be laid while the old one was still in existence with Emperor-King Charles at its head. Be that as it may, there were only moments available if an armistice were to be declared with Austria-Hungary as a state. Armistice committees were set up by the General Staff in early October, on the northwestern and southern fronts, but only the former received an offer. The terms were devised in Paris, and the document reached Diaz, the Italian commander-in-chief, on November 1. This stipulated a demarcation line that accorded with the promises that Italy had received in the secret Treaty of London. The negotiations were conducted by the Italian General Emilio De Bono with General Victor Weber, head of the Austro-Hungarian Armistice Commission. The armistice was signed on November 3 at the Villa Giusti, near Padua, and came into force at 15.00 on the 4th. A high proportion of the Austro-Hungarian forces, some 300,000 men, were taken prisoner of war after the signature. With the exception of a few intact units, most of the soldiers headed home in disorderly fashion. For the time being, there was no mention of the southern front, where Hungary was directly involved.[2]

Notes

1. Romania was also intended to play a role in future intervention against Soviet Russia.
2. A Serbian representative who complained about this was assured by representatives of the Great Powers that the armistice would allow the Allies to occupy the strategic points in Austria-Hungary.

2. NEITHER WAR NOR PEACE

1. The Aster Revolution

The war rapidly lost popularity in Hungary. Growing numbers of disabled veterans arrived home amidst constant reports of the dead and missing. About 3.4 million Hungarians had gone to war: some 531,000 lost their lives, another 500,000 were seriously injured, and over 833,000 were taken prisoner. There was a chronic labor shortage in villages and famine in cities. Refuges and soup kitchens could not cope with all the needy. The Central Powers had hardly managed to borrow enough from abroad to cover their war expenses, but they had raised huge amounts from their citizens and resorted to printing money. Now the war bonds people that had bought were becoming valueless. The currency—the crown—was shaken, and the ensuing devaluation could not be halted in Hungary until 1924. Meanwhile, the wartime Allied blockade continued after the armistice,[1] causing acute shortages of raw materials, especially coal, so that rail services could not be normalized or industrial capacity used to the full. Even deliveries from Germany stopped in the autumn of 1918. There was a prospect of mass unemployment.

The opposition inside and outside Parliament, having supported the military in 1914, soon began to claim the reward of universal suffrage.[2] The reputation of the political elite was shaken by blame for losing the war. On June 17, 1917, an electoral bloc was formed by Mihály Károlyi's Independence and '48 Party with Oszkár Jászi's Radicals, Vilmos Vázsonyi's Democrats and the Social Democratic Party of Hungary,[3] but only the first and third of these had even a modest representation in the lower house. By then, Károlyi was urging the earliest possible end to the war, and the

Social Democrats' congress in April had called for an immediate
peace without annexations or reparations. Despite every government precaution and countermeasure, there was a wave of strikes,
some economic in character, but many that were aimed at universal
franchise and an end to the war. The Dual Monarchy was collapsing as a Hungarian National Council convened on October 23–24,
with Károlyi in the chair. This institution, created much later than
needed, managed to consolidate as the one body offering hope to
the public. It could be expected to declare Hungary's independence,
provide the constitutional framework for an independent state, settle the land question, and introduce universal suffrage.

There was a prospect of fulfilling a century-old desire for full
state sovereignty, while renewing and modernizing the country's
political and social conditions, but behind these aspirations loomed
the danger that they would be accompanied by a dramatic decrease
in territory and population. Furthermore, the prospects for democratization were doubtful. "Embourgeoisement" of Hungarian society had begun quite late (in the years after the 1867 *Ausgleich* or
constitutional compact with Austria), and it had failed to spread
through the whole or even the majority of society, despite some
breakneck advances. Industrialization had been concentrated on the
capital and a few larger or smaller cities and belts of development,
leaving the peripheries unaffected, and involving agriculture only
to a small and uneven extent. Although Hungarian society and the
Hungarian political sphere had behaved in an open, receptive way
in the period of Dualism, causing substantial integration, the
economy and society with it had obviously split two ways. The new
sectors—industry, commerce and banking—and many modern services—the press, the entertainment industry, and so on—had
become dominated by the Jewish middle class, while the Gentile
economic elite remained tied to the soil and found it ever harder to
prosper. For the latter, the lines of escape were into the administration and the army. Even without the imminent national catastrophe,

this seemed obscure and uncertain to the coming generation, although the "old guard" kept its hold on politics, public administration and the armed forces for the time being.

A not inconsiderable proportion of the bourgeoisie and intelligentsia—partly older Hungarian intellectual families, and partly descendants of landowning families or noble families with small estates—supported the social changes, but remained largely unorganized politically. This non-Jewish stratum of bourgeoisie or those still undergoing "embourgeoisement" could not, then or later, become a decisive factor in the country. Its members could not exert themselves on the political scene and did not control the press. And as the great Jewish capitalists were also wary of any expressly political role, the bourgeoisie in general contributed only a pale tint to the political spectrum. They were prevented from becoming an integral force by their varying place and weight in the economy and society, while effective political intervention was forestalled by divisions of culture, history and outlook, above all between Jews and non-Jews. That was one reason why democratic and liberal ideas seemed, with a few exceptions, to be confined to the Jewish intelligentsia, while the "Hungarians" were grouped in an essentially conservative camp that was hard to define more closely. In the background stood a varied mass of people, exhausted and bewailing their human and material losses, the vast majority seeking land or an honest livelihood (pay and so on) and civil rights.

What emerges from all this is the absence of any extensive middle classes on which the democratic transformation of Hungary could rely, and of any influential and experienced parties. What parties there were most of the Hungarian elite viewed with suspicion, whereas those parties should have found a *modus vivendi* with the elite, to make up for their lack of support. Civil rights needed to be granted quickly, and above all, something should have been done about agriculture and the land question. The democratic republic had no long-term prospects without winning over the urban bourgeois or rural peasant classes and striking a compromise with the business elite. The instinct to avert danger was present in many strata and groups in society in the autumn of 1918, and that provided some chance of widening the base of support and reaching the necessary agreements. Even among fragments of the Hungarian armed forces, among landowners and even aristocrats and wealthy capitalists, there were many who became willing to support any government that averted the danger, or at least contained the risk. But the chance could only be seized via diplomatic success or effective military resistance. The support of the broad peasant masses might have been earned with a swift plan for land reform, and that of the urban working and other classes with a democratic move to widen the franchise.

Those were the social expectations and political conditions when the crowds on the Budapest streets forced the appointment of Mihály Károlyi as prime minister, on October 31, 1918. The Independence supporters were joined in the coalition government by Social Democrats and Radicals, while the National Council had a mandate to develop its own network and convene a Grand National Council to draw up a constitution.

But the People's Republic endorsed on November 15 and declared on November 16 was incapable of performing those tasks. It was prevented from doing so by outside military and diplomatic pressure, by administrative, economic and transport chaos at home, and by its own lack of political experience. The land measures and the electoral legislation were postponed. The institution of national councils fell foul of mistrust and differences among the parties, as did the prospect of a Grand National Council as a bridging institution to provide the new regime with legitimacy. The mistrust was particularly damaging in the military field. Some members of the government were averse to the old officers' corps, and so deployment of the remaining units and the formation of new ones were put off for months, although there was an urgent need for them for legitimate defense of assigned demarcation lines and for internal security reasons. Only in January 1919 did reorganization of the army begin under the direction of Vilmos Böhm, who paradoxically had to rely largely on the old officers' corps.

So the great popularity of Mihály Károlyi evaporated within a few weeks. Even in his own party, the "Red Count" was an original, an anomaly, and so it is hardly surprising to find that his party more or less abandoned their leader when the fever of revolution died down and unsolved or unsolvable problems had to be faced, meaning that Károlyi found himself in the political wilderness with only a handful of supporters. Coupled with that, the hopes of defending Hungary's territorial integrity soon proved to be illusory, and would not have been fulfilled even if a far better military policy had been followed. There are grounds for saying, incidentally, that anxiety over the territorial question and the military invasion that began in December and continued had the effect of paralyzing the government and Károlyi himself.

As for the Social Democratic Party, with its rock-solid base and dense network of branches, it was inundated with recruits, but its leaders became split intellectually into at least three camps, without any debate in the party or any organizational confirmation of the split. Only the intentions of the moderate believers in bourgeois democracy (Ernő Garami, Manó Buchinger, Jakab Weltner and Gyula Peidl) were known. It was quite unclear what the centrists (Zsigmond Kunfi, Vilmos Böhm, and so on) or the radical left-wingers (Béla Szántó, Béla Varga, József Pogány and Jenő Hamburger) wanted, or in some cases, what they were up to. It was as if the party's front line were advancing into battle blindfolded, without clarifying fully what position the party's governing body held.

All things considered, the bourgeois democratic coalition was like a ship without a keel, bobbing on the waves of a storm that might well capsize it. Indeed, signs of disorder and irregularity were increasing. The land reform was delayed and then postponed. That, coupled with the inadequacy or complete absence of law enforcement in many parts of the country, led to violent incidents, looting, arson and murder. The villages could have been a potential stabilizing force in the country, but they never gave their support to the bourgeois democratic administration. This was reflected politically in the fact that there were no contacts for a long time between the government and the Smallholders' Party.[4]

So the expectations behind the revolution were not met. Meanwhile, the army was breaking up, the country's territory being drastically reduced, and Hungary's forces suffering catastrophe at the fronts. Although some units arrived home in military order, many soldiers straggled back, especially to Budapest, to form idle crowds swelled by returning prisoners of war, although it was several years before all the latter were back.[5] The chaos was increased, not reduced, by a swift succession of ministers of defense. Two cardinal errors were made. The disciplined units were not retained, and in the feverish demobilization, the authorities failed to disarm the soldiers being discharged. The soldiers were not demobilized so much as scattered to the four winds. A hopeless tussle began between the army and the military council set up by the left-wing Social Democrats, with the army thwarted at every turn. By the end of the year, a million soldiers had been discharged in two months, which was tantamount to producing that number of unemployed or applicants for land. It was hardly surprising that some of these joined in provincial unrest in which country mansions were burned down, granaries and stores looted, and parish clerks and gendarmes attacked, while others hung about the capital, eagerly listening to any demagogue and ready to join any disturbance.

The cease-fire came on November 4, but the armistice concluded failed to define Hungary's territory. The government therefore conveyed to the Allies' Eastern Command a desire to negotiate, and when its commander-in-chief, General Louis Franchet d'Espérey, had received the terms for the southern front from Paris, he received a delegation headed by Mihály Károlyi. The scene at that meeting on November 7, often described and adopted as a grievance, certainly included insulting behavior by the victors' self-confident general, but there were encouraging signs as well. Above all, Károlyi was clearly the one prime minister with whom the official delegate of the victorious powers was prepared to negotiate personally, and that fact—as the British and Italians immediately protested—gave *de facto* recognition to his government. Furthermore, the general called on the Hungarians to rally round Károlyi, as the only man who could save the country. There was also some relief felt in the fact that strategic points in Hungary would be occupied by French troops, which seemed to mean that the armies of neighboring countries would not be allowed to invade.

After some hesitation, the Hungarian government decided to sign the military convention. This was done in Belgrade on November 13, on behalf of Hungary by Béla Linder, and on behalf of the Entente by General Paul-Prosper Henrys and Voivod Živojin Mišić. The convention drew the demarcation line above Beszterce (Bistriţa), Gyulafehérvár (Alba Iulia) and Déva (Deva), and below Arad, Makó and Szeged, and finally above Baja, Pécs and Barcs, after which it was to follow the River Dráva to the frontier.[6] It stated that the Allied and Associated Powers were entitled to occupy the strategic points in the country and use the country's land routes and waterways, and that the Hungarian army was obliged to disarm the German army returning home from the east that was commanded by General August Mackensen. The text contained the quotas of troops that could be kept under arms—six infantry and two cavalry divisions—and set certain delivery obligations. In fact Hungary, far from having eight divisions at the ready, could hardly have been said to have one.

Several sections of the convention's demarcation line were ethnically unfavorable—in the Székely Land, the Northwestern Banate, Northern Bácska and the Pécs/Baja/Komló triangle—but it could be seen just as a demarcation line. It could be hoped, as it was by many in Budapest, that the Hungarian government would have its say and put its arguments forward at the peace conference.

The war had been over for more than two weeks before the Allied and Associated Powers managed to smooth their differences over enough to open the peace conference at all. Meanwhile, every army had been using the time to improve its country's bargaining position as best it could. The carve-up of Hungary began at the beginning of December. The Belgrade Military Convention worked from the existing southern front line, disregarding the fact that Romania had become a combatant again since it was negotiated and taking less account still of the interests of the Czechoslovak state, which was just being shaped. That was a political question that the victors' politicians still judged in various different ways. The Belgrade Military Convention made up for these shortcomings to some extent, but it soon emerged that only Serbia was satisfied with it (the Kingdom of the Serbs, Croats and Slovenes had yet to be founded); the Czechs and Romanians would not resign themselves to the situation that it had created. Both had supporters in the Entente, which meant that their interests came to the fore and they were able to bury the convention.

In the final days of November and early days of December, the commander-in-chief of the Eastern Army received a dressing down from Paris. In the terminology of politicians from the victorious countries, Károlyi had changed from a Francophile politician into a treacherous imperialist. Mainly because of the claim that Romania was making on Transylvania, the French abandoned the idea of Hungary's strategic points being occupied by French troops. The military mission that had arrived in Budapest on November 25 and its head, Staff Colonel Fernand Vix, soon lost their original mission to prepare for French entry, and for want of anything else, Vix would wrangle with Hungarian representatives over some dereliction of duty or protest to his superiors about successive Czech, Romanian and Serbian infringements of the convention.

For the Czechs, Edvard Beneš, head of the émigré community, managed to persuade the French to issue a note calling on the Hungarian government to evacuate the northern Hungarian territories, more or less down to the line of the Danube. This was done despite the fact that Milan Hodza, the leading Slovak politician, had agreed on December 6 with Albert Bartha, the Hungarian minister of war, on a demarcation line that essentially followed the ethnic divide. Foreign Minister Beneš promptly repudiated the moderate Slovak negotiator and demanded that the Hungarians evacuate a much larger area. This was done, and on December 19, Georges Clemenceau, the French prime minister and minister of war, due soon to chair the peace conference, sent out French staff to draw the line. Vix protested against this, citing the Belgrade Convention, but to no avail, and on December 23, he handed the note to the Hungarian government.

By this time the eastern front was in motion as well. The Romanians made three advances. In November 1918, the army pressed forward to the demarcation line decided at the Belgrade Convention. A second wave of advance, with no legal foundation, began on December 15 and brought the Romanians up to the Szatmárnémeti (Satu Mare)–Kolozsvár (Cluj)–Déva (Deva) line. Some French officers in the area tried to halt the attack and prevent the capture of Kolozsvár, but it ensued on December 24. Despite subsequent talks, the Romanian forces started a third advance on January 15, 1919, but this time they met resistance and were temporarily halted. Certain French officers stationed in Romania blamed Vix for this, asserting that he had encouraged the Hungarians to resist a Romanian army that was under the control of French officers.[7]

By then it was clear that the Romanian army was determined to reach the western line of the territory promised to Romania in the secret treaty. On January 28, it reached the Máramarossziget (Sighetu Marmației)–Nagybánya (Baia Mare)–Zilah (Zalău)–Csucsa (Ciucea)–Zám (Zam) line, but there the front froze for about three months. All this occurred essentially without the Hungarian state putting up any resistance. An exception was the military resistance in the last stage on the Csucsa section, which was a factor behind the decision of the Romanian General Staff to stop any further advance.

In January 1919 Hungary's territory shrank to Transdanubia, the Danube–Tisza area, Subcarpathia and the Great Plain, which had serious consequences in addition to its ethnic and territorial effects. Refugees began to arrive in the straitened territory in huge numbers, the economic situation worsened, and the government progressively lost its support in society. There was an end to the accidental chance referred to earlier.

Flooding in from the lost regions of Transylvania, the Uplands, the Banate and Bácska into the remaining larger towns, especially the capital, came Hungarian landowners, officials, teachers and postmen, people whose property the new state was threatening to expropriate or had already done so, who had lost their jobs, their sources of livelihood, or simply did not wish to become citizens of an alien state. They joined with the returning prisoners of war, discharged officers and soldiers, and the army of unemployed to form a refugee mass that turned Budapest into a gathering place of the poor, the crippled and the bereft.

Má

Or

</

Notes

1. This was lifted in May 1919 for Austria, but only at the end of the year for Hungary, although Italy began to break the embargo regularly in May.
2. The struggle for universal suffrage in Hungary had become strong in 1907 and led to several huge demonstrations before the war.
3. The *Függetlenségi és 48-as Párt, Radikális Párt, Demokrata Párt* and *Magyarországi Szociáldemokrata Párt* respectively. Károlyi's party dated from July 17, 1916, when he and 25 others left the Independence Party.
4. *Kisgazdapárt.*
5. The Soviet government applied political criteria to the prisoner-of-war question. Initially, groups could return only if they were thought capable of revolutionary activity; most Hungarian captives were caught up in the civil war. Later prisoners, especially officers, were treated as hostages, to press demands against the Hungarian state— a method first used when Hungary's Berinkey government arrested Béla Kun and his associates.
6. The Serbian army soon stepped over the line to occupy the Muraköz (Međimure) district and Muraszombat (Murska Sobota), Letenye and some other places in the Murántúl (Prekmurje).
7. The campaign was led by General Petin, who listed supposed anti-Romanian acts by Vix in a lengthy memorandum.

2. Crisis and an Attempt at Stabilization

The occupations of territory, some authorized by the victors, some arbitrary, had grave domestic political consequences. As fast as opposition prestige had grown in the last months of the war, especially the personal popularity of Mihály Károlyi, it now shrank before the unresolved domestic issues, diplomatic defeats, and loss of the majority of the country.

Government and country divided politically at the end of 1918. The crisis in the government began with the dismissal of Albert Bartha as minister of defense, with which two ministers of Károlyi's party, Tivadar Batthyány and Márton Lovászy, disagreed. Their resignation initiated a process of disintegration in the governing party that later caused a split. Károlyi and a group that had become tiny were weakened within the government as well. Meanwhile, the Hungarian Social Democratic Party, uncertain in its leadership and confused in its policies, faced a new challenge. Among the returnees from Russia in November 1918 was a group of prisoners selected by the Bolsheviks, who had chosen while in prison to follow the banner of communism. The decisive personality among them was Béla Kun, a former Social Democratic journalist. After a short period of orientation, the group reached agreement with a few former members of the Social Democratic Party who had been expelled for leftism and with some other figures at home (among them such members of the intelligentsia as György Lukács) and established the Communist Party of Hungary.[1] The appearance of a radical revolutionary party backed by the success of the Russian Bolsheviks provided a center for the Social Democratic left wing; there was no telling how far sympathy for it had spread within the party.

Meanwhile, Tivadar Batthyány, having left the government, was striving to form a bourgeois coalition, in which the Independents would have been joined by the Smallholders' Party, relying on bourgeois and petit-bourgeois Christian Social and small landowner support. Its prime minister designate was Márton Lovászy.[2] Károlyi, however, hesitated about the coalition, and Lovászy failed to receive sufficient support in Entente circles, in practice from the Italian side. The crisis was finally resolved when the Károlyi-led government resigned and the executive of the National Council elected Károlyi as provisional president of the People's Republic (which it could equally as well have done at the beginning of November). Dénes Berinkey formed a government (on January 11) with four Social Democrats instead of two, and István Nagyatádi Szabó representing the Smallholders, but Oszkár Jászi was left out.

The ensuing efforts at stabilization were much impeded by the economic conditions, as well as the earlier problems. On January 1, 1919, the Austro-Hungarian Bank[3] ceased to issue money for Hungary, and money-related matters remained chaotic for some time. The Hungarian state began to print what became known as "white money," with the accustomed depiction of the crown on one side and the other side blank, but the public were suspicious of it. State revenues were lost and the coffers were emptied. Increasing amounts went on unemployment benefit, discharge gratuities to soldiers, support for the disabled, and other welfare spending. Inflation accelerated. Harvest prospects were poor, as many places had not done their sowing during the autumn upheavals. Wages rose, but their real value declined, and there was hardly anything to buy in any case. The misery of the public was increased by the appearance in the winter of Spanish influenza, a highly dangerous, unknown strain that claimed thousands of weakened victims.

One aspect of the stabilization was the fact that Vilmos Böhm, the new minister of defense, set about to restore the army, surrounding himself with trained regular army officers for the purpose. He managed to obtain some disciplined units, including the Danube Guard and a unit comprising the remnants of the Székely forces, described variously as a detachment or a division. Another sign of stabilization was the fact that the government acted against the extremists on the right and on the left. Among the bodies disbanded was the Hungarian National Defense Association (MOVE),[4] which had formed in mid-November 1918 as a democratic, pro-republican organization, but veered sharply to the right in January 1919 when Captain Gyula Gömbös was elected as its president. Thereafter, the leaders and some of the membership began toying with the idea of overthrowing the existing authorities and introducing a dictatorship. The government also moved against the Society of Awakening Hungarians (ÉME),[5] whose ambition was to organize a broad public movement on a nationalist basis.

A sharp attack was also launched against the communist movement, led by the Social Democratic ministers in January–February 1919. On January 28, the Central Workers' Council passed a motion expelling communists from the trade unions. A few days later, the government took over the headquarters of the Communist Party, and the idea was mooted at the government meeting on February 18 of outlawing the party altogether. On February 20, a serious atrocity took place outside the offices of *Népszava*, the Social Democratic Party newspaper, when armed protesters roused by the communist leaders attempted to break into the building, and several police and workers' guards were killed. This produced outrage in the Budapest working class, expressed in a huge anti-communist demonstration.[6] The government then ordered the arrest of the communist leaders, which the police carried out on February 22. The police avenged the deaths of their comrades on Béla Kun, the communist leader. A report of his beating in the evening newspaper *Est* sparked efforts to free the communists and some pro-communist demonstrations.[7] Although news reports and estimates at the time suggest that these fell short of the numbers mobilized by the Social Democrats by a factor of ten, the change of mood on the streets created a poor impression, with Béla

Kun suddenly put forward as a hero and a victim. Furthermore, a protest about the treatment of the communist leaders came from Moscow, which threatened to suspend the return of Hungarian prisoners of war.[8] This all led to the government ordering lenient treatment for the communist prisoners. Visitors could come and go at the Transit Prison in Budapest.

Yet the government curbed the extremist movements, and further stability seemed to come with the land reform and an electoral measure. Elections were announced for April 13.[9] It then emerged that some Social Democrats, whose party had campaigned for decades for a universal franchise and secret voting, were daunted by the not improbable prospect of failing to gain an absolute majority. There was certainly a chance that fair elections would bring gains for the Smallholders and Christian Socials, and even some seats for the Communists. But the Social Democrats had no cause for serious concern, first of all because the previous governing party, National Labor, and the great opposition Independent group had fragmented, while the new groupings had yet to show significant gains. The one who could really fear the elections was Mihály Károlyi. Realizing that his tiny party had no prospects, he envisaged running as a coalition with the Smallholders' Party led by István Nagyatádi Szabó.[10] Amidst these fears and guesses and electoral preparations, news reached Budapest of another note prepared for the forthcoming peace conference. This became known as the Vix Note.

Notes

1. *Magyarországi Kommunista Párt.*
2. Lovászy was editor-in-chief of *Magyarország.* He later featured in the Friedrich government, then settled in Vienna and edited the newspaper *Jövő.*
3. *Osztrák-Magyar Bank Rt.*
4. *Magyar Országos Véderő Egylet.*

5. *Ébredő Magyarok Egyesülete.*
6. An estimated 150,000 came out on the streets, according to the Social Democrats.
7. These involved a few thousand people.
8. The Soviets later used the method widely against other governments. In Hungary's case, it meant that most Communist leaders still in Hungary after the collapse of the Hungarian Soviet Republic were allowed to go to Moscow, along with others already in exile in Vienna.
9. Other probable factors behind this were the fact that Austria had managed to hold elections without great difficulty and the fact that the Hungarian government was being encouraged in Entente circles to do the same.
10. In Károlyi's view, the two parties would have gained 25–30 percent of the vote and the Social Democrats an estimated 55 percent.

3. The Note from the Peace Conference and Its Consequences

Mihály Károlyi, in his short period in government, altered the orientation of his foreign policy twice. He started with a "Wilsonite" pro-French line, but, finding that it led him nowhere, he turned towards Italy, and then, when that attempt failed as well, directed his attention to Soviet Russia.[1] The last possibility was beginning to interest one or two of the Social Democrats as well. That was the position in February and March 1919, when the conference arrived at a new decision about Hungary.

On February 26, the Supreme Council of the Paris Peace Conference decided to establish a neutral zone between the Romanians and the Hungarians, to be guarded and controlled by Entente military forces. The decision had been reached with difficulty against opposition from the American delegation, but it eventually proved to be possible to disarm Charles Seymour, chief of the Austro-Hungarian division of the US Commission to Negotiate Peace, by arguing that the Poles of Lemberg (Lviv), under threat ostensibly from the Bolsheviks but in fact from the Ukrainian nationalist forces, could only be helped by the Romanians if the latter were free to use the Arad–Nagyvárad (Oradea)–Szatmárnémeti railway.[2] This was precisely the line that the French delegation wanted to see as the Hungarian–Romanian border, and it was designated by the Supreme Council on February 26 as the eastern limit of the neutral zone.

The news reached Budapest well before the official announcement of the decision. The draft being prepared was mentioned by several Entente officers, and Böhm stated in a reply to General Henri Ange Alfred de Gondrecourt[3] that the Hungarian government could hardly meet the demands, and if it resigned, there would be no force left in the country capable of preventing a "Bolshevik turn." Debate on the tasks might have begun in the Hungarian government at that time but it is not known that it did so.

On the morning of March 20, Vix, accompanied by several members of the mission, handed the note to Károlyi, who received him in the presence of several government members. There are two disparate accounts known of this short meeting. Károlyi recalled that he immediately said no to the note, but Vix, in a telegram sent that day, stated that Károlyi had said "The Hungarian government will formally protest, but it inclines towards the conference decision." Then (again according to Vix) Böhm initiated a political debate that Vix did not wish to countenance, and so the scene ended with Károlyi's promise of a government reply on the following day.

There are several further signs that Károlyi was still not decided, which is to say that that he could not have given a categorical "no" on the morning of the 20th.[4] Everything points to the fact that Károlyi was seeking a way out on March 20–21 and had not yet ruled out accepting the note. But some of the Social Democrats in the government rejected the note out of hand.

The decision was taken not by Károlyi, but by some of the Social Democratic leaders, presumably a majority of them. Some of its left-wing, pro-committee leaders had made contact several days before with Béla Kun, although the leadership as such was unaware of this. Some leaders, such as Ernő Garami and Gyula Peidl, favored leaving a new settlement to a bourgeois coalition and keeping the Hungarian Social Democratic Party away from government responsibility in the near future. Some of the center, such as Zsigmond Kunfi, argued for retaining the governing coalition and rejecting the note. Vilmos Böhm, having put the possibility of a Bolshevik turn before Gondrecourt a couple of days earlier, resigned himself to that in reality. An important part was presumably played by his military advisers. According to Böhm's memoirs, Colonel Jenő Tombor felt that Hungary had to orient itself towards Russia: "The leadership of the country at present sees no other suitable administration than the Social Democratic Party capable of organizing the armed defense, but to this end it must reconcile itself and reach agreement with the Communist Party, so that Allied cooperation can occur with the Russian Soviet forces present on the northern border of the old Austria."[5]

Two factors seem to have coincided in the Social Democrats' decision: on the one hand, the clear wish of the left wing for agreement with the Communists, formation of a joint party, and accomplishment of traditional socialist demands, and, on the other, the national criterion of the centrists, focused on a Russian orientation. When the government met on the afternoon on March 20, Károlyi spoke of expecting a Social Democratic government taking over, with a Communist or two taking part, and how that would "open the opportunity for a new foreign policy orientation." However, he also announced that he wished to negotiate with all parties, and he actually prepared for such negotiations. In the case of a Social Democratic government, the prime minister designate would be Kunfi, but the list of possible candidates included Jászi, Lovászy, Batthyány, István Bethlen and Gábor Ugron as well. Károlyi's handling of the situation seems to have been rational at this point, except in one thing. He did not consider that for an orientation towards Moscow, the Social Democrats needed Béla Kun, Lenin's close acquaintance and comrade-in-arms, not Count Károlyi.

Meanwhile, some Social Democratic members of the government were also getting ready to negotiate with the Communists, which they duly began to do on the afternoon on the 21st, if some earlier unofficial contacts are discounted. The process of reaching a pact and the occurrences that accompanied it showed that the Social Democrats were acting hastily, in a situation of crisis, whereas Béla Kun knew precisely what he wanted, although he too made some slight concessions. Above all, Kun did not insist on the name Communist Party and was prepared for the merged party to be called Socialist. Finally, the leadership of the Social Democratic Party of Hungary, apart from some moderate figures who insisted on bourgeois democracy (Garami, Manó Buchinger and Gyula

Peidl), reached a decision, and on the afternoon of March 21, the negotiators signed the document merging the two parties and establishing a proletarian dictatorship.[6]

Looking at this timetable poses a question: whose work was it that created the Hungarian Soviet Republic?[7] Was it that of the imprisoned communists, whose basis of support consisted of a few thousand people and who made not a single initiatory move during the process? Or was it that of the Social Democrats, who could move about freely, were in the government, had organized a demonstration in the hundreds of thousands not long before, and sought Béla Kun with their proposal? The cause of that internationally exceptional Social Democratic behavior on the part of the decisive figures of the center could certainly be sought in the need for national defense.

The new government list was already decided when the old Berinkey cabinet met for the last time on the afternoon of March 21, without the bourgeois ministers or Károlyi having the slightest idea about the pact. The government endorsed the note rejecting the Vix Note, ordered the release of the arrested communists, and dispersed without the Social Democratic ministers having said anything about the pact with Béla Kun. None of them had the courage to look Károlyi in the eye and say that Béla Kun, not he, was needed for a Russian orientation. So it could happen that the president of the Republic was telling Kunfi that he intended to appoint him prime minister at the same time, perhaps, as he was confessing to the cabinet that he had in the meantime chosen the "left" alternative of the ones before him. Károlyi did not even know that a statement had been made on his behalf transferring power "to the proletariat of the peoples of Hungary." The statement was read that evening at the meeting of the Workers' Soviet, which also declared the existence of the proletarian dictatorship and accepted the composition of the Governing Soviet.

Although Károlyi had not signed the statement or even seen it in advance, he stayed silent on the matter for long time, believing that he could not find fault with an experiment directed against a type of "capitalism" whose representatives in Paris were "prepared to hand beggars' staffs to innocent millions of the Hungarian people." Károlyi was later charged with delivering the country into the hands of the communists and attacked for the territorial losses, the odium of which his opponents were determined should be borne by him. The first charge can be called quite groundless, while the second can be sustained only in part. It is certainly a fact that when the Vix Note produced a critical situation, Károlyi and democracy were left in a vacuum. The peace conference note acted as a catalyst. The majority of the Social Democratic leadership forfeited the independence of their party; then, partly for the attractive dream of socialism, but probably decisively to protect the country's territory, they set about implementing a program whose steps were largely dictated by the communists.

Notes

1. Several people had tried to get in touch with the Italians. Government contact was eventually made by Oszkár Charmant, with a mandate from Károlyi. The proposal for close Hungarian–Romanian cooperation under Italian leadership was supported by the Italian foreign minister, Giorgio Sidney Sonnino, but Károlyi broke off talks after a further Romanian attack on Hungary.
2. The French argument was that the Poles were being pressed by the Bolshevik forces, but in fact the Poles were being pressed by the Ukrainian nationalists in the area. The Red Army had captured Kiev on February 5 but then turned southwards. Furthermore, Lemberg was not a Polish city.
3. Gondrecourt was assigned to command the French forces occupying the control points in the neutral zone.
4. There are several signs that he was thinking of alternatives: either rejection, and a Social Democratic government including a few

Communists, or acceptance, with a coalition government open towards the right. Indeed, he began negotiating with István Bethlen and his circle.

5.   Based on these events, it cannot be considered fortuitous or mistaken that Hungarian Bolshevism was seen worldwide as a national issue, a sign of the Hungarians' extreme resentment, although this argument was later rejected vehemently by "Marxist-Leninist" historians.

6.   The signatories were Zsigmond Kunfi, Jenő Landler, Jakab Weltner, József Pogány and József Haubrich for the Social Democratic Party of Hungary, and Béla Kun, Béla Szántó, Béla Vágó and others for the Communist Party of Hungary.

7.   *Tanácsköztársaság*. This is otherwise known in English as the Republic of Councils, but the bodies that gave it this name were directly analogous to Bolshevik soviets and modeled on them, not "councils" in a normal English sense.

4. The Establishment of Soviet Power

March 21, 1919, is customarily seen as a second revolutionary turn of events, but no revolutionary events occurred, and the new power, the proletarian dictatorship, was really based on a merger of two political parties.

The regime could count on the support of the intelligentsia and a narrow stratum of officials, and the sphere might widen further depending on whether it managed to make contact with the villages or defend the national interests. In the early weeks, there were conspicuously large numbers of supporters from the intelligentsia, who expected the Hungarian Soviet Republic to pull down the barriers that were constricting Hungarian intellectual life and giving culture a measure of provincialism. Some officials supported the regime because an important part in its establishment had been played by the Vix Note, seen as the defense of the nation. This was supported by Kun's early statements. In his message to Lenin, for instance, Kun gave two reasons why the Hungarian Soviet Republic had formed: to solve the social problems, and to prevent mutilation of the country's territory and robbery of its assets, which the Hungarian people, Kun said, would not tolerate. In a second message, he expressly asked Lenin for support against the "imperialist bandits."

This matched the desires of many Social Democrats, but the Social Democratic majority in the Governing Soviet was forced from the start into a subordinate position, as it was felt that concessions had to be made, through Béla Kun, in exchange for Russian assistance. Communist radicalism therefore increasingly dominated the Governing Soviet's decisions and practical activity. Another contributing factor to this bias was the division among the Social Democrats and their ignorance of Bolshevik methods.[1] "Socialization" of the economy was conducted at breakneck speed: every factory or workshop employing more than 20 people was nationalized, and wholesale trading and educational and cultural institutions were placed under state control. Production fell sharply, partly because of incompetent interference, and partly because of shortages of raw materials and expertise, compounded after a time by acts of sabotage. The cost of the damage suffered by manufacturing was estimated later to have reached 1,500 million crowns.

The land question was still unresolved. An order of April 4 took medium-sized and large estates into state ownership without compensation, causing temporary chaos, as it emerged only later that this applied to estates of over 100 *hold* (57.5 ha). Medium-sized and small holdings of the peasantry (and to a lesser extent the nobility), making up 48 percent of the land, were unaffected, although some land went to the rural poor. Rural society had not supported the bourgeois republic. Now the vast majority of the peasantry became expressly hostile to the new authorities. General conditions and livelihoods were marked by blockades, shortages of raw materials, plunging production, and rural produce being held back for want of faith in the currency, as well as unemployment, and the fact that some of the territory that the peace conference intended to remain in Hungary was under foreign occupation.

The Governing Soviet certainly took some welfare measures. Wages and salaries were increased, compulsory insurance of workers was introduced and then extended to agricultural workers and day-laborers, holidays were organized for poor Budapest children, and the housing of large families improved at the expense of the wealthy urban population. But these measures in some cases were unrealistic under the general conditions that prevailed, and did not bring about a substantive improvement in the position of the working class, even according to Béla Kun.

The new regime replaced the police and gendarmerie with Red Guards, and replaced the previous judicial system with "revolutionary" and "summary" courts manned largely by laymen. The public administration also collapsed and the new system of elected soviets was installed only in patches. On April 7, general elections were called to establish a National Assembly of Soviets and elect local soviets. Those living off the work of others—businessmen, landowners and merchants, as well as priests and members of religious orders—were deprived of the vote. The National Assembly of Soviets was supposed to perform legislative functions instead of Parliament, but it was unable to do so, as it only met once. An important part was played instead by the Budapest Central Workers' Soviet, consisting of 500 representatives of organized workers in the capital, which had a say in the activity of the Governing Soviet from time to time. As for the soviets established to perform local administrative functions, they were extremely varied in composition and operation. In the larger cities, it was mainly Social Democrats and Communists who were elected, but in the country, the members included plenty of wealthy peasants, local members of the intelligentsia, or simply the old officials. The provincial soviets showed a lot of independence and often refused to obey instructions from Budapest.

It has to be concluded that the People's Republic, in about five months of existence, proved itself to be unable to lay the foundations of the new Hungarian state, while the verdict on the Soviet Republic must be that it managed to demolish the elements of statehood that were still operating: the public administration, and the law enforcement and judicial systems. These could certainly have done with transformation and overhaul, but the new Republic managed to replace them only with bodies that were socially limited and uncertain and unsupervised in their operation.

The state still possessed no army, while the Romanian High Command, according to news reaching Budapest, was busy with plans for the next offensive. On April 4, the day that assessment was made, Britain's General Jan Smuts arrived in Budapest to clarify any misunderstandings caused by the Vix Note. The assumption was that inaccurate wording of the Vix Note had led the Hungarians to misinterpret the neutral zone, by assuming that the future border would run down the middle of it, so as to coincide with the line recorded in the Treaty of Bucharest and consistently demanded by the Romanians. That was what the Hungarians were thought to have said no to. Smuts was empowered to push the neutral zone further east, but in such a way that the future border worked out in Paris would still fall within it. And indeed, according to the general's proposal, the country's eastern border was to run through about the middle of the neutral zone, not along its eastern edge.

But the people at the peace conference were mistaken in their scheme. Whatever they said afterwards, the Hungarians had understood the Vix Note perfectly: what they rejected was not the 1916 line, but the 1919 line devised at the peace conference. However, the maneuver by Smuts probably was misunderstood in Budapest. It was thought, as in the first case, that the future border would coincide with the eastern edge of the zone. They thought that it was a territorial concession, and that if Paris would go so far, it might go further as well. Again there were big differences in how the matter was assessed. Béla Kun, apparently, was against acceptance, emphasizing the point that after a "Brest Peace" of this kind, "nationalism helping the commune to victory" would sweep the new system aside.[2] There were some who were sorry to reject the proposal, but also commissars who also rejected Kun's demand for a return to "the original armistice" (in fact to the Belgrade Convention), because they saw that also as too great a concession. On April 6, Sándor Garbai reported on the negotiations to the Governing Soviet. He commented that the Székely would not accept the Smuts proposal, but he added that they would naturally reject the Belgrade armistice as well. On April 12, however, the Social Democrat Böhm reported that the Székely Division would not accept Kun's position in favor of the state described in the armistice of November 13, 1918. Böhm added "I will write them a letter tomorrow saying that we consider it our holy duty to recover

the Székely Land for the Székely." At the same meeting, the
Communist Jenő Landler announced that Kun's statement about the
armistice had to be considered null and void.[3] It can be concluded
from all this that the Governing Soviet was divided on the national
question, and, what is more, on the national question seen as the
reason for the existence of the Soviet Republic, and the borderlines
ran together in this regard, between the Social Democrats and the
Communists. For some Communist leaders, as well as Social
Democrats, attached primary importance to the national question
and thought little of Béla Kun's zigzag policy, whose main element
was to play for time in the hope that Russian assistance would
arrive, although it could be guessed from the early days that Lenin
was reluctant to offer such assistance. From what Kun let slip in his
notes and Governing Soviet measures, it can be concluded that his
ideal would have been to restore the former territory of the
Hungarian state, with autonomy for its national communities in a
federal or possibly confederative framework.

It has been mentioned that all this was occurring at a time
when the Soviet Republic had practically no military forces and the
Romanians were preparing for a new attack. The Romanian invasion duly began a few days later, on April 16. The defense lasted
about two weeks in confused circumstances, accompanied by hardly disguised ill feeling from the peasants of the Great Plain, and
ended when the Székely Division, in danger of encirclement,
stopped fighting and the other units fled. The Romanian army occupied the Great Plain as far as the River Tisza. In fact they could
have advanced on Budapest without much effort.[4] The catastrophe
was complete when the Czechoslovak army also advanced on April
27, crossing the demarcation line and pushing into Subcarpathia,
before occupying a succession of places (including Ózd, Miskolc
and Putnok) that had been awarded to Hungary at the peace conference. Thereafter the country's territory was confined to
Transdanubia and the Danube–Tisza region, and it was cut off from
its main bread basket, the Great Plain.

The Romanian and Czechoslovak military successes sent the Hungarian Soviet Republic into deep crisis, and news spread in Paris that it had actually fallen. Several commissars already thought that resignation was inescapable and recommended handing power over to a "directory,"[5] but Béla Kun was still able at that stage to persuade the leading committees that the situation was not hopeless, and only endurance and courage were required. Kun was actually waiting for a move by Russia, not entirely in vain, but not with full justification either. Hungary's Commissars' Soviet had issued an ultimatum to the Romanians, and that meant that the Romanian army called off any further advance into Hungary, because it was obliged to strengthen its eastern border. That kept the Kun regime alive for another three months. However, it did not guarantee the Hungarian leaders the Soviet Russian military support that they were looking for. Like Károlyi in Paris, Kun was disappointed in his eventually unfounded hopes in Moscow.

Notes

1. Kun, incidentally, wrote in an article in 1924 that Moscow's confidence was low, as Lenin and his associates suspected a Social Democratic maneuver behind the events in Budapest.
2. This shows that Kun had kept secret from the Governing Soviet the notes of his saying that he was ready to negotiate on the basis of the Vix Note or any other Entente proposal.
3. Governing Soviet members clearly knew nothing of Kun's statement that he was prepared to negotiate on the basis of the Vix Note.
4. After some hesitation they decided not to do so, because the Romanian military commanders thought that the territory occupied in Hungary gave enough of a guarantee that Romanian demands would be met. Meanwhile, it was preferable to bring greater forces to bear on Romania's eastern frontier, where the Red Army had won a succession of victories in March and April, as a result of which the British and the French decided to wind up their base at Odessa. The Soviet Union with its ultimatum really gave Budapest assistance that allowed the soviet system in Hungary to revive again.
5. This view was taken by Dezső Bokányi, Zsigmond Kunfi and Jakab Weltner, but it is unclear what exactly they meant by a directory.

5. Defense and Terror

The second stage of rule by soviets, from the beginning of May, was marked on the one hand by military activity and defense of the country, and on the other by heightened counter-revolutionary activity and a reign of terror.

Military organization was in the hands of an army High Command headed by Böhm, who took on Aurél Stromfeld to be his chief of staff.[1] Thanks to their actions, the enlistment of many young officers from the old army, and the initial enthusiasm of the Budapest workers, it was possible to send in a competent military force by May 9, to attack the Czechoslovak army, the weaker of the two invaders. The calculation worked. Hungary's Red Army retook a succession of places from the Czechs, crossed the demarcation line, and marched into many further towns and villages.[2] On June 16, the Slovak Soviet Republic was declared at a presumably none too representative meeting.

Hungary's successes caused consternation in Prague and excitement among peace conference delegates as well. The idea of intervention had been discussed from the beginning, but it had never been organized, for various reasons. One problem was the fact that the Great Powers could not involve themselves in any further warfare, for domestic political reasons. Another was the fact that they did not want to pay the bill that Hungary's neighbors would present to a now excessively mutilated Hungary. Instead, the conference swiftly closed the matter of Hungary's northern and eastern borders. The requisite committees had worked out their proposals before the Hungarian Soviet Republic was even declared. These were endorsed by the Committee on Territorial Questions, and on June 11 by the Supreme Council. The decision on the final frontiers was then presented to the Prague, Bucharest and Budapest governments. Negotiations took place about the southern and western borders, but the conference could not really expect Belgrade to

48

join in, as the Serbian army was occupying a greater territory than the conference intended that the Kingdom of the Serbs, Croats and Slovenes should receive, while Austria could not come into consideration for many reasons. Arthur Balfour, the British foreign secretary, could rightly complain that a tiny defeated state like Hungary was managing to defy the whole camp of the victors. Faced with a far from perfect situation, Clemenceau, president of the conference, thought it best simply to leave matters to time and Hungary's neighbors, but without promising them more than they had been led to expect already. However, it will emerge that the conference went on to use diplomatic means to support the solution that it saw as appropriate.

Meanwhile, there was mounting dissatisfaction in Hungary despite the military successes. Cases of conspiracy and rebellion against the regime were becoming more frequent. There was commotion among all the aggrieved strata and groups in society, not just the capitalists and landowners whose property had been expropriated (they mainly went into exile), but peasants, officer cadets, various townspeople, police, the priesthood, and so on. The terror initiated by the Soviet Republic alienated most of the members of the intelligentsia who had seen in it initially the dawn of a better future. The responses to all this were reprisals and terror, based on decisions of the Governing Soviet, but often depending on arbitrary judgments by quite unauthorized individuals. The hostage order was passed by the Governing Soviet (on April 19, and then repealed at the end of May), but official bodies were not the only ones to take hostages. The revolutionary courts were established officially, but they were not the only ones, or even the chief ones, to pass death sentences. The commander of the military summary court, Tibor Szamuely, put all formalities aside when passing death sentences not only on military matters officially within his province, but in cases of other kinds as well. Then there were those "rogue" individuals acting on their own, who wanted to avenge real or

imagined grievances and associated revolutionary activity with violence. The one who committed the most atrocities was probably a
young man of 26 called József Cserny, who set up a heavily armed
terror group on his own initiative. He picked hostages at will and
murdered those engaged in or suspected of being engaged in
counter-revolutionary activity. The gang was finally disarmed by
the army (on May 19), but some members carried on working as
investigators.

In areas beyond Governing Soviet control and outside the
country, political groupings arose whose leaders and members were
preparing to overthrow the regime and seize power. They generally described themselves as counter-revolutionary and sought to
foment a counter-revolution. On May 5, Count Gyula Károlyi set
up a rival government in Arad. Soon Romania's occupation of the
city led to a move to Szeged, which was under French control.[3]
There it merged with a local group and officially declared itself a
government on May 31. The French then gave leave for its Ministry
of Defense to recruit a military unit. It aimed politically at staging
counter-revolutionary actions in the zone controlled by the
Hungarian Soviet Republic. On the recommendation of István
Bethlen, Gyula Károlyi invited the high-ranking and respected
naval officer Rear Admiral Miklós Horthy to come to Szeged as
minister of defense, and he duly offered his services at the beginning of June. The man appointed foreign minister was Pál Teleki in
Vienna. Teleki was then flown to Szeged by the French. Also in
Szeged was Gyula Gömbös, although the French eventually
expelled him for his activity there. At Horthy's request, the
French allowed Hungarian soldiers to enter the Szeged zone of
occupation, provided that they were unarmed.[4] This allowed
Horthy to start assembling a land force that was later named the
National Army. It actually came together as a loose set of groups
of officers and subalterns, each commanded by a middle-ranking
officer. It had no structure in the true sense, or ranks, or weapons.

The French estimated that its strength was 5,000 in July, but others put it at 3,000 at the most.

Gyula Károlyi and his government did all that they could to win the favor of the French, but to no avail. The view at the French Command in Szeged was that the government was too reactionary and influenced too much by the "Viennese." In response to this pressure, Gyula Károlyi resigned on July 12 in favor of Dezső P. Ábrahám, an independent politician, who had served in Mihály Károlyi's government as state secretary for justice. Ábrahám brought in another state secretary of the earlier government from Mihály Károlyi's party, Aladár Balla. This gave the new team a more democratic look than the previous one. Teleki, however, remained in place. Despite great preparations, the Szeged government was blamed for inaction and dissolved itself without a successor on August 19. The Szeged group was not united. Some of the politicians were expecting Hungary to take a bourgeois democratic shape and did all that they could to demonstrate this intention, while many of the soldiers gathering in Szeged were preparing to introduce a dictatorship and sought to influence Horthy towards that end.

By the "Viennese" was meant a group of émigré landowners and army officers in the Austrian capital, headed by István Bethlen, who formed the Anti-Bolshevist Committee (ABC). Despite its apparent unanimity, the ABC embraced several currents of opinion. One of these, led intellectually by Bethlen, was seeking a solution to Hungary's problems by political and diplomatic means, relying on assistance from the victorious powers. Much more numerous were the legitimists grouped around György Szmrecsányi and György Pallavicini, who emphasized violent action, although other legitimists disagreed with that approach. Szmrecsányi and his associates organized a robbery of money held at the Hungarian Embassy in Vienna,[5] and then prepared an abortive military breakthrough at Bruck. Bethlen opposed these moves. He besieged

Entente missions in Vienna with petitions, and devised coalition plans for Hungarian consolidation after an expected foreign military intervention.[6] There were contacts between the Bethlen and Szeged groups, but it is very unlikely that any political negotiations took place.

On instructions from the Vienna group, a counter-revolutionary center also formed in Graz, organized by Colonel Antal Lehár, on the request of Antal Sigray. They were joined there by Szmrecsányi and his followers after a split occurred in June 1919 between the two camps in Vienna. The "Graz Command" used some of the money stolen in Vienna to buy weapons, and established a military unit of a few hundred men at Feldbach. The idea was that on receiving a signal, it would invade Hungary and take part in overthrowing the Red authorities, but this never happened. Instead, Graz became the base for a hard core that would give military support to an attempt to restore Charles IV to the Hungarian throne. The Graz group kept in touch with White officers who had stayed in Transdanubia and had a hand in the counter-revolutionary uprisings there. An attempt to take command of these units in the west was made by Gömbös, after he left Szeged, but this was resisted by Lehár, in an incident that foreshadowed later power struggles in the reorganizing army and in the political field.

The counter-revolutionary groupings went on to establish the Etelköz Association,[7] at a still unknown place and time. This was a secret society with initiation rites that included an oath. It elected a Governing Council and was divided into clans, and took various political decisions. The association's "visible" head was Bertold Feilitzsch, commander of the Johannite Order[8] and head of the group in Hungary, but Miklós Horthy was considered to be its concealed leader, although he never actually joined. Present knowledge of the association comes from scattered reminiscences and accidental remarks, as its written records have gone astray, if they ever existed. Somewhat later, it held meetings in Podmaniczky út,

Budapest, in the expropriated Freemasons' headquarters where MOVE was based. It is thought to have recruited members initially from a broad social spectrum, which may have been its downfall. The decisive forces in the association changed over a period of one and a half to two years, so that the conservative forces on the Governing Council managed to turn it against far-right radicalism. But it is very likely that the association initially was the main bastion of the forces alongside Horthy intent on freely choosing a monarch, although there were legitimist members as well.[9]

Notes

1. The High Command was set up on April 21.
2. The places taken or retaken: Fülek (Fil'akovo), Miskolc, Putnok, Losonc (Lučenec), Párkánynána (Nána), Ipolyság (Šahy), Szikszó (Siksava), Sajószentpéter, Abaújszántó, Rimaszombat (Rimavská Sobota), Edelény, Léva (Levice), Szerencs, Érsekújvár, Tokaj, Bodrogkeresztúr, Sárospatak, Sátoraljaújhely, Kassa (Košice), Korpona (Krupina), Selmecbánya (Banská Štiavnica), Zólyom (Zvolen), Eperjes (Prešov), Rozsnyó (Rožňava) and Bártfa (Bardejov).
3. The move had French permission, but the Romanian authorities arrested the government members on the train and would not let them proceed until the French intervened.
4. The permit was issued by Clemenceau in his capacity as minister of war.
5. However, the 150–160 million crowns stolen were divided, although great difficulties arose later over the settlement between the two groups.
6. Bethlen was seeking a broad coalition at the time. This is apparent from the fact that his political talks included several meetings with the émigré Social Democrat Ernő Garami.
7. The *Etelközi Szövetség* (*EKSz*) was named after the Hungarian term for a region of modern Ukraine inhabited by the Magyars before their arrival in the Carpathian Basin in 895.
8. The Johannite Order had been one of the main orders of chivalry in Hungary in the mid-twelfth century. Officially abolished in 1807, it

began to be reorganized at the end of the nineteenth century. Official reestablishment followed in 1924.

9.   Pál Prónay, in a memoir, described these conservatives as liberals and Freemasons and thought that they had all betrayed the anti-Semitic national idea. He included among them Bethlen, Teleki and Feilitzsche himself.

6. The Military Defeat of the Hungarian Soviet Republic

None of the counter-revolutionary groups reached the point of taking action, as the Governing Soviet resigned on account of the Romanian military victory.

The peace conference, in a decision dated June 7, called on Budapest to withdraw from its forward positions in the north, although it did not specify a line to which the Hungarian forces should withdraw. When Béla Kun asked about this, the conference feverishly laid down the northern and eastern borders of Hungary and announced these on June 11. They were accepted by the Czechoslovak prime minister, but not by Ion I. C. Brătianu, prime minister of Romania. This meant that it would not be easy to remove the Romanian forces from the line of the River Tisza. Nevertheless, a note was sent from Paris to Budapest that defined the northern border to be occupied (as Kun had requested) and raised hopes that the Romanians would be ordered to withdraw from the line that they were holding, as soon as the Hungarian government had complied with the conference's wishes.

On June 13, the government in Budapest was again divided by the Clemenceau Note. Kun requested a guarantee that the Romanians would withdraw. When he did not receive one, there was protracted wrangling on the Governing Soviet before it was decided to evacuate in the north in any case. This was ordered on June 24, and the Red Army withdrew in an organized fashion to the line that could now be considered to be a permanent border. It meant that the Hungarians had ceded some not inconsiderable territory. On the other hand, they permanently retained several places that the Czechoslovaks had occupied inside the zone awarded to Hungary by the peace conference, including Miskolc, Ózd, Sátoraljaújhely, Sárospatak and Tokaj, to mention just the larger ones. Nevertheless, the withdrawal conveyed an impression of weakness and defeat, which prompted several army officers, including Stromfeld, to resign and retire.

But the biggest problem was the fact that the Romanian army did not move back a yard, with tacit agreement from the conference. An alibi for this breach of faith was provided by British Foreign Secretary Balfour, who produced the formula stating that the Romanian forces should not be called upon to deploy along the designated borderline until Hungary had carried out disarmament to the extent laid down in the armistice agreement. However, nobody was capable of establishing the strength of the Red Army, on which there were only wild estimates circulating, and so the Romanian withdrawal could be postponed indefinitely on that basis.

Opinions in Budapest were again divided about what could be done. The main advocate of attacking the Romanians was Ferenc Julier, the new chief of General Staff. He explained his position with hindsight by saying that this would have been the most effective way of annihilating the Red Army and bringing down the regime. There certainly was little chance of victory, as the morale of the army had relapsed, it would be numerically inferior to the Romanians, and furthermore it would be facing a rested army. Some members of the Governing Soviet put forward counterarguments, but everybody's consent was obtained for an attack.

The Hungarian offensive along the Tisza began on July 20, as Kun in fact announced officially to the conference. The Hungarian forces enjoyed local successes in the early days, but failed to fend off a Romanian counterattack on the 24th. Defense was kept up until the 31st, when the Hungarian front became indefensible and collapsed. Then a headlong retreat began.

While the fighting took place along the Tisza, Vilmos Böhm, by then envoy in Vienna, was holding talks with the heads of the Allied missions there and with the Austrian government. His idea of an interim government to be formed under his leadership was unsuccessful, despite initial agreement from the heads of the British and Italian missions, because the conference did not want to commit itself in advance to a plan with an uncertain outcome.[1] However, Böhm did manage to ensure that the Austrian government gave political asylum to some leaders of the Hungarian Soviet Republic, presumably with the consent of the Allied missions.[2]

Between the morning of July 31 and the afternoon of August 1, the Governing Soviet members reached the conclusion that the struggle could not continue and the fate of the soviet experiment was sealed. The Governing Soviet decided to resign. This was accepted at the afternoon session of the Budapest Workers' and Soldiers' Soviet on August 1. Gyula Peidl, head of the printers' trade union, was charged with forming a new government purely of Social Democrats. The disbanding of the Red Army was ordered, although it had dissolved in any case by that time. Peidl realized that his government could only be temporary, but he probably did not expect it to last only five nights.

By this time, all the hopes placed in the Wilson Principles and the line to be taken by the Entente had been dispelled, along with the ideas of international revolution and the prospect of Soviet assistance. Hungary still stood alone in the world and now had nowhere to turn. Every one of its neighbors had claims against it and it had no Great Power support. That was the inescapable foreign policy conclusion to be drawn from the events of the previous nine months. Essentially it meant that there was no option but to accept the peace treaty prepared for the country. And it had to be applied as soon as possible, or the recovery of the remaining area of the country could not begin and there was no hope of the Romanian army withdrawing.

This was the case irrespective of how the responsibility for the country's fate was apportioned. As the debates of the time become more distant from us, it starts to become clear that Mihály Károlyi and his government made several political mistakes, but the victors distanced themselves for expressly foreign policy reasons, not domestic ones. Had the victors supported Hungary, the Slovak and

Transylvanian questions could never have been resolved to the satisfaction of their lesser allies.[3] The territory of a country surrounded by claimants and threatened by more or less organized armies could probably not have been saved even by much better military policies, but rather fairer conditions might have been won through reliance on the army and some intelligent diplomacy.

As for the Hungarian Soviet Republic, the regime, while and despite employing terror at home, did attempt the impossible by organizing resistance and save at least some of the territory, although it suffered defeat. Just as Károlyi came to rue his orientation towards France, so Kun and the Social Democrats supporting him were baffled in their hopes of Soviet assistance. For Hungary was left with very little room even for the best and cleverest maneuvers.

All things considered, the Hungarians had a role in producing what has come to be known as the Peace Treaty of Trianon mainly through their past and their distant past. The events of 1914–1919 influenced their destiny only by presenting them with a challenge. Hungary was tried and condemned for geopolitical reasons to do with national communities and power politics. The military defeat provided the chance to impose the sentence.

However, the Hungarians played the principal part in the domestic political confusion that lasted almost a year, from which the country alone could not find an escape. That remains so even though a part in the failure of the Károlyi experiment and the establishment of the Hungarian Soviet Republic was played by the territorial division of the country and by the Vix Note. The foundations of the new, independent Hungarian state could not be laid, and almost the entire Hungarian left crumbled away under the conditions of the "People's Republic" followed by the "Soviet Republic." A sizable proportion of the bourgeois democrats and the Social Democrats emigrated to Western Europe. A substantial group of left-wing Social Democrats and Communists went to the

Soviet Union, from which many were never to return. The political palette had hardly been filled in 1918 before it was scraped clean again. The ideas of democracy and republicanism were shaken too. These ideas were held by many Jewish members of the intelligentsia, *inter alia*, and a notably high proportion of leading figures in the Hungarian Soviet Republic were Jews, albeit secularized; thus anti-Semitism spread widely in society for the first time in Hungarian history.

Notes

1.   The Böhm talks have been seen as an agreement by some Hungarian historians, and the treatment of the Peidl government therefore as a breach of faith. This argument fails to consider the fact that encouragement from the heads of mission in Vienna did not amount to a conference decision. In fact, Böhm himself never claimed that the talks on the future government reached the agreement stage. This was still less possible as Béla Kun had not given his consent to them.
2.   Asylum was given to those whom Béla Kun had put on his list. This did not include Tibor Szamuely, who tried to escape but died near the border under unexplained circumstances, or some people's commissars who were being prosecuted in Budapest, although most were able to leave for the Soviet Union under the prisoner-of-war agreement. Nor was Mátyás Rákosi on the list. He nevertheless arrived in Vienna, where the Austrians gave him similar treatment to the others.
3.   Károlyi's reputation suffered when his statement of resignation was taken at face value and he was seen as preparing the way for the Communists, and when he began to associate closely with the extreme left wing.

3. THE STRUGGLE FOR POWER

1. The Months of Transition: Confusion and Uncertainty

On August 1, 1919, as Gyula Peidl's government took office, Hungary extended from the Austrian border to the River Tisza, but four days later, the Romanians took Budapest as well. They found no Bolsheviks there by then, but they set out to persuade the new government to sign a new armistice that contained some hair-raising demands. Peidl, who presumably was not conversant with the international legal situation, was inclined to sign, not least because he was expressly advised to do so by the Italian Colonel Guido Romanelli, the one Allied officer still in Budapest.[1] Luckily the peace conference forbade this move, arguing that an armistice agreement existed and there was no need for another.

By that time, the days, even the hours, of the Peidl government were numbered. It had just enough time to repeal most of the orders issued under the Hungarian Soviet Republic. On August 6, under cover from the Romanian army, a small armed unit of men from Christian (Catholic) circles broke into the premises of the Council of Ministers and forced resignation on the government, which was meeting at the time. They requested the *homo regius* or regent, Archduke Joseph of Habsburg, to appoint as prime minister István Friedrich of the Christian National Union Party,[2] after which in turn Friedrich declared the archduke to be regent.

This unusual procedure well reflected the public conditions in the country. But support for the Friedrich government was shaken before any such constitutional issues could be raised. It soon emerged that Friedrich would not sign the new armistice either, and so the Romanian Command ordered the occupation of northern

Transdanubia as well. This left a country hard to discern at all, with two self-appointed governments, an arbitrarily appointed person (Archduke Joseph) in charge of a legally non-existent authority (the regency), but without a constitution, a legislature, a police force, a gendarmerie, or even an army at the government's disposal.

Although Miklós Horthy had dissociated himself from the Szeged government, he would not subordinate himself to the Budapest one either. Instead, he announced the formation of a separate Supreme Command. Horthy was occupied mainly with politics in the days after the Soviet Republic collapsed, and contrary to common belief, his actions showed instinctive political sense. Taken together, the moves made by the rear admiral in 1919 place in question the idea that he was a "simple" officer of the armed forces, upright, but with a slightly stupid mentality generally thought to be remote from politics. First of all, he persuaded Archduke Joseph to establish the office of supreme commander. This legalized his position to some extent and disengaged him, while he immediately dissociated himself from those who sought to link the country in any way with the House of Habsburg, which made them unacceptable to the victorious powers. Thereby he consciously or unconsciously raised his chances considerably over those of the Friedrich group or the group of legitimist officers headed by Antal Lehár. Meanwhile, he reached agreement with the Romanian Army Command, which granted the national army freedom of movement in the Danube–Tisza region and southern Transdanubia. The first military units left Szeged on August 3 under the command of Pál Prónay, with orders to reach Budapest, but when this was opposed by the Romanian commanders, Prónay thought it better to cross the Danube at Dunaföldvár and make for the southern shore of Lake Balaton, which fitted in with the Hungarian–Romanian agreement that Horthy had made. Further units leaving Szeged on August 9 took that direction in the first place.[3] Not until after his negotiations in Budapest did Horthy move to Siófok, where he set up his headquarters. The Supreme Command (or parts of it) was centered on Kaposvár.

But in practice Horthy's group could only take control of a small part of Transdanubia. To the west, the Graz leadership appeared. Before the Horthyite forces could do anything about it, it had taken over the western counties with the help of the Feldbach men and local units. (They held Moson, Sopron, Vas, and Zala Counties, covering about 16,000 sq. km, while the Supreme Command controlled Baranya, Tolna, Somogy and Veszprém Counties.) Somewhat later, Lehár recognized the Supreme Command, but in practice he acted on his own account, all the more easily because he was able to cooperate politically and practically with Antal Sigray, the government commissioner for the area. Both Lehár and Sigray were legitimists, however, and they did not conceal their views from the Entente officers with whom they had built up relations in Vienna. That was one reason for their downfall, as that current of opinion was unacceptable to the Allies as a basis for establishing Hungarian statehood. So the group had written itself off politically, despite controlling a larger territory than the Supreme Command did, and operating faster and more effectively to restore and impose order. Meanwhile, the premium on the independent Horthy had risen, and his situation was given further stability, because Lehár had formally recognized his role as supreme commander.

The Supreme Command was soon engaged in lively political activity, and after the Romanians had withdrawn from Transdanubia, it took the whole of Transdanubia under its control in principle, with the consent of the Allies. This showed that Horthy intended that the military and he himself should play a decisive part in deciding the country's subsequent destiny. However, the question of what this would be remained open, and it remains unclear to this day what Horthy was preparing for at that time. Did he seriously consider imposing a military dictatorship? Many of his followers assumed so, but such a conclusion cannot be drawn clearly from Horthy's actions.

The Szeged government had lost its minister of defense and its military force, and it was clear that Friedrich would not hear of amalgamating with it. Drawing its own conclusions, the government resigned on August 19. This clarified the situation somewhat, but did not improve it. Another four months would pass before elementary conditions for consolidation came into being: a government able to judge whether to hold general elections and accept the draft peace treaty. They were marked by military occupation, confusion over power, arbitrary action, terror and political tugs of war.

The Friedrich government (of which there were really three, due to reorganization) would actually have been capable of becoming a coalition government and of organizing democratic elections, as it offered to do several times. And the free elections so desired by the peace conference took place in February 1920 more or less on the basis of an order that the Friedrich government had issued. Károly Huszár, who would gain Allied recognition and receive the peace treaty, was a member of Friedrich's party and government. All this shows that the trouble was not with Friedrich.

Ultimately, the one serious innate fault in the Friedrich government was its involvement with Archduke Joseph. Still a radical revolutionary in the autumn of 1918, by this time a monarchist, and soon to be an open supporter of the claims of Charles IV, Friedrich had not correctly gauged the antagonism produced by the appearance of a Habsburg as head of the Hungarian state. If Friedrich had not insisted on that pseudo-constitutional solution, he would probably have had a much easier political destiny. But once the anti-Habsburg tune began to be played in Prague and Belgrade, that innate flaw in his procedure could no longer be corrected.[4] It was no help that Archduke Joseph's family had broken off from the Vienna branch some time before, or that Joseph himself had become Hungarianized, or even that he resigned on sensing the animosity towards him. Nothing could ever wash away the stain of Friedrich's secret intention to restore the Habsburgs. That was an open secret, even if many have now forgotten that a kingdom (whether it be the South Slav one or the Romanian one) does not attack another dynasty, for reasons pertaining to the "system." It has been customary to list retroactively the real or imagined crimes of the Habsburgs over the centuries. But in terms of foreign policy, this was just a veil over a real, seemingly indelible fear that the dynasty's appearance would revive the unified Austro-Hungarian state or introduce a power factor able to gain priority over the Czechs, South Slavs and others. It was easy to estimate that such a unit might endanger their commercial, economic and political interests and even jeopardize the recent territorial gains from Austria and Hungary.

It was clear within days that the lesser Allies' protests meant that the peace conference would not contemplate recognizing Friedrich, but the prime minister closed his ears and procrastinated, believing that time was on his side. The minimum requirement for that was that some influential group in society should lend him support, but that did not happen either, for domestic political reasons. Friedrich's monarchist tendencies were unacceptable both to the extreme right wing that was developing and to the Smallholders' Party. Horthy had practically nothing to say to him, the aristocracy viewed him as a parvenu, and the Social Democrats had become suspicious of his political antics. At most, Friedrich might have been imposed on the country by the Allies, but they had not the least intention of doing so.

The tug of war was taking place before the eyes of an almost helpless commission of generals sent to Budapest at the beginning of August. The decision to send the Inter-Allied Mission had been taken in Paris while the Hungarian Soviet Republic was still in existence, and no change was made later to the generals' brief, which was merely to size up the situation and gather information. It was August 13 before all four members had assembled: Reginald St. George Gorton of the United Kingdom, Harry Hill Bandholtz of the United States, Ernesto Mombelli of Italy, and Jean César

Graziani of France. The mission's most important work from Hungary's point of view was the task of curbing Romanian requisitioning to some degree. The mission was the channel by which news of systematic plundering of the country reached Paris and the Allied capitals. On some occasions, one or other of the generals (usually Bandholtz) would personally prevent an illegal act of robbery, styled requisitioning. But such activity by the generals cannot have been too effective, as the asset value seized was later put at between one and a half and three and a half thousand million crowns. This plundering, especially the expropriation of rail rolling stock, was a sore point with countries claiming reparations from Hungary. So the Romanian occupation was hardly popular in peace conference circles, especially as its pretext—Bolshevik rule—ceased to be relevant the moment that Budapest was occupied. This caused constant friction between the mission and the Romanian occupation Command. The problem was compounded because withdrawal of Romanian forces was very hard to achieve without prior cooperation and assistance from the Romanian army.

For no country can be left without security forces, even under quite peaceful conditions, and conditions in Hungary then could hardly be called peaceful. So some kind of armed corps would be needed even before the Romanians withdrew. One big problem was the arms shortage. As for the conference's repeated calls since early August for some kind of Hungarian force to be formed, the Romanians failed to respond for self-explanatory reasons: that would undermine their arguments for being in Hungary at all. They wanted to complete the process of meeting their material demands and put more pressure on the conference or an emerging Hungarian government to meet some persistent territorial demands of theirs. So the Romanian Command ignored calls from the Inter-Allied Mission for the Romanian army to distribute small arms to the emerging Hungarian police, gendarmerie and army. Brătianu, in discussions with Sir George Russell Clerk, representing the Allies, simply shrugged his shoulders at the demand to evacuate Hungary, saying that Romania might do that, but it would be the victorious powers' problem to know what to do with a country descending into anarchy.

Once this problem was understood in Paris, a subcommittee of the Inter-Allied Mission was sent out, headed by US General Halsey E. Yates, to organize the arming of the future armed forces. This committee eventually received a consignment from the Romanians, the rest of the arms coming from Austrian arsenals that were delivered to Hungary. This procedure itself is evidence that the Hungarian arsenals and barracks were bereft of weapons and that to describe the national army as an army was euphemistic. But what had happened to the weapons? Where had all the small arms gone, ubiquitous from the autumn of 1918 onwards, especially on the streets of Budapest? And what had happened to the Red Army's weaponry? Much of it must have been obtained by the Romanian army, while the rest went individual ways into sheds, cellars and wells, or finished on garbage dumps.

The powerless government, the generals' commission short of a mandate, and the self-interested Romanian Military Command created between them a climate and conditions in which lawlessness could thrive. Into this power vacuum stepped the Supreme Command, exercising political rights, influencing or thwarting the work of government-appointed commissioners, introducing censorship, and checking trains and their freight. Far greater revulsion, which would cast a shadow over the army for a long time to come, was induced by the White Terror, which spread after the Romanian withdrawal from southern and western Transdanubia to northern Transdanubia, and then to the capital and the Danube–Tisza region.

The White Terror was identified for a long time with Horthy, but it is clear today that the question of blame cannot be resolved so easily. For one thing, the terror was conducted not only by the so-called national army, but by the initial separate and later still large independent units under Lehár, especially the Feldbach group, and by some Romanian units as well. For another, the "army" that was not so much commanded as hallmarked by Horthy was far from comparable to a real army. Naturally Horthy, as a rear admiral, had never had land forces under his command before. He had sound knowledge of the fleet, but no similar knowledge of the army. He was outstripped in this regard by the high-ranking officers who gathered around him. Nor did he arrange the recruiting, organization, posting, and so on. Horthy was not previously acquainted with most of the officers in his circle. That situation meant a great deal of freedom for agile operators, not least because Horthy did not press to take actual control over the reorganizing army. Nor did he take command.[5] So the "supreme commandership" operated mainly as a position of symbolic power, with far less military than political weight.

It is widely considered that Horthy's organizational work was done for him by one of his trusty followers, Staff Captain Gyula Gömbös, but there are doubts about this assumption as well. Gömbös appeared in the region at the end of April and had talks with Serbian and French officers aimed at getting them to allow a counter-revolutionary base to be set up in Pécs. That did not succeed, but he won the French over to the idea that organizing could begin in Szeged. However, some of the politicians gathered in Szeged were none too keen on Gömbös, and managed to get the French Command to order him out. While in Szeged, Gömbös worked in the offices of the Ministry of War (as did Tibor Eckhart.) But the real work of military organization was done by former field officers, such as Pál Prónay, for example. When Gömbös left the city on July 29, he went first to Graz, where he failed to take over command of the military forces organizing in the western region and hurried on to Vienna, before finally returning to Budapest. There is no sign at all of Gömbös playing any outstanding role in reviving the army, or of Horthy calling particularly for his assistance in the process of mobilizing the groups, which had already begun.

In any case, some of the units assembled in Transdanubia had never been to Szeged, which only enhanced the inclination of their commanders to act independently. This applied to the unit under the command of Antal Lehár, mentioned already, which constituted a separate army, and took part in the punitive actions, if not to the extent that Prónay's commandos did. An important part in the reprisals was played by Gyula Ostenburg, who was a committed legitimist and never really Horthy's man. It is not known at all when he appeared in Szeged, but he certainly commanded a larger unit.[6] This would lead in 1921 to a situation where the "royal" forces commanded by Lehár and Ostenburg more or less clashed at Budaörs with the official army under Horthy's command. There are indications that Prónay's detachment, later a battalion, had special authorization for actions, and it did not wait for orders or instructions from the supreme commander, which had already led to friction between Prónay and Horthy before the final breach came in 1921. However, there is no doubt that Prónay in 1919 considered that his units were under the wing of the Supreme Command. For despite the constraints on him, Horthy commanded respect, as he was the highest-ranking officer in the whole camp and had gained a name for himself in one or two actions during the war. But that respect was probably not unalloyed, particularly not in "professional" military matters, where it was strongly conditional on him whether his command was accepted by those at his disposal. In view of all these circumstances, it was highly questionable what would have remained of the national army if Horthy had got rid of the unit commanders who acted in an arbitrary way.

The units of that army, who had replaced the badges on their caps with a white feather (where available, a crane's feather), were united to a far greater extent by their mortally wounded nationalist fervor and desire for revenge. The army had no real command, no organization and no ranks, and, as mentioned before, no arms. The longing for revenge was what precipitated the White Terror.

According to present knowledge, most of the atrocities were committed by small commando detachments under the command of Prónay and Ostenburg, with full approval and encouragement from their commanders. Somewhat later, a great reputation for such acts was gained by a brigade on the rampage in the Kecskemét area, which had been assembled by Iván Héjjas and a local farmer, Mihály Francia Kiss. Héjjas worked closely with Prónay but was not recognized by Horthy.

Meanwhile, the government in Budapest was arresting the remaining leaders from the Hungarian Soviet Republic, who were put on trial during 1920. Seventeen "Red terrorists" (mainly members of the Cserny group and the Szamuely detachment) and four people's commissars were sentenced to death, but the latter were later exchanged with the Soviet Union for Hungarian prisoners of war. So apart from those terrorists, most of the leaders of the Hungarian Soviet Republic escaped retribution in one way or another. By contrast, hundreds of insignificant figures who had fulfilled some tiny function or other under the Hungarian Soviet Republic became victims over the next few months of a vengeance operating outside any legal framework and with no restrictions, in villages and small towns sometimes chosen at random. On more than one occasion, those selected were dragged out of the prison before the eyes of their helpless guards. The commandos were particularly fond of hunting out Jews, because they saw it as the main goal of their whole undertaking to rid the country of liberals and Freemasons—and that meant, in their eyes at least, the Jews.

When reproached by the government, Horthy acknowledged in a letter that reprisals of this kind were wrong, but he traced them back to the absence of lawful, legal proceedings. So, in other words, he defended the arbitrary murders. It can be established ultimately that the illegal acts were committed, apart from by the Romanian army, by certain small groups and commando detachments of the Hungarian military that was re-forming. They were done presumably on orders from above and without danger of retribution, in a general atmosphere for which the supreme commander must certainly take some responsibility, along with the historical events that were taking place at the time. Only later, when the army had been built up and consolidated to some extent, did Horthy set about ridding himself of those who had been compromised and who were compromising him. That was made easier because some of his lieutenants turned against him openly and took the side of Charles IV. If he had done that in 1919 (not that it had or could have occurred to him then), not much would have remained of the army. "He had to stick by the detachments," wrote Prónay about Horthy's behavior at the time, "and he dared not impede the punitive expeditions, which had as their purpose a thorough reckoning with the Jews, because otherwise the camp standing on a national basis would have turned away from him, and gathered around somebody else."

The national anarchy by this time was irritating the delegates at the Paris peace conference as much as the period of Red rule had done. So the idea was put forward of sending a further representative out, charged with arranging the withdrawal of the Romanians and putting an acceptable Hungarian government in charge. The British recommended for the purpose a leading British diplomat, and the French left them to it, as the French Foreign Ministry had no candidate or workable idea at the time. So Sir George Clerk set out to restore order along the Danube.

Historians have made several attempts to characterize the new state authority of that period. Some have discerned at the end of 1919 and in 1920 a fascism supported by the petite bourgeoisie, while others have sought to work with the concept of military dictatorship, and some have simply talked of a restoration of the old political system. But a dispassionate analysis of the situation and events shows that in the months following the complete turn of events in society, it was not possible to discern a firm political structure at all. Tendencies, trends and efforts were observable in that chaotic political situation, but no basis can be found for assuming that there was any kind of clear political system in existence to which any of the definitions above could apply. It will be seen later that the situation was quite fluid, and the acts of the participants marked by uncertainty.

Notes

1. Romanelli arrived as an envoy of the Italian military mission in Vienna, but his exact brief is unclear. He is known to have intervened on behalf of people arrested or taken hostage under the Hungarian Soviet Republic. He is likely to have had a hand in a trade agreement between the Soviet government and the Italian mission in Vienna, under which the latter undertook substantial deliveries to be paid for in gold crowns and paper currency. These deliveries began, causing a scandal when discovered. Soon afterwards, the Italian Foreign Ministry demanded Romanelli's recall, for "exceeding his powers," and this was obtained.
2. *Keresztény Nemzeti Egyesülés Pártja.*
3. It emerges from French records that Horthy's agreement with the Romanian Command came not long before that movement was made.
4. Romania only joined in the chorus somewhat later and more cautiously.
5. The commander of the main forces leaving Szeged on August 8 was General Kornél Bernátskay.
6. Ostenburg's movements are not known precisely, but he seems to have been in Vienna and then joined the Graz group before appearing in Szeged.

2. Laying the Foundations of Statehood

Sir George Clerk paid one visit to Bucharest and two to the Hungarian capital. He ultimately managed to accomplish both his assignments, although with the Romanian withdrawal, the credit is not really his, but that of the peace conference, which was still operating with gaps in its ranks. For the conference personnel sent several letters to the Romanian government, initially quite calm ones, followed by a long, fulminating missive like an ultimatum, ordering it to withdraw its army and containing threats.[1]

Clerk's visits to Bucharest and Budapest in September were simply fact-finding exercises. The substantive talks came on the second visit, decided by the conference on October 13. By the time that Clerk arrived in Pest, the Inter-Allied Mission had largely completed the equation for a political solution. It was decided that apart from police and gendarmerie contingents of 4,000 men each, Horthy should be allowed to form two infantry divisions and a cavalry brigade, and that these units should be armed. General Gorton, and the British Admiral Sir Ernest Troubridge, who had been playing an important role in the region, supported Horthy politically, as did the American General Harry Hill Bandholtz.[2] General Graziani of France had no views at the time, although he later came to know Horthy personally and found him decidedly congenial. Such was the news awaiting Clerk on his arrival in Budapest.

The same news finally spurred the French Foreign Ministry, which would have liked to avoid the Horthy solution, into action. Prompted by the Czechoslovaks, France proposed a broad coalition government in Budapest, to be backed by international armed forces that would include Czechoslovak and Romanian contingents. This proposal was met by the other members with general stupefaction. Apart from the French foreign minister, Stéphen Pichon, there was nobody at the peace conference or on the generals' commission in Budapest who believed that Czechoslovak and Romanian gendarmes could be of assistance in pacifying Hungary.

Once that plan had been swiftly disposed of, Clerk was on a one-way street in Budapest. His first task was to extract from Horthy a promise that the entry of the army into the capital would not be followed by illegality, let alone the introduction of a dictatorship. The supreme commander gave such an undertaking and issued a statement on November 1, firmly condemning persecution of the Jews and announcing that he had "initiated the strictest enquiry; I will place the criminals, the perpetrators and the instigators alike, if they belong to my army, before the military court, and exclude them permanently from the bosom of the Hungarian National Army..." Horthy's rapid, almost breezy, conversion to parliamentary government, from the military dictatorship of which he may have been thinking not long before, and his intervention against the persecution of the Jews, should have given his radical followers pause for thought, and that line of thinking may actually have begun. Having distanced himself from Friedrich, Horthy was now taking another decisive, and to many people unexpected, step, which incidentally shows again how the rear admiral thought mainly in political terms. Armed with Horthy's promise, Clerk and the Entente officers prepared a detailed and meticulous plan for every moment of the Romanian withdrawal and Hungarian entry. The Hungarian armed forces, whose organization and entry were in the hands of Antal Lehár,[3] took control of the capital on November 14 from the evacuating Romanians, according to a timetable prepared by the Yates committee. This was probably a deliberate concession by Horthy and again a sign of his political acumen. However, he insisted on the ceremonial entry. The later emblematic arrival of Miklós Horthy on a white horse took place on November 16.[4] Budapest had become Hungarian territory again, although the country still had only a government that was condemned to resign, and the delay in concluding the peace treaty meant that it had no accepted borders either. Indeed, it did not even exist under international law.

The negotiations on a government went ahead with great difficulty, partly because Friedrich was still obstinate and partly because the parties' representatives could not agree. In fact it was a unique and rather grotesque circumstance that the new Hungarian government had to be assisted into the world by a British diplomat, yet nobody seemed to be insulted by or ashamed of that. Why not? Perhaps the most important factors were the radical transformation of the country and more than a year of commotion. They meant that there was no political group that could point to clearly formulated views or a reliable body of support. The struggle for political power was beginning in a very murky, opaque environment. Furthermore, the conference assistance was not resented by the Hungarian politicians, because they knew very well that they could not obtain the withdrawal of the Romanian army without it. As for the Social Democrats, they were delighted at the prospect of the Entente imposing democratic conditions.

After several days of futile consultations, Clerk came up with the saving idea of placing all the political leaders of any substance and standing round the table to reach agreement. On November 16, at the first meeting of the parties, he read out a statement underlining the fact that there had to be a provisional government committed and able to conduct democratic elections. The left-wing bourgeois politicians, the Social Democratic representative, Ernő Garami, and a few aristocrats, including István Bethlen, Gyula Andrássy and István Rakovszky, supported Albert Apponyi for prime minister, and Horthy joined this group as well. But this idea was thwarted in the subsequent negotiations by the representatives of Friedrich's Christian National Union Party (CNUP)—Károly Huszár, György Szmrecsányi and Gyula Rubinek. The CNUP certainly did very well in the subsequent elections, but that political success came only because the others were afraid that Friedrich might remain, which they thought would mean that the Great Powers would carry on refusing to sign a peace with Hungary. So in the interests of lifting the blockade, concluding peace, and restoring normal relations, Horthy sacrificed the idea of a dictatorship and the political majority sacrificed the nomination of Apponyi as prime minister. They resigned themselves to a government dominated by the CNUP, with the hardly known Károly Huszár as prime minister.[5] The need to do this was enhanced by its contribution to curbing the activities of the extreme right wing. Once Horthy embarked on a course of general elections and legality, such groups had lost the potential figure to which they hoped to refer, even if there was no outward manifestation of that in their camp. They became increasingly isolated and fragmented as time went by, although some managed to regroup in the early 1930s.

Finally, Sir George Clerk presented a memorandum to Károly Huszár on November 23, authorizing him to form a government. This happened on the following day, when Huszár received a second memorandum provisionally recognizing his government. The latter included the conditions on which recognition was being granted: the Allied and Associated Powers expected democratic elections to be held without delay and civil rights and liberties to be ensured. It emerges from Clerk's report to the Supreme Council that he was aware that the new government was not a true "coalition," but he defended this by saying that no better solution remained, and he had to acknowledge that such a government could have no Jewish members. The conference endorsed his view, and not even the French sought any other solution.

The powers sent successive so-called high commissioners to Budapest in subsequent months, to ensure that they had some representation in the country before the peace treaty was signed and ratified. The first to arrive was Sir Thomas Hohler from Britain in December 1919, followed by Maurice Fochet from France and Vittorio Cerruti from Italy.[6] The high commissioners set up their own little conference in Budapest, which meant that they discussed every matter considered to be important among themselves, and wrote a joint report to the Conference (later Council) of Ambassadors, which had taken the place, and taken over the duties, of the peace conference.[7] So the high commissioners exercised great influence over issues to do with Hungary, although some rivalry could be discerned among them in 1920–1921.

The CNUP took six of the eleven portfolios in the Huszár ministry. One was taken by Károly Peyer of the Hungarian Social Democratic Party, but he soon left the cabinet. Preparations for the elections began on November 17 with a franchise order introduced by Friedrich, but it proved to be impossible to ensure peaceful conditions for the campaign. Further acts of terror were committed by the Héjjas group, and another unit in Budapest began to attack the offices of left-wing bourgeois newspapers and publishers. The government, on the other hand, made no attempt to disarm the commandos, but issued an internment order to enable further thousands of ordinary people to be molested. Various institutions and bodies began to expel members who had taken part or become involved in the previous revolutionary events, mostly left-wing bourgeois or socialist intellectuals. The Social Democratic Party was induced by the bad atmosphere and the hope of further Great Power intervention to announce that it would stay out of the elections. That possibly understandable, but certainly wrong decision meant that the numerous working class remained unrepresented in the first National Assembly, in spite of the universal franchise, and the Social Democrats became more isolated than ever.

The turnout in the elections held on January 25–26, 1920, was almost 81 percent of an electorate of over 3 million. The Smallholders won 77 seats and the CNUP 76, and the so-called "booted" Parliament convened.[8] But the new National Assembly was far from reflecting the real political power relations in the country, not just because of the Social Democratic boycott, but because the CNUP was an umbrella party with no chance of sticking together. Its disintegration duly began in April. The long transition to a politically stable, independent country was far from over with the formation of the Huszár government. In fact, the battle for power was only just beginning.

The two most urgent tasks facing the government were to prepare to negotiate the peace treaty and to settle the matter of the head of state. On December 1, the peace conference sent the invitation and a delegation led by Albert Apponyi set out on January 5. Its credentials were presented on January 14, along with documents setting forth the Hungarian arguments on the peace treaty, maps showing ethnic distributions, and so on. The Supreme Council of the conference received the delegation on the following day, handed over the draft treaty, and on January 16, heard the contribution of Albert Apponyi. The official Hungarian position reflected in the submissions and addenda can be summed up as an appeal for the mainly Hungarian-inhabited areas adjacent to the proposed borders to be left to Hungary and for plebiscites to be held in some other areas with a mixed population.[9] The maps to back up the suggestion were later used again by Hungarian governments. However, it was not fortunate that Apponyi kept returning in his speech to the demand for a plebiscite. It is not known whether this had been agreed in advance or whether it was Apponyi's own decision.

The peace terms were thought to be unacceptable in Budapest, but the government nevertheless requested a 15-day extension of the period for reply, which it received, and also requested that the Hungarian question should be decided not in the Conference of Ambassadors, but at the Great Power negotiations (a kind of substitute conference) to be held in London on March 1. This was granted as well.

Meanwhile, talks continued on the question of the head of state, which seemed far from easy to resolve. There had been no royal Hungarian dynasty for centuries, the idea of a republic had few followers, and King Charles IV had resigned his powers and withdrawn into exile. Still, there were plenty of legitimists about, eager to see Charles on the throne again—but, in the main, exclusively with the Hungarian Crown on his head. More numerous still were monarchists who wanted a free choice of a king, who would not necessarily have to be Hungarian-born. Imaginations went to work, but before long they were being constrained from two directions.

The originator of the international campaign of protest against any member of the royal House of Habsburg assuming the Hungarian throne had been Hohler, the British high commissioner, who sought to kill two birds with one stone. He wanted to do a favor for the governments of countries neighboring Hungary, these being of importance for the current Anglo-French rivalry in the Balkans and the Danube Basin, and to assist Horthy, with whom the high commissioner was on very good personal terms. On January 30, Horthy issued a military order stating that a "provisional" head of state should be chosen immediately, and nobody could be in any doubt about who was seen as suitable for the post. In the fluid political situation at home, that declaration of will by Horthy proved to be decisive. On February 2, the Conference of Ambassadors passed a resolution banning the Habsburgs, as a result of which a "provisional" formula could be accepted by everybody. Horthy's election seemed to be a settled matter; only the rights and powers attaching to the head of state's function still had to be clarified. The excitable atmosphere in which the talks to reach a conclusion on this were held was stirred further when commando officers on February 17 murdered two Social Democrat journalists: Béla Somogyi, responsible editor of the Social Democratic daily newspaper *Népszava*, and Béla Bacsó, a young colleague of his. The clues led to Ostenburg's brigade and a strong suspicion arose that they went further, up to the Supreme Command or Horthy himself. The latter charge could not be proved, but the matter was certainly hushed up as far as possible and the perpetrators were let off lightly.

On February 27, the National Assembly passed, by a large majority, Act I/1920, stating that the National Assembly would temporarily elect a regent until the question of a head of state could be finally settled. The assumption was that the final settlement would soon be forthcoming, and so the term of the regent was not stated; indeed, the "regency" as a state form was not defined. On March 1, the day of the election, military officers appeared at the entrances and in the corridors of Parliament, and some even entered the chamber. These commando officers were demonstrating in favor of Horthy superfluously, as the parties had agreed in advance to his election, and his extra demands in connection with the task would have been met without them. The appearance of the officers, in fact, did Horthy more harm than good, but his adherents had to be given such a chance, just as Mussolini's had been during the pseudo-advance on Rome. Horthy became Hungary's regent, but few thought that he would remain so for over 24 years. Advocates of freely choosing a king expected him to conduct the great royal Hungarian election, while legitimists trusted him to preserve the situation and hand power over to the legitimate King Charles IV. Only a few foreign observers doubted whether the regent was inclined towards either solution.

Hungary, during the crisis, became a radically different country. It broke away from the Dual Empire and gained independence, as a country of medium size, a kingdom in principle, but headed by a regent, its multiethnic character lost, and its economy facing a new, more difficult situation. The framework of the state emerged early in 1920, but it was still unclear what forces and groups within it would take the centers of power or how the power structure would look. It was still doubtful whether the parliamentary system could consolidate. The full power structure would wait for about six years and then some years later would be challenged all over again.

Notes

1. The Great Powers halted all deliveries to Romania for a time.
2. There is no evidence for the assumption that the British involved were seeking a democratic solution and tried to pass Horthy over.
3. This contribution was never mentioned in the Horthy period after Lehár fell from favor over his part in the second Carlist coup attempt in 1921, and was forgotten by everybody later.
4. There is an ancient belief that a good ruler sits on a white horse, as opposed to the evil ruler's black one.
5. The Huszár government, incidentally, included Friedrich.
6. The last was replaced by Carluccio Castagneto in the autumn of 1920.
7. This organization consisted of the Paris ambassadors of the Great Powers. Its task officially was to take up a position on matters unresolved in the peace treaties, but in practice it considered every major foreign policy problem to do with the defeated powers.
8. A reference to the peasant boots "worn" by the Smallholder politicians.
9. The reason for the difference between Apponyi's speech and the documents is not known.

3. The Peace Treaty

On March 1, the day on which the regent was elected in Budapest, the Great Powers meeting in London began to discuss the Hungarian question again, and there was some hope that the original draft might be amended. David Lloyd George, the British prime minister, argued in general terms against detaching several million Hungarians from their country, while Francesco Nitti, his Italian counterpart, recommended altering the southern border in Hungary's favor. But their pronouncements were met by strong protests from the small states concerned and the French representatives at that time, and even resistance from Lord George Curzon, the British foreign secretary, and from some Italian diplomats. Lloyd George, incidentally, conceded that he had given his consent to the peace treaty on one occasion not long before. Nevertheless, the rapid British retreat was a response to French concessions in a longstanding dispute between the two countries over Asian oil, or at least the two developments coincided. Eventually, the only result of the Anglo-Italian intervention was the fact that the Great Powers appended to the peace treaty a letter expressing their good intentions.

This document, known as the Millerand Letter,[1] stated, *inter alia*, that small adjustments to the border might be made through the intercession of the League of Nations. Initially, more significance was attached to this sentence in Budapest than it would bear, or at least some people acted as if it had a serious import. Much more promising were the talks that began in Paris in the same month. French foreign affairs at the time of the London conference were still in the hands of Henri Mathias Berthelot, a great promoter of Romanian and South Slav interests, but Maurice Paléologue was in charge at the Quai d'Orsay by the time that the Hungarian delegation stopped over in Paris on their way home from London. Paléologue differed on the Central European question from his

81

predecessor, which allowed wide-ranging economic, financial, political and military talks to begin between France and Hungary in the second half of March. These were concerned primarily with a large French capital investment, the establishment of a Polish–Hungarian–Romanian bloc, and some easing of the terms of the peace treaty based on French goodwill. The last was concerned with easing the ethnic injustices and rationalizing the military requirements.[2] That turn of events placed the issue of the peace treaty in a new light.

Meanwhile, there had been a change of government in Budapest, as the provisional government resigned, as it was obliged to do, having completed its task. On March 15, Horthy appointed as prime minister another CNUP man, Sándor Simonyi-Semadam, who two days later read out to the National Assembly a letter from Albert Apponyi in Paris, calling for the illegalities of the military commando detachments to be ended in the light of the harmful effect that the terrorist acts were having on opinion abroad. An important change in government ensued on April 19, when Pál Teleki took over the foreign affairs portfolio. Although Teleki did not dispute the fact that the peace treaty had to be signed, there was a difficulty, because nobody with political ambitions wished to put their signature to it. Albert Apponyi and his whole delegation resigned, Teleki protested at the task, towards which the representatives of the Great Powers showed understanding, and Minister of Defense Károly Soós first agreed to do it and then refused. It was finally signed by two people of no political importance: Ákos Benárd, the minister of welfare, and Alfréd Drasche Lázár, ambassador extraordinary and minister plenipotentiary. The time and place were nominated by the Great Powers, and the signing took place accordingly in the Grand Trianon Palace of Versailles early on the afternoon of June 4.[3]

The Peace Treaty of Trianon reduced a country of 282,000 sq. km and 18.2 million inhabitants to 93,000 sq. km and 7.6 million people. About 30 percent of the Hungarian ethnic community became subjects of other countries. On the other hand, a previously multiethnic state became largely homogeneous.[4] Part V of the treaty covered military matters, stating for example that the professional army could be based on 12 years of service and was not to exceed 35,000 men. The treaty contained the principle of reparations, although the question of the amount of these was left to the Reparation Commission, which had already been established.[5] Mixed committees were to be established to settle inter-state and private legal disputes. The treaty allowed Austria, Czechoslovakia and Hungary to conclude a preferential trade agreement for five years, in other words to grant each other tariff concessions not available to other countries. That was a big concession compared with the hitherto rigid application of the most-favored-nation principle, and served to substitute for the customs union, which Italy and Czechoslovakia vigorously opposed. However, that logical and beneficial provision in the peace system met with rejection by the states concerned, in favor of an economic policy based on autarky, on seeing which, the Great Powers swiftly returned to the most-favored-nation principle. The peace treaties' articles on the principle of war crimes and punishment of war criminals were not applied either.[6]

The country lost not only territory and population, but an urban network, including the fastest-growing cities after Budapest—Pozsony (Bratislava), Kassa (Košice), Kolozsvár (Cluj), Temesvár (Timişoara), and so on—as well as mines, forests, waters, hills, upland pastures, roads, railways, raw materials, prosperity and scenic beauty. The oft-chided great common market and community of the Dual Monarchy also disappeared. Pozsony or Kolozsvár could only be visited with a visa, and goods could not be sent there at all, because Hungary had no commercial treaty with any neighboring country or any tariff legislation. Agricultural exports in 1920 amounted to 21 percent of their pre-war volume and industrial exports to 40 percent. The period was over when the gentry of Pest could travel over for an evening at the Vienna Opera. The independent Hungarian state set up in 1920–1921 was a different country from its predecessor, which meant that it had to think differently about its future.[7]

The debate on the peace treaty held in the National Assembly in November 1920 included some passionate outbursts and irredentist statements, but everybody knew that there was no alternative, and the house passed the text by a large majority. It was then ratified as Act XXXIII/1921. This process was assisted by the accompanying letter and by the expectations of the League of Nations. There were great hopes initially of the talks in Paris, but these proved to be a disappointment. The Hungarian side expected that the great opportunities being offered for French capital[8] would be rewarded with immediate, or at least very rapid, territorial concessions. The idea of Paléologue and other leading French figures, for French capital to gain financial and transport control over the whole region by a relatively long process, was probably based on using the economic position to influence a reorganization of political matters, including some territorial ones. This proved to be illusory for both sides.[9] Nevertheless, serious efforts to obtain it were made in Paris and in Budapest over several months. Hungarian politicians were stimulated particularly by the willingness to cooperate that they found in Warsaw. Since the Polish government was decidedly anti-Czech for various reasons, some had great hopes of the Hungarian–Polish grouping as a means for rapidly changing the northern border.

The fragmented and disorganized state of the post-war apparatus of authority and administration left opportunities for unsuitable, even irresponsible, people to intervene in foreign affairs. This was all the more possible because Hungary could only send representatives to the main capitals before the peace treaty was ratified. It still had no diplomatic or consular service, and the Foreign Ministry itself was still at a rudimentary stage. There were various plans for incursions, even for a joint Bavarian–Austrian–Hungarian attack on the peace treaties.[10] Others began to print crudely forged foreign currency,[11] and various unrealistic plans were made for retaining the whole of the "western counties," which were due to be annexed to Austria as the province of Burgenland. Others saw the Paris talks along with a Polish interest as a basis for retaking Subcarpathia (Ruthenia) by force. It has to be noted that Miklós Horthy, having dipped into politics and enjoyed some success in domestic affairs, also showed some foreign policy dilettantism in that period. He was ready to negotiate on the Ludendorff Plan, wanted to challenge Tomáš Masaryk, the Czechoslovak president, to a duel, and prepared great plans for revising the borders of Hungary as fast as possible, although Pál Teleki, initially as foreign minister and later as prime minister, managed to restrain him from taking such risky steps.

The situation seemed to be particularly favorable from the military point of view when Poland's attack on Ukraine faltered and the Soviet Red Army pushed the Poles back as far as Warsaw. With the situation becoming critical in mid-July, several Western European governments were inclined to avail themselves of the Hungarian offer to help the Poles, but their enthusiasm was curbed by the knowledge that the Hungarian favor would come at a price. Eventually the Polish army overcame the crisis with some aid from France, while the Franco-Hungarian rapprochement foundered in other regards as well. The amicability was clearly over when Paléologue fell in September, as Budapest knew that it could expect nothing from Berthelot's return to the Quai d'Orsay. Thereafter, the Hungarian Foreign Ministry turned steadily towards Britain, which the British Foreign Office took in good part, having taken a poor view of the earlier talks with Paléologue and tried to ensure that the plan failed. The Hungarian government could thereafter count for several years on discreet but effective support from leading circles in Britain.

Notes

1.   It was so named after its signatory, Prime Minister Alexandre Millerand of France.
2.   Not even the Allies' military experts agreed with the military restrictions in the peace treaties, but the will of Clemenceau in particular prevailed over their proposals, which would have conceded the defeated countries about twice as much as the treaties eventually permitted.
3.   Several writers have wrongly placed it in the Small Trianon Palace, which was quite unsuitable to hold the assembled Hungarians and delegations of the Allied and Associated Powers present when the act was carried out.
4.   The Hungarians made up about 54 percent of the population before Trianon and 92.1 percent after it (a 1930 statistic).
5.   Hungarian reparations were dealt with in the first instance by the Vienna subcommittee. The Hungarian government later requested that a Budapest subcommittee be established, but this never happened.
6.   The article, accepted only after long legal debate, was never implemented, because the Netherlands was not prepared to hand over the "main criminal," Kaiser Wilhelm, who had sought asylum there.
7.   Ratification took place on July 26, 1921; the United States and Hungary signed a separate peace treaty on August 29, 1921.
8.   There was talk of a 99-year lease of Hungarian State Railways, big construction projects on the Csepel branch of the Danube, and purchase of a large block of shares in the Credit Bank (*Hitelbank*).
9.   In France's case, this was not just due to resistance from the lesser Allies or from strong groups in French political life. It was also because France's potential was far from sufficient for such an undertaking.
10. On the German side, the plan was associated with General Erich Ludendorff, who had acquired a great name as a military commander, and so even Horthy and the Foreign Ministry became embroiled in the discussions.
11. At first Czechoslovak currency was printed in Austria, but the forgery was so poor that the organizer, Gyula Mészáros, was prosecuted twice. He went on nevertheless to take part in forging the French franc as well.

4. Pál Teleki's First Term as Prime Minister

Prime Minister Simonyi-Semadam proved to be thoroughly incapable of soothing tempers and creating calm. The one and only sign of pacification for the time being was disbandment of the Héjjas detachment. However, the detachments of commandos based at the Britannia Hotel continued to spread fear in Budapest, while the country's reputation abroad was sullied by the internment camps, the censorship, the regular curbs placed on freedom of assembly by uncontrolled groups, and above all the way in which illegal acts went unpunished.[1] This had all led by June 20 to the transport workers' unions declaring an international boycott of Hungary, covering mail and telegraphy as well as freight haulage. The government resigned. After long negotiations, the regent on July 19 called on Pál Teleki to form a government.

Teleki, a well-known geographer from a celebrated Transylvanian family, had rarely intervened in politics before the fate of Transylvania threw him into the fray. István Bethlen had encouraged him to join the Szeged government, and he had helped to prepare the materials for the peace negotiations before becoming foreign minister in April 1920. He was a monarchist, but almost certainly not an unmitigated Carlist. His primary aspiration in 1920 had been to see Archduke Joseph on the throne, but if that should not prove to be feasible for international reasons, he inclined towards a British candidate. Teleki was a conservative, religious figure, and a believer—even on biological grounds—in restricting the role of the Jews in the economy and the arts, although he refrained from animosity or incitement. His efforts during his first term of office as prime minister, up to April 1921, were spent mainly on reinforcing legality, in which he could point to some greater and lesser achievements.

Teleki managed to rid Budapest of most of its commando detachments. The number of atrocities fell and life began to return to normal. The prime minister held successful talks to end the boy-cott of Hungary by the transport workers, made easier because it was not hurting only or even primarily Hungary. He concluded the talks with the Soviet government on exchanging people's commis-sars for prisoners of war and allowed convicted people's commissars to leave for the Soviet Union. In December that year, the first amnesty regulation allowed lower officials of the Hungarian Soviet Republic to be released. Investigation into the Vienna robbery began, although the perpetrators could never account for some of the money.

The Romanian army had retreated only as far as the River Tisza in November 1919. There they had halted, and it took a fur-ther intervention by the peace conference before the Romanian prime minister, Alexandru Vaida-Voevod, would agree to evacuate the whole territory of Hungary.[2] The Romanians finally left the region beyond the Tisza on March 30, 1920. The elections that could be held there at last reinforced the Smallholders' Party, giv-ing them 91 seats to 59 for the CNUP (a number reduced also by splits), but a government could still only be formed by a coalition of those two parties, neither of which held a National Assembly majority.

Restoration of sovereignty over the Great Plain meant also that the new farming year looked more secure, although bad weather in 1920 brought catastrophic harvests, and livestock herds had been reduced drastically by the war, the armistice terms, and requisition-ing by the Romanian forces. These would take a long time to build up again, especially in the case of horses and cattle. Milk and dairy products remained a rare treat in the capital city, and there were great shortages of meat and fuel as well. The poor suffered heavily.

Legislative work began. The most important piece of legisla-tion was the draft land reform named after István Nagyatádi Szabó, although drawn up, collated and introduced by Minister of Agriculture Gyula Rubinek. It was preceded by much debate, because the organization of great landowners, the National Hungarian Farming Association,[3] found it too radical, while Nagyatádi Szabó's Smallholders' Party was dissatisfied, and the far right-wing "racial protectors" also attacked it for its limitations and uncertainties. Nagyatádi Szabó, who became minister of agriculture just before the bill came up for debate in Parliament, decided to defend it nevertheless, probably on the grounds that little was better than none. The act provided for 8.5 percent of the farmland to be redistributed over ten years to about 300,000 landless peasants and those with dwarf holdings, to veterans who had been decorated in the war—holders of the gallantry medal granting the title *vitéz* (or "warrior") and others qualifying for a "*vitéz* holding"—and to war victims (widows and orphans). To the total of about 400,000 receiving a landholding there can be added 260,000 who were granted a building plot. The act did not set upper or lower limits to the sums of compensation, which were expressed at the 1913 currency rate. The area of land available was very small, and the procedures originally accepted were very cumbersome. The latter were amended by the Bethlen government, but this did not help the fact that the reform was increasing the number of peasants with dwarf holdings unsuited to market production and too small even for subsistence farming. The land reform gave the villages some relief, but without increasing the number of viable farms or essentially altering the structure of land ownership. This was probably the greatest omission in the period, as it damaged every branch of the economy and the labor market, while constraining economic modernization. The question of how to settle the system of large estates in the country so that land reform could become a motor for development remained unanswered.[4] At least in theory, something better than the very meager Hungarian solution might have been found, but there was neither inclination nor incentive to do so.

The National Assembly did not have to deal with legislation introduced under the People's and Soviet Republics, which had been set aside by the Peidl and Friedrich governments. However, it extended the exceptional powers (up to July 26, 1922), defined the legal province of the regent,[5] and on September 29 voted through the so-called *numerus clausus* act.[6] The latter prescribed that "certain races and ethnicities" were to partake proportionately in higher education and that admission procedures had to take into consideration criteria of "loyalty to the nation." Only Jewish students were overrepresented in the universities and law schools, and so they were the only ones affected by the act, which was also insulting, because the Hungarian Jews interested in higher education considered themselves to be Hungarians practicing the Jewish religion, not a separate race. This segregation law was attacked not only by the Jewish population, but by the far right wing, for ostensible leniency, while turning public opinion in Western Europe against the Hungarian regime. Ultimately, new legislation introduced into the National Assembly by István Bethlen replaced the curbs based on "race and ethnicity" with limitations on certain occupational groups, while requiring university admissions to take geographical proportions into consideration as well.[7] But the symbolic significance of the *numerus clausus* act lay not in proportions, but in heralding a period when the Hungarian state would abandon its earlier approach of national accommodation and integration. Since large-scale Jewish capital controlled a decisive proportion of the Hungarian economy, and furthermore the modern, bourgeois branches of it (finance and commercial and industrial capital), the discrimination displayed threatened to bring about a split in society that would extend to its upper reaches.

Another move by the National Assembly that aroused consternation at home and abroad was the decision to impose sentences of flogging for profiteering. In the event, this act with medieval antecedents was rarely applied, probably because the judges did not want to make the law a laughing stock. However, Act III/1921 "on more effective defense of state and social order" had or could have had very serious consequences, as it covered not only those committing acts against the state but those failing to disclose knowledge of them.[8]

Meanwhile, Teleki tried to place foreign affairs on a firmer footing. He dropped the German–Bavarian plans from the agenda and began official talks with the Austrian and Czechoslovak governments. No progress was made on the Burgenland question, but negotiations with Edvard Beneš, the Czechoslovak foreign minister, began promisingly at Bruck in mid-March 1921, although they were soon jeopardized by the attempt of Charles IV to regain the Hungarian throne.

Since the office of government was a provisional one, Miklós Horthy pledged loyalty to Charles, with an assurance that he was only safeguarding the status of head of state for its legal owner. This must have persuaded Charles and his advisers that the appearance of the king would suffice to restore the old situation. After a hazardous journey, Charles was taken by his boyhood friend Count Tamás Erdődy from Vienna to Szombathely, where he was received by Bishop János Mikes. On the following day, the ex-king continued on his way to Budapest to take over from Horthy. But the astonished regent failed to behave as Charles had expected. Citing reasons of foreign policy, he categorically refused to meet his monarch's wishes and talked him into returning to Szombathely forthwith, after which he did everything to secure his permanent departure.

Debate still goes on as to whether Horthy rejected the restoration simply for fear of neighboring countries and possible occupation, or whether he had additional reasons. Certainly the attempt, despite its failure, made for diplomatic unpleasantness on a scale large enough to explain why the regent acted as he did. He would even have had to avert Charles's occupation of the throne if he had otherwise shown the full fidelity of a subject—for political reasons. However, there are several signs that this was not Horthy's only criterion. Horthy's entourage consisted largely of those who supported a free choice of king, while he, coming from a large family of medium landowners, supported mainly by his career as a military officer, and a member of the Reformed Church, had still not been accepted by the legitimist aristocracy. The majority of the National Assembly also favored a free choice of king. Memories of wars of independence from the Habsburgs and absolutist acts of savagery were alive among the general public. People had grown accustomed to the long reign of Francis Joseph, but fond memories were still not attached to him. Although his young successor had proved to be congenial, he had remained largely unknown in Hungary, where convinced Carlists made up only a tiny group. Characteristically, when Minister of Welfare József Vass caught sight of the king in Szombathely, he did not know who he was. And the country had spent over two centuries struggling for independence (or sometimes greater self-determination), and now Horthy was supposed to take responsibility for reversing with a stroke of the pen the one positive outcome of the wartime devastation. The line taken by the regent in 1921 lays open to question his "loyalty to the court" in the past. Finally, Horthy gave no sign then or later of wanting to resolve the question of the king, and his personal objectives and ambitions may have played a part in that as well.

Charles arrived in Szombathely on March 26, negotiated with Horthy on the 27th, and returned to Szombathely to await government clarification of the foreign political situation. The king claimed that his move had the support of Aristide Briand, the French foreign minister, and Charles seems likely to have received some encouragement from ministry circles, if not the minister himself. French diplomacy was deeply concerned by the risk of *Anschluss*, annexation of Austria by Germany, which it wanted to avoid at all costs, and one possible means of avoiding this was to bring Austria and Hungary under one monarch again. But Charles IV's adventure had a severe internal contradiction. He could expect outside support if he could obtain the Austrian as well as the Hungarian crown, but he could not mention that eventuality in Hungary, where most legitimists opposed reviving Austro-Hungarian cohabitation. Not long beforehand, the legitimists had proclaimed that Charles could only wear his country's crown exclusively as King of Hungary.

The wrangling went on for ten days, giving neighboring countries a chance to intervene as well. While the Great Powers worked to persuade the Austrian government to grant Charles a transit visa and Switzerland to receive him back,[9] Czech Foreign Minister Beneš issued an ultimatum, and a feverish reconciliation of viewpoints began between Prague, Belgrade, Bucharest and Rome. This gradually gave the impression that these countries alone had worked to remove Charles, and the embarrassed Hungarian government said nothing to deny this, although it knew that the truth was radically different.

Although it remains uncertain what policy the prime minister pursued in those difficult days, Teleki resigned, the Czechoslovak–Hungarian talks foundered, and the Little Entente was formed. The ring around Hungary had in fact begun to form in 1918, but there had been too many differences among the neighboring countries at that time to let them conclude such an alliance. The first anti-Hungarian treaty was signed on August 14, 1920, by Czechoslovakia and the Kingdom of the Serbs, Croats and Slovenes.[10] This was followed on November 12 by the Italian–Yugoslav Treaty of Rapallo, which included a rejection of Habsburg restoration and prescribed consultations in the case of a Hungarian or Austrian threat. After the attempted royal coup came a Czechoslovak–Romanian treaty (April 23, 1921). The circle closed when Yugoslavia and Romania set aside their differences over the division of the Banate to conclude a treaty of alliance on June 7. Unsurprisingly under the circumstances, the Czechoslovak–Hungarian talks came to nothing.

Notes

1. The last was possible because the detachment members collaborated with police circles or readily destroyed the evidence against them, as for instance in the Somogyi–Bacsó murder case.
2. However, the Allied Powers recognized Romania's annexation of Bessarabia.
3. *Országos Magyar Gazdasági Egyesület (OMGE).*
4. If the intention had been to grant land to those who could pay for it (via compensation) and had the means to till it, the mass of rural poor would have remained, but if a radical reform had been carried out, the fragmentation of land ownership would soon have created great new problems.
5. Act XVII/1920 empowered the regent to adjourn the National Assembly, order the army into foreign service in time of danger, and exercise the power of clemency.
6. Act XXV/1920.
7. Act XIV/1928. The universities did not always or everywhere observe the spirit of the new law, whose main practical effect was to give children of the non-Jewish middle class access to higher education. Many Jewish young people were sent abroad to study (for instance to universities in Fascist Italy), at no small cost to their parents.
8. The act even allowed for capital punishment, although this was imposed only in the cases of Imre Sallai and Sándor Fürst, based on government emergency regulations of September 19, 1931.
9. The obstacle was the Swiss view that Charles had abused their hospitality. In the end, the Swiss government agreed to have him back, but assigned as a place of residence Wartenegg, which was further from the border than Prangins, and requested an undertaking from him not to cause further political embarrassment.
10. Length meant that the name of the state was used only on protocol occasions and the name South Slav or Yugoslav gained ground. The Kingdom of the Serbs, Croats and Slovenes officially became Yugoslavia only in 1929, but the name is used below for convenience.

4. RECOVERY: ISTVÁN BETHLEN'S TEN YEARS

1. Orientation

The new government was formed on April 14, 1921, by István Bethlen, whose ten years in office as prime minister have justifiably been called the Bethlen era. Like Teleki, Bethlen was a Transylvanian count, a small-scale magnate with 5,500 *hold* (3,135 ha) of land and a modest mansion, who had lost everything in 1918 and escaped on foot with his family from a partly armed crowd intent on pillage and robbery. Even in peacetime, he had taken part in national and still more in Transylvanian politics, but he gained a decisive role only when he managed to organize the counter-revolutionary forces in exile in Vienna. The question of appointing him prime minister had come up during the negotiations with Sir George Clerk, and he had been Horthy's first choice in July 1920. Now Teleki's resignation had opened up the way for him.

The new prime minister was firmly convinced that politics is the art of the possible, and he wanted to found his foreign policy on a realistic assessment adjusted to the mood of the period. Up to 1928, he did not even let the word "revision" (in a territorial sense) escape from his mouth, and thereafter he championed peaceful revision. At the same time, he consciously strewed the path that might lead to revision one day. (It is another matter that he made mistakes in doing so and only recognized them much later.) In domestic policy, he sought a firm state dedicated to law and order, one in which the "licentiousness" of democracy could not lead to upheaval and in which authority would be respected, but social movement was not restricted to a degree that might cause an explosion. Although he personally stood close to agricultural circles, he

knew very well that the economy could not be built up without promoting the interests of big business as well. So he sought a balance
by representing the rights and interests both of the traditional aristocracy and great landowning elite and of capitalism, and brought
members of the upper middle class into the sphere of executive
authority.

Bethlen did not disguise his "counter-revolutionary" past. He
emphasized nation-building and economic advance as tasks for the
state. He called his policy a national one, but he added that the
nation could only be served across a broad horizon, and it had to
retrieve the horizon that the self-involved Hungarian nation had lost
under Habsburg rule. He pointed out from time to time that this
country belonged to the cultural circle of Christianity, although he
seldom employed the "Christian national" label, and if he did, he
would quickly add that, as he saw them, neither the word
"Christian" not the word "national" bore any connotations of
excluding citizens of the state. He was roundly criticized by the far
right-wing opposition as a bargainer, a traitor, a liberalizer and a
Freemason for this reason, and for allowing in international capital
and supporting the interests of domestic Jewish capital. Bethlen
was no great speaker, but he proved to be an excellent negotiator.
He rarely wore the *díszmagyar*, the ceremonial dress of a
Hungarian nobleman, but he could convey what he stood for well
enough wearing Western clothes.

Bethlen was in a very difficult position after his appointment,
because he did not possess a government majority to suit his tastes
and aspirations. He was still obliged to head a coalition, in which
the Smallholders were in a strong majority, and the prime minister
had no wish to wear Smallholder leading strings. The other serious
problem was the fact that the prospect of economic progress would
elude him until the confused financial situation had been remedied.
The first to make an attempt to refloat the country's finances was
Minister of Finance Lóránd Hegedűs, who sought to tap domestic

resources and increase tax revenues through what was termed a "wealth ransom": a way of taxing wealth. He also wanted to stimulate investment, but this was impeded by the measures that he took to improve public finances. As a result, he met with very strong resistance and resigned soon afterwards. (His efforts are discussed again in more detail in the chapter on the economy.) Hegedűs was followed as minister of finance by Tibor Kállay and then Frigyes Korányi. They increased the propensity to invest with an initially mild dose of inflation, which also helped gradually to soak up unemployment. There can be no doubt that the prime minister endorsed and embraced this policy. However, it could do nothing to relieve the shortage of capital or the rising indebtedness of the state.

Before addressing this difficult issue, Bethlen wanted to clarify his government's situation in Parliament. He had thought originally that he could squeeze back the Smallholders and build a broad conservative camp, a kind of "law and order" party that would encompass both the free-choice-of-king and the legitimist camps. His efforts to fragment the Smallholders were helped along by the Eskütt affair: Lajos Eskütt, personal secretary to István Nagyatádi Szabó, had been selling export permits from the Ministry of Agriculture. News of this corruption scandal was released by the prime minister in an attempt to discredit Nagyatádi Szabó, even though a fairly insignificant matter was being blown up out of proportion. He appeared to imagine that the scandal would help to rid him of the "booted" Smallholders once and for all, but that is not how things eventually turned out.

Nor did the negotiations with the legitimist political leaders end as they had begun. At a meeting with Gyula Andrássy and his associates, Bethlen conceded in principle that Charles had a right to the Hungarian throne, although he made exercise of that right dependent on how circumstances developed, in other words postponing it to the Greek Calends and emphasizing the exclusiveness of the Hungarian Crown. Bethlen rightly considered that the two provisos made it impossible for the idea of Charles ascending the throne to be treated seriously. Cautious enquiries abroad convinced him that Charles's cause no longer met with understanding anywhere. Indeed the French Foreign Ministry, which in 1920 (in a complete reversal of its position a year before) had warmly supported the idea of crowning Archduke Joseph king,[1] was now against that as well. Regent Miklós Horthy was of the view that for Charles, the Hungarian Crown would simply be a springboard to Vienna, and Bethlen was coming to similar conclusions. He was also sure that the *Anschluss* was inevitable,[2] which meant in itself that he could not support Charles for the throne. The agreement with the Andrássy group was designed more to promote the domestic political solution that Bethlen envisaged than to settle the question of kingship.

Notes

1. The main exponent was Maurice Fochet, the French high commissioner in Budapest.
2. The Foreign Ministry was soon of the view that the inevitable *Anschluss* should be opposed so that the price of approval could be exacted from Germany in due course.

2. Sopron and Charles IV

The government faced some serious foreign policy issues at the end of the summer. Bethlen wanted to see the already illegal Yugoslav occupation of the Pécs–Komló–Baja district ended, not least because it contained the country's most important coalfield. Belgrade, on the other hand, was doing all that it could to retain the area, believing that the left-wing forces there—based on the strong miners' movement and the Communists and Social Democrats who had fled there after the fall of the Hungarian Soviet Republic— would support those organizing to oppose Hungarian sovereignty. Nor could there be further delay in settling the so-called Burgenland question in the West, now that the peace treaty had been concluded. Moreover, Bethlen wanted Hungary admitted into the League of Nations, correctly seeing this as a first step towards ending his country's international isolation.

The first step by Foreign Minister Miklós Bánffy was to have the Ambassadors' Council agree to link withdrawal of the Yugoslav army with the Burgenland handover. The Yugoslavs did in fact evacuate the Baranya zone at the end of August after the Great Powers had intervened, but there was no success in the bargaining with the Austrian government. Budapest, however, was aware that the French government would not rule out a slight frontier adjustment at Austria's expense, as long as it was peaceful, as a way of chastising the Austrian government for failing, in France's view, to do enough to curb the *Anschluss* movement that had flared up in the country. So there was little difficulty about making a small concession to one defeated country at the expense of another. Bánffy had pointed out the possible solution to the French by mid-July: Hungary would hand over Burgenland peacefully and securely in exchange for retaining the city of Sopron and its environs. This the French Foreign Ministry had not rejected, and Paris also knew that the Italian foreign minister was inclined to accept it as well, although he attached the provision that Hungary should first hand over the whole territory and then begin negotiating the concession. Bánffy did not think that this was a feasible procedure, no doubt because he did not trust in the generosity of Austria, once it was in possession. The recommendation from the French Foreign Ministry was that Hungary should take that detail up with the Italians. In fact that "detail" became responsible for all the complications, but it appeared to the Hungarian foreign minister to be the most important issue at stake.

The government handed over to the Austrians the bulk of the territory (Zone "A"), but allowed it to be infiltrated by so-called insurgents, mainly former commando detachments from other parts of Hungary,[1] who created conditions in which the Austrians were obliged to leave the field. The western Hungarian uprising began on August 27, with clashes first at Pinkafő (Pinkafeld) and then Ágfalva. The incidents proliferated in September, culminating in a battle at Ágfalva on the night between the 7th and the 8th, in which several men were killed. After the subsequent evacuation of Zone "A," the Hungarian government came up with a new formula: it would only be able to order the insurgents out if it had a concession with which to appease them. But Pietro Tomasi della Torretta, the Italian foreign minister, was immovable. He recommended sanctions against Hungary in early September and did all that he could to prevent Hungary's admission to the League of Nations at its September Assembly.[2] It seems that the Italian envoys in Vienna and Budapest eventually persuaded Torretta that a prior concession had to be made to the Hungarians, and he abandoned his hard line on September 14.[3] On September 15, Bánffy officially informed Vienna, Rome and Paris of the "Sopron formula." It had been clarified that the Hungarian and Austrian governments would both accept Italian mediation gladly, but nothing happened for some days, probably because Torretta was waiting to hear the British position.

However, the Ambassadors' Council was officially demanding evacuation, and there were threats attached to that, based on the earlier Italian proposal. Bánffy then turned to the Czechoslovak foreign minister, Edvard Beneš, who readily agreed to mediate. That proved to be enough to move Rome, which announced its intention of mediating in the Ambassadors' Council on September 29. However, there were further delays because the British Foreign Office first expressed reservations and only agreed to the concession of Sopron to Hungary and to the Italian mediation on October 6. Meanwhile, one of the insurgent leaders, Pál Prónay, had proclaimed a Banate of the Lajta (Leitha) on October 4, with the intention of organizing opposition to the handover in the entire Burgenland zone. This again raised a danger that the Hungarian government would have trouble controlling the detachments, as the concession proposed would appear very meager.

Finally, the Austrian chancellor and the Hungarian delegation were invited to Venice for October 11. There Johannes Schober was presented with a decision by the Great Powers and could change it only to the extent that the Hungarian government accepted the principle of a plebiscite. It was stated in addition that Austria would accept the proposals of the commission during the designation of the border, or, if it were unable to do so, it would abide by the recommendation of the Council of the League of Nations. The Hungarian government undertook to hand Burgenland over to Austria, with the exception of the area where the plebiscite was to be held, and to have the irregulars withdraw to that end.

However, armed reinforcement was needed in the Sopron area, as the local guard was small and the victorious powers did not want to send in any sizable military force. So Gyula Ostenburg's brigade of gendarmerie was dispatched for the purpose. Antal Lehár's unit was also in the area, and having the two legitimist commanders near the border proved to be risky indeed.

The lesson drawn by King Charles IV from the Easter debacle was that a further attempt to regain the throne would need the backing of military force and pressure. Those who assisted him in his plan, apart from Colonel Lehár and Captain Ostenburg, included

Count Sándor Hunyadi, Count József Cziráky, Gusztáv Gratz and István Rakovszky. Legitimists such as Gyula Andrássy and Albert Apponyi, with whom the prime minister had reached agreement, were not initiated into it. After thorough preparations, a plane bearing Charles, Queen Zita, Aladár Boroviczény and several pilots landed on October 20 on Cziráky's estate at Dénesfa. However, there seems to have been a mistake after all, as the king arrived earlier than expected, causing great haste and eventually a serious delay.

Bánffy established retrospectively that if the king had not delayed, but left straight for the capital, he could have occupied it on the 21st or 22nd with no trouble, as there was no military force available to the government in the area. Instead, time was spent on ceremonials, swearing in troops, receiving delegations, and so on, and the moment for the coup was missed. By the time that the first of four royal trains, bearing Ostenburg's gendarmes, arrived at Budaörs, the government had managed to cobble together a unit of civilians, mainly association members and university students. These Ostenburg swiftly dispersed, but he halted his unit nevertheless, for want of an order from the king to advance to Kelenföld station, which was 10–15 minutes away. On the following afternoon, government troops arrived from other parts of the country, and on seeing the numerical superiority of these, some of the officers who had sworn allegiance to the king gave him poor information. The king relieved them of their oath and the soldiers began to desert from the king's troops. Ostenburg announced that he was not capable of continuing the struggle. The king would then have liked to return to Szombathely, but the train was cut off by government forces. He then sought refuge in the Esterházy mansion at Tata, but there the government arrested the royal couple and their entourage and sent them to Tihany Abbey, where Charles waited for the Great Powers to assign him a new place of exile and means of transport to it.

The king was under arrest, and a louder campaign against him than ever began in Prague and Belgrade. Beneš demanded compensation for the costs of mobilization and the planned partial occupation, and also insisted that the Venice Agreement should be set aside and that the Little Entente should take part in military control of Hungary. The diplomats looking into the sense of these measures, well aware of the situation and knowing how the Hungarian government had taken up arms to disarm a ruler otherwise recognized as legitimate, something unprecedented in modern history, realized that there was no sense in the mobilization and found only one answer. The Czechoslovak and Yugoslav governments were intent on ousting the Bethlen government.

The Council of Ambassadors rejected the demands. Once the danger had passed, the French Foreign Ministry tried to find some consolation for Prague, but managed only to express the demand for dethronement and for military intelligence about Hungary gathered by the Little Entente states to find its way to the Military Control Commission. However, the Hungarian government had already decided about the dethronement and the Little Entente already had a right to make submissions to the military controllers.

The Hungarian government handed Charles over to the Allies, and a British cruiser, *HMS Glowworm*, took him by agreement with the Portuguese government to Madeira, where the monarch, the Emperor of Austria-Hungary and King of Hungary, died on April 1, 1922. Back in Budapest, the National Assembly passed the act of dethronement of the House of Habsburg by a large majority.[4] This was the third occasion on which Hungary had dethroned the Habsburg dynasty,[5] but the form of state legally remained a kingdom. Hungary was not alone in being a kingdom in Europe, of which there were several, but it was alone in leaving the throne vacant. No serious opportunity arose to place the Holy Crown on anybody's head in the period up to the proclamation of a new republic. "You are a bold, but slightly bizarre, nation," one French prime minister remarked.

The Vienna Agreement luckily rode out the storms. The plebiscite was held on December 14–15, when a majority of 72.5 percent in Sopron and 65 percent in the whole disputed area voted to remain in Hungary.[6] The chance of obtaining the Sopron decision had been obtained by a decision of the Great Powers and by Hungarian government policy reliant on the insurgents, but the decision itself was made by the local population. That was the one revision of the peace treaty allowed to Hungary with the consent of the victorious powers, and it has not been challenged in a serious way since. Although the Hungarians and the Austrians had delivered a great many wounds to each other during the upheaval and the election campaign, the storm soon died down again.

Notes

1. Pál Prónay arrived with a brigade, as did István Héjjas and his brother with their men, and even István Friedrich came with an armed group that he had recruited.
2. In practice, the British and the French advised the Hungarian delegation to withdraw its request, which the government did to prevent loss of face.
3. He traveled to Vienna on that day and held talks with Austrian Chancellor Johannes Schober as well as with the two envoys.
4. The act was augmented, at the request of the Ambassadors' Council, by a declaration that the dethronement referred not only to the royal branch, but to all descendants of the House of Habsburg. This excluded the claim of Archduke Joseph and others to the throne.
5. This was done first in 1707 by the delegates to the Diet of Ónod, headed by Ferenc Rákóczi II, and secondly by the National Assembly on April 14, 1849, during the 1848–1849 Revolution and War of Independence.
6. It was assumed for a long time abroad that Hungary had won only by massive fraud. But the scattered cases of fraud, perpetrated mainly by college students, involved far too few voters to upset the decisive victory in Sopron. There was no chance of anything of the kind in front of the Allied officers. The Sopron committee of generals affirmed that the voting had taken place legally and in good order.

3. The Basic Domestic Political Equation

The attempted royal coup ruled out Bethlen's original plan to form a united conservative party that would include the legitimists. Some of the legitimist leaders were in custody. Cooperation would no longer be possible with what was a broken political force. Although the intellectual current of legitimism survived in various self-styled "Christian" parties and revived in the 1930s, it would never play a distinct political role again.

The far right had also weakened to some extent. The prime minister had drawn on the assistance of the commando leaders during the settlement of the Burgenland–Sopron question. Later he had taken firm action to ensure their departure, and Ostenburg was prosecuted for his part in the attempted coup. The far right-wingers who supported a free choice of king, such as Gyula Gömbös and Tibor Eckhardt, stayed on the government side for the time being. This prevented the Gömbös group from acting independently. All that it could try to do was to influence government policy according to its lights.

Bethlen gained strength at the end of 1921, through the success of the Sopron plebiscite and the reoccupation of the Baranya region and Új-Szeged. In April 1922, Hungary was able to take part in the Genoa Conference on the problems of the world economy. Although the discussions did not achieve their purpose, Foreign Minister Bánffy, like Walther Rathenau, the German foreign minister, made contact with Georgy Vasilyevich Chicherin, the Soviet foreign policy commissar, and agreed to prepare for commercial and diplomatic relations between their two countries. Closely questioned by Chicherin, Bánffy stated that Hungary, according to its strength and conditions, would support a Soviet military move against Romania and remain neutral in the event of a similar move against Poland.[1] The documents on these negotiations warrant our making a radical reassessment of the relative weight accorded to aspects of foreign policy based on ideological considerations, strongly though those considerations were voiced at the time.

Although the government's prestige had grown, the question of its parliamentary support remained unresolved, as Bethlen continued to find his Smallholder majority unpleasant and unreliable to work with. He first found a *modus vivendi* with the Social Democratic Party. This seemed inescapable from the international point of view as well, as Bethlen sought in several regards to meet Western European norms.[2] He also thought that the Social Democrats' widespread foreign connections might be helpful with certain problems, and as he admitted himself, they supported him on national matters. Bethlen, incidentally, often later pointed out to Hungarian Social Democrats the example of their counterparts in the West, comparing the behavior of those with what he saw as the rigid, orthodox program of Hungarian Social Democracy.

Be that as it may, there was hardly evidence of orthodoxy in the talks that the Social Democrats held with the government or in the agreement reached with it on December 22, 1921, although this remained secret for the time being. This much-debated document certainly restricted the freedom of action of the Social Democratic Party, but it had the advantage of bringing it out of the ghetto to which it had been consigned by its part in the Hungarian Soviet Republic, the ensuing White Terror, and its boycott of the general elections. It was now entering the political scene again by the back door. It renounced political strikes, republican propaganda, organization of state employees, and the possibility of political cooperation with the bourgeois opposition. At the same time, it espoused support for Hungary's foreign policy interests and cooperation with the bourgeoisie on economic matters. The government, meanwhile, was to ensure the party and the trade unions freedom to operate, and promised a swift end to the accelerated legal proceedings, an imminent partial political amnesty, and reform of the social insurance system. The government immediately fulfilled the first three promises, but the insurance question was not resolved for a long time. The government did not make concessions on the internment system, as the Social Democrats wished, or on the question of Social Democratic exiles, for which the Social Democrats sought a chance of immediate repatriation without consequences. However, the number of internees was substantially reduced, and the system was abolished in 1924. The émigrés were allowed home only later and selectively.

The document known later as the Bethlen–Peyer Pact was a compromise that left room for Social Democracy to retain limited legality up to 1944. Perhaps the toughest of its stipulations was the ban on political cooperation with the bourgeois opposition, which characterized the absurdity of the government policy for dividing society. Like all agreements, this pact could have been shifted in theory in several directions, but conditions in Hungary and the political approach of the Social Democratic Party meant that the shift was at the expense of Social Democracy, not in its favor.

There is no avoiding the fact that the Social Democratic Party steadily lost electoral support, winning only five seats in 1939, as opposed to 25. The loss of support happened under conditions in which the party had no appreciable competition in organizing the workers in the second half of the 1930s. The outlawed communists kept their own organizations and tried to distribute their propaganda throughout the period, but they remained very few in numbers and their chances were all but non-existent. If they had managed to recover, the police would have come down on them immediately. They were unable to exert any appreciable influence at any time during the period. As for the efforts of the parties organized on a Christian basis, they made temporary gains only initially: the Christian trade union movement remained embryonic. The far right-wing organizations, as far as can be judged, were attractive to the workers up to the mid-1930s and still more at the end of the 1930s, but they placed little emphasis on organization until Ferenc Szálasi set to work in 1938.

Even so, the workers' left wing of the Social Democrats never reached a stage where they could shift the regime towards formal democracy, let alone consensus democracy. They saw survival and criticism as their main tasks, fearing that activation of the workers and an autonomous Social Democratic policy might endanger the scope for operation that the pact had ensured for them. That extreme caution was sharply criticized even by so moderate a representative of the émigrés as Ernő Garami, and caused mounting dissatisfaction among the party's followers. What the pact won at least for the party, for the time being, was a moderate representation in Parliament and the chance to keep its branches, offices and press. It is hard to judge whether it was right to make the pact or not. There hardly seems to have been any alternative to signing it in 1921, but that of course does not mean that there was no alternative by 1925 or 1929, although by then the system had consolidated and it may have been difficult to shake it off.

Towards the end of 1921, when the organizers of the royal coup and those who had taken part in it were awaiting their release from prison, Bethlen entered into dialog with the Smallholders. He visited the party's club at the end of January 1922 and made it known that his CNUP would like to merge with the Smallholders. That meant in practice that on February 22, 1922, the prime minister and a couple of dozen followers joined the Smallholders' Party and formed a new organization known as the Christian Smallholders', Agriculturalists' and Citizens' Party.[3] This new governing party became known as the United Party,[4] rather than by so long a name. Bethlen announced that he would accept the principles of the Smallholders' Party, which was nothing but humbug. The proclamation was far from resembling the prime minister's true convictions. The Smallholders, for instance, were after radical acceleration and greater effectiveness for the accepted land reform—not Bethlen's intention at all. In other words, the difference over the land question was too great for the viability of this combination even to be assumed. The maneuver on Bethlen's part made sense because he was convinced that he and those with similar personal weight (connections, knowledge, political technique, and so on) could gain supremacy over the "booted" Smallholders and then dictate the tasks.

The problematic sphere of the Hungarian village was not resolved. Bethlen speeded up implementation of the land reform somewhat (with a program styled the *novella*), but its basic parameters were unchanged. The fragmentation of the Smallholders' Party carried out in 1921–1922 meant that the problem would not be solved in the future either. The village retained its old character. From the economic point of view, it remained a repository of masses of superfluous agricultural workers and owners of dwarf holdings. The far greater restrictions on emigration meant that the rural poor had no means of seeking a new job or home abroad. The vast concealed rural unemployment was among the reasons why the agricultural sector became an express obstacle to general economic development, while the sector itself suffered increasing difficulties.[5] Meanwhile, the state of the agricultural sector maintained the antagonism between landowners and capitalists, although this was concealed initially, and this antagonism had an influence on how political life developed. The tension heightened from 1930 onwards, as the mass rural poverty placed even greater burdens on politics and became a permanent problem for the political atmosphere of the 1930s. It formed the basis for the subject matter and campaigning of the *népi* group of writers concerned with the lot of rural people, and became a feature of all kinds of far right-wing outbursts and demagoguery.

The end of 1921 and beginning of 1922 brought political conditions in which Bethlen, as head of the United Party, could expect victory in the new elections but still thought it advisable to tighten the current electoral law. His draft sought to reduce substantially the number entitled to vote,[6] but the aspect that met the greatest resistance was the idea that the ballot was to be open again, not secret, except in the capital and the municipal boroughs. The response in the National Assembly was obstruction, but its mandate ran out on March 1, 1922, before the new electoral bill had been passed. The obstructive members trusted that the election would have to be held under the old law, but that did not happen, as the prime minister issued a decree on the franchise instead. This flouted parliamentarian principles, of course, although Bethlen managed latterly to set up an expert body prepared to state that this illegal measure was constitutional after all.[7] After the political vacuum (described already) that followed the events of 1918–1919, democracy had few chances, but this was the point at which it formally bled to death.

The proportion of the population included in the electorate under the new franchise order resembled those in the rest of Europe at that time. Its biggest anomaly was its decision to reinstate open voting in small towns and villages, which left the voters subservient to administrative officials and landlords. It concurrently eroded the vote of the Smallholders and increased the chances of those who supported Bethlen's policies. So too did the fact that Bethlen's new umbrella party began to be joined by the "gentlefolk"—owners of large and medium-sized landed estates, high-ranking administrative officials, and discharged and reserve officers.

The election campaign began, with Gömbös as the main organizer for the government party. It was a merciless struggle, one of the bloodiest events being the bombing of the bourgeois liberal club premises in the Erzsébetváros district of Budapest. It was a professionally made bomb that did huge damage and killed several people. The police swiftly announced that the perpetrators had been arrested and then that the suspects were innocent after all. After a long silence, new suspects were found and given harsh sentences in a show trial, but the charge of causing an explosion was overturned on appeal.[8]

The general elections held on May 28–June 11, 1922, gave 143 of the 245 parliamentary seats to the United Party, 25 to the Social Democrats, and 20 to the CNUP. It was a serious defeat for the Christian political movement, for one thing because it had split after the attempted royalist coup, and for another because it failed to present a new program pleasing to the broader electorate. The other seats went to smaller parties and independents. The government party now had a comfortable parliamentary majority, but that was not the essential difference, for there had been a radical change in the structure of the party's representatives. The real Smallholders, the "booted" peasant farmers, were largely eliminated, leaving them only with spokesmen in the National Assembly. Their places had been taken by Bethlen's men: landowners, high sheriffs and high-ranking functionaries. Alongside these were a minority representing the radical right-wing Gömbös group, and the remaining true Smallholders. The transition, it seemed, was over, and the conservative Hungarian miracle had occurred: a stable conservative state imposed forcefully, but essentially without violence. That view of the matter was soon belied. There was an important match still to come.

However, the basic domestic political structure was in place. For a long while, it was customary to describe it as "fascist," but there is little point now in taking issue with that label, as the majority of historians have long forsaken it, and the same can be said of such hard-to-define expressions as "fascistic" and "quasi-fascist." Nor are there grounds for calling it a dictatorship, which obviously makes no constitutional sense since the nation operated under parliamentary conditions, even though the parliamentarianism was severely restricted. It is also questionable whether the epithet "counter-revolutionary" is justified, commonly though it is applied to the period. It has already been mentioned that no counter-revolution in the strict sense had taken place in the country, only a witch hunt by groups styling themselves as counter-revolutionary. The leading groups of the period were indeed "counter-revolutionary" in politics and outlook, insofar as they set about the political task of forestalling a recurrence of the events of 1918–1919. Thus far it is justified, but as an epithet to be applied to the period, the baggage that it brings renders it grotesque, or even absurd. Firstly, it implies that the country lay in a state of permanent counter-revolution, which needs no refutation. And secondly and subordinately, it suggests that the prime purpose of the state authorities was to avert revolution, which strongly diminishes the importance of its actual activity. Neither suggestion coincides with the reality of Hungary at that time.

Finally comes the possibility of calling the Hungarian system authoritarian, like the Polish or Spanish one. Here the verdict depends on what is meant by it. If it refers to an autocratic system, or to dictatorial rule by one person or a small clique, the concept certainly does not fit. But if it is taken to mean a system that seeks to have its subjects behave with respect for their superiors and the state, and consistently restricts the opposition's conduct, the concept appears useful—in every regard in social terms, and well worth considering in terms of the state as well. With the latter, it might be worth examining the symbolic and presumably varying authority of the regent, as well as what seems at first sight to be the widely fluctuating authority of heads of government. The prestige in the Bethlen period seems to have centered on the prime minister, rather than the regent, but the situation changed later. Horthy's symbolic authority increased in the 1930s, but was ultimately greatly curtailed, to the extent that he and his family might be humiliated or maligned, or his orders ignored, more or less with impunity. But it is hard to describe any of the prime ministers after Bethlen as ruling in an authoritarian way, as all but Miklós Kállay were thrown out by Parliament, even Gömbös. On the other hand, the Hungarian state tried consistently to impose "law and order," a main aim of authoritarian government. This can and should be understood to include subservience and averting revolution, and from 1938 onwards, restraint and rejection of far-right lawlessness.[9] The concept of order underwent great changes as time went by, and the Gömbös ministry interrupted the continuity, but this effort can be seen as a decisive feature of the Hungarian system from Teleki's administration up to Kállay's. This rested to a large extent on the way in which the Bethlen government placed tight restraints on the political stage, of which the system itself eventually became the victim. The concept of order and the effort to maintain respect for authority could be seen clearly in the whole framework and operation of society, while it was much shakier and more variable in terms of state power.

Historians have identified the influence of a third group on Bethlen's decisions, although the constituents of the triad consisting of the great landowners, big business and the upper administrative elite were not equal in influence: the bloc did not consists of partners with equal strength or rights. After the Upper House had convened, Bethlen himself raised the question in a speech as to which class was the basis and determinant of the Hungarian state. He excluded the middle class from this function, saying that it was not financially independent, and he excluded big business as well, alleging that it was "not Hungarian." So there remained the landowning class, mainly the large-scale landowners. This precept of Bethlen's did not preclude state attention to the interests of the other groups mentioned—or in the case of the middle class, those of its elite—or the authorities cooperating with one or another of them, but it signified that the weights given to these groups were unequal.

Bethlen would have had little trouble deciding about the first, the elite of the middle class. The surprise would have been if it *had* been able to play any decisive autonomous role. In practice, it played the same part as elsewhere, placing its knowledge and expertise at the authorities' disposal, receiving in return the conditions for performing that task and a high standard of living. Its increasing presence obviously tinged the means and techniques of exercising power. As for the lower reaches of the middle class, Bethlen used every available means to curb its inclination towards independence, and succeeded for a while. Far more problematic was the position of big business and its role in Hungarian statehood. Big business interests undoubtedly coincided with those of government policy in the 1920s. The prime minister did not take a single step that aroused opposition from the great financial, commercial and industrial groups. But the interests of big business were not represented by a distinct political party. They were asserted through the National Association of Industrialists (GYOSZ) or indirectly through personal connections. Behind this still lay the decidedly Jewish character of big business. It has been mentioned how Sir George Clerk noticed in 1919 that a future Hungarian government could not have a Jewish member, and that remained the case, regardless of the decisive proportion of the Hungarian economy that big business represented. The government assisted new investment in the years before the economic rehabilitation by using inflationary maneuvers. It then introduced high industrial tariffs to show that it was really pursuing a policy favorable to industry and commerce. So the power position of big business appears to have been firm in economic terms, but very limited in political and intellectual terms. That presumably had an almost automatic effect on the whole bourgeois sphere, since its influence on public life could hardly be imagined without effective participation by its strongest group. In fact, Hungarian power and public life were far less "bourgeois" in that period than they might have been, given the country's economic level and social structure. Characteristically, the active leading capitalist group was represented in the Lower House in the 1920s solely by Ferenc Chorin. (The situation changed to some extent in 1931.) These circumstances raise again the problem of the division in Hungarian society, which points, along with the unsettled agricultural question, to unresolved internal strife within it.

If this feature seems to leave political life and the power sphere somewhat "truncated" and lame, then how much more conspicuous is another shortcoming: the absence of a military elite. In terms of exercising power, this means that such a political system lacks a supportive, reliable military elite capable of looking after the maintenance and development of the army. The absence of such a body seems to have arisen for various personal reasons, as well as the terms of the peace treaty. Some members of the Hungarian officers' corps were tied to the old state and the old order and customs. Others had been rendered unreliable by their part in the Hungarian Soviet Republic. Yet others had been sidelined by their legitimist commitments or activities. Finally, a remnant had been excluded by their actions in the White Terror and in right-wing radicalism of other kinds. One remaining question in Hungarian history is when this situation altered, and how, by what means, and with what content it did so, right up to the point where it is possible to question, with regard to 1938, the common assumption that no essential change occurred in Bethlen's structure of power before the German invasion of 1944. For the military elite certainly emerged in 1938 and thereafter as a distinct factor, with an often decisive influence on decision-making, but it did so in the light of a radically new transformation, not of the state structure developed in the Bethlen period or in defense of the order that Bethlen established.

Bethlen admitted the opposition into politics, but with tight restrictions. His restrictive weapons included pressure, threats and political guile, along with agreement and compromise. But he was careful never to let anybody from the bourgeoisie or working class slip behind the lines of power. So the left-wing opposition largely regarded him as a stubborn reactionary representing class and clique interests, arrogantly dismissing all proposals for widening democracy or enhancing social security, or if making such a promise, invariably breaking it. Meanwhile, on the far right wing the prime minister was seen as a liberal traitor and hireling of the Jews.

Notes

1. The cooperation of the two countries against Romania was concerned with Bessarabia on Chicherin's side and Transylvania on Bánffy's. Bánffy stated that, if warned in advance, Hungary would provide volunteer units.
2. A memorandum by Ernő Garami, written in 1919 while in exile in Vienna, tells how Bethlen sought him and tried to convince him of the need for a government that would include the Social Democratic Party of Hungary and Garami himself. This Garami stated that he rejected.
3. *Keresztény Kisgazda, Földműves és Polgári Párt.*
4. *Egységes Párt.*
5. Agricultural gloom became general in Europe in that period, due to competition from American goods, backed by high capital inputs and technical levels. The problems of the agricultural countries with selling their grain and livestock became persistent. Germany was to profit from this phenomenon in the 1930s.
6. Restricting the electorate to 58 instead of 74 percent of citizens over the age of 24.
7. Bethlen was quite aware of the illegality, as is clear from the way in which he later put the decree to the National Assembly again and had a vote taken on it.
8. According to the French investigation authorities, the explosion was organized by the police, with the chief of police, Imre Nádosy, himself being involved.
9. The police in the late 1930s set up a special unit to watch leaders and members of far right-wing parties. A similar unit keeping the communists and the "left" under surveillance had little to do; the "right" unit had greater prestige.

4 Financial Recovery; A Break with the Far Right

On September 18, 1922, the Assembly of the League of Nations unanimously elected Hungary to its ranks, and not long afterwards the protocols enabling Austria's financial reorganization were signed. That encouraged the Hungarian government to look into obtaining a loan, and prompted hopes that the reparations problem might be solved. The minister of finance and the prime minister reasoned that if the country's catastrophic impoverishment were revealed, it might provide international organizations with grounds for canceling Hungary's reparations, or reducing them to a kinder figure, and for allowing the country to raise substantial loans to set right its public finances and stimulate investment. The government's economic package also included settling the inherited state debt, preparing and instituting an act on customs tariffs, and establishing a separate Hungarian currency.[1]

Preparations for the package began at the end of 1922, with the active cooperation of a British banker, William Good.[2] The Hungarian government's actions were hastened by the Franco-Belgian occupation of the Ruhr district, on the grounds that Germany had been late with its reparation payments. After thorough diplomatic preparations, Bethlen set out on a tour of European capitals (London, Paris and Rome), during which it became possible on April 6 to put a Hungarian loan request before the Reparations Committee. Despite the cordial reception given to this, it soon emerged that the promised British support did not extend to every detail of the plan, and the French government was decidedly cool because of the strong opposition of the Little Entente countries. The resolution eventually adopted on May 23 envisaged the Reparations Committee supervising the loan to be granted and stipulated preferential payment of the reparations. That decision suited neither Hungary's interests nor Britain's approach. The latter was contradicted on two points: the British government had wanted to place

117

the loan under League of Nations supervision, and the British financial world objected to an international loan being used to cover reparations. There began a long period of parleying and exercising diplomatic and financial pressure. The main weapon was the way in which London tied support for loan applications by other small countries to acceptance of the conditions that it supported for the Hungarian loan.

It also emerged that the sum of the loan was far less than the Hungarian state had requested, its uses were limited, and Hungarian citizens had to make big sacrifices in exchange. And a chorus of protest came from the far right when it became clear that the process would be supervised by a commissioner sent by the League of Nations. There were cries of treachery from inside the United Party and from nationalists outside it, who blamed the government for sacrificing the country's sovereignty and handing the economy to foreign capital, when (they claimed) it could heal itself. This view was taken by Gyula Gömbös and his group within Bethlen's party, which caused irreparable conflict between the two politicians. In June 1923, Bethlen made his position as prime minister conditional on the regent's support for his program. When Bethlen received that assurance, Gömbös had to draw his own conclusions. On June 19 he resigned as the United Party executive vice-chairman, and on August 2 he left the party with some of his supporters (including Endre Bajcsy-Zsilinszky and Tibor Eckhardt). A year later, Gömbös set up his Hungarian National Independence Party,[3] generally known as the Racial Protection Party.[4]

With that, the Bethlen government dissociated itself from the far right and it seemed as if the extremist groups had been excluded from power permanently. For a while, Gömbös really found himself on the fringes of politics, although subsequent events showed that the strands linking the conservatives and the far right had not broken. Gömbös, for instance, still received government monies from the sum allocated to irredentist and revisionist propaganda, which was directed incidentally by Pál Teleki as head of the League of Social Associations.[5] Meanwhile, certain events showed that Gömbös may have applied for personal protection from certain government organizations. These more or less invisible strands made it possible for him to return to politics later.

However, the League of Nations loan went ahead. The Reparations Commission passed the matter on to the League of Nations (on October 17), whose Finance Committee endorsed the plan (at the end of November), and a subcommittee traveled to Hungary to examine local conditions. The members of the subcommittee pressed on the Hungarian people statements about the need for sacrifice and thrift. Finally, everybody concerned signed the two protocols on the Hungarian loan and the reorganization conditions between March 5 and 14, 1924. The loan of roughly 250 million crowns could be taken up by the state in installments over two and a half years, during which reparations did not need to be paid. In each of the following twenty years, Hungary was obliged to pay an annual average of 10 million crowns in reparations, which was not an alarmingly large sum. During the reorganization, the economy would be supervised by a League of Nations commissioner, the American banker Jeremiah Smith, who found nothing objectionable in the Hungarian public finance system over the two and a half years. In addition, a central bank of issue had to be created, without which the country could not have financial independence. The Hungarian National Bank[6] held its inaugural general meeting in June 1924 and had beside it as a foreign adviser Royall Tyler, who advised the bank's directors for several years while discreetly monitoring their activities.

The inflation was curbed (causing a temporary money shortage) and the budget ended 1924 without a deficit. The process of setting the finances to rights ended with a currency reform. On December 27, 1926, the *pengő* became the unit of a currency of medium strength tied to the pound sterling. Disregarding occasional and partial issues of money, this was the first credible independent Hungarian currency to exist since the sixteenth century. (More financial detail appears in the chapter on economic development.)

The diplomatic and financial successes of 1924–1925 opened up the way for Bethlen to complete his consolidation in domestic policy. Although the left-wing opposition had very little chance of influencing government policy, it made a strong effort to do so in 1924, in response to government efforts to restrict its freedom of action and expression in two regards. One method that Bethlen chose involved the parliamentary standing orders, where he set out to curb the endless debates and to prevent the opposition from using the National Assembly as a platform for publicizing its views. The other means of bridling the opposition (left and right) was to introduce and ensure passage for a bill on capital city, where the prime minister hoped to increase government influence and reduce Budapest's scope for independent action. Hitherto, the Christian Community Party[7] had been in a majority, and there was a strong chance that the Hungarian Social Democratic Party would also do well in the 1925 elections.

Concern to avert these two threats by Bethlen led the Social Democrats, the National Democratic Party[8] and the Kossuth Party to form the National Democratic Alliance.[9] During the ensuing parliamentary debates, one Social Democratic spokesman was sent out of the chamber by the speaker. The opposition bloc then copied the example of Mussolini's opposition, the Aventino.[10] Although 44 Alliance members left Parliament on December 1, this passive resistance did not even produce a latent crisis in Hungary. Instead it led to further government ruses. Bethlen thought that the Social Democratic Party had broken the 1921 pact by allying itself with the bourgeois opposition, and so he began to allow rumors of the secret agreement to spread. These forced the Social Democratic Party to publish the text of the pact, which did a lot of damage to the party's reputation among the domestic working class and abroad. Furthermore, official talks began on starting a new labor party. Initiated by domestic "opposition" Communists and left-wing Social Democrats, this was to be called the Hungarian Socialist Workers' Party.[11] At the head of the move was István Vági. The government allowed the new party to form on April 14, 1925, hoping that it would counteract the influence of the Social Democrats. The new party stood officially for "democratic dictatorship" and land reform (of estates over 100 *hold*—57 ha—with no compensation for the wealthy classes). It was then tolerated by the government for as long as it could be used against the Social Democrats, but its leaders began to be arrested in 1926.[12]

It also proved to be a government ruse when the Somogyi–Bacsó murder case was brought up for discussion. Bethlen now permitted a new enquiry, which had long been an opposition demand. Among those who gave evidence was Ödön Beniczky, who had been minister of the interior at the time. Beniczky's accusations also involved the regent, and thus led to a slander trial, which he lost for want of evidence for such an involvement.

Despite all this activity, the left wing won the local elections held in Budapest on May 21–22, 1925. (The Democratic Bloc won 128 seats, 52 going to Social Democrats and 71 to the National Democratic Party.) This showed that the capital did not belong to the government, and that only Budapest was inclined towards the democratic forces. The bloc's absolute majority meant that the government could only improve the situation by drawing its appointed delegates to the council almost exclusively from the government party. The same election was also a serious defeat for the Christian Community Party.

On May 26, 1925, the National Democratic Alliance left off its passive resistance to confront the prime minister in Parliament over a further move to restrict people's rights. Bethlen presented a franchise bill that encompassed an earlier regulation, along with measures to organize the upper house of the legislature, turning the

National Assembly (*nemzetgyűlés*) into an Assembly of the Nation (*országgyűlés*). This was undoubtedly the keystone of Bethlenite domestic policy.

It was certainly an omission that the National Assembly had failed to discuss for six years the question of the earlier structure of the legislature. The former House of Peers had neither been confirmed in its existence nor abolished. Bethlen's proposals for reestablishing an upper house were passed by the National Assembly on November 11. Its 242 members were to act as a further brake on the system, but its structure would change to reflect the alterations in the political elite of the country. Most of the seats were to be filled by election, but 47 would be *ex officio* and another 40 the regent's appointees, while male members of the House of Habsburg would have perpetual seats if they were resident in Hungary. This significantly reduced the proportion of aristocrats and great landowners in the house and admitted representatives of business and the upper stratum of the middle class.

That completed Bethlen's consolidation, by creating a self-contained conservative political system in which the opposition was restricted without being abolished. At around this time, Bethlen openly dissociated himself from liberalism, as something liable to lead to "unlimited" democracy and thereby Bolshevism. He expressly emphasized the system's conservatism. He named landed property as the repository of power, but in practice he continued to ensure that the interests of big business would not be infringed, even though they were pushed to the background in power terms.

The year 1926 was a turning point in the history of post-war Hungary and the Bethlen period, because development of the structure of power, administration and politics was completed, financial and economic reorganization had been carried out, and the hitherto energetic and dynamic Bethlen government slowed down, so that domestic politics became stable, even stagnant. There was hardly an event worth mentioning in domestic politics before 1930. In those and in subsequent years, there was a state in which the prime minister commanded an unchallengeable respect that reflected also on the strata that backed him. He also enjoyed the almost symbolic prestige accorded to the regent, who eschewed everyday politics altogether at that time. The government turned its attention to educational and social matters and to foreign policy. The ensuing years of calm were not to be interrupted until the economic crisis.

The next parliamentary elections, on December 14–15, 1926, brought the successful prime minister his greatest victory. His party won 170 seats and the supportive Christian National Farming and Welfare Party another 35, making more than 80 percent of the seats between them.[13] The losers were all the other parties and groups outside the government bloc.

Notes

1. Up to the beginning of 1920, "quasi-"Hungarian currency was produced by overprinting Austro-Hungarian banknotes in crowns, but that could only be a temporary method.
2. Good spent several years as an adviser to the government, having a hand in all the foreign loan transactions. His work seems to have ended when Gyula Gömbös was appointed prime minister, but there is little detail available about the details or what remuneration he received.
3. *Magyar Nemzeti Függetlenségi Párt.*
4. *Fajvédő Párt.*
5. *Társadalmi Egyesületek Szervezete.* The government's budget transactions were certainly not clear. Major sums were paid under various labels for unspecified purposes. For instance, large sums went towards covering the expenses of Charles IV and his court, principally to ensure that penury did not become a reason for retaining a desire for restoration. The government funded the insurgents of western Hungary, which led, incidentally, to the resignation of Foreign Minister Miklós Bánffy. Monies were regularly disbursed to domestic revisionist organizations and associations of Hungarians abroad.

Greater or lesser sums were probably devoted from time to time to
military purposes, but the charge that the government wanted to
break the peace and maintain a large, well-armed army was quite
without foundations.

6. *Magyar Nemzeti Bank.*
7. *Keresztény Községi Párt.*
8. *Nemzeti Demokrata Párt.*
9. *Országos Demokratikus Szövetség.*
10. The left-wing parliamentary alliance in Italy formed after the murder
    of the Socialist MP Giacomo Matteotti, in an attempt to precipitate
    an enquiry and thereby a government crisis.
11. *Magyar Szocialista Munkáspárt (MSzMP).*
12. Connected with this was the first trial of Mátyás Rákosi, who was
    back from Soviet exile by then.
13. *Keresztény Nemzeti Gazdasági és Szociális Párt.*

5. The Years of Stability

The loan backed by the League of Nations broke the country's isolation, and Bethlen began to speak of active foreign policy overtures in 1924. He was certainly right in the sense that his government developed rational relations with the Western Powers and dialog with the politicians of neighboring countries.[1] This led to numerous outstanding inter-state questions being settled. The discussions with the Yugoslav foreign minister were more promising still, and continued on a more serious level in 1926.

A relatively modest, but discernible, spurt of economic growth also began. Sizable amounts of foreign capital arrived in the country in loan form, although foreign capital investment remained small. The key stabilizing factors were education and welfare policy, both of which unfolded in the second half of the 1920s. The general standard of education was improved greatly by the work of Kunó Klebelsberg, minister of religion and public education. His program called, of course, for higher budget allocations, and the legislature began in 1925 to vote him very high sums indeed, amounting to 9–10 percent of annual public spending. Klebelsberg's educational and cultural policies were intended to bolster Hungarian preeminence, and this the government and legislature supported as well, although the ostensibly excessive spending of the education portfolio would come under heavy parliamentary attack as the economic woes increased. Klebelsberg's plans pointed in two directions. On the one hand, he wanted to raise the general level of education, with the elimination of illiteracy as the starting point. This meant an elementary school program, using broadcasting for popular education, opening public libraries, and many other moves. On the other hand, he wanted to strengthen and improve the intellectual elite, through secondary school reform, a broader basis of university and scientific work, and various schemes for scholarships and foreign studies. (Implementation of these plans is returned to later.)

Klebelsberg took a conservative national line of policy, which he styled "the new nationalism," and viewed the mood of the times with increasing pessimism. While defining knowledge and culture as the pledge of the nation's recovery and advancement, he wanted to open the gates of the schools and universities quite widely. Knowledge was to be placed in the nation's service, but acquiring it was a human right and duty. His plans were to educate people in that service. Taken all together, they meant that by the end of his term as minister he was being attacked not only for high educational and cultural spending but also, from the right, for ostensible liberalism.

Public conditions were also improved by the government's welfare measures. Compulsory accident insurance was introduced in a 1927 law. In the following year came compulsory insurance for old age, disability, widows and orphans, but only for wage and salary earners. These were to have covered agricultural workers as well and there was to have been a scheme of unemployment benefit, but the Great Depression intervened. (Further detail on welfare policy appears later.)

Yet social mobility remained minimal despite the major education and welfare measures. The demand for labor increased in the manufacturing industry and associated fields, but the attraction was too small to have an appreciable effect in the villages. The increased demand for labor in the service industries was supplied mainly by urban families, largely as their social position dictated. The school gates were open in principle, but very few of those passing through them hoped for social advancement. The children of the poor aspired to complete the elementary school, those somewhat better off a trade or civil school, while the academically oriented middle schools known as gymnasia and universities remained the preserves of the upper middle, landowning, and big business classes. There were exceptions, but those conditions were the rule. The sons of artisans, traders, peasants and manual workers made up

24–25 percent of university entrants, of whom some 2 percent were of worker origin. So there was no major shift in society, and the impression created, then and later, was that nothing had altered since the Dual Monarchy, when in fact a great deal had begun to change.

Too little is known of the history of the army in the 1920s, not least because it framed many of the socially very sensitive changes that occurred in the period. Under the terms of Trianon, the strength of the army had to be cut to 35,000, of whom 1,175 could be officers, which meant that the chances of a military career were severely restricted for the sons of landowning and middle-class families, who would have willingly chosen it earlier. In 1925, there appeared General Kocsárd Janky, as a commander-in-chief who doubled as chief of the General Staff, but what that actually covered, what the General Staff was, and how the peace treaty terms were circumvented to allow it to appear are unclear to say the least. Next to nothing is known about officer training and education. The records of the Military Control Commission have not been researched, and the reports of the foreign military attachés in Budapest are unknown as well. However, it is clear that the military strength up to 1927 covered 62–63 percent of the quota permitted, and the men could not be supplied with modern arms. The weapons and parts later gathered into Italian stores for possible delivery to Hungary were remnants of Austrian weaponry plundered in the Great War. The risky venture of delivering them to Hungary failed twice, but not without confirming that no appreciable arms manufacturing could have been taking place in the country at that time. Hungary in the 1920s lacked not just an appreciable army, but any army worthy of the name.[2] One reason for this was the twelve-year period of service: few young people were prepared to commit themselves for so long. But there were also problems of financing. Over this decade, or rather the second half of it, the Ministry of Religion and Public Education received many times the public funding that went to the Ministry of Defense. The situation changed only in 1928, after Gömbös became state secretary at the Ministry of Defense, and still more when he became minister of defense in 1929. The change was obviously connected with the activation of foreign policy and the initial stages in the building of Hungarian–Italian relations, of which more will be said later.

The intellectual and political atmosphere of the period is customarily characterized as the "Szeged idea" or "Christian national" ideology. The old Szeged people often did refer to the Szeged idea and there were plenty who were wont to use the epithet "Christian national." But the expressions need further scrutiny. There is every sign that many people thought in many different ways in Szeged, but nobody has stumbled upon any kind of rounded, clearly expressed idea, program or world view, or even an embryonic version of one. You could bet your bottom dollar that Dezső Pattantyús Ábrahám did not think the same way as Gyula Gömbös, or that Pál Teleki and Miklós Horthy differed. Everybody was a counter-revolutionary against the Hungarian Soviet Republic and everybody had national feelings against the prospective truncation of the country. But the government included some who thought it possible to institute bourgeois democracy, and those who still did not think it wise to present the most democratic of faces to the Allied governments and to the many French officers to be found in Szeged. Count Gyula Károlyi, prime minister of the rival government, stated in writing that for his own and his government's part, he recognized the decisions of the peace conference, and added a hope that the Hungarian side might still be heard there.

Meanwhile, another group of Szeged people, consisting mainly of young military officers, put the appearance of Bolshevism down as a crime of the People's Republic, and would hear nothing of any kind of democracy or liberalism. They were pondering a military dictatorship, and thought that Miklós Horthy and the national army were destined to produce one. But their ideas were only expressed fragmentarily, let alone publicized. The group even thought it conceivable that the nature of the peace treaty might be changed swiftly and violently by some kind of international grouping (German, Austrian and Bavarian). It is not right to blur the distinction between these two groups.

As for the intellectual character of the Vienna and Graz groups, both were likewise anti-Bolshevik, but there were big differences in the ideas and methods of the two, leading later to the events of 1921 discussed already. Bethlen disagreed in matters of principle and of tactics with the legitimist Graz group, prone to use violent methods, but he also stood a good distance from the radicals among the Szeged people. With the latter, he later established two points of contact. One was the fact that Bethlen strove steadily to narrow down the democratic system of institutions, and he eventually rejected liberalism because he felt that it would lead to "partyless" democracy, which opened up the way for Bolshevism and anarchism. The other point of contact arose when Bethlen broke with legitimism due to various considerations, which brought him into one camp with the radicals intent on having a freely elected king, or if it did not quite do that, at least it left him close to them. It has been seen, however, that these strands did not prevent Bethlen from resisting the Gömbös position, as contrary to the country's interests. At least temporarily, he preferred to break with them rather than make concessions. To all this it must be added that Bethlen and Pál Teleki, so often mentioned in one breath, did not have identical political complexions either. This was not just because Teleki was a scientist and Bethlen not, Teleki religious and Bethlen not, nor even exclusively because their ways of doing things differed. It was also because they thought differently about the nation, the ethnic community, and religion, and used different methods in politics. In disposition, Teleki was hesitant, Bethlen pragmatic, Teleki constantly struggling in politics with his own convictions, Bethlen airily putting aside convictions that clashed with his practical tasks. Essentially, however, Bethlen denied a leading role to a community with a non-Hungarian identity, specifically to the Jews, but he would not go as far as Teleki, who sought biological pretexts for limiting them strongly in numbers and in the positions they held.

As for "national," there was hardly a legal party that did not espouse the idea—and hardly a country in Europe where nationalism was not advancing. But the national question and national interest, proclaimed by all, were interpreted differently by each. The noisiest, those who proclaimed the slogans "No, nay, never!" and "Everything back!"[3] hardly stretched beyond the far right. They hoped for immediate, rapid solutions, while more responsible political factors sought paths towards possible compromise, and the bourgeois and Social Democratic opposition saw territorial revision on ethnic lines as the solution. Meanwhile, the nationalist-irredentist group and the anti-Semites, who overlapped, soon began to cool down. They lost their position in the Bethlen period as the decisive political and intellectual factor.

The epithet "Christian" also meant several things according to who applied it and for what end. Some linked it with deeper ideas from the history of philosophy. Some saw it as a civilizing factor. Some used it to lend legitimism greater intellectual weight. Some politicians who called themselves Christian combined basically conservative views with strong social policies and organization (of labor unions and later professional corporations). Often, although not always, an emphasis on Christianity meant nothing more than opposition to ungodly, un-Christian, Bolshevik atheism and to the Jews, seen as vehicles of that. These approaches could also be combined. So "Christian" as a political epithet was in the same position as "national," not forgetting that in Hungary's case there was a huge difference between Christian in a Catholic sense and Christian in a Reformed sense.[4] For there were constantly repeated reactions to the fact that a country with a Catholic majority had a regent who belonged to the Reformed Church, as prime ministers often did as well.

Although the epithet of "Christian" was never as widespread as it was in that period, no effective Christian political force emerged. A short period of expansion was followed by fragmentation, accompanied by a shrinking base of support. One reason was probably the fact that the Christian platforms were divided over the form of state and on agrarian and social questions. Another may have been the fact that political activity was shown mainly by Catholic groups, while the rest abstained from direct participation. Moreover, there was no cooperation or even rapprochement between the various churches, as the Catholic church leaders would have nothing to do with ecumenical ideas. In fact there was an effective competitive struggle, in which denominational allegiance became a factor in various appointments and decorations. Yet the Catholics made up only 65 percent of the country's population (in 1930). Finally, the political perplexity and ineffectiveness of the Christians was enhanced by the failure of the upper hierarchy of the Catholic Church (apart from a few bishops) to support the political autonomy of the groups close to them. Instead the church was content to give general support to the government, accompanied by mild criticism according to church criteria. Although not all of these warnings were effective or reached their target, they contributed to constraining and isolating the church leaders who held more modern views.

The epithet "Christian" was sometimes assumed also by the far right-wing opposition, although for them it meant almost exclusively anti-Semitism, sometimes in its new biological guise and interpretation. Those active in politics were capable of phrasing or presenting their views in a more socially acceptable form, but they also possessed a less visible background of support where murderous passions were still shown. That deeper stratum began to disappear from the political stage in 1922 and become marginalized, but its basis remained. The Etelköz Association broke up in political acrimony, and Horthy, whom its supporters saw as their invisible leader, wanted nothing more to do with them by 1922. Nothing was heard of MOVE, and ÉME, with imposing influence and membership in 1920, had shrunk to insignificance. One blow, perhaps the final one, came in 1924, when an ÉME group featured in 1924 as the main accused in the trial over the Erzsébetváros bombing. However, Gyula Gömbös, who went into opposition in 1923, kept up his ties with several members of the "old guard," and he was able to put forward his views in Parliament and in the press. All in all, the Christian national idea for the far right at that time was primarily anti-Semitic and irredentist.

These differing interpretations of the ideological slogans became merged in daily life, so much so that the average person could hardly distinguish them. The general mood was clearly nationalist and anti-Trianon. Although the anti-Semitism retreated, it continued to exist under cover.

Throughout the period, the intellectual and political spectrum included left-wing bourgeois trends and Social Democratic leaders and journalists. They were joined on certain issues and occasions by the legitimists. They found common cause in defending and promoting democratic rights, although they seldom managed to act together for the purpose. They sought progressive reform of voting rights. They demanded that those committing acts of terrorism be brought to justice. While the internment system lasted, they called for its abolition, along with the chance for bourgeois and Social Democratic exiles to return home. The Social Democratic Party of Hungary was also pressing for effective welfare measures.

It has been seen that the Bethlen government was in no danger from the right or the left-wing opposition, which allowed, perhaps, an authoritarian, law-and-order administration to manifest itself, but the government by no means dominated the intellectual sphere. The intellectual and political picture was much more varied and colorful than that of the "course." The opposition held much more intellectual ground than political. Its representatives may not have received lucrative posts in public life, higher education or the Academy, and may even have thought it best to leave the country, but the liberal and the Social Democratic opposition retained positions in the press. Public taste in literature was being shaped most effectively by *Nyugat* (West), a thoroughly nonconformist periodical, and there was plenty of modernity appearing in the arts—if less in the fine arts than in music. Despite all the pedantry and obstacles, new scientific and scholarly approaches were appearing and new disciplines gaining strength.

Notes

1. Bethlen remarked on how "the road to Prague runs through Paris"—in other words, pressure could be brought on Little Entente countries with help from the Great Powers. Once that was done, they proved to be willing negotiators.
2. The Little Entente countries frequently alleged the opposite, prompting frequent checks by the Military Control Commission in Hungary. The latter in its reports did not preclude the possibility of measures being taken that breached the peace treaty, but never obtained any concrete information about such measures.
3. *"Nem, nem, soha!" "Mindent vissza!"*
4. *Keresztény* was the Catholic term for Christian, *keresztyén* the Reformed.

6. A Change of Foreign Policy Direction

Hungary's series of diplomatic successes came to an abrupt end in 1925. It turned out that large quantities of thousand-franc bills had been forged in Hungary, and suspicions spread that the government's hand was behind this. The first to be caught with the forged money was an army officer called Arisztid Jankovich, at a money-changer's in Amsterdam. The Dutch also found on him a carefully kept diary, detailing what he knew about the forgery and naming all who were implicated in it, including Prince Lajos Windischgrätz, Imre Nádosy, the country's chief of police, Gyula Gömbös, and many others. There was no glossing over the matter under the circumstances, although several people in Budapest thought for a time that there was. The investigation, also involving the French police, of course, brought down two successive commanding officers of the Cartographical Institute, where the forgery had been carried out. It became apparent that several army officers, active and retired, had been used to distribute the money, and that Gömbös had played a preeminent part in that. It did not take much imagination to see strands extending from there towards the General Staff and the regent. It even became clear during the interrogations that Pál Teleki had agreed with the plan in its initial stages, and even that the prime minister knew of it. It also emerged that Teleki had tried to stop the forgery in 1925 and Bethlen had forbidden distribution of the bills, but the opposition saw this as a chance to bring down the government. The idea was floated in Paris that the French state should press for this, as the injured party, but ultimately nothing was done, lest Gömbös should be Bethlen's successor.

The forgery scandal culminated in 1926 in a trial where the events and some perpetrators were presented, but all the strands broke off just where higher figures—the General Staff or the government—would be implicated. In fact the scandal was far more than the amusing interlude that it was treated as being. The diplomatic repercussions were extremely damaging and its effects in Western Europe lasted almost two years. Hungary was frozen out again for a while and there were no more chances of substantive talks in Paris until the end of 1927.

And the scandal coincided largely with a change in Britain's financial and foreign policy direction. This was a response by the Bank of England when Britain's financial capacity was clearly proving to be too small for it to assist in further rehabilitation of the Danube–Balkan belt, in the light of Britain's Imperial commitments. Thereafter, Britain largely withdrew from the region in financial terms, and this had its effect in politics as well. In Hungary's case, this was apparent in the fact that Britain had subscribed most to the 1924 League of Nations loan, but the British money market hardly contributed at all to subsequent loans (municipal, county, and so on). In 1925, the lion's share in handling Hungarian loans passed to the American bankers, including some whose reliability was being questioned (the Speyer house). There were fluctuations and alterations in British behavior in later years, but this is essentially when Britain began to ignore the region's problems.

Meanwhile, the two countries that Bethlen had really expected to raise the issue of territorial revision, Germany and Italy, showed no signs of doing so. Germany was concerned with trying to gain a place for itself among the Great Powers, and if Foreign Minister Gustav Stresemann had other plans, an active policy towards the small states of Eastern Europe was not among them. The Italian Fascist government had just survived its first serious test, when the murder of the Socialist MP Giacomo Matteotti had precipitated a crisis. Mussolini began to concentrate early in 1925 on consolidating Fascism from within by building up the structure of dictatorial administration. His government showed caution in foreign policy and took practically no initiatives for the time being.

For Hungary, the world had narrowed to an extent that precluded an active policy in any direction. However, the Foreign Ministry had long nursed a design to break out of the Little Entente encirclement by making a pact with one of its members. Czechoslovakia did not seem appropriate for this, not just because its government took every opportunity to attack the Hungarian system, but because Foreign Minister Beneš on each occasion had called the proposed concessions put forward by President Masaryk an error and simply repudiated his remarks. This happened so often that the Hungarians became convinced that this was a kind of ruse devised by the two statesmen and that the president was not taking his proposals seriously either. There Budapest was probably wrong. Masaryk, after all, had not only brought up the need for Czech–Hungarian rapprochement up before the Hungarians and did not only intend the proposed concessions simply as a sweetener. There are French notes to show that he also talked about the plan in 1925 with French and British politicians, who did not withhold their support for it, as long as Czechoslovakia could have it accepted by its partners.[1] This, events showed, it could not.

The essential, underlying idea of reaching agreement with Romania began to crop up repeatedly at the beginning of 1919, in the form of a personal union, but these Hungarian notions never found a sufficiently strong or prestigious negotiating partner,[2] and in any case, problems of far smaller weight could not be resolved either. The government always placed great emphasis on improving the situation of the Hungarian national minority, most seriously with Romania, where there was a Hungarian population of almost two million. So the first Hungarian condition would be a fairer solution to the minority question, which regularly ran up against barriers from the other party. Nor was it possible to resolve the so-called option issue. This concerned the matter of whether compensation was due under the Romanian land reform to those losing land only if they chose Romania as their country of residence, rather than "opting" to move to Hungary. István Bethlen, the Hungarian prime minister, was himself one of those whose land had been expropriated and did not want to leave it at that, but he was thwarted by the stubborn Romanian refusal to discuss it.

This left Yugoslavia. Up to 1927, Yugoslavia had no treaty with France, but bad relations with almost all its neighbors, including Italy, despite some temporary improvements. So there was justification in believing that the Little Entente did not represent a very reassuring solution for Yugoslavia. And apart from Austria, Yugoslavia was the country against which Hungary had the fewest grievances. Croatia and Slovenia had not been part of the territory considered to belong to the Hungarians, and so claims arose only with the Banate, Bácska (Bačka), the Danube–Dráva Triangle and the Muraköz (Međimurje). Yugoslavia therefore had the smallest annexed population of Hungarians of any Little Entente country.

Bethlen had noticed the Yugoslavs' willingness to negotiate earlier, during preliminary debates on the League of Nations loan. Foreign Minister Lajos Walko began initial talks with his Yugoslav counterpart, Momcilo Ninčić, in Geneva at the beginning of 1926. These proceeded encouragingly, and on August 29, the 400th anniversary of Hungary's Battle of Mohács against the Ottomans, Regent Miklós Horthy spoke warmly of the heroic Serb struggles against the Turks and called for Yugoslav–Hungarian rapprochement. This began well but then became stalled. The other two Little Entente countries made various demands that Belgrade could not ignore, and on realizing that Hungary was seeking territorial concessions, the Yugoslavs immediately began to back out.

So the Yugoslav–Hungarian talks were foundering by the time that the prime minister received an invitation in December 1926 from the Italian government to visit Rome to discuss Hungarian–Italian relations and conclude a treaty of friendship. This invitation was presumably seen as the big prize in the Foreign Ministry,[3] for Italy was the first and only important power to extend the hand of friendship to the Hungarian government. The chance could not be missed, even though Rome had done so in the hope of frustrating any Yugoslav–Hungarian agreement, notably because supervision of the League of Nations loan was ending at about that time (mid-1926) and so was military supervision.[4] Now only Royall Tyler, the National Bank adviser, remained. This prompted Budapest to try a bolder approach towards diplomatic issues, and Bethlen set out for the Italian capital early in March 1927 with that purpose in mind.

What the Hungarian and Italian prime ministers signed on March 5, 1927, was only a treaty of friendship, but the exchanges of views pointed further. Mussolini and Bethlen agreed that the post-war status quo could not be sustained in the long term and they expected international life to become more fluid in about 1925, for which both states would need to prepare militarily. Here Mussolini promised to supply Hungary with a quantity of arms. Bethlen did not rule out the possibility that France or even Russia might have a role in altering European relations, but he thought it most likely that Germany would take the lead. Here they also agreed that the annexation of Austria to Germany was inevitable, although the *Anschluss* would have to be opposed ostensibly so as to collect the price of agreeing to it from the Germans.[5] Mussolini suggested improving relations with Romania to the Hungarian prime minister. This Bethlen did not rule out, but he added that an improvement in the position of the Hungarian minority there would be a requirement.[6]

These closer Hungarian–Italian relations set revisionist policy and propaganda in motion, but Bethlen decided to wait for a while. He probably assumed that Rome's opening to the East would arouse interest in Hungary in other states. He began putting out feelers to Berlin, London and Paris as well, but there were no official reactions, at least in official circles. But there was an unexpected move by an English press baron, Lord Harold Rothermere, who began a press campaign for revising Hungary's borders.[7] One outcome was the formation of the Revisionist League on his initiative, but the Hungarian government found this embarrassing rather than helpful. It knew that the campaign would muddy relations in official London quarters, and it found also that Rothermere's plan for ethnically based territorial revision did not match the Hungarian concept. Yet some people in Hungarian public life went out of their way to embrace the peer's dubious initiative. They gave a sumptuous reception in his honor, from which the revisionist Hungarian government did not dare to absent itself, partly for fear of losing face at home, and partly because Rothermere, however gauchely, had brought the question of revision to international attention.

That explains why the Foreign Ministry issued a decisive statement saying that it was not worth aiming for ethnic revision in installments. The aim should be "optimal revision": the revision that the future international situation would make optimally possible. This also expressed in a nutshell Bethlen's political concept: politics was the art of the possible. When Rome's lead was not followed by any other power, Bethlen actually went over to an active policy of revision early in 1928. He announced in a Debrecen speech at the beginning of the year that Hungary could not accept the peace in perpetuity, for peace could not rest on the basis of the borders that it laid down. "On these borders a prison can be built," he said, "in which we are the guarded and the victors the guards." At about the same time, Kunó Klebelsberg was formulating his "new" nationalism, whose main goal was "strengthening of the race and resurrection of our home country." The Revisionist League launched a big campaign, not always in the spirit of Rothermere.

Meanwhile, on January 1, 1928, a train at Szentgotthárd was discovered to be carrying machine guns and components to Hungary. The opposition, the exiles and the Little Entente tried to turn these into a weapon against the Hungarian government, but the slight value of the consignment, which consisted only of handguns, escaped further scandal with only a murmur from the League of Nations. But the scandal showed that Austrian deliveries were not

safe while the left wing there was still strong and influential. Not
without reason, Austria was on the agenda when Bethlen sought
another meeting with Mussolini in early April 1928, this time in
Venice. The meeting was supposed to be kept secret, but that did
not succeed.

On the subject of Austria, Bethlen and Mussolini agreed to
give joint support to the *Heimwehr*, a militia that espoused fascist
ideas and showed a willingness to orient itself and the nation
towards Italy, the idea being to stage a coup and take power. The
two countries went on to supply the *Heimwehr* with sizable sums of
money and quantities of advice, but the attempted coup was aborted.
Meanwhile, there was reorganization in Austrian domestic politics,
which left *Heimwehr* rule superfluous from the Hungarian–Italian
point of view. There was also agreement in Venice to help the
Croatian separatists to break up Yugoslavia. The Hungarian government had been in touch for some years with the Party of Law
headed by Ante Pavelić, and as a continuation of that, intensive
relations were built up with the leaders who went into exile and
later brought the *Ustaše* into being. At Mussolini's request, Bethlen
undertook to assist the Italian head of government with his plan for
a *Pacte à trois*, in which Bulgaria, Greece and Turkey were to take
part under Italian leadership. Bethlen duly visited Ankara, Sofia
and Athens, although the Mussolini plan foundered. Mussolini also
promised Hungary a sizable military loan to buy aircraft from Italy,
which were to be kept at the Udine air base, where the Hungarian
pilots would be trained.[8]

The Balkan visit led to some rapprochement with Bulgaria and
Turkey. As for Bethlen's trip to Warsaw, it was decidedly successful,
and a Treaty of Polish–Hungarian friendship was signed at the end
of the year, as was a similar document with Austria early in 1931.

The political leaders of the countries with which Hungary
entered into treaty relations in 1927–1931 agreed that the status quo
could not be maintained, but none of them thought that the time had

come for action. All except the Poles were convinced that Germany would give the signal for this in due course. Meanwhile, the revisionist group had formed in opposition to the Great Powers and smaller powers keen to maintain the status quo. That did not mean that the Hungarian government had slammed or wanted to slam the door in London or Paris. Relations with Britain were unimpaired, insofar as British commitments in other directions allowed. After two frosty years, Bethlen also managed to make a move in Paris, where he took up with Aristide Briand a grand French investment scheme and establishment of a Hungarian cultural institution in Paris. Relations became especially close after the economic crisis blew up, as the Hungarian government was looking out for a further foreign loan.

Hungary had another unsettled issue left over from the peace treaty, which had to be arranged in conjunction with the former Allied Powers. The question of reparations had only been arranged temporarily, along with the League of Nations loan. The Reparations Commission, having reached in principle a final settlement on German reparations in 1928, turned in 1929 to the question of the smaller countries. This was fairly easy with Austria and Bulgaria, which were relieved of all further burdens, but with Hungary there were complications deriving from the option affair. A solution was not found until 1930, at the Second Hague Conference, when Bethlen agreed that Hungary would lay aside for settlement of optants' claims a sum of 13.5 million gold crowns a year for 23 years, in addition to the commitments agreed in 1924, of which 240 million would be earmarked to cover bonds that the optants received as compensation.[9] Although all inter-state repayments were interrupted and steadily ceased in 1931 after the world economic crisis, that could not be known in advance. The measures taken by the prime minister over the option affair caused widespread outrage at home, all the more so because some of the oppressive signs of the crisis were already becoming apparent.

Notes

1. All that is known subsequently of the initiative is that Masaryk aired his plan at talks with Romanian and Yugoslav politicians, with results that can only be guessed at. He probably met with the same refusal as at home.
2. This possibility was first aired in January 1919 by Mihály Károlyi to the Italian government. Bethlen, Teleki and Imre Csáky had held talks on it with the Romanians. The idea kept cropping up later in the press in suggestion or proposal form.
3. Mussolini's regime, incidentally, had a good name among conservatives all over Europe at that time.
4. Bethlen had originally wanted to achieve that in 1926, but failed.
5. This principle defined the approach to Austria from the Hungarian Foreign Ministry for years. As the phrase went, Austria was seen as a *Kaufobjekt* or bargaining counter.
6. This recommendation was later forgotten by Rome when close Italian–Romanian cooperation came to an end.
7. Rothermere conducted the campaign in the columns of his *Daily Mail*. He built up very wide connections in Hungary. In the end he was carrying on open polemics with the Hungarian government in the columns of the Hungarian press (*Népszava*).
8. The negotiations on the military loan went on for years, and the practical results are not known. The Hungarian air force subsequently established certainly consisted of Italian aircraft.
9. Some Hungarian option bonds were involved in a scandal that broke out in France in February 1934, leading to a government crisis and formation of a popular front. It appears that Alexandre Stavisky, the main figure in the scandal, was also marketing bonds with no financial cover.

7. The Economy in the 1920s

The wartime defeat and the peace treaty of Trianon left Hungary a different country. For one thing, it became internationally and constitutionally independent at last. But its area shrank from 282,870 sq. km to 92,607 sq. km (93,073 sq. km after the Sopron plebiscite), and its population from 18 million to 7.5 million. About 3.2 million of the inhabitants lost were self-declared Hungarians. The population in the area of post-Trianon Hungary rose by 373,172 between the 1910 census and the 1920 one, mostly through the arrival of over 300,000 refugees, for 250,000 had died in battle, and previously, about 60,000 had emigrated between 1910 and the outbreak of the war. Only ten of the 63 historical counties were unaffected by the territorial change. The density of the population in the parts of Hungary annexed to neighboring countries had been lower than the national average. So the national average population density of 64.6 per sq. km in 1910 jumped to 85.9 in 1920—a huge increase, especially when ten years' natural increase had been wiped out by war casualties. Subsequent demographic figures show a satisfactory increase that raised the population density further (to 93.4 in 1930 and 100.1 in 1940), bringing the population to almost 8.7 million in 1930 and 9.3 million in 1940.

The population increase was due mainly to falling infant mortality and improving health. An infant mortality rate of 223 per thousand in 1900 was down to 130.1 by 1940, a major improvement, although Hungary still lagged behind the Western European average. The mortality rate for the under-20s fell from 20 per thousand to 14 over the same period. As the population rose, so did the average age: from 36.6 years at the start of the century to 55 in 1940 for men, and from 38.2 to 58.2 for women. That did not mean that people lived much longer, but simply that infant and young child mortality was lower, although there was some increase in life expectancy with the spread of health care and welfare provisions.

Marriage remained the decisive form of cohabitation, but the number of single people increased, especially among women (from 4.5 percent in 1900 to 8.0 percent in 1940) and the number of divorces per hundred marriages rose (from 3.7 percent in 1900 to 7.9 percent in 1940). The average size of household decreased from 4.7 persons in 1900 to 3.8 in 1940, due to a lower propensity for multi-generation cohabitation and the fact that families moving to urban areas ceased to run farms. There was a falling propensity for households to absorb more distant relatives or auxiliary labor (servants and farm laborers), except among the upper middle class and the elite.

Female employment rose modestly in the first half of the twentieth century. Women made up 25.2 percent of the workforce in 1900 and 27.3 percent in 1940—figures rather lower than the Western European average, although some countries in the West, such as the Netherlands, Belgium and Italy, had fewer women working than Hungary did. This shows that female economic activity is not influenced solely by economic development, but also by ingrained mentality and custom. One important factor behind Hungary's figures was the fact that village women only went out to work until marriage. Thereafter they were not recorded as earners.

Trianon radically altered Hungary's ethnic composition. Old Hungary had been a notably multiethnic state, in which almost half the inhabitants did not deem Hungarian to be their native language. The proportion of the latter in post-Trianon Hungary fell to 10 percent, then 8 and finally 7 percent, due to a natural increase in the Hungarian-speaking population, but also due to state-sponsored "Hungarianization.". The country essentially became a nation state. The biggest minority was that of the half a million Germans ("Swabians"), followed by much smaller groups of Slovaks, Croats, Romanians and Serbs. The Gypsies were not counted as a national minority; estimates of their numbers ranged from 60,000 to 100,000. So a great political dilemma, which had occupied great minds in the 1830s and 1840s (such as Miklós Wesselényi and István Széchenyi) and held politicians spellbound under the Dual Monarchy, had suddenly disappeared. Only one of the fragmented national minorities living in Hungary between the wars caused serious political disruption: the Germans did so in the 1930s, when German Nazism lay behind the problem.

The denominational structure of the population also changed. The Orthodox and Greek Catholic churches almost entirely vanished, bringing increases in the proportions of Roman Catholics (from 49 percent to 66 percent) and Reformed (from 14 percent to 21 percent). The proportion of religious Jews was unchanged (5 percent) and that of the Evangelicals (Lutherans) decreased (from 7 percent to 6 percent). The Catholics exerted the greatest influence on public life; the disputes between churches were more about such influence than about religious or doctrinal matters.

Finally, the great territorial change affected the structure of employment. Post-Trianon Hungary was more highly urbanized, thanks to the relative dominance of Budapest, with its population of almost a million. Other cities with about 100,000 inhabitants (Szeged and Debrecen) remained in the country, as did several more with over 50,000 inhabitants, although the fastest growing cities—Pozsony (Bratislava), Kassa (Košice), Kolozsvár (Cluj), Temesvár (Timişoara) and others—were lost. Development in Debrecen, Szeged and Pécs gained impetus in the 1920s from major university- and hospital-building programs. While 41.6 percent of the overall population remained in Hungary, 62.7 percent of the urban population did so. Budapest and its immediate surroundings (since then part of Greater Budapest) contained 15.6 percent of the total population of post-Trianon Hungary, which indicates the capital's relative economic importance. All in all, inter-war Hungary was the world's eighth most densely populated country, with all the accompanying advantages and drawbacks.

A higher degree of urbanization meant greater industrialization as well. Over 51 percent of the industrial workforce and 57 percent of the manufacturing workforce remained in the truncated territory. These changes also affected the structure of the economically active, with agricultural employment losing ground to other sectors:

Table 1. Branches of employment, as percentages

	Before the War	In 1920
Agrarian	64.5	55.8
Mining and Industry	17.1	21.4
Commerce and Transport	6.5	8.7
Other	11.9	14.1

But despite modest relative growth, mining and industry made up the sector that faced the greatest difficulties. Traditional mining and settlements where it took place had mainly been lost, including all salt mines and all known oil deposits—Nyitra (Nitra), Transylvania, and the Muraköz (Međimurje). The salt was never replaced, and finding crude oil called for extensive prospecting, while refining capacity was left idle. Nor was there much of a market, as motorization only became appreciable a decade later. So the refineries initially concentrated on petroleum for rural lighting. Also lost was the one bauxite mine (in the east of Bihar County), although that caused little harm, as Hungary had not possessed any processing capacity. Bauxite mining, like oil extraction, livened up later in new areas: the Bakony and Vértes hills. The country lost all its gold, silver and copper mines, as well as those for rare metals such as manganese, antimony and mercury. A bigger blow to industry was the scarcity of iron ore deposits, of which production fell by a third (from 3.9 million metric quintals to 1.2 million), and the low-quality remainder could not be used in the big foundries (at Ózd and Diósgyőr) for want of enrichment. Four years passed before Czechoslovakia agreed to supply Slovak iron ore to Hungarian firms, even though it had no local processing capacity of its own. The coal situation was better. The peace conference had rejected claims to the Salgótarján and Pécs coalfields by Czechoslovakia and the future Yugoslavia respectively, and almost 73 percent of the black coal and 71 percent of the brown remained. However, much of the Pécs production still had to go to Yugoslavia for five years after Yugoslav occupation of the area ended.

Other serious problems arose because the country retained industrial capacity unusable for want of raw materials or of a market. Trianon Hungary retained a disproportionately high proportion of the industrial capacity, especially in engineering and printing. While about a third of the territory of the country remained, the proportion was 60 percent for industrial production, 90 percent for printing, and 82.2 percent for manufacturing. Only 22.3 percent of the timber processing remained, yet that capacity could not be utilized fully for want of woodland.

The most developed branch of engineering was vehicle production. Hungarian industry had supplied the Monarchy with most of its railway locomotives, rolling stock, track, points, and so on, and served Hungarian maritime and river shipping. These were threatened after the war by raw material supply and market problems. Even the maintenance work was reduced along with the length of the rail system and smaller numbers of locomotives and rolling stock. The reduction in territory brought a decrease of 35 percent in the rail network but a proportionally higher decrease in locomotives and rolling stock. This had come about as the German forces retreating across Hungary commandeered capacity, as had the Romanian occupation troops, to such an extent that even the Czechoslovak government objected, fearing that the share due to Slovakia might end up in Romania as well. This expropriation without legal grounds was only remedied to some extent through the courts. The shipbuilding industry suffered from the loss of the country's one port, at Fiume (Rijeka), while the length of the navigable waters was down to 35.4 percent. The existing merchant fleet became unusable as well, and much of it had to be handed over to successor states after arbitration.

Great harm was done not only in industries connected to iron and steel, but in flour milling. Hungary's internationally famous milling industry had been processing large quantities of Balkan grain as well, but it lost most of its suppliers after Trianon. Budapest before the war had been the world's second-largest milling center, with 13 large mills grinding about 10 million quintals of grain a year. Its capacity sufficed to serve the whole of the remaining area of the country, but the rest of the country was full of other mills, large and small, in country towns and even villages. This left the mills idle for much of the time: utilization seldom reached a quarter of capacity after the war, and in worse years not even that. The situation later improved to some extent, but not to the extent of a recovery for the industry.

Along with the fundamental changes already mentioned, there were many other industries of lesser importance that suffered a loss of supplies of raw materials. Some others were brought down by the post-war wave of inflation. This benefited certain types of investment, but not longer-term construction projects, and so the construction industry was hit hard for several years. This, coupled with the long period required for transport to normalize, explains how much of industry was bankrupted after the war for non-economic reasons and how mass unemployment ensued.

The peace treaty did not affect the prospects for agriculture as much as it did those for industry and transport. The best farmlands in the Bácska, Banate and Csallóköz districts were lost, but a high proportion of the arable lands remained, even if much of these called for soil improvement (for being saline, lime-deficient, and so on). The structure of cultivation shifted strongly from meadow and pasture to arable, and the loss of upland pastures was especially unfortunately for stockbreeding. One consequence was a big increase in the production of rough fodder and Lucerne grass. Modernization of agriculture-type production was promoted by the fact that majority of the vineyards remained—about half of the hillside vineyards and 80 per cent of the sandy soiled vineyards—and some wines also found foreign markets. But the loss of woodland acquired catastrophic proportions. Hardly any pine forest remained (less than 3 percent) and less than half the oak, beech and other deciduous forest. This loss of the woodland belt damaged the timber-processing industry, which had to work with expensive imports, and it made water management difficult as well, as most of the rivers had their sources beyond the borders, where the Hungarian authorities had no control over timber production.

Another change to the economy was in the structure of land ownership. Inequality became even more pronounced, with the proportion of arable holdings of more than 100 *hold* (57 ha) rising from 30.66 percent to 41.15 percent. These large estates were concerned mainly with extensive grain production with low labor requirements, which increased the demand for jobs at a time when industrial and transport crisis precluded the cities from absorbing surplus labor. At the same time, the safety valve of emigration was all but closed by a new quota system introduced in the United States in 1921. Canada, meanwhile, was regulating the number of immigrants accepted according to its varying demand. This prompted the Hungarian government in the early 1920s to seek solutions in Europe, but there the demand was for industrial workers and miners, although that did not preclude some rural Hungarians from acceptance. Larger numbers of Hungarian workers found work in France and Belgium, but smaller groups also went to Turkey, which was modernizing strongly at the time.

As for livestock, 35 percent of the cattle, 45 percent of the horses, 52 percent of the pigs and 31.3 percent of the sheep remained. In terms of stock per head of population, there were fewer cattle and sheep, a few more horses, and a good many more pigs.

There was another consequence of the peace treaty that the reduced country had to cope with. About 200,000 people resettled in Hungary from Romania and about 125,000 from Czechoslovakia, because they had lost their jobs or did not want to take an oath of allegiance to the new state. There were some great landowners among them, but most were state employees, teachers, school directors, postal employees and officials. A high proportion had no home or relatives in Hungary. Building was still out of the question due to the state of the construction industry, mentioned already, and so many of these refugees were reduced to living in over 4,000 railway carriages, which had been made available. By the end of 1922, the state had managed to build 3,869 dwellings, mainly consisting of just one room and a kitchen, which reduced the number living in railway carriages. A further problem was the fact that many of them wanted jobs, but the market for labor in the remaining area of the country did not permit this. The whole state apparatus was narrowing, so that it was more a question of laying off staff than of hiring new people. The issue was eventually resolved by granting them state pensions, which was an added burden on the pension system.

All in all, the war damage and peace treaty terms sent Hungary's economy into a serious crisis, forcing the country to alter its economic foundations in several regards. A way out of the crisis was not found for about six years. This was made harder still because the state sector went into crisis, just as the private one did. Hungarian State Railways and the engineering industry were largely in state hands, and the war, coupled with excessive welfare spending under the People's and Hungarian Soviet Republics, upset the public finances and fueled the inflation that had started during the war. Subsequent governments met the deficit by printing unbacked money.

It was all the more tempting to increase the money supply because the state had unexpected new expenditures to cover, for tasks that had not been within its remit to carry out before. There were no sources of funding for the shaken system. Earlier, Hungary had attracted considerable investment capital from abroad, but this ceased and the country suffered a lengthy economic blockade after the armistice had been signed. However, foreign capital was already well embedded in the Hungarian economy: 36 percent of the engineering stock and 55 percent of the big banks' capital was foreign, mainly from Austria and Germany, which took up 60–70 percent of the state paper and railway bonds issued.

One outcome of the blockade for a while was a tendency to equate foreign trade with smuggling. Czechoslovakia was not allowing German or Polish coal deliveries through, while the Pécs– Komló coalfield was under Yugoslav occupation (up to August 1921). So the country had practically no coal, without which it was impossible to run the trains, let alone the factories. The Romanian occupation forces also impeded postal, telephone and telegraph links as well for a while. The cost of the damage done in the military occupation that followed the war was estimated at 24.5 billion crowns. Although this is probably exaggerated, there can be no doubt that the systematic pillaging by the Romanian occupiers caused untold harm. The greatest damage was done in the munitions factories, especially the Csepel factory and Győr ordnance factory of Manfréd Weiss, the second of which was dismantled down to the last screw, along with all the raw materials and even the scrap iron, leaving only the bare walls.

Meanwhile, the specter of reparations appeared on the horizon. The peace treaties had stipulated that the defeated countries had to pay for the damage that they had done to other countries, but as the peace conference could not agree on any figures, a Reparations Commission was established and charged with arriving at the totals. Even then, the problem was not solved, because the representatives of the victorious powers took different positions. First, the commission decided on various payments in kind, or clarified obligations that had already been laid down in the peace treaties.

Up to the end of 1926 Hungary had to deliver 880 tons of coal a day to Yugoslavia and provide a total of 28,000 head of livestock for slaughter to Yugoslavia, Italy and Greece. The victorious powers seized as a pledge for the future reparations all the country's state revenue and wealth, which meant that Hungary had nothing to offer as collateral for a foreign loan. The sum of the reparations alone was the subject of the same arguments as in Germany's case. The main scene of action by the Hungarian army had been Russia, but Russia was not part of the reparations process, and so the debates were between Italy and Yugoslavia, which were directly concerned, and Britain and France, which were not. The Italians were the most merciless initially, wanting Hungary to pay 3 billion crowns. This compared with the sum of 1–2 billion that would have satisfied the more moderate representatives of France, while the British put the total at 480,000–600,000 crowns. In the end, the French agreed with the Italians on 2.135 billion crowns, and the issue was resolved provisionally along with the question of the rehabilitation loan.

The Hungarian state had to deal first of all with the money question, for there could be no thought of economic reorganization or recovery without orderly monetary relations. Up to 1918, crowns issued by the Austro-Hungarian Bank[1] had been the legal tender throughout the Austro-Hungarian lands. Although the bank ceased to issue money for the seceding states, there was still a very large quantity of paper money on the market. All the successor states were obliged under the peace treaties to overprint these bills until they could establish their own currencies. Liquidation of the Austro-Hungarian Bank was placed in the hands of an international committee (from France, Italy and Romania), after which its transactions (assets and liabilities) were split among the successor states in proportion to area and population. By the time that the division had been completed in October 1920, Hungary had received about 11.9 billion of the 36 billion crowns in circulation.

At that point, the Hungarian side of the original bank ceased to trade, and the Royal Hungarian State Banknote Institution[2] opened on August 1, 1921. However, overprinting of the crown had taken place much earlier—in most successor states in 1919 and in Hungary in the spring of 1920, after the political transformation. By that time, Hungary had to do it at great speed, as large quantities of non-overprinted money were flowing into the country from neighboring countries where overprinting had been done earlier. The banks overprinted these notes with the word "Hungary" and the state took half the nominal value in the form of 4 percent state bonds. This paper issued against the compulsory loan could be used to pay taxes and liabilities to do with the agrarian reform. So the 8.87 billion crowns overprinted lost half their nominal value, but the state gained a means to reduce its debt.

But this was not enough to halt the inflation. A new wave ensued after only a short period of falling prices. Nor did the central bank perform the classic function of a bank of issue. Although it took over its proportionate share of the functions and assets of the Austro-Hungarian Bank, it remained dependent on the state, simply an office issuing the paper money, and it was under the control of the minister of finance of the day. So in practice, monetary policy was dictated to the bank of issue by the government.

Inflation was not avoided by any of the belligerents in the First World War, as they covered their mounting military expenditure with foreign loans, domestic state paper, and the issue of paper money. The last procedure was most pronounced in the Central Powers, the countries without access to foreign (usually American) loans. The Austro-Hungarian crown had been one of the most stable currencies in the region before the war, but it faltered immediately when war was declared. The Hungarian government borrowed 14 billion crowns from the bank of issue during the war and raised another 18 billion from crown-denominated bonds known as war loans. These were bought with their savings by many ordinary people, who lost them entirely in the galloping post-war inflation. Governments were covering such loans only with unbacked paper money, and so inflation had reached a rate of about 60 percent a year by the time the war ended. Thereafter it really began to gain speed, one impetus being the regimes of Mihály Károlyi and of the Hungarian Soviet Republic, through their financially unbacked welfare measures. The situation was worsened when the Governing Soviet scattered the country's gold reserves as well. With matters worsening rather than improving, Lóránd Hegedűs, the minister of finance of the Teleki government, introduced an anti-inflationary recovery program.

Hegedűs, president of the National Federation of Industrialists,[3] started from the assumption that Hungary's finances could not be reorganized through foreign loans while the country's revenues and assets were still mortgaged. The remedy had to come entirely from domestic sources. He therefore devised a stabilization program on that basis at the end of 1920. Bearing in mind the fact that some French consortia were still displaying interest in the business opportunities in Hungary, he wanted to christen the future currency the Hungarian franc and tie its rate of exchange to the French franc. His first step was to try to restore budgetary equilibrium by making drastic cuts in expenditure and increasing revenues. He wanted to encourage thrift above all in state institutions, even seeking to control the price of the automobiles used by ministry officials. He sought to raise more revenue with a wealth tax, speculating that capitalists who had earned high wartime profits and businesses shedding their earlier debts easily thanks to inflation would easily bear this one tax levied on wealth. In addition, he raised the rates of existing taxes and introduced new ones, including a general turnover tax, and a luxury tax on certain goods. The general turnover tax proved to be exceedingly successful and was a source of pride to the minister for many years.

The planned wealth tax would have been levied according to an extremely complex system of separate rates for different types of property. In some cases, it could be paid on property in kind. The levy on agricultural land, for instance, was to have been 26–240 kilograms per *hold*, according to the size and quality of the holding, but it could also be paid by handing over to the state 6–20 percent of the property's value. There was an auxiliary order stating that landowners possessing over 1,000 *hold* (570 ha) were obliged to pay the levy in land. It was calculated that this would transfer 1.5 million *hold* of land into state ownership, and so assist in carrying out the land reform.

But the 24 billion crowns expected of the levy did not materialize; only 0.5 million, not 1.5 million *hold* were transferred to the Treasury. Hegedűs later argued that the program had been sabotaged by the landowners. There was some truth in that, but the failure had several contributory causes. The essence of this financial policy included deflationary measures that hardened the crown, raised interest rates, made it harder to obtain investment loans, and impeded exports, which were already extremely meager. Put another way, the minister was not offering compensatory means to the actors in the economy in return for levying them, but reducing their chances in every regard. Furthermore, the smaller sum that actually materialized had to be used for current expenditures, and so the levy made no appreciable contribution to stabilization. Although the minister of finance managed to halt inflation in the second half of 1921 and improve the exchange rate of the crown (from 572 to the US dollar to 240 a few months later), the price had been paid by the real economy, and so Hegedűs came under increasing attack and resigned in September 1921.

Inflation speeded up again after the abortive attempt to stabilize the economy using domestic resources. This was seen as a great advantage by debtors and by some investors. Landowners and others could pay off debts in rapidly depreciating crowns, freeing themselves of all their old mortgages for nominal sums after the war. Landlords and tenants borrowed a nominal, unfixed sum of about 3 million gold crowns up to 1924. The financing of almost the whole economy was done by the bank of issue in such loans, which could hardly have been more lucrative for borrowers, who repaid the *nominal* loan, after its real value had been eroded. Although government policy in late 1921 and 1922 was not expressly inflationary, the policy of the government-run bank of issue was a serious inflationary factor, which feeble efforts by the Ministry of Finance failed to offset.

There were still no countermeasures at all in 1923—the amount of paper money in circulation multiplied several times over by the beginning of 1924. The 17.3 billion crowns in circulation in the summer of 1921 became 46.2 billion a year later, 400 billion by the summer of 1923, 931 billion by the end of that year, and 2.52 trillion by May 1924. The inflation in some months reached 100 percent and bills in new denominations had to be issued. The 100,000-crown note was followed by the 500,000-crown one. As a result, the exchange rate of the crown also sank steadily, to 0.009 Swiss centimes by March 1924. It is impossible to imagine that such galloping inflation could not have been connected with government policy, not least because Prime Minister Bethlen is known to have thought that the country should present as poor a financial picture as possible at the loan and reparations talks taking place at the time.

But that scale of inflation no longer served the interests of any stratum in society. The biggest losers were the masses of wage and salary earners, whose income failed miserably to keep up with the price rises. The prices of staple foods in Hungary rose at the second-fastest rate in Europe, while average wages rose at only half that rate. Nor did the salaries of clerks and officials do any better. Officials and workers alike, poorly paid even before the war, were reduced to penury in the years after it. Other big losers on account of the inflation were holders of war loan stock and any other fixed-interest savings. Once Hegedűs's stabilization had failed, people began fleeing with their money into gold and foreign exchange, until the process was halted by establishing the Foreign Exchange Center,[4] to prevent the purchase of foreign currency and the movement of funds abroad.

The false boom produced by the inflation broke off at the end of 1923. Some of the fortunes obtained by speculation collapsed. Restrictions on exports and on the free flow of foreign currency curbed imports, which made life difficult for many import-dependent industries, although this created good markets for some Hungarian products that would not have been competitive internationally. This, along with the 50 percent fall in wages mentioned already, placed some industrialists in highly lucrative positions of monopoly. The inflationary period arrived at a stage where all rational calculation was impossible and the economy was utterly disorganized, causing increasingly strident demands for order and financial stabilization.

A start could be made with stabilization in May 1924, after the prime minister's successful diplomatic and foreign policy campaign. The so-called international loan was arranged, along with provisional settlement of the reparations. Although these fell far short of Hungarian expectations, they provided sufficient foundations for restoring financial law and order. The main elements in the strategy were plans to stop printing money, to found a central bank independent of the government, to restore the budgetary balance by mid-1926 using the international loan, and to augment financial reconstruction with a general plan of economic development. Some of the huge deficit in 1923–1924 had to be covered by a 523-billion crown domestic compulsory loan from half a million individual and corporate payers of wealth tax and income tax, of which most was duly advanced. Meanwhile, large Hungarian corporations raised a 20-million Swiss franc loan that could also be used to relieve the state deficit. These and some other transactions meant that the first installment of the loan was not consumed entirely by the budget deficit.

But the terms of the international loan were extremely unfavorable. The government was talking initially of 550–600 million gold crowns, but it soon had to abandon that figure. Eventually access would be obtained to 253 million of the 307 million that featured on paper, and although the bonds later appreciated on the international market, the final sum was still only 267 million gold crowns. The British, American, Swiss, Swedish, Dutch and Czechoslovak banks charged 7.5 percent and the Italians 8.05 percent; this meant that the annual installment payment came to 30 million gold crowns. In fact the subscription to the loan was not too successful. All the big finance houses except the British ones had reservations. Eventually the Hungarian banks had to join in, to the tune of 11.6 million gold crowns, but the tranche was soon resold to the American bank Speyer, which in this way built itself a good basis for further business.

Despite the initial difficulties, the practical transaction of the loan went very well. Even the first installment of the loan did not all need to be spent on covering the current deficit, and none was used for that purpose in later years. Jeremiah Smith, the League of Nations supervisor, recommended releasing successive sums for investment purposes. Behind this thrift, however, lay great increases in taxation and drastic reductions in state expenditure. The main target was land tax, but the government did not forget income and wealth tax, company tax or the various duties and fees, either. Furthermore, towns were permitted to levy local taxes to cover their deficits. So the pre-war mean tax yield of 45 gold crowns *per capita* became 72 gold crowns *per capita*. The operating losses of Hungarian State Railways were eliminated by raising fares and charges by about 30 percent. Royall Tyler, the US adviser to the National Bank, had grounds for saying that the reorganization had been the work of the Hungarian taxpayer.

The cuts on the spending side began with major redundancies in officialdom. The government had committed itself originally to trimming 15,000 jobs, but in fact 33,000 people were dismissed from state employment; however, most of them were pensioned off, and so the saving was not great in the short term. The slimming of the bureaucracy was needed after the huge reduction in the country's area and population, but it continued in subsequent years. The National Economy Commission[5] set up by the government in 1925 devised further plans for rationalization, including the closure of several redundant institutions, such as the Ministry of Public Nutrition, the Price Examination Office and the Government Commission for Coal. The idea of modernizing public administration was also raised, but the commission failed to agree on how it should be done.

What has been said so far shows that the government based its budgetary and financial stabilization on the country's domestic resources. But there were two other questions that it was unable to resolve. One was the question of reparations, while the country was still saddled with a mortgage on state assets and future revenues. Both were patched up temporarily by the reconstruction memoranda. The reparation payments were to be made over twenty years, with nothing to pay during the reconstruction years, followed by annual payments, starting at 5 million gold crowns and rising steadily, but not to exceed 10 million. The memorandum stated that within the reparations, there should be priority for so-called "peace treaty expenses." These included costs incurred by various committees working in Hungary (the Vix Mission, the Smith Committee dispatched in 1919, the generals' committee, the border commissions, the military committee supervising the Sopron plebiscite, and so on), as well as sums for prisoners of war and for treatment and transport for wounded prisoners. According to internal estimates by the Ministry of Finance, the figure for this alone, up to 1929, regularly exceeded the full allocation, and no reparation payments in the original sense were made. After that, in 1929, the experts set about making a final settlement of the question, of which more will be said later.

The most important result of the loan talks with the League of Nations was certainly the temporary lifting of the mortgage. It allowed other large foreign loans to be raised, which managed to revive the economy. The League of Nations commissioner established guidelines for utilizing the investment loans: the projects had to be productive and yield at least enough to cover the interest on each loan. This was not always attained. One of the main brokers for the foreign capital that poured into the country after the reorganization was the American house of Speyer, mentioned already, which did not have an immaculate international reputation. However, one factor that often lay behind the "unproductive" investments to which contemporaries objected was the fact that only a smaller part of the foreign loans was taken up by industrial firms, landowners, and so on. The greater part was taken up by the state or, more specifically, counties and cities, with a state guarantee. The state would only invest in its own firms, and in line with the spirit of the time, did not have any interest in general economic development or feel competent to promote it. So most of the sums borrowed went on infrastructural development, educational and cultural purposes, and improvements in health care. There would have been no Klebelsberg program of people's schools without the loans, and no university-building, and no new clinics, hospitals and sanatoriums. County and city loans went mainly on improving roads, leveling farmland, electrification, improving local transportation, paving roads, providing medical facilities, and so on.

There were big debates on the question, for those involved in industry classed all such projects as unproductive luxury spending, while the Ministry of Finance argued that improving education and the health of the workforce were productive for the economy as a whole. People joked about the "water-beetle smithy"—the new Ichthyology Institute at Tihany on Lake Balaton—and scoffed at money being spent on a grand hotel at Lillafüred, intended to cater for the top end of the tourism market. In fact the efficiency of the loan utilization was reduced primarily because about 40 percent had to go on servicing pre-war debt. Only about 20 percent of these monies went on truly unproductive consumption.

But private business and landed estates were also prominent in the wave of borrowing that began in 1925. The state and public institutions accounted for hardly more than 50 percent of the oft-mentioned 4.1 billion gold crowns (or according to other estimates 4.5 billion) of indebtedness that had accrued by 1931, and a high proportion of that was still rolled-over debt from before the war. Almost half the remainder was owed by various agricultural interests. All in all, Hungary had become Europe's most indebted country, thanks for one thing to rising confidence among foreign lenders. Even in 1928–1929, this process was being interpreted in different ways. Some experts saw it as being far from tragic: the dynamic growth of the economy at the time would sort out the temporary difficulties. Others, looking especially at the trade figures, reckoned that the debt spiral was becoming irreversible.

The economy certainly took off. This could not yet be felt in 1924–1925, as the spending cuts and tight monetary policy caused a money shortage that impeded investment. The new National Bank of Hungary[6] followed a very cautious policy that built up its reputation for decades. On taking over the task of handling state debt from the government-controlled bank of issue, it stated definitively that it would not give unsecured credit to the government or any other public institution. Nevertheless, lack of demand from domestic business investors forced the government to buy large amounts of bank stock, giving it a stake of almost 40 percent in the sector.

The National Bank of Hungary also took over the country's gold and foreign exchange reserves and established an operational fund to complement its own registered capital. The latter was topped up by the Bank of England, which made £4 million available for

three years, and also undertook to exchange crowns to any amount
for pounds sterling, provided that the Hungarian currency was tied
to the pound. The original rate was 346,000 paper crowns to the
pound, but after the price of a gold crown in paper crowns had
soared to 17,000, the crown-to-pound rate changed with the stabilization, and the divisor changed again to 12,500 when the *pengő*
was introduced as the new unit of currency. There were 27.82
pengő to the pound sterling in 1929, along with 5.7 to the US dollar and 1.4 to the German mark. There was no gold coinage issued,
and the silver coinage of daily transactions had a copper content of
almost one third. There were some technical reasons for substitut-
ing the *pengő* for the crown, but it also had prestige-related significance for the independent Hungarian state.

The National Bank was so cautious in issuing money that its
reserves greatly exceeded the value of the amount in circulation.
This was a factor behind the "rehabilitation recession" that ensued
after the stabilization. Interest rates were jacked up by the general
shortage of money, and some firms began to reduce their output,
which led to redundancies and wage cuts. Employment declined
and unemployment, which had been declining, started to rise again.
The small firms, mainly trading firms, that had sprung up in the
inflationary period began to fail in large numbers. This was not
confined to the weaker ones. Business failures in 1925 were six
times as many as in 1924 and compulsory settlements increased by
a factor of twelve. Behind these alarming figures lay two agricultural developments as well: exceptionally bad harvests, and the
beginnings of a general agricultural crisis in Europe.

After what has been said, it can be appreciated that the value
of Hungary's post-war industrial output, according to most
researchers, had risen by a total of 12–13 percent by 1929. Discounting the first two post-war years of hardly any growth at all
and considering the way in which the partly illusory achievements
of the inflationary period were reversed by the rehabilitation

recession, it is clear that most of the increase fell in the period of three or three and a half years from 1926. Dividing the increment among ten years gives an annual average growth rate of 1.2–1.3 percent, but bearing the fluctuations in mind, there seems to have been a growth rate of 3 or more percent starting in 1926. This was no worse than the European average, and exceeded the rates in several established industrial powers. In fact, it can be seen as a great success in the light of the initial conditions and the ensuing post-war situation.

The survival of industry was helped by the speed with which earlier regional and international cartels reestablished contact with each other after the war. The Rimamurány–Salgótarján Ironworks Co. (RIMA),[7] for example, was already receiving assistance with raw materials from former Czech and Austrian partners, in exchange for supplying foodstuffs to Czechoslovakia and Austria over and above the inter-state quotas. In 1925, the large corporations concerned, which became known as the Central Europe Group,[8] agreed among themselves to defend and divide their national and international markets. The Central Europe Group went on in 1926 to join the International Steel Cartel formed by French and German interests and was granted an annual quota of 7,272,000 tons, of which 300,000 tons went to RIMA. In 1927, the Central Europe Group also reached an agreement on refined steel, but both the International Steel Cartel and the Central Europe Group were swept away by the worldwide Depression, the former winding itself up in 1931 and the latter in 1932.

The dark side to the economy in the 1920s appeared mainly in agriculture. Agricultural output in 1925 was still only 75–80 percent of what it had been averaging before the war. Behind this lay an increase in the amount of land lying fallow, due to a shortage of draft animals and manpower. The yields of all grain crops, corn, potatoes and sugar beet were down on what they had been before the war, and continued to decline until 1922. The worst year was

1920, when the government was obliged to import grain and flour from the United States and Argentina. The agricultural export surpluses of the pre-war period accordingly fell to nothing. Exports revived in 1921, with Austria as the main destination, with sizable deliveries of grain to Czechoslovakia, and livestock for slaughter and for draft to Italy and Germany. International trade, incidentally, continued according to the earlier common tariff with states that were prepared to accept it as a guideline. But there was a clear need for new trade agreements based on new Hungarian tariff legislation, all the more so because protectionism had come to reign across Europe, despite all the arguments and proposals against it.

There were some intellectuals, business people and even politicians, in all countries, who recognized, as the peace treaties were signed or just afterwards, the threat posed to Europe by the isolation of countries behind autarkic economic policies and the tariff wars that these would entail. Several lecturers at meetings of the Hungarian Cobden Society[9] in 1921–1922 argued for European or Danubian economic cooperation. The well-known financial expert Professor Elemér Hantos, for instance, was not alone in Hungary or in Europe in pressing, in a lecture in December 1921, for a single European currency and consumption-oriented economic policies. But the expert advice on modernization and European economic cooperation was drowned out by the rabid nationalism of the period, above all in Central Europe, the Balkans and the Baltic states, where establishing and protecting the independent, sovereign economic entity of the newborn, or newly enlarged, state was seen as a prime duty. Where agriculture lay in the background, the intention was mainly to gain advantages for that sector; where industry had to be developed, that is where the state preferences mainly went.

Hungary belonged to the second category, which put its stamp on the new customs tariffs devised and introduced at the beginning of 1925. This also involved changing the whole logic of the previous Austro-Hungarian tariff policy. The Imperial customs duties levied in the Dual Monarchy favored Austrian industry and Hungarian agriculture, although the system was not so biased as to prevent industrial development in Hungary or any part of the Empire. Those devising Hungary's independent Hungarian tariff system certainly based it on the premise that the country's economic prosperity depended on rapid industrial development, for otherwise the whole economy would be condemned to vegetate, as "open prey" for any neighboring country, and eventually would dwindle into a "raw material-producing colony." This prophecy by an official at the Ministry of Finance was certainly vindicated later by the economic policy of the German Nazi regime, but in its time, in the 1920s, it aroused passionate debate and began to lead the groups whose interests were opposed to Bethlen's economic policy to line up.

Nevertheless, the new Hungarian tariff was expressly supportive of industry. The agricultural protest against it was initially muted, as the high protective tariffs for industry left enough scope for Hungarian negotiators to gain some concessions for agricultural exports. Such tactics were effective against Austria and Czechoslovakia for several years in the 1920s. But the "agricultural peace" at home did not last long, as export prospects rapidly deteriorated with the onset of worldwide economic crisis. The strongest cries came initially from the wholesalers, for whom exports of agricultural produce and raw materials and imports of manufactures had traditionally been a lucrative business, but they were soon joined by the farmers. The tariffs were expressly designed to encourage import substitution, which meant, *inter alia*, that the industry supported in this way would produce for the home market, at least initially. The whole scheme was a spur to those setting up new industries, as it allowed protection of factories once they had been set up. Logical though this idea was, it unwittingly posed a danger that protected industry in a situation of near-monopoly would dictate high domestic prices, and that is what happened. The high prices imposed then prevented consumption from rising fast enough to encourage further industrial growth.

The tariff legislation covered far more product groups than its predecessor had done, and set an average tariff of 30 percent on industrial imports. High protection went to the fledgling textile industry, which was important because textile products accounted for 35–40 percent of all imports in that period. There was also firm protection for iron and steel, notably agricultural implements, vehicles and electrical machinery, and for leather, paper, and food processing. But important raw materials for industry—wool, raw leather, timber products, jute, coke, petroleum, and so on—were allowed in duty free. The tariffs were later adjusted to varying extents several times, to account for policy changes in neighboring countries, but the logic of Hungarian tariff policy remained the same. It was obviously not by chance that industrial development tended to appear first in the industries that received special tariff protection.

Hungary's main trading partners in the immediate post-war years were the neighboring countries, of which Austria and Czechoslovakia remained the most important up to the end of the 1920s: in 1927, they accounted for 17.5 and 24.2 percent respectively of Hungary's imports and 34.8 and 19.4 percent of its exports. These proportions deteriorated rapidly in 1929, and lower trade volumes were typical also for the other two neighboring countries, Romania and Yugoslavia, with some fluctuations. Having introduced the tariff legislation, Hungary went on to conclude a succession of trade agreements that backed the industrial development of the next few years.

Industrial production leapt forward in the later 1920s, especially large-scale manufacturing. Manufacturing raised its production value by an unprecedented 70 percent in five years, but all modern branches of the economy showed sizable growth. Industry and mining accounted for 25 percent of national income in 1913, but 31.1 percent by 1929, or 37.4 percent if transportation and trade are included, so that it hardly fell short of agriculture's share of 39.7 percent. This spurt provided the aggregate growth of 12–13 percent since 1913, mentioned earlier.

The development was especially strong in textiles, vehicles, electrical power generation, and the electrical industry, but the food industry lost its share (temporarily) despite the concessions, and so did iron and steel and mechanical engineering. Textiles contributed 4.8 percent of manufacturing production in 1913, but 14.2 percent in 1929, giving it three times the weight and allowing it to supply 75 percent of the domestic market for finished goods. This growth was interrupted by the Great Crash, but the industry did not suffer great losses and managed to resume its growth later. Similar sudden increases were experienced in the paper industry, whose volume of production increased from 2,000 tons to 34,000 tons, to cover 40 percent of domestic demand.

Some products of the engineering industry fell back for want of a market, but others increased. The manufacture of private automobiles was abandoned and that of commercial vehicles limited to short-run assembly of trucks at MÁVAG and the Győr Wagon and Machine Factory.[10] On the other hand, the manufacture of motorcycles and bicycles at Csepel experienced growth. Particular importance was attached to the Ganz diesel-powered railcar, which enjoyed international success. But the successes in vehicles could not offset the decline in engineering as a whole. This affected railway rolling stock, which had been made in large quantities, and agricultural machines. Within the latter, only tractor-making really increased, but about half the production could only be sold abroad. Nevertheless, the general situation in vehicles was marked by capital shortage, which meant that many Hungarian inventions went unexploited, for want of the money to install mass production facilities. That applied to the helicopter that Oszkár Asbóth designed, and to the jet engine of Albert Fonó.

While the situation in engineering was mixed, the electrical industry retained and improved its position, thanks to new products. The tungsten-filament and then the krypton-gas bulbs of the United Incandescent Lamp Works broke into the international market. Orion radio valves and radio sets also acquired a good name, although relatively few of them were sold at home. In telecommunications, mention can be made of the Hungarian model of television, made in the mid-1920s, but destined to have same fate as the helicopter and jet engine mentioned earlier. The idea of starting television broadcasting was considered from time to time, but always postponed for want of capital.

There was obvious progress in electrical power generation. The pre-war output had risen tenfold by 1929. Nine new power plants had been built and the length of the grid of electricity cables increased from 1,000 to 2,500 kilometers. It has been seen that mining lost ground under the peace treaty and its lack of prospects was alleviated only by the discovery of bauxite deposits near Veszprém. The chemical industry expanded with the opening of the Pét Nitrogen Works.[11]

All in all, the industrial reorganization required by the radical changes in the country's territory and economic structure was completed successfully in the 1920s. Transport conditions improved and international trade resumed. The number of industrial installations rose by 165.3 percent between 1921 and 1929, and the industrial workforce expanded by 155.2 percent. The development was matched in the closely related fields of transportation, telecommunications and electrification. Hungarian State Railways introduced new, modern steam locomotives and electric locomotives designed by Kálmán Kandó for the newly electrified Budapest–Hegyeshalom line towards Vienna. The rail network was not increased, as it was thought to be sufficiently dense. The fact that a planned ring line was never built was partly because the political elite, counting on territorial revision, envisioned it as running outside the Trianon borders. There was a modest increase in the number of motor vehicles, mainly motorcycles. Car ownership was still a luxury at the end of the 1930s and most freight still went by rail or on horse-drawn drays or carts.

The biggest leap in communications was the start of radio broadcasting in 1925. This expanded nationwide after the Lakitelek transmitter was completed in 1928. Listening became general among the lower middle classes and even in the villages as cheaper radio sets became widespread towards the end of the 1930s. The automation of telephone exchanges began in 1928 in Budapest, followed by other large cities. This meant that more lines could be served, and telephony spread very rapidly, except in rural areas.

The increasing power generation allowed electric street lighting to become general and streetcar services to expand. Domestic electricity supplies spread even to small towns and villages. About 27 percent of the country's communities were lit by electricity. The piped water and sewage systems did not increase, however, and most of the population still lacked a healthy water supply at the end of the period.

Most domestic trade was still conducted at general stores and other retail shops and stalls, but the capital and other large cities began to gain department stores and chain stores as well. The Hungarian Fashion Hall,[12] which opened in Budapest in 1925, was followed five years later by the Corvin department store. Meinl of Austria built up a chain of grocery stores and Bata of Czechoslovakia established a chain of shoe shops.

This picture, optimistic in several regards, is darkened by the continuing problems in the rural economy, which still accounted for 40 percent of national output even in 1929. Problems persisted with the structure of ownership, outmoded farming production methods were still used, and the supply structure failed to match demand on foreign markets. It has been seen already that the peace treaty shifted the ownership structure in favor of estates of more than 100 *hold*

(57 ha) and that the land reform under the Bethlen government did not help. Most of the land reforms in the region were more radical than Hungary's, but they were carried out mainly at the expense of foreign great landowners, German ones in the Baltic and Hungarian ones in the countries neighboring Hungary. Hungary, on the other hand, did not have non-Hungarian great estates to expropriate, and this made the government cautious.

Under a reform protracted over several years, 1.3 million *hold* (741,000 ha, 9 percent of the cultivated land) was redistributed, of which more than two thirds consisted of land offered under the Hegedűs "wealth ransom" scheme. About 200,000 *hold* (114,000 ha) of the land were used for public purposes (housing for clergy, teachers and gendarmes, sports grounds, holdings for ex-servicemen with the rank of *vitéz*, and so on). Some 155,000 *hold* (65,550 ha) were turned into tenant smallholdings, so that the freehold ownership remained the same. The remaining 930,000 *hold* (530,100 ha) went on 260,000 freehold building sites averaging 400 square ells (1,428 sq. m) and 425,000 freehold smallholdings averaging 1.7 *hold* (0.97 ha) each. So fewer than half a million new smallholders were created, and they gained holdings that were hardly viable, or in the best cases just provided a family with a subsistence. In 1895, 53.7 percent of farms had been "dwarf holdings" of under 5 *hold* (2.85 ha), but in 1935, 72.5 percent were. Meanwhile, the number of farm servants and day laborers was 1,810,000 in 1930–1931; in other words, there was still that number of people of landless left after Bethlen's land reform. So it is apparent from the structural change described that the land reform failed to swell the stratum of viable peasant farmers. It has to be added that the sums of compensation were not agreed until 1928, and these were soon impossible to earn from the holdings received, due to the Depression, the fall in agricultural prices, and the consequent servicing and repayment costs. Most of those who received such holdings went bankrupt and had to say goodbye to the "property" that they had received so recently.

This happened despite government efforts to assist the new owners of housing sites and dwarf holdings, as the assistance took the form of loans. Housing site owners were offered loans to build and smallholders to buy machinery and livestock. But if they did so, they faced mounting repayments. Another form of assistance in theory was a 10 percent discount on tractor purchases by those farming fewer than 100 *hold* (57 ha), as long as the new holders agreed to plow another 100 *hold* at a reduced price. A relatively successful side of the land reform was the distribution of housing sites, under which 43,000 families received house-building loans. This program was augmented in 1941 by the National Fund for People's and Family Protection.[13]

Another factor worsening the situation of agriculture, apart from the anomalies in the ownership structure, was retention of the traditional product structure. Hungary had long been growing wheat and corn in the main, and there were also good export markets for meat products, although not poultry or fish. But after the war, strong competitors in these appeared: US and Canadian wheat, and Argentine beef, for instance. The agricultural supplies from overseas were produced a good deal more cheaply, thanks to developed methods of production, than were those from Hungary or other parts of Central and Eastern Europe. Furthermore, European prices in the midst of the Depression were beaten down even further for two years by "Russian dumping," that is to say, Stalin's notion of covering the costs of his great industrialization program by selling Russian agricultural produce at less than world market prices.

The alternative or complementary solutions proposed by Hungarian experts were to change the product mix in agriculture and give preference to smaller-scale items such as vegetables, fruits and poultry, while providing the means to modernize for this and in the agricultural sector as a whole. That was to include further expansion and improvement of the road and rail systems,

forestation and sewage programs, soil improvement, better credit
provisions, expansion of agricultural education, establishment of
people's colleges, extending the program for consolidating holdings
from the Great Plain to Transdanubia, and encouraging peasant farmers to join cooperatives. The prime minister is known to have
looked into a loan scheme that would have secured the water supply on the Great Plain, but nothing came of that or any of the other
proposals. There were timid changes in the product structure, but
only in the latter half of the 1930s. According to calculations by one
great landowner, there were only 19 great estates in Hungary that
were being run in ways that matched the standard of the times. By
that he meant adequate mechanization and fertilizer use, with much
of the output utilized on the estate itself, and with adequate measures taken to bring the produce to market, in other words adequate
capital, expertise and commercial connections. Over 90 percent of
farms lacked these, and thus the proportion of intensive farming did
not grow, use of artificial fertilizers increased only on large estates,
and poor, saline or acidic soils were not improved. So it was hardly surprising that the wheat yield per hectare in Hungary, a typical
agricultural country, was lower than in any European country
except Yugoslavia. The situation was similar with all grains, corn,
potatoes and sugar beet as well. Hungarian agriculture was falling
ever further behind not only America, but the developed parts of
Europe. By 1930–1932, it was capable only of 40–60 percent of
Danish, Belgian or German yields, and it had been overtaken by
Czechoslovakia, Poland and several other countries.

The initial picture in livestock farming was even worse. The
stock of horses had been eroded by wartime requisitioning. The territorial changes then lost the country its best breeding and pasture
lands. Further blows came with the Romanian occupation and the
livestock delivered as reparations in kind. The aggregate number
of horses, cattle, sheep and pigs per head of population in 1927
was only 87 percent of the pre-war figure. The hardest and most

time-consuming task was to make up the horses and cattle. Most of the new studs and breeding stations required were not established until the 1930s. They were successful, though, as the number of horses in the country rose by over 800,000 by 1938, which placed Hungary high up internationally again. One positive development in cattle was the fact that the herds were made up with better dairy breeds, such as Simmental and Hungarian Red Speckled, which doubled the average milk yield. Sheep were still bred mainly for wool, but some young lambs were also being sold for slaughter on international markets. The biggest change with pigs was an increase in the proportion bred for meat, although demand remained also for the Mangalica, the common Great Plain fattening breed.

The biggest problem for the Hungarian economy could hardly have been solved under the conditions of the period. Hungarian agriculture, having fallen behind internationally, had to compete with the production of far more advanced Western European and American farms, while European farming began to face mounting difficulties in 1925. Despite industrial development, agriculture still accounted for over 60 percent of Hungary's exports (50–57 percent grain, 12–15 percent livestock), but these were decreasingly lucrative and finally could only break even, meaning that the state had to pay an export subsidy, so that the produce did not remain with the producers and the National Bank received some foreign exchange. An additional problem was the fact that the imports of neighboring countries from Hungary fell dramatically. Austria was the one exception. Although its imports from Hungary showed a tendency to decline, its 40 percent share of Hungary's exports was still above 20 percent in the year before the *Anschluss*, whereas Czechoslovakia's 17–18 percent was down to 5 percent by 1938. Romania and Yugoslavia also accounted for less in that year. The question of agricultural exports was particularly pressing during the Depression, when all European countries were reducing their purchases. This obliged the Hungarian government to do some market research. Efforts were made mainly on the German and Italian markets, which had been far less important than the Austrian and Czechoslovak ones in the 1920s.

Notes

1. *Osztrák-Magyar/Österreichisch-ungarisch Bank.*
2. *Magyar Királyi Állami Jegyintézet.*
3. *Gyáriparosok Országos Szövetsége (GYOSZ).*
4. *Devizaközpont.*
5. *Országos Takarékossági Bizottság.*
6. *Magyar Nemzeti Bank.*
7. *Rimamurányi–Salgótarjáni Vasmű Rt.*
8. *Közép-Európa Csoport.*
9. *Magyar Cobden Társaság.*
10. *Győri Vagon- és Gépgyár.*
11. *Péti Nitrogénművek.*
12. *Magyar Divatcsarnok.*
13. *Országos Nép- és Családvédelmi Alap (ONCSA).*

8. Society

The changes in employment, ethnic background, and religious affiliation produced by the peace treaty did not greatly alter the structure of Hungarian society. It has been seen that life expectancy increased and changes occurred in marriage customs, household size and female employment, but these were not pronounced. The persistence of earlier social conditions appeared most clearly in the marks of a rigid hierarchy and caste structure, expressed in barriers of lifestyle and culture, although these began to loosen slightly. There were still high walls dividing city from village, and barriers between groups in various degrees of poverty and prosperity. The official and economic links between these hardly extended to human relations at all. There were some noticeable changes occurring within certain subgroups, brought on by the conditions of the war and the peace, structural alterations in the economy, and the demands of modernization, but these remained internal: they failed to democratize the social climate.

The owners of great estates of over 1,000 *hold* (575 ha) had coincided traditionally with the aristocracy. Although this was not entirely true even in the period of the Dual Monarchy, there was no significant change until after the Great War. Then many aristocrats lost their great estates; a good many had all their lands expropriated and only received some paltry compensation for them several years later. Among those affected in this way were Albert Apponyi, István Bethlen, Miklós Bánffy, István Csáky, Imre Csáky, Gyula Károlyi, Pál Teleki, and many other celebrated men. They were allowed to retain their title of count or baron, but they had to forego their illustrious lifestyle and find jobs that afforded them a much more modest way of life. So the concepts of aristocracy and ownership of great estates ceased to coincide, while some of the surviving great estates were reduced, including all of those whose lands had extended beyond the country's new borders. The wealth dwindled and the operating conditions changed, and not everybody proved to be capable of adapting. Some aristocratic landowners went bankrupt after ignoring the new requirements and continuing their old lifestyle. There were frequent cases where part of the estate was sold or some or all of it let to tenants. There had been over 2,000 great estates owned by 800 aristocrats at the turn of the century. By 1930, there were only 745 great estates and 350 aristocratic owners. But the reduced numbers and social weight of this stratum did not mean that the predominance of the great estates disappeared or faded, for they still contained 30 percent of the cultivated land in 1935.

Politically, the aristocracy was divided into two main groups. The old "court" aristocracy largely retained its old beliefs, becoming Carlists or Legitimists; they were mostly Catholics from Transdanubia. They did not have much to say to the "parvenu" society around Miklós Horthy, and they did not play a political role, with a few exceptions. They largely retained their estates, since the border changes affecting them were mainly in favor of Austria, which did not begin confiscations. They shut themselves up in the country mansions, mixed with their own kind, and if they went out, visited Western Europe rather than Budapest. The other group consisted of the "more Hungarian" aristocrats of the Great Plain and Transylvania, a group that included the impoverished as well. The vast majority of the aristocrats listed earlier, who lost their estates, were from Transylvania. All but Apponyi held ministerial posts after the war, and three of them—Gyula Károlyi, Bethlen and Teleki—became prime minister. Several of them, including Bethlen, belonged to the Reformed Church, and so the former courtiers and the Catholic hierarchy looked askance at them. Their point of reference sooner or later became Miklós Horthy. They paid little heed to Charles or, after his death, to the heir apparent. They were the ones who preserved some influence for the aristocracy, although increasingly they had to share political power in the 1920s and still more in the 1930s.

The Catholic Church grew in size relative to other denominations, but its estates dwindled from 2.2 million *hold* (1,254,000 ha) to 860,000 *hold* (490,000 ha). But it was still the largest landowner in the country, which continued to offer it great opportunities, financially and in public life. Although the decisive figures in the Catholic hierarchy were inclined towards legitimism, the church was discerning and cautious enough to cooperate with the existing system and enjoy the advantages of cooperation in return for its spiritual support. The Calvinist Reformed and Lutheran Evangelical Churches did not lose lands, as they had not possessed any. Politically, their leading clergy saw it as advantageous for the country to be headed by the Reformed statesmen Miklós Horthy and István Bethlen, rather than a Habsburg. So there was no shortage of political support from their side either. The Christian churches could agree on the Christian national bases, although there were other disagreements between them. But it emerged during the 1930s that the willingness to abide by a peaceful coexistence in power was largely confined in all the big churches to the high clergy.

Far from being shaken, the position of big business consolidated, despite the anti-Semitism that flared up in 1919–1920 and in the *numerus clausus* legislation. Many people had realized during the war that the policies of individual countries and their international systems of relations were dominated by economic questions—commercial and financial ones, and those to do with economic development and social matters—on which no progress could be made without the representatives of the modern branches of the economy. Bethlen relied on the expertise and connections of Jewish big business during the reorganization period and in the subsequent loan transactions. Indeed, several Jewish big businessmen joined Horthy's and Bethlen's circle of friends. Bethlen initially proposed as his own successor János Teleszky, who was the president of several banks and on the board of numerous industrial corporations, and no less importantly, had played an important part in devising all the financial legislation under the Bethlen government. The haute bourgeoisie in Hungary was obviously dominated by the Jewish big business community, which had a kernel of 50–60 families. The richest of these were the Chorin, Weiss and, more recently, Vida and Perényi families. Except among the far right wing, Hungarian anti-Semitism was not directed at this big business group, for rational if not other reasons, for the Hungarian economy would have collapsed without them. The target of the anti-Semitism among the leading political figures of the day was the "little Jew," whom they liked to represent as homeless, a wanderer, and so on, or accuse of aiming to disturb the social peace. Nevertheless, the big business community rarely accepted a direct political role, preferring to exert its influence in the background, primarily on economic matters.

Such influence was exerted, for instance, on the tariff law, which clearly favored industry and big business. While the problems were still not dominant in agriculture, the agricultural/ mercantile antagonisms were not heightened, but the peace was soon broken as the Depression claimed its victims. The agriculture lobby then began to demand protection and sure markets, and some people had good reason to say that every landowner was pro-German, because Germany was where the greatest selling opportunities were. The industrialists had different concerns: the potential markets for them were in the industrially backward countries. The change in the international situation meant that big business stood to lose this passionate debate, because the huge agricultural exports had to be sent somewhere and there was no chance of further credit to liven up the economy. So the position of big business weakened in the 1930s, but it still managed to protect its interests up to the German invasion, despite the Jewish laws. In fact it began in 1938 to do conspicuously well out of state contracts. It follows, therefore, that in spite of its anomalous position, big business was one of the pillars on which the system rested politically, although nobody, not even Bethlen, wanted it in a position of power.

Going down the social scale, the next group below the great landowners and big business was the middle class, numbering 780,000, 360,000 of them earners and the remainder dependants, making up about 9 percent of the population. This consisted of several distinguishable strata. The decisive upper stratum consisted of landowners with 200–1,000 *hold* (114–570 ha) and those in high positions in the state and public administration, including the upper ranks of the army, the police, the gendarmerie, Hungarian State Railways, the postal service, and so on. They did not live in mansions, but they could boast country manor houses or fashionable urban apartments of five or six rooms, and occupied the highest salary bands.[1] They knew no financial hardship, and their children were often able to study abroad. From this social stratum came Miklós Horthy, who made use of the Royal Palace of Buda Castle and of the summer palace at Gödöllő while he was regent, but also resided on his own estate at Kondoros. The middle class included many non-aristocratic noble families, who held high positions in the ministries and public administration: for instance, they provided numerous county high sheriffs.

One definable group among the well-to-do middle class was made up of its urban, bourgeois members. They did not exceed 6,000–7,000 people, but they owned factories with 10–100 workers, stores with 5–20 assistants, or tenement houses for rent. Their situation was less stable than that of their counterparts in state employment, but they were wealthy enough to ride out the difficulties and economic fluctuations that arose. Their life was similar to the other groups financially, but they differed sharply from the landowning or noble groups in lifestyle and culture.

The latter privileged group in the middle class numbered only about 52,000, or 0.6 percent of the population, but they earned about 20 percent of the aggregate income and enjoyed an income more than 33 times greater than average. This index of prosperity (although Hungary's national income was comparatively low) can

be seen as exceptionally high by international standards. In 1930–
1931, during the Crash, the average income of the group was
17,800 *pengő* a month, slightly before the time when, according to
the popular song, you could "joke at ease" on 200 a month.

The main body of the middle class consisted of a much bigger
stratum, with much lower incomes, divisible into several subgroups. Its members included senior (but not leading) officials in
the various business houses, a similarly high, but not highest, layer
of state employees, a stratum of high-ranking members of the
uniformed services, and some of the intelligentsia—such self-
employed intellectuals as successful authors, artists, architects, medical doctors, lawyers, university professors and school directors.
They numbered about 300,000 in 1930, or more than 80 percent of
the 360,000 members of the middle class. People in the various
subgroups showed wide income differences, and some of the
exceptionally successful authors and artists might be placed in the
higher category on these grounds. They included the author Ferenc
Herczeg, the artist Károly Kernstock, the composer and conductor
Ernő Dohnányi, the composer Jenő Huszka and the writer Ferenc
Molnár, as well as such stage stars as Pál Jávor, and even a historian such as Gyula Szekfű in 1942. It is interesting to see that the
income of Prime Minister Pál Teleki in 1940 was about half that of
Ferenc Herczeg. However, such privileged positions were only
obtained by a few.

This transitional layer of the middle class would live in
apartments with full modern conveniences consisting of three or
occasionally two rooms, and keep a staff of a single maid-of-all-
work. However, their situation would change over time, as their
salaries were affected by years of service, rank and position,
according to the automatic system of promotion of state employees.
The initial salary of a new official or teacher would hardly exceed
the 200-*pengő* mark, but it might increase to double or even treble
that figure as retirement approached. The situation was similar in

the uniformed services. The initially weak, but later stronger inflationary pressure that began in 1938 pushed salaries upwards, but
not enough to protect their purchasing power.

The segregation of the Hungarian "gentry" was reflected in the
gentlemen's clubs. The National Casino[2] remained the preserve of
the aristocracy that it had always been. The younger Countrywide
Club[3] was frequented mainly by those of ministerial or high-
sheriff rank, high-ranking public officials, and the non-aristocratic
landowning stratum, but not the bourgeoisie. Both institutions were
right-wing in their politics. Urban groups of the upper middle class
formed clubs too, but members of the first two groups were not to
be seen in them. There were also club-like institutions that did not
call themselves casinos, one of which, the Cobden Society, tried to
transcend the bounds of caste, but only liberals or those who were
liberal on certain issues appeared there. Then there were numerous
professional bodies, which confined themselves to their own
spheres.

Finally, the members of the lower middle class had very weak
financial foundations, and among the worst paid of them were the
staff of middle schools, and still more elementary schools and
kindergartens. The starting salary of an upper school teacher was
hardly more than 200 *pengő* a month and that of a lower school
teacher 163 *pengő*. Nor would the periodic automatic raises pay for
social advancement. Still worse was the position of the refugee
public officials and intellectuals, who had often left well-paid posts
beyond the borders and failed to find anything similar in post-
Trianon Hungary. Even in the 1930s, large numbers of them were
still living in emergency apartments, if no longer in railway carriages.
After extremely difficult years just after the war, the standards of
living of this sizable lower group of the middle class began to
improve in the second half of the 1920s, but was so shaken again
by the Crash that subsequent improvements never restored it to the
position that it had held before the war.

The main body of the middle class formed the main body of consumers of the cultural goods that could be called modern in that period. They made up most of the audience at the opera or theaters, they attended concerts and exhibitions, they bought most of the newspapers and periodicals, they acquired the first radio sets and telephones, and their sports habits first extended to car driving and motorcycling. They were also the first stratum to take up vacationing on a mass scale, showing a strong preference domestically to the Balaton resorts.

As for the clergy, their status was spread out across the upper and lower strata of the middle class, with the difference that only the top of the Catholic hierarchy could dispose over sizable wealth, although it was not their own, of course. They belonged to the upper middle class, while the leading strata of the other churches enjoyed far smaller stipends and a lower standard of living. There was less difference among the lower clergy of the various churches. The Reformed Church clergy working in education, health or welfare services had a standard of living similar to that of their lay counterparts, while the stipends of the Catholic priests were usually laid down in the states of the religious order to which they belonged. But the income of parish priests and ministers depended greatly on their congregations and on whether the parish was rich or poor, as the proportion of church taxes that they received was very low. The personal status of a provincial priest resembled that of a country doctor, while differing according to his personality or the degree of local religious fervor as well.

On the lowest level of the middle class were the urban and rural petit-bourgeois, who were not generally thought of as belonging to the middle-class category at all. There was much variation among them, and they may be divided into several subgroups. The petite bourgeoisie made up 12–13 percent of society and numbered about 1.3 million. Most were small businessmen, artisans or traders, and a smaller proportion on the lower rungs of the state and

private employment ladder: junior clerks, porters, conductors, postmen, concierges, subalterns, and so on. The fortunes of small-scale
industry and trade fluctuated over the period. A large number failed
during the reorganization or the Depression, although some managed to rise into a wealthier world of medium-sized business firms.
Small-scale industry and trading were relatively open to entry;
diligence and long hours could lead to advancement. Most petit-
bourgeois lived modestly, often drawing on the labor of family
members. Families were thrifty, usually living in small homes of
one or two rooms, although they sought educational opportunities
(in civil or trade schools) for their children. They were forever
under the threat of uncertainty. However, the reorganization of the
economy and steady growth of big business did not eliminate the
petite bourgeoisie. In fact their numbers grew, along with demand
for their services.

The petit-bourgeois in state employment did not face uncertainties of livelihood. Those who started a postman's or switchman's
career were likely to finish as such; the pay was secure, there was
a modest retirement pension, after a while they received free or
low-cost medical care, and some organizations offered accommodation or other benefits in kind. Hungarian State Railways, for
instance, built housing, and its employees and their families
received travel concessions. Several private companies erected
housing developments as well. (The system of benefits in kind and
provision of accommodation were not rare in other social strata
either.) Pay, on the other hand, was low. Salaries towards the end of
the period started at 80–100 *pengő*, and the average was actually
around 200.

For a long time, the urban petite bourgeoisie was associated
with the radical far right, but in fact the picture was more varied.
There were petit-bourgeois on the left and the right, and a good
many were indifferent. Every political strand found support among
the petite bourgeoisie, but most people contented themselves with

adjusting to the prevailing situation and regime. Political affiliations, as in higher middle-class strata, were much influenced by
whether the person was a Jew or a Christian, and how far the
Christians could keep under control the sometimes virulent, sometimes milder, anti-Semitic groups that appeared. The latter sought
to persuade the middle classes that their problems had two origins:
the Jews as a pestilence and ubiquitous obstacle to the advancement
of Christian Hungarians, and Trianon, likewise attributed mainly to
the Jews.

The standard-bearers of this school were young men of good
family who had not been able to continue their previous comfortable life in the much reduced state administrative service or officers'
corps. They thought that the lucrative business jobs, the places in
prosperous law firms, the enticing medical practices and the edito-
rial jobs in the press had been snatched from them by the Jews. This
was true to some extent, but largely because the young men from
middle-class homes lacked the qualifications for business, banking,
and so on. The Jews certainly were overrepresented in some professions, notably in business, trading, the law, journalism and
acting. The *numerus clausus* legislation was intended to change
that by restricting the proportion of Jews studying at university. The
universities did not enforce this uniformly, but the proportion fell to
the 8–11 percent range. But the consequences of this had not
reached the employment market in the 1920s, and when the Crash
came, many fresh university graduates could not find jobs. It was
not by chance that anti-Semitism, having cooled in the Bethlen
period, flared up again. On the other hand, the Christian artisans or
lower school teachers had hardly any Jewish competition. Their
interests clashed only in small-scale trading, and then not ubiqui-
tously. The village publican was almost always a Jew and the village shopkeeper often one, but these positions were not disputed by
locals and urban jobseekers had no aspirations in that direction.
And most of the Jewish retail traders served the rural population.

As for the rural population, it remained at the end of the period at about the 4.4 million that it had been at the beginning, but the intervening increase in the country's population meant that its proportion decreased from 55 percent to 48 percent. All social categories, from the destitute to the wealthiest, could be found in the villages, and the farmers and stockbreeders known collectively as the "peasantry" covered several strata whose ways of life differed strongly. Over all were the landowners, who owned the village mansion or manor, whether they were residents or absentees, but not every village had one. However, each village had a narrow stratum of intelligentsia, to which the doctor, the recorder, the *szolgabíró* (district administrator), the priest and the schoolteacher belonged in a larger village. All these, except the teachers, would have houses in the middle stretch of the main street. Order was kept by mounted gendarmes, whose barracks were normally in a nearby town. The center of intellectual life was the church (sometimes churches), but the school also played such a role. The petite bourgeoisie were represented by a few artisans—a doctor, a smith, a cobbler, and so on—and retail traders.

With the peasantry, the bulk of the rural population, the most important distinction was between those who owned land and those who did not. There were further differences among the landowning peasants according to the size and quality of their holdings, and where their production went. The upper limit of a peasant holding can be put at about 100 *hold* (57 ha), as "gentleman" landowners seldom farmed less, although some peasant farms approached that size. This was also the lower limit for the holdings of the Debrecen *cívis* (the wealthy people of the towns in the Hungarian Great Plain who lived from agriculture). Holdings under 100 *hold* made up 44.2 percent of all holdings before the war, but this increased after the war, reaching 51.9 percent in 1935. However, the greatest rise was in the smallest category of holding, up to 5 *hold* (2.8 ha), whose number increased by 34,000 in ten years.

Peasants farming 20 *hold* (11.4 ha) or more might have their own team of two horses, a cow and a sizable stock of poultry. Some of the produce would be taken to market. He would not have a tractor, however, let alone a threshing machine. No tractor would be used and the thresher would be hired. A vineyard owner would be in a similar position even with a much smaller holding. Good results were also obtained, especially in the 1930s, by farmers who went into vegetable or fruit growing (for example, peppers, onions and peas, or apples, apricots and plums), but only if the farm lay near a successful processing factory, cannery or distillery. Nor was it immaterial whether the farm of 20 or more *hold* lay on the Great Plains or in Transdanubia. The plow land on the Great Plains was usually in one piece, but work was impeded because the holding would often be far from the farmer's village home. Transdanubia was held back by its settlement pattern of tiny villages, which often lacked the intellectual stratum mentioned and the necessary industrial and commercial services. The greatest obstacle, however, was the fragmentation of the land holding, which wasted valuable time for a peasant with a horse and cart.

Anybody farming 10–20 *hold* (5.7–11.4 ha) obviously had less room for maneuver, and if a money profit was made, it would be spent by preference on adding to the holding. The owner wanted to buy land, not machines. Twenty *hold*, incidentally, was a kind of psychological threshold, inspiring all who approached it to make further efforts to expand. Such a family mainly saved money on food. Although they had a pig in the sty and poultry in the yard, they would only eat meat once a week; baking almost always consisted of leavened pastry, sweet or savory; the rancid fat bacon from last year was all eaten up. Although the cow gave milk, most of it was sold, as was the butter, sour cream and curds. Fruit appeared on the table and jam was made only when the orchard produced it, and again only if it was unsuitable for the market.

With a holding of under 10 *hold* (5.7 ha), there was little point in saving to prosper. Peasants in that category were pushed into that category by circumstances, especially if they had a plow and a larger family. However, it made a big difference to life and livelihood whether the holding was 5 *hold* or 10, what quality the soil was, and what kind of cultivation was done on it. Peasants with holdings of up to 5 *hold* and indeed the majority of the peasantry could not make a living out of their land unless they concentrated on grapes or fruit, for which much of the land in the country was unsuitable. Such peasants regularly had to take on extra work for others, such as woodcutting, harvesting or carting, if they had a cart.

Finally, there were villagers who had no land at all, whose property consisted only of the house in which they dwelt. Those who did not even own that lived in a cottage provided for farm servants by the local estate or simply had a bed somewhere. The landless made up 46 percent of the peasantry in 1930, and if those with holdings of up to 5 *hold* are included (24 percent), it can be claimed that 70 percent—2.8 million out of a rural population of 4.4 million—lived in penury, on incomes well below the national average. The farm servants were in a better position, because their subsistence was provided for them, while the day laborers had to seek work. But the farm servants were at the mercy of their landowner's and employer's whims. Some landowners built fine rows of cottages for them, each with at least a room and a kitchen, where geraniums flourished in the windows. Elsewhere farm servants would be huddled together in hovels like stables. The pay was normally paltry, well under 200 *pengő*, but with benefits in kind that allowed families to subsist. The outdoor servants developed a hierarchy as well, headed by the coachman. The situation was different for those in service at a mansion or manor (as a manservant, chef, cook, chambermaid or cleaning woman) or in auxiliary industrial establishments on the estate (flour mill, sugar beet mill, distillery or wine cellars), and again for those only doing field work or tending livestock. But even a horse herd was a lord compared with somebody looking after the chickens.

The biggest problem for day laborers was the fact that much of their working potential was wasted. They could only be sure of a job at harvest time, and even then, they might have to travel a long way for it. There was rather more scope for navvies who formed gangs to carry out earthmoving tasks. They were welcome at ditch-digging and road-building sites and dug the foundations for buildings—all work for which there was plenty of demand in the second half of the 1920s. But conditions changed with the Crash, which in Hungary affected the construction industry worst.

The people of the scattered Great Plain *tanya* or homesteads formed a special category. The statistics classed them according to the land that they owned, and thus it is not possible to say accurately how many there were, but it is certain that a sizable proportion of the inhabitants of several Great Plain towns lived in *tanya*—one third in Szeged, for example. The dwelling and barns of a *tanya* stood in the middle of its land, and so it might be a considerable distance from its neighbors or the nearest town. The advantage was being close to the fields, but the drawbacks were poor access to the market without proper roads and the lack of any other modern facilities. There was no mail service, electricity or access to medical services or doctors. It was almost impossible for *tanya* families to send children to school regularly, and they benefited little from the Klebelsberg program of school-building.

This divided rural world of peasants was held together most of all by its isolation. Although few communities were far from a railway station, it was used at most to attend markets in the nearest town or to buy goods not available in the village. Otherwise there was still a gulf separating town and village. A village was a village above all because it lacked the amenities of a town. Rural electrification had hardly begun and most rural homes were lit with petroleum lamps or candles. Cooking was done on traditional stoves, as gas was still unknown. Water supplies might consist of one well for a street, and it would only be used for drinking, as nobody could carry home and store enough water for other purposes. Waste water went into a ditch by the road. Most roads were unpaved and most cottages had floors of beaten earth. Where there was a "best room," it was kept for honored guests or special occasions, while the family lived in the smallest space possible, not least so as to save fuel. The privy, if there was one, would be in the yard, and often had no brick or concrete pit beneath it, which led to it polluting the ground around it. Only well-to-do families began to acquire radio sets in the 1930s, and the telephone was unknown. Very few villagers subscribed to a newspaper. So the common denominator in villages was backwardness compared with the towns. The villagers did not include the "gentry," to whom the "peasants" were expected to show subservience, expressed in modes of greeting, address and behavior. Hungarian society in general suffered from a rash of titles and ranks. It depended on the pay scale whether somebody should be addressed as "your honor," "your worship," or "your excellency." The malaise became comic when it required a well-to-do village farmer to lift his hat to any town clerk or petty official, simply because he wore pants instead of breeches. Yet the peasant's pantry might be full, while even the mice were starving in the pen-pusher's home.

The common features in the way of life of all villagers were faint and few. Almost everybody went to church on major festivals, all the children went to the same school, whoever their parents were, and everybody except the handful of intelligentsia and petite bourgeoisie in most villages (but not all) eschewed fashionable urban dress. Some peasant farmers wore riding boots, others ankle boots or shoes, and yet others went barefoot for much of the time. Riding boots were the decisive factor in village dress. Ornamental dress would come out on Sundays and holidays—embroidered or braided men's coats and breeches, and lavish, richly decorated women's costumes with several skirts, made of fine materials, but most people had only modest clothing, and a good many walked about in tatters. The only people excluded from this village society were the Gypsies. They had no seats in church, their children did not go to school, and their hovels were on the edge of the village. They usually pursued some kind of craft (adobe brick-making, woodwork or raffia) or commerce (trading in horses or other animals), but they might beg on occasions.

The agricultural world was as divided as the urban, but to the detriment of the villages, the differences were in the cultural field, not the technical. There were no rural middle schools, which impeded the education even of children whose parents could have afforded the fees and did not have to rely on the work of their adolescent children. There were no specialist doctors in the villages, and many people died unnecessarily because a woman in labor or a sick patient had to be carted to hospital over long distances. (There were no motorized ambulances.) Many women in labor prepared to give birth at home, relying on a local doctor or midwife. There were no libraries, of course, and theater was just a word to the peasants. The only cultural events were school celebrations, and the system of people's colleges had not spread in Hungary. Only in the 1930s did movie shows become widespread, with a projectionist arriving to show a movie perhaps once a week, although the success demonstrated the rural demand. Motorization was advancing in the country, but it had not reached the villages, where young people cycled, not motorcycled, and draft animals provided the haulage. Only the owners or tenants of large farms owned trucks. Even the wealthy gentry still preferred a fine horse and carriage to an automobile.

Yet the Hungarian villages were not ossified or uniform. There were big differences according to how far a village lay from the town and its markets. If they were near, the process of marketization was beginning. Village men and women would go into town on foot or by train to sell their dairy products, vegetables, fruit, small animals, day-old chicks, force-fed geese, surplus wheat or corn, or spare piglets, calves and foals. Those who paid regular visits to the town would inevitably pick up some urban ways, which were also brought back to the village by peasant girls who had been in domestic service. Villages near the market began to see the spread of urban clothing, young people learning popular songs and urban dances. Films were already becoming familiar in any case. Furthermore, they were visited by representatives of medical services such as the public medical officer and staff of the Stefánia and Green Cross[4] charitable organizations, who assisted the midwives, monitored infants, held health courses, and so on.

The political preferences of village people fluctuated widely. The large numbers who voted in the general secret elections of 1920 seem by all accounts to have plumped for the Smallholders, but after Bethlen had managed to fragment that party, the relatively prosperous peasants who still had a vote obediently voted for the government candidates in successive elections. This was altered somewhat by the revival of the Smallholders' Party in 1930, but the new party was never as effective as the old, not least because the poorest districts in the 1930s became greatly influenced by far-right agrarian demagoguery. Rural poverty had much to do with the electoral advances of the fascist Arrow-Cross in 1939. Then and thereafter there was also an increase in support for the opposite end of the political spectrum. To simplify somewhat, some of the village poor at the end of the period sought redemption from the far right and others sought it from the left-inclined Smallholders' Party and other peasant organizations.

Other strata in the lower ranks of society, such as the village owners of dwarf holdings and the farm servants, made up most of the urban workers and "servants". These numbered a round 900,000 in 1920, but had increased to 1.15 million ten years later, that is, from 24 percent to 29 percent, and ten further years later they passed the 30 percent mark. But only about 57 percent of these

(660,000 people) worked permanently in mining or industry. The others were employees spread out over other categories (banking, commerce, public services, and so on), including the long-distance commuters. Taking the whole period as a basis, the number and proportion of female workers rose mainly to meet the needs of the textile industry (from 26 percent to 32 percent), while there was a shift from skilled workers to semi-skilled and casual labor. The women and the semi-skilled and casual laborers were first-generation workers, who had arrived from the villages or moved into industry not long before, and so they lacked working-class traditions and attitudes.

Average real wages for workers peaked in 1929, but even then they were only 80–90 percent of what they had been in 1913. The hardest years were 1922–1924 and 1929–1933. Average wages never attained their 1929 level again. In 1939, the average annual wage of workers in manufacturing was around 1,200 *pengő*. That was exceeded significantly only in mining, printing, and iron and metalworking, while workers in the textile, building and timber industries earned less than the average. Stratification was under way as well, as the Hungarian working class developed its own "aristocracy" of skilled workers, including some categories whose standard of living matched that of the urban lower middle class, rather than that of the proletariat as a whole. A locomotive engineer or a compositor, for instance, could afford a two-room home with some amenities. His family would dress like the average urban citizen, and if he put his mind to it, he could educate his children. But this group was tiny compared with the hundreds of thousands of manual workers for whom finding their day's food was a problem.

Members of the politically conscious segment of the working class would be union members and voted in the first part of the period for the Social Democratic Party. But this line broke in the 1930s: the votes won by the Social Democrats steadily declined. Analysis of the results of the 1939 elections leads to the conclusion that the Arrow-Cross did particularly well in the expressly working-class districts of the capital.

All societies became differentiated in that period, with various strata and groups becoming separate. Nor did the principle of equality of opportunity apply in the most developed countries of Europe either. But in Hungarian society, the barriers between strata and groups became so impenetrable that the chance of movement between them remained minimal, and the scale of upward mobility was extremely modest as well. The structure of society became exceptionally rigid and therefore failed to turn into an organic whole. An important part in this was played by the deep differences in social provisions and by the education system. Both played a role in the maintenance of the barriers in society, although great progress was made in both regards during the period.

Notes

1. The salary bands of state officials ran from XI to I, with the latter as highest. Other regulations applied in certain categories, and then it was customary to talk of ranks. The distinctions between the two were not easy to follow.
2. *Nemzeti Kaszinó.*
3. *Országos Kaszinó.*
4. *Zöld Kereszt.*

9. Welfare and Education Policy

During the First World War, it was realized in the political world that the problems of the general public could not be ignored any longer. This applied to everything from political rights to society, health and education—the whole area of life—but it appeared most decisively in the demand for welfare provisions. One concrete sign of the change in thinking came when the post-war peace conference instigated the foundation of the International Labor Organization, which was to serve as the main forum for social policy issues in the inter-war period. The ILO convened numerous international conferences and adopted conventions and recommendations. The first such International Labor Conference was held in Washington DC in October 1919, where it was decided to found the International Labor Office as its secretariat. Hungary became a member in 1922. Other recommendations of the Washington conference included an eight-hour day and a 48-hour working week, unemployment insurance, and a ban on night work by women and minors. Social problems were also covered in the peace treaties: the basic social principles appeared in Part XIII, Article 355, of the Hungarian peace treaty. They provided for adequate wages, an eight-hour day and 48-hour week, and unbroken weekly rest of 24 hours.

The Hungarian government was aware that this article was obligatory, like the others, but it could not deal with it substantively, even if it had wanted to, before the economy was on its feet again. Such social questions affected not only the urban working class, but also clerical employees and the rural masses, but the demands came mainly from the Social Democrats, who represented the urban working class. So many came to see social policy as something to do with the workers, to whom there was widespread antipathy in the aftermath of Béla Kun's Hungarian Soviet Republic. This social psychosis impeded the introduction of welfare measures.

Some hasty moves were made after August 1919 to reverse the welfare measures of the previous year and move towards nationalization of the rudimentary insurance system. With the convening of the second National Assembly in 1922, social policy took a new direction under József Vass, minister of labor and welfare. Vass kept his portfolio for some ten years, pursuing a Christian–conservative policy line. He also had influence over the system of requirements being devised continually at the International Labor Office, which did not handle social well-being as simply a "workers'" question, but as something concerning society as a whole, meaning that a full insurance system would be required, covering sickness, accident, old age, widows, orphans, the disabled and the unemployed. The government also had to consider the fact that this program had the support of the 25 Social Democratic members of the legislature and of several other not inconsiderable groups, who regularly spoke up in favor of implementing it.

Bethlen promised when he became prime minister to broaden the social insurance system considerably. This recurred in the 1922 election manifesto of his United Party. Albert Apponyi called the problem the most important that the age had to solve. With unemployment high and wages near starvation level, the Ministry of Labor and Welfare drew up a plan for unemployment benefit based on employers' contributions to a fund. This failed, as big business was determined to push the costs onto the state, mainly in the form of government-funded public works.

But the state was still burdened with a chronic budget deficit. Although public works were needed, there was no money to pay for them. Despite regular insistence and debate in Parliament, it was 1925 before the question of pensions for workers and dependants was resolved, and then only for those in mining and associated industries. Despite the earlier failure, draft legislation on unemployment benefit was put forward in 1926. This augmented contributions from the government and the insured with the proceeds of a payroll levy of not more than 4 percent on the employers to provide a dole for a maximum of 13 weeks. The draft was debated first at a meeting of the Hungarian Economics Society,[1] at which opinion was sharply divided, as it was at Minister of Labor and Welfare József Vass's consultations, first with employers' representatives and then with those of employees. Vass then dropped the matter and concentrated on other pressing issues instead.

Meanwhile, the country's finances had improved and the budget was in a temporarily good state. The new parliament that met in 1926 ushered in a golden age for inter-war welfare legislation. First came accident and sickness insurance (Act XXI/1927), then insurance for old age, disability, widows, and orphans (Act XL/1928), as well as ratification of eleven international conventions. Almost everybody in the parliamentary debate held in the spring of 1927 agreed with sickness and accident insurance, but the left wing criticized it for not covering the whole of society, especially for neglecting the agricultural workers and self-employed artisans. It can be added that the scheme neglected the villages as a whole and the private traders. The thinking behind this was that people doing business on their own account should solve their insurance problems on their own account as well. Unfortunately neither the farmers of dwarf holdings nor the artisans and retail traders could do so with the country in the condition that it was in at the time.

Eventually passed by a large majority, the act provided for necessary funds from three sources: employees' contributions (3–7 percent of wages), the employers and the state. The Ministry of Labor and Welfare became the supervisory body for all insurance institutions. The act established a National Social Insurance Institution[2] to handle the money and organize the provision. The body had to overcome some serious temporary financial problems and political wrangling before managing to perform its task satisfactorily. Alongside it was an Insurance Institution for Private Employees and a National Officials' Sickness Benefit Fund,[3] while some larger corporations or groups ran insurance schemes of their own. This insured a sizable proportion of the population against medical and hospital treatment, but it still left the majority uncovered.

Parliament ratified several international conventions in the autumn of 1927, the most important of them covering industrial accidents and provision of a period of 24 hours' continuous time off each week. Early in 1928, the government submitted its bill on insurance for the elderly, the disabled, widows and orphans, which the National Federation of Industrialists was prepared to accept, as compensation for having opposed the unemployment benefit. Before the bill came before Parliament, the National Social Insurance Institution held a debate on the matter lasting several days, where it was criticized for its narrow scope and for the small part that the state was accepting in it. The same criticisms came up in Parliament as well, but there was no real opposition to the bill. The pensions were to be financed from the same three sources: the insured, the employers and the state.

These measures certainly marked an advance in social questions, but there were still no provisions for the lowliest strata: the agricultural day laborers, the farm servants, and those with dwarf holdings, as well as the retail traders and the unemployed. The issue of unemployment suddenly became urgent, as the Great Crash hit Hungary hard in 1929 and 1930. This prompted Bethlen in February 1930 to hold talks with a delegation from the Social Democratic Party, at which Károly Peyer pressed for an eight-hour day and a system of unemployment insurance. All that the prime minister promised for the time being was to continue the negotiations. The unions then sent a memorandum calling for the commencement of public works, which the government debated, again without reaching a decision. At that point, the Social Democrats decided to take the workers out onto the streets. A protest march on September 1 was broken up violently by the police. By then there was no time left for Bethlen to pay more real attention to social problems.

The health side of the welfare question improved greatly over the ten years of Bethlen's government. Clinics and medical schools attached to Debrecen, Szeged and Pécs Universities were built or were begun. This increased the numbers undergoing medical training—there were 31 medical doctors per hundred thousand population in 1913 and 117 in 1938—and provided new research facilities. Several thousand new hospital beds were made available (33 per 10,000 in 1920, 47 in 1930, and 54 in 1938). Lung sanitariums were established at Mátraháza and Pécs.

Ground was gained in health care by the kind of preventive medicine that had grown up in Western Europe in the nineteenth century, for instance through the Stefánia clinics, devoted to the protection of mothers and children, which began to appear after 1915. These established so-called "milk kitchens" where mothers' milk was distributed, as well as day nurseries and after-school centers. In 1927, the Rockefeller Foundation contributed to the foundation of the National Public Health Institute[4] under Béla Johan, which linked the municipal medical officers and their auxiliaries, offered training, and financed research into methods of combating epidemics. Thanks to the institute, the practices of isolating infectious patients and of compulsory vaccinations were introduced. It also initiated the development of the Green Cross organization, which had a broader program, extending the protection of mothers and babies to schoolchildren's health, offering care of patients with neurotic and venereal diseases, advising on marriage and occupational problems, campaigning against alcoholism, and propagating awareness of the importance of cleanliness and domestic hygiene. The Green Cross trained district nurses and ran campaigns of aid, mainly by distributing sugar and milk to the needy. The organization also held cookery classes for rural women, and initiated an allotment-garden movement, which it encouraged by distributing sowing seed, saplings and plants.

There was inevitable competition between the Stefánia and the Green Cross, with the Green Cross, backed by the National Public Health Institute, the absolute winner, as Béla Johan was backed not only by the initial Rockefeller capital, but also by regular support from the state. It gave the momentum to the whole institution of medical officers, although it was a state concern. A combination of these measures ensured that the health and health prospects of the public greatly improved. Nevertheless, the rate of infant mortality was still higher than the average for Western Europe at the end of the 1920s, the campaign against tuberculosis had only just begun, rural housing remained unhealthy (with earth floors and crowding), and only a fraction of households had mains water, almost all of them in the towns and cities. Most of the wells provided water containing unacceptably high amounts of harmful substances.

Another big contribution to the general state of society was made by education. Great strides were made in social policy under the Bethlen government, but the system remained incomplete. Education policy, on the other hand, was expressly successful, although it did not manage to increase social mobility as a whole. Up to 1925, the minister responsible, Kunó Klebelsberg, like József Vass, could do little, but after that, his Ministry of Religion and Public Education produced a flood of reforms. The minister pursued two basic principles throughout his period in office. One was to broaden access to basic knowledge, in other words to overcome illiteracy. The other was to encourage a high-level stratum of intelligentsia by expanding and modernizing the university and research sector. In connection with that, he also strengthened and broadened the secondary-level institutions that would lead from elementary education to employment or higher education. He backed his prolific and costly plans in principle by arguing that there were opportunities in the existing world only for nations with a high cultural standard. He spoke frequently about the cultural ascendancy historically enjoyed by the Hungarians in the Danube region, calling on all who spoke on scholastic, university, scholarly and scientific questions to help maintain that ascendancy. The slogan of cultural ascendancy was certainly taken ill in neighboring countries, although the campaign for "schools instead of swords" was, after all, progressive and favorable to them, as it was better to compete in the cultural field than in arms manufacturing.

Klebelsberg had battles on his hands but always had the support of the prime minister. He began in the 1925–1926 financial year to obtain a regular 9–10 percent of the budget allocations for his Ministry—an unprecedented proportion never to be matched again. One factor behind his success was the fact that Klebelsberg surrounded himself with high-quality experts (the most famous being Zoltán Magyary) and founded all his innovations on consultation and advice.

There was little opposition to his efforts to expand the elementary school system, supply teachers for it, and provide housing for the teachers. The illiteracy rate at that time was about 15 percent, which was much better than in areas to the north or south of Hungary, but worse than the 10 percent average in Western Europe. One problem was the fact that a sizable 15 percent of children of elementary school age were not attending school regularly, for want of the requisite clothing and footwear or because they lived too far from the school. The latter was the case mainly with children on isolated *tanya* homesteads. Further problems arose because it was only possible to have a class for each year in schools in larger communities. Pupils in rural areas were taught in one big class, or at best two. This applied to 73 percent of schools when Klebelsberg launched his reform.

In 1926, Klebelsberg's Ministry of Religion and Public Education introduced its first bill, calling for construction of 3,500 new classrooms and 1,750 dwellings for teachers. Priority was to go first to providing schools for *tanya* districts, then for villages without schools, and then for crowded suburban areas. This program the

Ministry managed to carry out completely by 1930. The number of schools increased according to plan, and the number of teachers rose by more than 2,000 (60 percent), partly through changes in teacher training. However, the price was that elementary school expansion absorbed more than half of the Ministry's budget allocation. The reform did not resolve the problem of *tanya* children, but the illiteracy rate sank. However, the program was cut short in 1929 by the Crash. The Ministry's allocation of 60 million *pengő* in 1926–1927 fell to 46 million in 1932–1933.

The elementary school course lasted initially for six years, but those whose parents could send them to civil school or gymnasium left after four. In principle, the six years were followed by three years' further education, but that system scarcely operated, and where it did, the low number of weekly lessons (5–7) meant that it could hardly be effective. In 1928, Klebelsberg toyed with the idea of raising the period of compulsory education to ten years, of which eight were to have composed the basic course, but the plans to do so had to be shelved because of the Depression.

The Ministry also took up extramural adult education, as there were high rates of illiteracy among older age groups in rural areas, and most of those engaged in farming had low levels of specialist knowledge. People's halls began to be built or supported and people's libraries established (there were some 1,500 by 1927–1928, with a total stock of 200,000 volumes), and the first people's colleges appeared. There had been similar initiatives before the war, but neither then nor in the 1920s was there any real success, although many people were keen to see the people's colleges expand. People's colleges in Hungary provided vocational and cultural classes, but failed to find forms and methods that would really attract rural people. The minister also initiated educational broadcasting, but early attempts were clumsy.

Vocational training remained a neglected field. Trade, commercial and agricultural apprentice schools were few, as were their students and the numbers of classes: nine a week, but only four a week in agricultural schools in the spring and autumn. The situation was better in the civil schools, which took pupils after the fourth grade. The original number of 253 civil schools had increased to 397 by 1929–1930, and continued to grow slowly in the 1930s, and there was an initially dramatic rise in the number of pupils. The popularity of the civil schools later decreased greatly as the eight-year middle schools became widespread and the period of compulsory education increased to eight years at the end of the 1930s. Civil schools in themselves did not train pupils for anything, but those who completed them had slightly better chances of employment in the lower ranks of administration, or they could go on to a four-year upper commercial or three-year industrial training school. Upper commercial schooling led to a school-leaving certificate and entrance into university in certain subjects, while the industrial schools awarded a trade certificate.

In 1924, Klebelsberg introduced three types of gymnasium instead of the previous two. The modern school[5] remained, with its emphasis on natural sciences and languages, rather than a classical education. Alongside this he established the *humángimnázium*, offering a broad education in the humanities, and the *reálgimnázium*, which offered modern languages rather than Greek. Two years later, the middle schools for girls were also divided in a similar way, as the girls' gymnasium and the lyceum respectively. However, the system was overly complicated, as each type led to a school-leaving certificate and allowed entrance into higher education. There were several subsequent modifications, therefore.

Nevertheless, secondary education flourished. The number of schools rose from 129 to 156 in 1929–1930, and enrollment from 58,000 to 70,000. Educationalists considered that the standard matched that of Western Europe. The high standard of staff remained, with many teachers excellently qualified and sometimes engaging in scholarly and scientific work. Most middle schools had a library, a laboratory, a map collection and a gym, and sometimes there was equipment for other special activities. Educational films began to appear in the gymnasia towards the end of the 1930s. These schools, found exclusively in towns and cities, were openly providing an elite education. Their weakness was the great difficulty with which talented children from lower down in the social scale gained admission.

Education for those seeking a military career was supervised by the Ministry of Defense, not the Ministry of Religion and Public Education. Future subalterns and officers went to military middle schools, of which only three remained after Trianon, at Pécs, Sopron and Kőszeg. They were known as upper and lower *reáliskola* or popularly as *cőgeráj*,[6] and qualified students for admission to the military academy. The military middle schools made high demands. All the gymnasium subjects were included, alongside greater emphasis on physical education and sports. However, they had very few students in the 1920s, when the number of army officers was heavily restricted.

All the school types (people's, civil and middle) received new syllabuses during Klebelsberg's period as minister. These differed from the old mainly in placing some general ideological elements into the arts subjects and geography, and adding irredentist passages to some of the material. The children were to be brought up in an expressly nationalist, religious spirit, and have before them constantly the old, "true" Greater Hungary and its values. The subjects in literature and history courses were to be selected according to whether they met the Christian national criteria. This trend appeared strongly in the 1920s and redoubled in the 1930s.

The education system placed great emphasis on physical education, especially for boys. Efforts were put into school gymnastic and sporting activities and into developing both the Boy Scouts and the Levente movement, founded in 1921. The Scouts recruited mainly middle-class boys (45,000 by 1930), and as in other countries, set out to make them self-confident, religious, physically fit and self-sacrificing young people, organized along military lines, and engaged in exercises and activities that appealed to young people.

The Levente movement was founded by Act LIII/1921, primarily to give military training to broad sections of youth while evading the restrictions contained in the peace treaty. The movement targeted boys aged 12–21 who were outside the school system, and obliged them to take part in regular weekly physical exercise, drill and shooting practice. Most of the Levente instructors were professional, reserve or retired army officers. The Levente, unlike the Scouts, was never a popular institution, perhaps because it was compulsory, and it was not fully imposed in the 1920s.

People's schools and middle schools raised no storms in Parliament or public life, but higher education caused the minister constant trouble. MPs in their initial patriotic fervor gladly voted to move the universities of Pozsony and Kolozsvár into Trianon Hungary, but as the costs emerged, they began to think that four universities (with Budapest and Debrecen) were too many. Klebelsberg was almost miraculously successful in defending what were now the Szeged and Pécs Universities from the anti-university campaign that broke out in 1925. The attacks were led by the racial protectors, whose financial objections were compounded by two other factors. One was the fact that they had failed to match their support in Budapest universities with any real headway among students of provincial universities; they had failed to predict the outright opposition aroused by the 1928 amendment to the *numerus clausus* act, especially in Debrecen. The other was the fact that the heads of the provincial universities had not won their favor with the way in which they had applied the *numerus clausus*. The act had not made it clear whether the 6 percent of Jewish students referred to the number of places available or to the number of students admitted, as provincial institutions, especially the two new universities of Szeged and Pécs, could not expect many applicants. So the universities had chosen the first interpretation, which meant that the proportion of Jews in the student body was much higher than 6 percent. The antagonism of the tiny racial protection group and its demands for the closure of the two universities would not have been a problem if the same demands had not been voiced by the Budapest University lobby and the committee of experts that it had consulted.

The National Austerity Committee[7] appointed to put the public finances to rights set up a three-man subcommittee to examine the question of higher education. This published in May 1925 a majority proposal that the needs of the country's intelligentsia should be satisfied at one university (Budapest) and one provincial medical school (Debrecen). The report was confidential, but the Ministry of Religion and Public Education leaked its contents in an attempt to exploit the publicity. The provincial universities had their say, of course, and although the hesitation lasted a while, the National Austerity Committee rejected its subcommittee's proposals and voted to keep the four universities. Klebelsberg had won, and with him his aim of cultural decentralization. In one of several statements that the minister made there was one to Parliament in February 1925: "Where there is one university chair [in the country] for one subject, it is impossible to speak of scientific work, for one man does not amount to scientific work—there is no exchange of views or debates, no friction between ideas." Klebelsberg tried to put practicals and seminars in the forefront of university teaching, to stress the role of universities as urbanizing and civilizing factors, and to point to their regional significance.

The debates and attacks treated him fairly lightly. The construction work on Debrecen University, mentioned earlier, would have to be completed in any case, and efforts had to be made to find appropriate premises for the institutions being moved to Szeged and Pécs. This proved to be difficult mainly in the case of Pécs. The teaching had to take place temporarily in Budapest in

1922; the university could only open its doors in Pécs itself in 1923, mainly because Pécs and its citizens were less than happy about the horde of noisy young people being settled on them and did not want to open the city purse. Another factor was the fact that no preparations had been possible before the Yugoslav occupation forces left in August 1921. Later, when Pécs people began to see the advantages that the university would bring and complain of being treated shabbily, Klebelsberg acknowledged that Pécs had been a Cinderella and refrained from reproaching its citizens for their initial doubts. Attacks on the ostensibly oversized university system resumed in the Depression and were aimed mainly at the University of Pécs. The situation was only saved in 1930–1931, when the city, at the height of the difficulties, spent 1.3 million *pengő* of its own on the university building.

In the end, teaching at all four universities was uninterrupted, but the standards failed to become equal. The provincial universities did not manage to endow the requisite number of chairs, and the staff shortage meant that the outstanding personalities found themselves teaching next to people who made no contributions to science or scholarship over many years. And signs of partiality and denominational interests began to appear. Catholic professors at Debrecen were sidelined on professional matters, and Pécs did not want to admit staff who belonged to the Reformed Church. Keen to protect and raise standards, Klebelsberg gained for his Ministry the right to depart from university recommendations when appointing full professors. That allowed him, for instance, to recruit the celebrated botanist Rezső Soó for Debrecen and bring two superb Jewish experts, József Frigyesi and Lajos Ádám, to the Budapest medical faculty. The minister also did his utmost to turn the universities into research institutions, on the grounds that they would not be universities in the full sense if scientific work did not flourish there. Incidentally, he also saw the archives and museums as research institutions, on which were based the so-called Collection

University,[8] in a not wholly successful merger. But Klebelsberg also recognized that separate research institutes had to be established for certain kinds of specialist research where Hungary proved to be particularly adept. Mention has been made of the Ichthyology Institute at Tihany, to study the fish of Lake Balaton, which became a focus of protests against Klebelsberg.

Aggregate university enrollment peaked in 1922–1923, with a surge of applicants whose education had been held back by military service in the war. Thereafter, the number of university students and their proportion of the population fell back, stabilizing at 16,000–17,000 up to 1930. The course structure initially changed to the detriment of law and in favor of almost all other subjects (medical, economic, technical, and so on) except the arts and natural sciences, but the earlier proportions were gradually restored. Law regained the lead, with major growth in the arts and natural sciences, and in educational training and divinity, as other subjects dwindled. Klebelsberg acted to curb the overproduction of law graduates, but with a lack of success that exacted a heavy price during the Depression. The bulk of the students, about 60 percent, came from the middle classes, with the children of the intelligentsia most prominent. Some 14–15 percent of students came from artisan or retail trading families, 1.3 percent from those of agricultural workers, and 5.3 percent from those of industrial, commercial or transport workers. This did not differ much from the structure in other European countries.

However, there was great resistance in Hungary to the admission of women students, to whom Western European universities were much more open. When the question came up in a serious form in 1923, the Ministry consulted the universities. Budapest University of Sciences gave a decisive no, while the Technical University was prepared to accept up to 2 percent of female students—in economics, and where the places could not be filled with men, this latter meaning that a small number of places were available in architecture. All the provincial universities but the Debrecen medical school were willing to take female students. The debate, joined on one side by Gyula Kornis, the Budapest professor of philosophy, and on the other by Klebelsberg, showed what a gulf separated two otherwise similarly conservative, "Christian national" personalities. Kornis advanced some biological arguments and some ostensible experience to support his view that university education was not appropriate for women, who were unsuited to it. Klebelsberg declared several times that the arguments were untenable, and that "it shows that they were devised by men, they contain a great amount of prejudice, and unacceptable male self-ishness shines out of them." He recalled that the post of minister of education in Britain was held by a woman and that many women were teaching at Western European universities, while "in this country we do not even want to send women to the university as plain students." The eventual result of the debate was that the 1926 act on middle schools for girls stated that the school-leaving certificates obtained there qualified students for university education. Then subsequent executive order then retained some restrictions, under university pressure. The minister later had to argue in favor of female appointments to university lectureships. The first was made to the Debrecen medical faculty in 1930.

Klebelsberg did not see university education as the completion of his program for training the scholarly and scientific elite. He argued that the most talented students should be offered the chance to gain experience and build up connections abroad. This threw a rope to some existing institutions, such as the Hungarian Historical Institute founded in Rome by Vilmos Fraknói, the German-run Hungarian Institute at Berlin University, and the Hungarian Historical Institute in Vienna. The Ministry first applied and received budget funds to establish a college in Berlin to accommodate students sent out on meager scholarships. In 1924, a Collegium Hungaricum opened in Berlin and Vienna. In the same year, the

Rome institute was turned into a college that also undertook research, for which the Hungarian government in 1928 purchased the Falconieri villa, where it operates to this day as the Accademia d'Ungheria in Rome.

The government intended to establish further colleges in Zurich and Paris. Plans for the latter seemed to be outlining themselves in 1927–1928. A Hungarian–French Information Bureau was established in Paris in 1927 for scholarship students studying there, and Bethlen had talks with Prime Minister Aristide Briand on a future Collegium Hungaricum for Paris. But the idea was swept away by the Crash and never revived for several reasons in the 1930s.

Education, including the development of higher education and scientific training, was probably the most successful field for the post-war Hungarian government, even though it mainly assisted the elite training of the sons of the middle classes. The impetus was lost, however, in 1929. The Ministry suffered a chronic deficit in the next two years, and the initially successful Klebelsberg became a disillusioned, skeptical man, who died not long after the government resigned.

Notes

1. *Magyar Közgazdasági Társaság.*
2. *Országos Társadalombiztosító Intézet (OTI).*
3. *Magánalkalmozottak Biztosító Intézete (MABI)* and *Országos Tisztviselő Betegsegélyezési Alap (OTBA)*, respectively.
4. *Országos Közegészségügyi Intézet (OKI).*
5. *Reáliskola*, cf. the German *Realschule*.
6. Cf. the German *Zögling* (pupil).
7. *Országos Takarékossági Bizottság (OTB).*
8. *Gyűjteményes Egyetem.*

10. The Crash

The Great Crash began with the Wall Street collapse of October 1929 and soon developed into a general crisis of finance, production and trade. The decisive factor was the American stock market, credit system and advertising policy, all of which rested on fictitious financial foundations divorced from solvent demand. The most perilous consequence for Europe was the fact that the Americans immediately began to demand repayment of their loans, which many European banks had lent on as short-term high-interest credits. The chain of lending broke and the market suddenly shrank. The sales problems soon brought about cuts on production and a seemingly unstoppable spiral of Depression. This was compounded when the French state suddenly blocked an already negotiated loan transaction in March 1931, in protest at plans for a German–Austrian customs union. That loan was urgently needed to rescue the Creditanstalt in Vienna, the leading bank in Central Europe, and so its failure caused the other banks in the region to topple like dominoes. The Hungarian government on July 13, 1931, had to close the banks for three days, to prevent the gold and foreign exchange reserves from being depleted. However, Bethlen sought new loans to bridge the problems with the public finances.

The Crash brought about an agricultural, industrial and credit crisis in Hungary, with an oppressive increase in the country's indebtedness. This has been variously estimated by experts at 4.1–4.5 billion *pengő*. It has already been pointed out that about half of this was owed by the state, and half the state's obligations took the form of pre-war debt. The other half of the debt was owed by the private sector. Like most grain-exporting countries, Hungary had faced regular sales problems since the war. These began to climb inexorably after 1928, with a dramatic situation developing in 1930. As sales prices dropped, the gap between relative agricultural and manufacturing prices doubled. Nor would the grain even sell at the depressed prices, due to the contraction of demand. Only 11.5 percent of the grain crop could actually be sold at valuation, as opposed to 25–30 percent before. A sizable proportion of Hungary's exports were of agricultural goods, and thus export prices as a whole fell sharply. The discrepancy between the agricultural and industrial price indices widened by some 30 percentage points in the worst stage. Most agricultural exports consisted of wheat and flour. The production cost of a quintal of wheat in Hungary was about three times as much as it was in the United States or Argentina, the two biggest rivals. Hungarian exports were affected most severely by the drastic measures taken by Czechoslovakia, and the slower but likewise damaging steps that Austria took. Prague reneged on its commercial treaty, and a veritable tariff war was waged against Hungarian goods. Having been forced to backtrack by French intervention, Czechoslovakia then brought in a range of restrictive regulations and eventually tripled the tariffs on its agricultural imports. All these developments meant that the price of wheat fell from 32 *pengő* in 1927 to a low point of 11.2 *pengő* in 1933. Despite strong efforts to enter the Italian market (Bethlen's 1931 proposal for a so-called Brocchi plan and its signature), Italy's share of Hungarian exports fell from 12.8 percent in 1930 to 8.6 percent in 1933. Improvement only began in 1934, when the effects were also felt of the 1931 Hungarian–German agreement. This favorable change was due partly to the end of the Depression and partly to the extra quantities of food required by Italy and Germany for military consumption. (The Italian government began to prepare at that time to intervene in Abyssinia, while the Germans set out to produce a modern mass army.)

Globally, agriculture became incapable of servicing its debts, with the hardest consequences being felt by the smallholders. Masses of indebted peasant holdings were put on the market because the expected income had not materialized and the debts had not been serviced. In the summer of 1930, the government

introduced what was known as the *boletta* system. The *boletta* was
a grain coupon received by the producer from the buyer, along with
the cash price. It could be used for paying taxes or being cashed in.
The *boletta* on a quintal of wheat was three *pengő* above the market price from July 1, 1930, six *pengő* from July 1, 1931, four
pengő from July 1, 1932, and three *pengő* again from July 1, 1932,
to July 1, 1933. The system was abolished in 1934. However, this
rate of government assistance was too meager for the producers and
expressly detrimental to the consumers, to whom the cost of the
boletta was passed on.

The small use of advanced technology fell back. As production
had to go on in agriculture even at a loss, producers tried to reduce
their losses by cutting inputs: fertilizer use and machinery purchases. Average use of artificial fertilizers plunged from 12 kilograms
per *hold* to 1.5, causing yields to fall from 8.08 quintals to 7.34.
There was no improvement in either statistic before 1938. The failure to modernize farming became a drag on the whole economy.
Backwardness was also apparent in the structure of production. The
proportion of fallow fell fairly steadily (to 5 percent and then 2 percent), but cereals continued to lead, despite the market difficulties,
and fruit and vegetable production hardly rose. The opportunities
for Hungarian wheat were worsened further because over a hundred
strains were still being grown in the 1920s, which precluded an
even quality. Some improvement in this regard came later with the
establishment of a wheat registry and state sowing seed campaigns.
But the problems all came together during the Depression and
worsened the country's economic position. The agricultural pro-
ductivity rates of 40–50 years earlier became entrenched. These
had counted as modern initially, but meanwhile a veritable revolution in production had taken place elsewhere in the world.

The 135.4 million *pengő* debt-servicing cost for agriculture in
1925 reached 2 billion *pengő* in 1932, which exceeded sector earnings by 229 percent. The high figure consisted not only of borrowing

but also of tax arrears. Measures to protect debtors had to be introduced, including interest reductions and the declaration of certain estates as protected. The Bethlen government initiated lending rate reductions of 8–10 percent in 1931 and the policy continued under the Károlyi and Gömbös administrations. Protection, which landowners could request if a debt exceeded 15 times the net registered earnings, meant that the estate could not be possessed and auctioned off, some debt was settled out of state resources, and a repayment moratorium was granted. Of the owners in the dwarf holding and smallholding categories (under 10 *hold*—5.7 ha), there were 84,000 who qualified to request such protection but failed to do so for some reason, probably inadequate information. Sixty-one percent of the funds associated with protection went to landowners with over 100 *hold* (57 ha). Other assistance to farmers included concessionary rail freight rates for agricultural produce, price reductions on manufactures important to farming, and sale subsidies. This system operated with some amendments for the ten years up to 1941, during which time the credit institutions and the state devoted 650–800 million *pengő* to agricultural purposes. The cost of rescuing agriculture, like that of bailing out business, was borne by the taxpayer.

The Depression had caused a fall in industrial production of 18 percent by volume and almost 40 percent by production value by 1932. Its ravages varied according to whether the industry manufactured for direct consumption or for investment purposes. The concerns that lost most were those producing means of production or serving the construction industry (the iron, metallurgy, timber, and building and building materials industries). The food industry rode out the crisis rather better for four years, while the chemical, textile, tanning and paper industries were hardly affected. Industrial output fell back sharply by volume and by value, so much so that *per capita* national income fell by $30 up to 1932. So the Depression deducted twice the increase that the economy had strained to produce in the 1920s. The penury in much of society worsened, with those on its fringes suffering the worst deterioration in their standard of living, meaning that hundreds of thousands stood on the brink of starvation.

Those in the worst predicament were the day laborers, but only the more prosperous among the peasantry managed to get through the Depression unscathed. The working class suffered unemployment rates of up to 35 percent without a system of assistance (for Gyula Károlyi's administration introduced unemployment benefit but swiftly abolished it again) and wage cuts averaging 25 percent. At the deepest point in the recession, there were 205,000 industrial workers unemployed. The self-employed artisans and retail traders were as crippled by taxation and debt as the peasants were. Masses of them shut up shop or ceased to ply their trade. But the Depression was not accompanied by inflation, and so the officials and intelligentsia who did not lose their posts suffered least. White-collar unemployment was found mainly at entry level, which was the source of most of the "graduate unemployed."

The disruption to the economy and mass impoverishment and insecurity inevitably had effects on society. There were unusual shifts in the cities and the countryside, as discontent spread among sections of society, especially in agriculture, that had hitherto given strong support to the regime. There was a wave of strikes, and the leading circles in society were especially uneasy when the Social Democratic Party managed to bring about 100,000 Budapest workers out onto the streets on September 1, 1930.[1] The Social Democrats seemed in other regards also to be breaking with their stance since 1922 of confining themselves to parliamentary activity and the opposition role available to them within the municipality of Budapest. Its agrarian policy, which appeared in the autumn of 1930, included a plan for land reform, in which lay holdings of more than 200 *hold* (114 ha) would be taken and redistributed with compensation and all church holdings would be taken and redistributed without compensation. The party made some advances in the villages, especially in the region beyond the Tisza.

The peasantry had lacked real representation since the formation of the United Party and its absorption of the Smallholders' Party. The Depression was obviously a factor behind the formation in December 1930 of the Independent Smallholders', Agricultural Laborers' and Citizens' Agrarian Party, known generally as the Independent Smallholders' Party.[2] Its founders were Gaszton Gaál, owner of a medium-sized estate, and Bálint Szijj, a landowning peasant, who did not hide their ambition to take over the heritage of István Nagyatádi Szabó's old party. When Gaál died, the presidency of the Independent Smallholders' was taken by the former racial protector Tibor Eckhardt, a friend of Gömbös.[3] The party then entered dangerous waters in the first part of the Gömbös government's term, but from 1935, it took to an opposition line again.

There was movement on the far right as well. The Society of Awakening Hungarians emerged again, and so did MOVE. In January 1931, the Hungarian National Fascist Party was formed under the leadership of Pál Prónay and Gyula Ostenburg.[4] The secretive Etelköz Association also gave signs of life, but the old "coalition" spirit was no longer dominant in it. The conservatives and liberals were shed and the far right came to set the tone.

Calm based on a balance of interests was no longer possible in the governing party either. Ever stronger criticism from the agrarian side was endorsed by the right wing within the party as well. A typical example was the latest change of political complexion by Gyula Gömbös, who was forced to realize in 1928 that his racialist position would condemn him to inaction and jeopardize his political career. He dissolved his party, abandoned his anti-Semitic program, and sailed back into the governing party. Bethlen rewarded him generously by appointing him state secretary at the Ministry of Defense and a year later minister of defense. Bethlen probably wanted Gömbös in his administration as a man who could revive the dead question of the army. Gömbös was not knowledgeable in the field, but he certainly advanced the army's cause, although it is not certain how. However, he had taken a critical position within the government by 1930–1931 and was trying to turn the prime minister back towards internal "rehabilitation," using a firm hand and a policy of restricting the Jews.

1931 began with an unusual move by Regent Horthy, who convened the so-called Crown Council,[5] which differed from a normal government meeting because he took the chair and some people outside the government were invited. His purpose appears to have been to induce Bethlen and the government to make changes in financial policy and take firmer measures against the expressions of social discontent. For the first time under the Bethlen government, Horthy was trying to turn his personal prestige into direct political influence, but unsuccessfully for the time being. Horthy followed Gömbös in calling for summary judicial proceedings, prevention of Jewish immigration, restrictions on freedom of the press, and a change in the interest rate policy of the National Bank. The last was important mainly to the landowners, but lower interest rates could have livened up the whole economy, except for the fact that that the whole financial world, from Washington to London, was against any such move at that time. On March 5 came another meeting of the Crown Council for similar purposes, but it failed to gain prime ministerial acceptance of any of the proposals on the agenda. Bethlen viewed the Depression as global and saw insufficient reason why the government should be called upon to revise its policies. He continued to go his own way, but thereafter he had to acknowledge that the regent's ten-year confidence in him had been shaken.

Nothing of that was changed by the fact that the regent and the prime minister were marking ten years in office in 1930–1931 with much celebration and honor. On February 21, the upper house passed an act enshrining Horthy's merits, whereupon the Boráros tér bridge and a number of public buildings were renamed after him, while famous men published appreciative analyses in the press about Bethlen's decade at the helm.

The prime minister certainly erred in thinking that the economy could be restored simply by introducing economic restrictions and raising new loans, although it has to be added in fairness that most other statesmen and politicians made the same mistake. Bethlen produced a cartel act to protect free trade and impede the formation of further cartels, and went on to introduce National Bank permits for exports of foreign exchange. On August 4, the National Assembly agreed to the minister of finance's having special regulatory powers that bypassed Parliament. It also agreed to appoint a Committee of 33 to supervise the government's financial and economic activity and offer advice. Its 22 members elected by the lower house and 11 by the upper house convened on August 7,[6] and it became a forum for criticism of the government, although neither the Social Democrats nor the Independent Smallholders took part.

The dwindling state treasury was rescued in November 1930 by a loan of 87 million *pengő* from British banks and in August 1931 by a loan from French banks of about 150 million *pengő*. But these were just emergency measures, as state indebtedness assumed catastrophic proportions and the customary international financial flows came to an end for several years. The only state in 1931 still able to advance loans and even do business was France, but it too had to cease doing so a year later. In June 1931, US President Herbert Hoover proposed a one-year moratorium on international commitments, so initiating a process that ended by canceling all such commitments, after a long period of soundings, negotiations and agreements. The moratorium did not apply automatically. Each state was examined on whether it sought a moratorium and on what commitments the moratorium was sought. Bethlen refused to submit such an application, but at least the process of reparations was ended worldwide in 1932. Most of Hungary's other international commitments were written off, but thereafter there would be no more loan transactions either. There was a change in the whole logic of international economic activity, to which most countries found it difficult to adjust.

The first lesson was that governments had to play a much greater role in the economy; in Hungary that meant especially in stimulating exports. This Bethlen only half understood, or if he understood it, he failed to see its implications. He failed to revise his financial policy in a way that would stimulate production and trade, although no other government did so while Bethlen was still in office.[7] But he had the new needs in mind as he set out to sell wheat towards the end of 1930. His talks in Berlin in November led to a Hungarian–German trade pact under which Hungarian wheat would enjoy in principle a 25-percent tariff concession on the German market, although this made little practical difference as the Depression prevented Germany from buying any.

The other lesson from the Crash largely learned in Western Europe, after some squabbles and bargains, was the need to expand the home market. The government had to contribute to stabilizing the labor market, by working with employees to create jobs and producing a redistribution that would ensure an increase in solvent demand. The new procedures included legalizing labor bargaining, introducing collective contracts, and encouraging workers (also on the land) to join associations to that end, which furthermore might eliminate wildcat strikes and other surprise events. But such things were unheard of in Hungarian government and political circles. Instead another model soon appeared: state controls over the market, to eliminate labor unions and introduce a corporative system.

A further conclusion was that general economic agreements between countries had to be sought, to reduce economic damage. The experiment began with regional cooperation. There had been several politicians in the 1920s who had reached the conclusion before the Crash that Europe could be defended from a competing outside world and some dangers at home only if European countries were to create a uniform economic system. Intellectual preparation for this idea had been provided first by the French foreign minister, Aristide Briand, at the autumn assembly of the League of Nations, in the form of what he called the United States of Europe or the Pan-European Plan. The first version of this, which put the economy to the fore, was received well (by Hungary too), but the later version of May 1930 placed political agreement in the forefront and was rejected by most states.[8] An attempt was made to establish regional cooperation between Belgium, the Netherlands, and Luxembourg, but that was vetoed because of the most-favored-nation principle. Almost the whole of Europe opposed the German–Austrian customs union, even Hungary, which had not been invited to participate. Efforts led mainly by France were made for years to organize a league of agricultural countries, but plans for cooperation always ran up against rivalry over the Danubian and Balkan countries between France on the one hand and Germany and Italy on the other.

Hungary had many good advocates of European union in the 1920s and the beginning of the 1930s. One of the earliest and most decisive apostles was the Social Democrat Ernő Garami, then in exile, who besieged his party's newspaper, *Népszava*, with ideas for creating economic unity. Another advocate was the liberal legitimist Albert Apponyi, and Pál Teleki contributed a long analysis to the review *Magyar Szemle,* arguing that European union was inevitable. Another writer of regular articles on regional and continental unity was Elemér Hantos. But the efforts at union in Europe and regions of it were swept away by events in the 1930s, only for them to be revived again during and after the Second World War.

The efforts at agreement among the agricultural states were a governmental concern in Hungary as well, but ideas of political union in Europe conflicted with the foreign policy goal of territorial revision, which meant that eventually the Briand proposal met with a politely evasive response.

Bethlen's last important act at home was to hold general elections on June 28–29, 1931. The results can hardly have been much comfort to him. Although the governing party retained its overwhelming majority, it lost 12 seats. The liberal parties and the Social Democrats held their ground, and the new Independent Smallholders entered Parliament with 10 seats. So the elections showed some shifts, but no change in the political structure. Nor were there any other storm clouds suddenly apparent when Bethlen announced his intention of resigning and met with incredulity. The joke in Budapest had long been that Bethlen would go like somebody coming. Still, the unbelievable happened on August 19, when Bethlen resigned and the regent accepted his resignation.

The prime minister was probably exhausted by ten years of unbroken political struggle. He wanted to leave to others the unpopular measures necessitated by the Depression, and he was particularly averse to taking the kind of political measures that the regent desired. As for the financial changes that Bethlen wanted to make, he saw no chance for them under the valid international rules of the time. Had the September devaluation of the pound sterling occurred while he was still prime minister, he might not have resigned, but immediately weakened the overly strong *pengő* and ordered a substantial cut in interest rates. This would have been logical from the monetary point of view, as the *pengő* had been tied originally to the UK pound sterling and the Bank of England had undertaken to exchange *pengő* for pounds any time on that basis. Valuing the Hungarian currency lower would not have been inflationary, simply a reaction to international reality. But in August 1931 Bethlen still saw no room for financial maneuver. By resigning, in fact, he was trying to save his reputation for better times, for he remained head of the United Party. Splitting the premiership from the party presidency of the party opened up scope for factionalism, making it possible for Bethlen to cause his successor great discomfort. Be that as it may, August 19, 1931, closed the Bethlen era, even if the man after whom it was named was still unaware of it. The question was whether Hungary would have another head of government with prestige such as Bethlen had built up. His successor, Gyula Károlyi, certainly did not and would not have it.

Notes

1. An important factor may have been the return of Ernő Garami from exile in 1929. But the party leaders failed to adopt his ideas for active autonomous policy-making, and he left again in 1931.
2. *Független Kisgazda, Földműves és Polgári Agrárpárt* (*FKgP*).
3. Eckhardt had already been playing a leading part in the party.
4. *Magyar Országos Fasiszta Párt*. This was banned by the government, but founders and followers soon reappeared with another little fascist-type party.
5. *Koronatanács*. Horthy had not exercised this right hitherto.
6. An initial mandate of five years was extended in 1938: Acts XXVI/1931 and XV/1938.
7. This conclusion was drawn first by the British government, but only in September 1931, by which time Bethlen was no longer prime minister.
8. Briand seems to have been pressed into this shift by the Foreign Ministry, seeking to fix the present situation. The dissension also ruled out economic agreement, although there were other reasons for that as well.

11. An Interlude

The outgoing prime minister's idea was that his successor should be a non-party financial specialist. His candidate was János Teleszky, president of the National Financial Council, for Teleszky was already seeking an antidote to the "borrowing policy" followed so far and preparing the requisite financial measures. But Regent Horthy decided otherwise. He turned to his family and friends and appointed the 60-year-old Gyula Károlyi instead.

Károlyi had some beneficial traits, but some that hampered him in addressing the very grave problems that faced him. Apart from a few ineffective months chairing the government in Szeged, he had kept out of politics, which was now an advantage rather than a drawback. Never having been implicated in corruption, he had a reputation as a lily-white puritan, which increased the demand for him. Furthermore, he ran his estates in an exemplary fashion, which gave decided hope to the large agricultural lobby. However, all that Károlyi really understood about money was that you had to be thrifty with it, and this left him disoriented when he had to choose between alternative proposals and inducements. He thought that he was setting a good example when he got rid of all the automobiles at the ministries and began himself to walk into work, or when he restricted the amount of paper to be used. His gestures attracted attention, but people smiled rather than followed his example. In addition, he gave the impression of being a malleable, uncertain, indecisive prime minister. His situation was all the harder because István Bethlen still headed the governing party, which meant that the prime minister could rely decreasingly on his own party's support.

This seems to offer ample explanation for the brevity of Károlyi's term as prime minister. Yet there remains doubt as to whether those were the real reasons for his rapid departure. There seems to have been another, more important reason, hitherto neglected by historians. It can be seen in a moment that he was probably troubled less by the domestic difficulties than by the crumbling of the accustomed international financial and economic conditions, perceptions and relations and the emergence of a radically new situation. To put it as tersely as possible, Károlyi probably stumbled over the *pengő* and interest rates.

The new cabinet certainly started badly. Károlyi could find nobody to take on the finance portfolio, which was a key position, and this gave the impression that the prime minister himself knew not which way to turn. (Frigyes Korányi eventually became minister of finance in mid-December.) Károlyi's introductory address was accordingly non-committal and bland, while the political field positively resounded with tension, and Miklós Kozma, president of the Hungarian news agency MTI, described it as "a complete madhouse."[1]

The government had hardly formed before it was taking the unpopular measures that Károlyi's predecessor had sought to spare himself. At the end of August, it set about trimming the pay of state and administrative employees, and then raised income tax to 50 percent. In other words, it took measures that met the requirements of traditional financial policy. But before any substantive economic measures could be taken, the country was shaken on September 13 by an unexpected event. One Szilveszter Matuska managed to plant a delayed-action bomb under an express train crossing the viaduct at Biatorbágy on its way to Vienna. The train plunged into the valley and 22 people were killed. Amidst the general fear and agitation that this caused, the government introduced a state of emergency that was later to be applied only when it came to communists. There was also a political attempt to blame the atrocity on the communists as well, but that possibility was excluded by the police enquiry. Matuska, who had already tried to cause explosions in Germany and Austria, was given a death sentence, but this was commuted to life imprisonment on compassionate grounds.[2]

Meanwhile, steps were taken by the Committee of 33. On August 25, it charged a Committee of Five, later increased to six, to examine the budgets of each ministry, mainly for cases of over-spending. The lead was played by two former ministers of finance, János Teleszky and Tibor Kállay, who represented and enjoyed the confidence of the financial world. The influence of the Committee of Six and of the banks lay behind the way in which the govern-ment, in setting out its financial policy, turned again to the League of Nations (on September 7) and requested an examination of Hungary. It was hoped that this would lead to a further rehabilita-tion loan and foreign backing for the country's financial plans. The League of Nations decided quickly to meet the request, and a com-mission was sent out to begin work in Budapest almost immediately.

Concurrently, however, came an event of great importance to the whole continent, even to the world: London's announcement on September 20 that the Bank of England was coming off the gold standard. The reaction was a sharp drop in the sterling exchange rate, causing several European currencies to falter and bringing many other complications. But floating the pound had a stimulating effect on British trade and helped to pull the country out of its recession. Liberal orthodoxy in financial matters had fallen, in its birthplace, from which it had been dictated to the world. Thereafter, there were rival schools of financial thought. Some countries immediately followed the British example; others still followed the old British model, which was borne off by France and still backed by American practice. Paris stood by the value of the franc, and luckily, managed to hold it until 1936. It certainly seemed in 1931 as if Britain would collapse and France would stay on its feet, as the one power able to bail others out. Washington was still following its principle of isolation from Europe, although financially it remained a continual influence on events there, as was shown by the American handling of the Depression, the moratorium idea, and the decisive circumstance that it continued to pursue a tightly liberal financial policy until 1933. In other words, it opposed moves by governments to meddle with exchange or interest rates or otherwise intervene in the economy.

All the signs were that Hungary had chosen to follow France's lead, for a number of reasons, not least the convictions of Hungarian financiers. While Kállay continued to dominate the Committee of Six, Korányi was appointed minister of finance in December. These two men had championed the inflationary policy of the early 1920s that had managed to revive investment and start the engines of production running. They if anybody knew that cuts and savings alone would not pull an economy out of recession, and that cautious loosening of the money supply would do more for trade (and thereby production) than any diplomatic agreement. But they dared not make a move, because of the international conditions already alluded to and perhaps out of fear of another wave of uncontrollable inflation.

The League of Nations financial report submitted on October 27 was phrased according to classic financial principles. It estimated the internal and external debts of the state, judging that these exceeded its real needs.[3] It recommended putting the trade balance in surplus, in other words raising exports, but almost precluded that by calling on Hungary to maintain the stability of the *pengő* and the National Bank to *increase* the base interest rate.[4] It also advised further public expenditure savings, with a reduction in the number of public employees. The commission did not see any prospect of obtaining a foreign loan to set the Hungarian budget to rights. This deluge of advice was akin to squaring the circle.

The report of the Committee of Six that appeared two days later did not contain any concept, which was not its task, but set about criticizing some specific aspects. For instance, it attacked the "separate funds" from which extra-budgetary spending was financed, the illegal extra earnings obtained, and the loss-making state-owned corporations. In connection with the proliferating cases of corruption, it raised the question of conflict of interest, which it wanted to resolve.[5] It performed a cleansing task, therefore, but it did not set out to produce a financial-cum-economic plan. And it warned against radical change, saying that it would cost a lot of money.

A choice had to be made: to maintain the overvalued exchange rate and continue honoring payment commitments, or to devalue, begin a policy of moderate inflation, take up the moratorium offer, reduce interest rates (which the National Bank had started to do), and so pursue a policy of livening up the economy. The debate became focused on the moratorium. Many felt that suspending or reneging on financial commitments was required for the recovery of a government of national "concentration" (that is, coalition). Exchanges began on this but remained inconclusive. The main obstacle was the fact that a viable coalition could not be formed without the Independent Smallholders, whose adhesion would have entailed meeting at least some of the peasants' demands. The need to choose became quite clear. Ferenc Chorin, general manager of Salgótarján Colliery[6] (and later president of the National Federation of Industrialists) warned the government that it could not simultaneously shoulder the debt burden and serve the interests of the economy: fulfillment of payment obligations had to end. But the government still hesitated and held talks in Geneva. Nor did a speech by Prime Minister Károlyi on November 4 bode well. He more or less followed the line of the two reports, and while mildly criticizing the previous government policy he advocated continuing it. He underlined the importance of maintaining the *pengő* exchange rate, avoiding inflation, and continuing to meet foreign commitments, on which, he argued, the country's future creditworthiness depended. Meanwhile, he raised the prospect of further cuts and redundancies. So Károlyi, no doubt with the approval of the minister of finance and other financial advisers, still believed that another foreign loan could be obtained, and based Hungarian policy

on the loan conditions. That program caused general disenchantment in all parts of the political spectrum.

Meanwhile, there was a political tug-of-war; this was backed
by ideological arguments too, but the main forces behind it became
the economic and financial issues. The agrarian bloc, embracing
legitimists, conservatives, liberals, democrats and fascists, still
agreed on one thing: the government was duty-bound to support the
economy (primarily agriculture) and this should manifest itself in
fiscal policy, concessionary loans to farmers, and a policy on tariffs
and trade. It was hoped initially that Károlyi could be won over, as
he was a landowner, and every means was tried of driving a wedge
between him and Bethlen. They eventually succeeded, but quite
differently from the way that they had envisaged.

The attacks with "anti-capitalist", anti-Semitic overtones were
led by the far right. After the banned Prónay organization mentioned earlier came the Hungarian Legion Association, the
Hungarian Party and finally the Opposition Bloc.[7] The Hungarian
National Party was revived by László Budaváry. Its supporters
were known as the Blue Shirts after the uniform that they wore. An
insurance salesman called József Korom set up a little fascist-style
national party, some of whose branches and members came from
the old Szeged hard core, including men who had stood out in the
acts of terror committed by the commandos. Just as they had
become disenchanted with their first leader, Miklós Horthy, so they
became disenchanted with Gyula Gömbös, whose subtler politics
they could hardly understand, although some still hoped that he
would return to the fold one day. So after several years' quiet, they
began to rebel again and one group even tried to overthrow the government.

The handful of men arrested on the night of November 27 for
preparing a coup and a takeover of power were headed by László
Vannay, a supply officer formerly in Prónay's battalion, as well as
an activist in ÉME, MOVE and the Turanian Hunters. He and a few

companions had come into contact with Lieutenant General Károly Raics and Gendarmerie General Ferenc Schill, both retired. Schill was arrested by the police on December 7 and found dead in his cell early on the morning of the 13th.[8] According to police leaks and the judicial judgment, the conspirators had planned to arrest Horthy and the entire government, and to murder Imre Hetényi, the chief of police, and Gömbös. They had drawn up a plan of action specifying which public buildings they would occupy (barracks, railway termini, the radio, post offices, and so on).[9] Based on the fact that all this had remained at the planning stage, some of the 19 arrested were acquitted and others got off with light sentences. Neither during the investigation nor during the trial did anybody try to look behind the scenes and discover what further connections this group had. However, it was clear to the general public that the police had gathered information on such connections. (Among the provocateurs was Gendarme Captain László Baky.)

The domestic political disputes were only heightened by Károlyi's indecision and extreme caution. While the authorities were doing all that they could to curb and break the Social Democrats and the agricultural protests, the prime minister agreed with the Social Democratic leaders to transfer a sum of assistance for the labor unions to distribute among the unemployed. This move at a time of general parsimony caused outrage, with even the liberal Károly Rassay protesting. Károlyi backed down and withdrew the measure on December 8, which duly elicited bitterness among the Social Democrats and the workers.

The prime minister went on to cut public employees' pay again, without any consultation. This forced even the Christian Farming and Welfare Party to react, although it had so far backed the government and provided a minister, Sándor Ernszt. On December 12, the party left the Committee of 33 and called on Ernszt to resign, which he did. Tactically, the party could hardly have done worse. It dissociated itself from the government without going into opposition, a hesitant, shiftless course that the electorate could not fathom.

Frigyes Korányi and Béla Imrédy had some success at the international talks in Geneva. They gained the agreement of foreign creditors to a twelve-month payment moratorium on everything but servicing of the League of Nations loan and some other, smaller debts. This allowed the treasury to be recharged. On December 16, Korányi accepted his appointment as minister of finance; the government order on the moratorium appeared on the 23rd. This was not applauded by everybody, because of the exceptions, but it soothed tempers for a time. The government was able to act in this way because US President Herbert Hoover's moratorium proposal had made it harder to resist general pressure internationally for payment concessions. But the government still kept to tight principles of financial policy and abstained from measures to liven up the economy, in the hope of obtaining another loan.

So the domestic calm could only be temporary. On February 11, 1932, the agrarian bloc of the United Party gave the government a memorandum listing their demands like an ultimatum. It covered everything that the smallholders and great landowners alike wanted, from priority for agricultural loans, through raising the *boletta* value and extending it to other products (corn, oats, and so on), and capping the prices of manufactures, fuel, and so on, to reducing interest rates.

Since the government did not dare either to begin "diluting" the currency—Korányi obviously not, for foreign policy reasons— or to go against the interests of capitalism, there was nothing left but to continue seeking a solution to the problems with agricultural exports. It was mentioned earlier that French governments since 1930 had been dealing with these intensively, with Louis Loucheur as the guiding spirit. It became clear in the spring of 1931 that Budapest had looked down its nose at the German–Austrian customs union and not even Hungarian and Italian policy had been coordinated in this regard. Another blot on Hungarian–Italian friendship was the fact that nothing had yet come of the Italian loan for military development, despite several discussions. For the time being, Mussolini was confining his assistance to words, as the ministries resisted any calls. However, it was agreed to devise a Hungarian–Italian–Austrian system of preferences, and a draft was completed, thanks to Iginio Brocchi, but that had no practical consequences either. In mid-January, István Bethlen paid a private visit to Rome, apparently for the purpose of getting Hungarian–Italian cooperation moving again. Bethlen claimed later that he did so with the agreement of the government and the regent.[10] He put forward a proposal for a triple customs union of Austria, Hungary and Italy, with the Brocchi preferences as the first step. Mussolini may have been concerned about possible German opposition to this, but the Italian government voted to accept the draft. But it was buried after all by the fall of the Austrian government and the fact that the new Austrian chancellor, Karl Buresch, did not accept the idea. There was also a difficulty with the 25 percent concession on the wheat tariff that Bethlen had agreed on with Germany, although the German government never managed to avail itself of the concession, despite the agreement. All these circumstances gave extra value to the French connection.

On March 2, the French prime minister, André Tardieu, presented to the Finance Committee of the lower house his reorganization plan for the Danubian countries, in which Austria, Czechoslovakia, Hungary, Romania and Yugoslavia would grant each other preferential tariff treatment. Tardieu later added that the remaining surplus of grain could be bought by the Western Powers, again on preferential terms. The Hungarian government hastened to begin negotiating on the plan, based on drawing all commercial advantages possible from the system of preferences, but not blocking Hungary's paths in other directions. The envisaged system of regional cooperation also suffered from internal difficulties, as the industrially backward states (Yugoslavia, Hungary and Romania) were concerned for industry, while the countries engaged in agricultural development (Austria and Czechoslovakia) had fears for agriculture, but it was not rejected out of hand. There were no longer difficulties with the British based on the principle of the most favored nation, as Britain itself had introduced a system of imperial preferences, but London was hardly likely to give wholehearted support to France's Danube Plan. The representatives of Germany and Italy attacked it strongly, as a threat to their own plans and to their interests in the Danube Basin. The German government proposed bilateral agreements with all the countries involved except Czechoslovakia, while Italy speeded up the Hungarian–Austrian–Italian negotiations. The Tardieu plan had failed even before Tardieu himself stood down in May.

The plan indicated that the policy of international loans had plainly come to an end and France too was putting trade policy to the fore instead of financial methods of extending its influence. It has to be added from the historical point of view that this was the last great effort by a French government to take charge of Danubian and Balkan issues and it marked an expansion of the zone concerned, in that France was now counting on Austria and Hungary as well. The attempt failed, and as the negotiations had indicated, Germany was preparing to move into the area economically and would do so the moment that its economic situation permitted.

So for Hungary, there was no way open after the Tardieu plan for creating a regional system of preferences, and the stalling of the Hungarian–Italian talks showed that no great results could be expected of Italy, due to its agricultural protectionism.[11] This meant that the domestic political strife would not cease either.

The Ministry of the Interior, the police and the gendarmerie were using increasingly merciless methods against the mass movement, the Social Democratic Party and the illegal communist organization. There were successive arrests, confiscations of newspapers, and closures of workers' hostels and other institutions, and on April 5, the minister of the interior banned the newspaper *Népszava* after it had published a fairly bold article. The police tried to break the printers' strike and demonstrations with a wave of arrests, and the *Névtelen Lapok* (Anonymous Sheets) that appeared instead of the *Népszava* were confiscated. Having taken several communists into custody, the police got their hands on some of the Communist Party's leaders as well. Imre Sallai, Sándor Fürst and Frigyes Karikás were arrested on July 15 and charged with activity that imperiled state and social order. Despite petitions and protests at home and abroad, the one and only session of an emergency court was held on July 28. Sallai and Fürst were sentenced to death and executed immediately.[12]

The police also kept the far-right movements under surveillance, but their intervention was incomparably milder than it was with the left. One newcomer was Zoltán Böszörményi's movement, later dubbed the Crossed Scythes,[13] which targeted the peasantry and cited Hungary's historical greatness and historical figures held in general respect in support of its "national, socialist, independent, anti-Semitic" program. Zoltán Meskó, however, announced in Parliament on June 16 the formation of a National Socialist Party.[14] An attempt to merge the two parties was unsuccessful, as Meskó relied on the middle classes and Böszörményi on a broader popular base. Adding up all the parties and movements of a fascist or Nazi type to appear in 1931–1932 suggests that they were not a sizable force, but the tendency that they marked cast a shadow over the future.

The wrangling continued in Parliament and in the United Party. The real problem was the fact that neither the League of Nations nor Royall Tyler, the US adviser at the National Bank, had yet changed their view on financial activity by the state. The government and Korányi did not need to fear the country's missing the opportunity of a sizable loan if it broke the internationally recognized norms—there was no chance of one anyway—but it might still fear for the moratorium, without which the country's position would worsen. Tyler and the international creditors (mainly Americans) rejected the idea of reducing interest rates and manipulating the exchange rate, and indeed every kind of state intervention, whether to remedy the grave difficulties in agriculture or to solve the problems of other sectors.

This put the government under increasing pressure. The attack in the spring of 1932 was directed by István Bethlen. The policy that he demanded was one that he himself had not managed or even thought possible as prime minister. Standing at the head of the agrarians was one who during his term had been accused mainly from that quarter of preferring big business interests over theirs. Now as he stood up for the agrarian bloc, nobody noticed that he was actually championing big business interests as well. The dispute between agriculture and industry existed only in the rhetoric of conflicting interests. When it came to expectations of state financial policy, the interests diverged far less than the debates would suggest. However, only the landowners had parliamentary representation suitable for applying pressure on the government, and so the battle over state intervention appeared to be only about agriculture. Károlyi, opposing the landowners as prime minister, came from one of the greatest aristocratic families, who defended the interests of the state and had gained a reputation for neglecting agriculture in favor of financial capital mainly for international reasons. On May 4, Bethlen spoke in Parliament against the policy of Károlyi and Korányi, before 87 United Party members introduced what were known as the farmers' demands:[15] reductions in interest rates, settlement of the encumbrances on the land, an increase in the price of wheat, and concessions for those who had just gained land. The governing party's attack on the government was joined by the Independent Smallholders, and thus Károlyi's position deteriorated. The change of mood could also be gauged by the result of a by-election in Mezőcsát, where Minister of Agriculture Emil Purgly, the United Party candidate, was defeated by the Smallholder Tibor Eckhardt.

After the Mezőcsát debacle, Bethlen ceased to pretend that he was attacking his government as head of the governing party. On September 3, he addressed a letter to Károlyi stating that he could no longer "curb" his party if the government failed to meet its elementary demands. He wrote that this would not be done by the minister of finance, with his fear of foreign bankers, and so the prime minister had to act to avert worse troubles. Bethlen would have known from his own experience that a minister of finance (the same man with whom he had cooperated on the same policy) could go against foreign opinions only with the backing of his prime minister. Károlyi then announced that he would not give way to dictation. On September 21, he drew his conclusions and resigned. Many thought that Bethlen would be reappointed, including Bethlen himself, but the reward went to Gyula Gömbös, who had stayed very quiet throughout the storm.

The parliamentary base for Bethlen's style of politics was overturned during the transitional period under Károlyi, and the governing party group in Parliament split. Initially in the background, there appeared a far-right grouping that targeted the lower middle strata, the petite bourgeoisie.

The departure of Károlyi can also be seen as a change of generation. The main figures who had salvaged themselves from the Dual Monarchy (Apponyi, Andrássy and others) were dead or retired. Decisive contributors to post-war stabilization and reconstruction such as Klebelsberg were no longer alive, Bethlen was sidelined, and neither Korányi nor Tibor Kállay would play a decisive part again. For a few years at least (before something of a comeback by the old guard), the rising stars came from a younger generation and largely from lower down on the social scale. But Károlyi's efforts failed less for domestic social and political reasons than because international conditions left the government so little room for maneuver in economic policy. There was a wind of change blowing through Europe and the world, and the regent's next choice of prime minister seemed to be a kind of response to the new situation.

Notes

1. Kozma had been on the far right in Szeged but had come over to Bethlen's side. He raised the news agency to the standards of the time. The Film Bureau that he set up produced newsreels and most of the educational materials in use then. He left a vast quantity of records, which constitute a valuable historical source.
2. This was done under an agreement with the Austrian state. Matuska was a resident of Vienna, and Austrian law did not recognize the death penalty.
3. The debt stock of about 18.5 billion *pengő* included a foreign debt of over 4 billion. Annual interest and repayments came to 300 million *pengő*.
4. In fact the National Bank made a mild decrease in its rate at that time.
5. Parliament considered the question several times but without legislating.
6. *Salgótarjáni Kőszénbánya Rt.*
7. The *Magyar Légió Szövetség, Magyar Párt* and *Ellenzéki Blokk*, respectively.
8. The official statement said that he had hanged himself.
9. Vannay later withdrew most of his police confession on this.
10. There is no sign of such an endorsement in the Foreign Ministry archives.
11. Mussolini's so-called "wheat battle" had appreciable results, as Italy became almost self-sufficient in cereals. So the country had no interest in buying sizable quantities of Hungarian grain.
12. Karikás was sentenced to life imprisonment, but was later allowed to leave for the Soviet Union, where he became a victim of the terror.
13. *Kaszáskeresztes.*
14. *Nemzetszocialista Párt.*
15. *Gazdakövetelések.*

5. PERILOUS EXPERIMENTS

1. Gyula Gömbös—A Corporate State?

On October 1, 1932, the regent chose a strong man to fill the prime minister's place: Gyula Gömbös. His choice, by accident or design, reflected the fact that Bethlen's financial and economic policy of cooperation with Western European and American financiers was over. It had come to an end with the Károlyi government and its Bethlenite efforts to find a solution in a European framework. Gömbös, by contrast, had been advocating a separate Hungarian solution since 1923, and now sought an alternative to the European situation produced by the Depression. With no further prospect of an international financial remedy for Hungary's problems, the idea of a separate financial policy became more attractive. This meant promoting "national self-interest," involving domestic "national" production, foreign trade, and sales of agricultural produce, notably wheat, as the country's biggest surplus product. These conditions presumably fitted in with Gömbös's system of views, at least in part.[1]

Before going into detail, it must be said that Gömbös's administration was lucky in spite of itself in its first period of almost two years. 1932 brought an end to the reparation debts, which made life much easier, financially speaking. Then the Depression began to ease, which improved the chances for trade, especially selling grain. But it must be added that 1934–1935 (again independently of Gömbös) brought international events that did not favor his plans, and indeed caused him serious additional difficulties.

Gömbös, incidentally, was a quite new type of prime minister. There had already been three non-aristocratic prime ministers in 1919–1920,[2] but they were from the lower ranks of the landowning

236

classes, and public opinion saw them as temporary. Gyula Gömbös was not and could not be thought of in any such terms, although it is not easy to say why. He had not held any post where he could display his toughness, endurance, capacity for work, tactical sense, good negotiating manner or mercilessness in politics. However, anybody expecting such qualities of him anyway would not have been disappointed.

In terms of his father's profession (a village schoolmaster), Gömbös hardly started higher than Mussolini or Hitler.[3] But unlike them, he had received a regular military education, including training for General Staff officers. Nor did he preach rebellion against the leading groups in society. On the contrary, he had oriented himself upward in society, to the highest echelons, which gave him advantages, but did not qualify him to be a people's leader. In fact there is no evidence that he aspired to be one. He would make reference to the people, but he actually represented the middle stratum of the middle classes. He made speeches, but he did not step forward as a spokesman, and he was visibly repelled by tavern politicking. Among Gömbös's advantages was the fact that he had managed to retain the regard of state and political leaders even while in opposition. He had remained in the circle on which Horthy relied. He had managed to slip smoothly back into the governing party in 1928, and in 1932 his path from the defense portfolio to the premiership seemed almost logical. This career certainly points to flexibility and tactical ingenuity in Gömbös. But the close relations that he had maintained with the political elite of the 1920s stood between him and any prospect of launching a mass opposition party based on his own ideology. He had to be content on taking office with the party that he inherited, where István Bethlen called the tune.

Yet Gömbös's behavior set a new style and purpose from the outset. Instead of Bethlen's gentlemanly image in a civilian suit of English cut, the type of dress that he cultivated was the Hungarian style known as the *diszmagyar*, or expressly informal wear, and he liked to keep his hands in his pockets. His travels were not to London, Paris, the Hague or Geneva, as his predecessors' had been, but to Rome and (more rarely) Berlin. Bethlen had stressed firmly how the new Hungary had to find its place in existing Europe. Gömbös often spoke of the "self-aimed"[4] Hungarian nation, a phrase hard to interpret directly, as every nation has aims in some sense, but referring obliquely to an aim of distancing itself from Western European values and ways of life. This concept accorded with Italian Fascist ideology of the time, which saw the ultimate principle and purpose in life as the nation (equated at the time with the state.)

Gömbös was the first Hungarian prime minister to follow up his appointment with an extensive, structured program—the famous national plan of action, under 95 points. There was nothing magical about this, as he had been expecting to take office for several months and his followers would have been drafting the plan for some time. But it was quite unusual, and although some people joked at it, quite a large number found it a pleasant surprise. The new tone and the reforms promised attracted attention beyond the middle classes on whom Gömbös normally relied for support, among all who considered the country to be ripe for reform. He had drawn into his team during the weeks before his appointment several potential ministers who had good professional reputations, such as Béla Imrédy and Bálint Hóman.[5] Another feature of the new style was the fact that the prime minister made a strenuous tour of the country to advertise his program, although this did not become a habit. A further feature was the sensitivity of the Gömbös staff to publicity. The new prime minister attached importance to personal influence and used new techniques of obtaining it, including radio broadcasting.[6]

The 95 points were essentially a "dream-book," as his more malicious contemporaries called it, in the sense that a country still in the grip of recession could not realistically expect to satisfy the conflicting desires and demands of all groups and strata at once, as the program promised. But it probably contained details of a long-term idea: in other words, the prime minister was planning a thorough transformation of the system. The main questions to consider are what Gömbös really envisioned, how far he got in realizing his vision, and why he got no further.

The plan of action included the key expression for organizing a dictatorship: it referred to reorganization of power whereby "maximum national forces can be made available to the nation's leaders for realizing the national goals." This sentence in the national plan might equally have come from Mussolini or Hitler, and stated clearly enough that Gömbös was preparing his "leaders" for a great national mobilization, one not based on a multi-party parliamentary system. Gömbös did not need to seek an example for the "self-aiming" question of the nation, as he had referred to this himself during and after the war. The national plan of action did not state directly that a single-party system would be introduced, but if the Gömbös in opposition (at the end of 1934) is compared with the prime minister who openly engaged in organizing a corporate state (in 1935), there are strong grounds for suspecting that this kind of state structure had been intended in 1932 as well. The situation was more complex, however, due to the question of anti-Semitism.

Caution is advisable here, as very little is known of Gömbös's intellectual horizons or the images of society that they contained. Of his reading, historians usually mention the racial theories of Houston Stewart Chamberlain, which he certainly read as a young man. He is also known to have studied works by Lajos Méhely, a Hungarian exponent of the biological theory of race. But it is not known what he adopted from these, nor what else he read of the quite extensive literature on race or of the Nazi authors, nor how familiar he was with the Italian Fascist ideology and system.[7] So it is not even possible to say what brand of anti-Semitism Gömbös stood near to, or what changes his views may have undergone in this regard. Another question is whether he really laid aside his anti-Semitic policy, whatever it was, as he promised Bethlen that he would in 1928. He certainly repeated this publicly in 1932. Nor did he not initiate any anti-Semitic propaganda or take any measure against Jews during his four years in office.

Having said what is not known, it is now time to summarize what is actually known about Gömbös's "world view." He certainly developed at the end of the First World War a concept of the organic nation that he took as axiomatic, semi-"divine," and therefore the ultimate goal. Starting from the interests of the nation, he came to oppose first the Vienna leadership and the House of Habsburg, and then, influenced by the military defeat and the revolutions, liberalism, the working-class left, and the Jews, whom he identified with liberal and socialist democracy, and with communist inclinations. He saw the soil and those who tilled it as the decisive, cohesive force in the nation, and so he wanted to transform and influence the country's economy in their favor. To this end, he advocated a strong state and "spiritual dictatorship." He also turned away from the West and its culture, as representative of damaging liberalism. The program included excluding, or, as he put it on one occasion, "annihilating" the criminals and the Hungarian traitors who supported them. On the other hand, it included a range of economic, welfare and education measures designed to support the "healthy" part of the nation. There was no essential change in his views even after his party and his own position had begun for a while after 1924 to embrace a "racial" spirit. All that happened after he broke with Bethlen was that he expressed such views more freely and openly. But he did not define the concept of race in a National Socialist spirit, partly because of Hungary's foreign policy aspirations and partly because of his own origins.[8] He could not speak of a *magyar* race (pertaining to the Hungarians) and so spoke of a *magyarországi* one (pertaining to Hungary) instead.

Analysis of the government program, the statements of Gömbös, and, perhaps most significantly of all, the documents and orders surrounding the party organization all suggest that a Nazi-type anti-Semitic program was not part of the corporate single-party system that Gömbös espoused. It might be said that he wanted to pursue a positive policy in favor of the "Hungarian (*magyar-országi*) race" that would automatically squeeze out the undesirable Jewish element, without special punitive measures. After 1928, he no longer used the concept of race, returning instead to a national policy. His desire seems to have been an "indirectly" anti-Semitic policy, designed to strengthen the Hungarian landowning and middle classes and give them more scope in business and in cultural and intellectual matters. There are signs of a distinction being drawn under his premiership (as earlier) between Jews long native to the country and recent immigrant Jews. This ties in with the way in which an office for control over aliens was developed under his administration and guidelines were sent to the Ministry of the Interior on how to treat recently arrived Jews. There would only be sense in this if some special fate were intended for the recent immigrants.[9]

The prime minister certainly did not put his cards on the table when he came to office. One obvious reason for his caution was the fact that nobody would have stood a chance of becoming prime minister of Hungary in 1932 with a program directed at dictatorship. Another seems to have been the fact that Gömbös was far removed from the radicalism that the racial picture of society and the program of National Socialism represented, not least because it held no place for the Hungarians.

However, Gömbös's declared views on the state, society, politics, and so on, which still caused no confusion in domestic politics, fitted in well with the Italian Fascist ideas of the period. Mussolini in the mid-1920s identified the nation as the ultimate meaning in life. He too wanted to subsume into the nation the individual and all its manifestations, and he too cited the nation's needs when erecting a strong, homogeneous, centralized state unbroken by conflicts. (Somewhat later, the sequence was somewhat reversed in Fascist ideology, with the state becoming the nation's embodiment, expression, and mainstay.) The Italian corporate state also provided the pattern for the corporate type of organization that Gömbös proclaimed no much later. As for the Jewish question, Mussolini had also spoken of "race" and racial interests, but not in the Nazi sense. Whatever he may have claimed later, he had no knowledge of anti-Semitism up to 1938, and the *Duce* continued for a long time to dissociate himself and his system from the racial hatred of National Socialism. These things could easily have influenced Gömbös, who clearly had a high opinion of Mussolini irrespective of his desire to deepen relations for diplomatic reasons. Nor could any prime minister ignore the damage to the country's economy that a violently anti-Semitic policy would do. Taking all this into account, it is easy to imagine that Gömbös's Jewish program remained sublimated in the background of his ideas.

There can be no doubt that Gömbös was expecting Hitler to come to power in the autumn of 1932, bringing international relations to the boil and opening up prospects of territorial revision. Nor was the Hitler phenomenon new to him. Relations between the National Socialist German Workers' Party and Hungarian groups on the far right dated back to 1920. Sporadic data suggest that these groups gave some financial help to the Nazis.[10] In the autumn of 1923, for instance, a known associate of Gömbös's, Ferenc Ulain, was caught on the Hungarian border with a suitcase full of money to help the coup that was being prepared in Munich. It is simply inconceivable that Gömbös should not have enquired again into the ideas and propaganda of the Nazis, at least after their first electoral success in 1930, but there is no information available on how he stood in relation to Hitler's views. Once Hitler was in power, Gömbös must have seen a path opening up for Hungary towards territorial revision, although this was to prove to be a disappointment. However, Gömbös seems to have stood closer to the Duce and his Fascism than to the Führer and his National Socialism.

The political structure inherited was not suited to the main purpose of making "maximum national forces" available to the nation's leaders. The prime minister was in practice a prisoner of the governing party. He had neither a party nor a mass movement of his own behind him. He could not dismiss the parliamentary majority, because the regent would not have given him a free hand to do so, and for the time being not even the regent had powers to dissolve the legislature. He could not turn things around with military pressure either, because most of the army was under the command of old-style officers. So in terms of method and tactics, Gömbös could not even follow the Polish or the Portuguese model, let alone the Italian or the German one.[11] He was unique in working from within to throttle the system or make it monolithic, using its own means. This proved to be no easy task, but it was not an impossible one. Gömbös knew he could produce a decisive change in parliamentary power relations by swinging and controlling elections. There before him was the example of 1922, when Bethlen made his breakthrough largely under Gömbös's management. Party and Parliament, so dependent on the public administration, began at just that time to avenge themselves, and Bethlen, architect of that dependence, was more or less powerless to prevent that.

For Gömbös, there was still a long time before the next elections. It was easy enough to rename the United Party the National Unity Party, and as Bethlen raised no objections, Gömbös took over its leadership, but the composition of the party was unchanged. The Gömbös supporters remained a tiny minority within it. The government had no trouble in gaining acceptance for a sequence of populist, morale-improving measures, but made no headway with its own objectives. It ended the emergency measures and the ban on assembly. It did what everybody had castigated Károlyi in vain for not doing and brought down interest rates, giving something of a stimulus to the economy. It granted special preferences to certain industries. It eased the position of indebted smallholders, reduced transport tariffs for agricultural produce, and improved contract terms for farm servants. It also thought of the workers, showing that the prime minister's remarks on national reconciliation were not empty words. It introduced a 48-hour week, at least in principle; it did not apply to corporations automatically, but it was a move towards settling the general issue of working hours. It decreed a minimum wage, to be introduced progressively in various industries. This series of measures temporarily raised the prime minister's popularity and the hopes attaching to his actions.

Let us note here for the benefit of those who see a single-party system—fascism, Nazism, Stalinism, or any kind of dictatorship—as a kind of ultimate evil, incapable of bringing social or cultural improvements, that this idea is erroneous. Included in the essence of all the twentieth-century dictatorships, alongside their contempt for the individual, is the fact that they did not confine themselves to social "demagoguery" when trying to maximize mobilization for the nation, the community, the race, and so on. For various reasons and in various ways, they stabilized and improved the lot of the masses, at least temporarily, while making available to them the culture and ideology that they wanted to impart. Conversely, people in many states whose political structures and state systems did not qualify them as dictatorships suffered greater social misery than their counterparts in a smoothly running dictatorship. The poverty may have been greater, the ignorance more widespread, and the lower classes more neglected. Hard though it is to believe, one of Hitler's great objections to the Hungarian ruling classes was that they went in for old-fashioned exploitation of the people. Nor was there peace and plenty in many of the "pure" democracies either. Collective worker–employer bargaining began at the earliest in the 1930s. There was nothing approaching a welfare state anywhere.

Governments fell on the issue of unemployment benefit. Nor was corruption or police brutality unknown in them. Welfare policy in the hands of a dictatorship worked as a means of furthering the goals of power and stabilization. In the case of Gyula Gömbös, he was trying to follow a similar policy as a way of making his plans for a dictatorship palatable to society.

One requirement for economic recovery—a slow improvement in world economic conditions—came about irrespective of Hungary's endeavors, meaning that the state benefited from something that it had not had anything to do with. In addition, the recovery was helped by government policy: deliberate development of certain industries, and utilization of the new situation in Germany. The government gave its support to power generation, the radio industry, aluminum production and the carbohydrate program, which encouraged modernization and transformation of the industrial structure, helped these industries to find their feet, and soaked up unemployment. So far "Jewish" big business had no reason to complain.

These measures enhanced the government's reputation, and so did some greater or lesser diplomatic successes that Gömbös scored. But the scale of success with this new, more "dynamic" foreign policy has been exaggerated, by the government at the time and by some recent historians. Gömbös did well primarily as far as an increase in grain exports was concerned. Otherwise, his government let go of the ties in Western Europe that had existed and operated to some extent up to then. It also lost what had seemed to be secure Italian support for its long-term plans (due to a temporary change in Italy's orientation), while failing to gain support elsewhere, as German ideas at the time were far removed from the basic thinking in Hungary.

István Bethlen had already put some effort into agricultural marketing, but neither his nor Károlyi's government had anything practical to show for it. There had been Italian–Hungarian negotiations for several years on various aspects of economic cooperation, and there were some agreements concluded, which provided in principle preferential treatment for Hungarian exports in certain types of product. But nothing came of this in practice until the economic agreement forming part of the tripartite Hungarian–Italian–Austrian pact of 1934 regulated the details of the actual transfers. Italian purchases of grain and meat did perk up for a while for that reason and because of the Italian military venture, but they never approached the scale of exports to Austria or Germany. Austria, on the other hand, had long been Hungary's biggest buyer. All that happened in 1934 was that a temporarily disrupted Austrian market was restored and stabilized.

Gömbös managed to revive the Hungarian–German agreement of 1931, with additional agreements in 1933 and early 1934 that specified quantities for agricultural imports to Germany (for grain, livestock, fat, and so on) and these were actually purchased by the Germans. This was connected with the end of the recession, with the beginnings of German rearmament, as armies always mean greater food requirements, and finally with a radical change in Germany's trade policy. Sales to Austria outstripped those to Germany in 1932, but by 1937, they were hardly more, and according to some calculations, Germany had taken the lead.

It could be thought until the end of 1934 that ties with Italy were also becoming more intensive politically, especially after the tripartite agreement of March 17. Gömbös had reservations about Austria, due to conflicts of commercial interests,[12] but tighter relations with Italy were his main hope when signing. Yet there was little of the return awaited. The Italian regime soon committed itself in other directions, entering on a military campaign that made it much harder to meet other commitments, and altered power relations in the Danube Basin.

In other regards, the tripartite agreement caused the Hungarian government more discomfort than joy, at home and abroad. It was not pleasant for Gömbös at home to have the alliance greeted mainly by the left-wing opposition, as a guarantee that Austrian independence would remain. Nor was it pleasant when the same accusation was made in Berlin. Gömbös had managed to ensure that the tripartite agreement left open the possibility of *Anschluss*, but the prime minister, the foreign minister, and the head of the Hungarian mission in Berlin had weeks of explaining to do there. Hungarian–German relations deteriorated and became expressly tense somewhat later,[13] and the tripartite agreement did not lead to perceptible advantage. This was not just because Chancellor Engelbert Dollfuss was assassinated in July and his successor much more cautious about making commitments, or because the Italian government's African policy was pushing it towards France and this conflicted with Hungary's interests.[14] As a result of the Abyssinian crisis, Italian policy became expressly anti-British and pro-German, but by that time, Gömbös was gravely ill and unable to profit from the change. The "axis" that he had eagerly awaited came into being, although he did not survive to hear the concept that he had advanced adopted and advertised by Mussolini.[15] But he probably realized that power relations had begun to change at Italy's expense and in Germany's favor, which can hardly have been reassuring.

The final months of 1934 presented Hungarian diplomacy with the following immediate problems: offense taken by Nazi Germany, a decline in the worth of Italian "friendship," and League of Nations accusations over the Marseille assassination, whose target was the Yugoslav King Alexander, although the French foreign minister was killed as well.[16] The Hungarian government and Foreign Ministry constantly did penance in Berlin or complained of German behavior, while making reproaches and applying pressure in Rome, to no avail, against Mussolini's commitment to France.

Mussolini promised that he would continue to support Hungarian territorial revision and try to gain France's support as well, but Budapest had little faith in his success. Gömbös handed

Mussolini a map of ethnic distribution marked with Hungary's
claims, and the Duce thought that these were realistic and moderate, but neither side attached much importance to the occasion.[17]
The preparation of the map and the prime minister's initiative suggest that the government had abandoned diplomatically the idea of
an "optimal" revision that would restore all lost territory to
Hungary and fallen back on the ethnic principle. (Bethlen obviously got wind of this and immediately attacked the new approach.)[18]
The significance of the issue was much reduced by the fact that the
Italians began to put all their energy into their African enterprise
after the beginning of October 1935. As for the Abyssinian campaign, the Hungarian High Command thought that it would tie
down Italy's army for a long time so that Germany could supersede
Italy in the Danube region.

And so it came to pass. Budapest faced the unpromising
prospect of German expansion. Then there were the tensions mentioned and Berlin's lack of interest in acting as a third party in
Hungarian territorial revision, whether "optimal" or ethnic in basis.
Chancellor Hitler, Alfred Rosenberg, head of the Nazi Party foreign
department, Foreign Minister Konstantin von Neurath, and others
were quick to point out to Gömbös and other Hungarians that their
country could only expect support for its territorial plans in relation
to Czechoslovakia, as Germany sought to pursue a policy of friendship towards Romania and Yugoslavia. It is still unclear whether
this was digested at the Hungarian Foreign Ministry, or when it was
realized that Nazi Germany was not pursuing a policy of third-party
territorial revision. But it soon emerged that German policy did not
embrace revision in general, from the Hungarian, Bulgarian or
Italian point of view.[19]

All in all, the frequent visits of the Hungarian prime minister
to the Italian and German capitals and his demonstrative reception
did not cover any great diplomatic success. The Marseille atrocity
of October 9, 1934, on the other hand, brought press attacks on the

prime minister, worldwide and among left-wing exiles. As for Gömbös, he had a big hand while still minister of defense in building up relations with the terrorist *Ustaše* organization, which was allowed to rent some houses and isolated farms, and hide exiled members in Hungary, where they could even receive basic military training. But under pressure from the Foreign Ministry, efforts began early in 1934 to remedy the situation and remove the *Ustaše*.[20] So Hungarian government circles played no part in preparing or organizing the October 9 outrage. But international forbearance shown to Rome and Berlin left only the Hungarian government in the dock, in Geneva before the League of Nations, and in France when the case came up for trial.[21] All that Gömbös could manage through mild blackmail of the Duce[22] and moderation by Western governments was to keep the tone of the sentence mild. Although this did nothing for the country's international reputation, the unfounded charges did help to produce broader and deeper sympathy for the government at home.

The atmosphere helped to facilitate a rapprochement and eventually a meeting between the prime minister and some representatives of Hungarian letters. The connection was made by Lajos Zilahy, through Miklós Kozma, an old friend of Gömbös, who headed both the Hungarian news agency MTI and Hungarian Radio at the time.[23] As such, he had created broadcasting possibilities for László Németh, and through him, for many other Hungarian writers. Those concerned primarily represented a new literary generation, whose members were of rural, peasant origin or were concerned with rural matters for other reasons, known as the *népi* (common people's) writers. This general term reflected the shared purpose of an otherwise heterogeneous grouping. It mainly included, apart from authentic villagers, members of the intelligentsia, and it was joined by some writers with an expressly urban bent, and even some Jews. This was a quite novel sphere and occurrence in Hungarian literature. It was also novel for a group of writers to appear as an expressly political force. Although the members differed in their approach in many regards, they agreed on two criteria: they wanted to advance the peasantry, seeing it as the most valuable constituent of the Hungarian community, and to defend or save Hungarian culture from German and Jewish influence. In foreign policy, they mainly stood for ethnically based territorial revision. These writers with the cares of the village and the need for reform close to their hearts were temporarily dazzled by hearing the authorities, in a way quite unknown in Hungary, make the same noises about the peasantry as they did, and some of the measures that the writers took show that they thought that these noises were sincere. But the meeting at Zilahy's home on April 16, 1935, took place in a different atmosphere. By then, the ill-fated elections had been held, in which peasants had been beaten up and even killed, Endre Bajcsy-Zsilinszky, who stood close to them, had had his election invalidated, and the benign veil of uncertainty had begun to slip from Gömbös's real plans. It seems likely and hardly surprising that the meeting took place in an insipid atmosphere, failed to advance mutual understanding, and produced nothing of the rapprochement that Kozma had promoted so enthusiastically.[24]

The prime minister should have been able in principle to rely on the army in pursuing his goals, but again there were barriers not easily overcome. In Gömbös's favor was his own background as an officer, his thorough knowledge of the people in this sphere, his previous service as state secretary and then minister of defense, and strong support for his views among younger officers. There were also high expectations of him in those circles. But there was a legal prohibition against political activity by the Hungarian army, reinforced by tradition among the old corps of officers. While people brought up in that tradition remained at the head of the army and its chiefs of staff and in the important commands, there was no way that the army could exert pressure for a dictatorship. Gömbös began to build up his connections, probably consciously, in 1928, and to subordinate to his purposes the decisions on retirement and replacement, but this had not been wholly successful before he died. He was able to remove the old-guard Kocsárd Janky as commander-in-chief and chief of General Staff, but his replacement, Lieutenant General Vilmos Rőder, was hardly better for Gömbösite politics. Although Rőder had very good German and still more Austrian contacts, he could not be persuaded to assist in a turn to the far right. In 1935, Gömbös launched an assault on the old guard in the army, pensioning off 22 generals, and this "rejuvenation" promoted many Gömbösites. The prime minister even managed to dismiss Rőder, but the real success was to appoint as deputy to General József Somkuthy, chief of General Staff, the far-right Jenő Rátz, who replaced Somkuthy soon afterwards. But all in all, Gömbös had to be satisfied with having his preferred candidates appointed to a number of high positions, and he failed to reach the decisive stage, or reached it too late for his own purposes. It seems that his efforts bore fruit three or four years later, reaching a stage in the war where Gömbös's cadres could influence not only the army, but the fate of the whole country.

Ultimately Gömbös approached both government and the model of a corporate society in a single-party system of state in an exceptional way, all of his own, as mentioned earlier. He turned the governing party that he inherited into a starting point, hastily renamed the National Unity Party, in line with his ideology. The maneuvers were conducted for years in secret by his confidant Béla Márton. Gömbös wanted to make the National Unity Party the one party by organizational and propaganda means, so that it would become a formation that fitted into a firm, hierarchical structure and was suited to controlling and directing social organizations that would be rendered uniform at a future date. Bearing in mind the great influence of the governing party, this did not seem impossible at all. As early as 1932, there began a vast campaign to found local party branches, recruit members and ensure ideological preparation.

This campaign had some success. Successive branches were started, which divided the population into various groups of 40–45 people, on which card indexes were kept, as they were on almost everybody. The members were instructed to obtain leading positions in local government and social organizations. A national list was made of the latter in 1934, as an aid to insinuating party members onto their executives, where they could play an initiating role and bring the organizations concerned under party surveillance. The Organization of Social Associations[25] was assigned the task of integrating its member societies.

The need to create "self-aiming" and unity was the main idea brought out by this great campaign. This would lead to "a society organized in a planned way," as Béla Béldi, publicity chief of the National Unity Party, put it. The party statutes drawn up at the same time make it clear that a dominant role in this disciplined, planned society would be played by the "leader," to whom lower leaders and members would owe unconditional obedience.

While the organization continued at lower levels, it led at a higher political level at most to a couple of parliamentary questions and to opposition from some high sheriffs, without exciting Parliament. This changed when Gömbös set about extending the power of the executive at the expense of the legislature. He sought to introduce several pieces of legislation to create conditions for "calm government." The first big storm came over a plan to establish a superior ministry for the economy, which aroused so much opposition from the National Hungarian Farming Association and the National Association of Industrialists that Gömbös was obliged to withdraw his proposal, at least for a while. Nor did the bill to increase the powers of the regent again go through smoothly, although Act XXIII/1933 was eventually passed by both houses, giving the regent royal powers of adjourning, suspending, and dismissing Parliament. This act also showed the ambiguous position in which Gömbös found himself. He certainly had ambitions to be leader, but he knew that he could not obtain that status without Horthy's support, and so he tried strengthening the regent's powers in return for support for his own power, for instance against Parliament. His behavior and procedure over this was again reminiscent of Mussolini's. After that, Gömbös wanted to get his hands on the capital and prepared a bill on municipalities for the purpose. This caused outrage among the opposition, leading to the formation of a "constitution-defending bloc," and divided the governing party as well. The Smallholders were preparing to overthrow the government when Bethlen came to the prime minister's aid, almost at the last minute, and the majority in the National Unity Party agreed to accept the proposal after some amendment.

After that, any tiny government move remotely to do with promoting centralism and a single-party system met with further storms and opposition from most of the National Unity Party. Nor could the regent be induced to use the powers that the prime minister had won for him and dissolve Parliament. Gömbös, although party chairman, continued to bear the burden of a parliamentary group in which the decisive word and influence still belonged to István Bethlen, who began at the end of 1934 to dissociate himself from Gömbös's line and criticize government activity in public. It became clear that the conservatives in Parliament agreed with the left in not being prepared to follow Gömbös's road. It would inevitably come to a clash, and it was high time for Gömbös to look for allies.

One natural ally seemed to be the Smallholders' Party, whose leading figure was now Tibor Eckhardt, an old friend and comrade in the counter-revolutionary and racialist movement. But the views of the early "Gömbösite" far right had come to differ over the years. After the incident to be discussed here, Eckhardt turned the Smallholders' Party into a strong force of opposition and he himself left for the United States during the war, to seek help for the Hungarian government in bailing out of the conflict.[26] Another early supporter, Endre Bajcsy-Zsilinszky, became a decisive figure in the anti-Nazi opposition, who eventually paid for his activity with his life. Of the important figures in that earlier group, only Miklós Kozma remained by Gömbös's side, supporting his main policies, although he too disagreed with some initiatives and eventually came into conflict with him.

Despite his tactical quibbles, Eckhardt was prepared in 1934 to enter into an alliance with Gömbös, the bait being the prospect of an end to the Bethlen group's political hegemony. But he certainly did not think that the point of the alliance was to make it easier for Gömbös to move towards one-man rule. He aimed to strengthen his own party, make it capable of governing, and open up for himself the way to a ministerial career.

Gömbös, with the tripartite agreement, the grain sales, and the bargain with the Smallholders behind him, announced that he would speed up his reforms, only to admit some months later that he could not carry this out. This was because of the diplomatic difficulties and failures discussed earlier and the resistance with which he met in Parliament. Talks began on the settlement program and reform of the entail system;[27] then the question of electoral law came into the political focus. Several versions were circulated and debated, but the one that appealed to Gömbös failed to gain the necessary majority. The number of unconditional supporters that he had in the lower house ranged between 20 and 25.

A veritable political explosion was created when a bill for introducing a system of compulsory representation appeared in January 1935. This followed the lines of Italian corporate law, making it compulsory to join one of the representative associations known as chambers, which were to operate under government-appointed executives and have the right to conclude collective contracts for their members and control recruitment. If the bill had become law, they would also have settled employment disputes.

This exposed the political crisis in the National Unity Party. Bethlen emphasized, in a speech in Debrecen at the end of January, the point that he wanted neither "unbridled" Western democracy nor "any kind of dictatorship either." Two years earlier, Bethlen's wing of the United Party had clashed with Prime Minister Károlyi over practical matters of policy (mainly financial). Now the dispute ran much deeper, as it affected the whole apparatus of state, the existing political rights in Hungary, and the scope for more or less autonomous movement by the various social groups. At the party meeting on January 29, Gömbös, after all the sharp attacks on him, could again thank Bethlen for the vote of confidence that he received, but by then everybody had come to realize that this was only a momentary political gesture on Gömbös's part. This emerged in any case at conciliatory talks between Gömbös and Bethlen, arranged by Horthy. Bethlen presented some tough demands, ranging from respect for the majority opinion in the party, through an end to the far-right agitation among young people, to making the mandate of the House of Representatives sacrosanct. The last meant that Gömbös would abandon his plans to dissolve the house (which Horthy would not endorse in any case) and hold premature general elections. Again Gömbös had to backtrack, and he abided for a while by the undertakings that he made at the talks. He did not stint his reassuring pronouncements, while passing the task of attacking Bethlen and his group to the Smallholders.

Not long afterwards, Gömbös produced a rabbit out of a hat. On March 1 he ordered a ban on public assemblies, and on March 4 his government resigned. Then as the head of a new government, he managed to persuade Horthy on the same day to dissolve the lower house. The order was kept secret and the prime minister disappeared for a few days, and thus nobody could do anything about it. However, this coup demonstrated that Gömbös had no choices either. The wall of opposition to his program in the National Unity Party and the lower house could be demolished only if he could conjure a majority out of his supporters in the general elections. So he gave up his franchise plans and put his trust in a swift result, allowing the elections to be held under the old legislation. It is not known, incidentally, how he persuaded Horthy into this move.

Bethlen immediately left the National Unity Party, explaining his detailed reasons in an election speech on March 17. He attacked Gömbös for his leader behavior, his production of "discredited racialists," and above all, for plans that would endanger public order and the rule of law. It had to be feared, Bethlen said, that the Hungarian system "will become a guinea pig for immature, bizarre ideas imported from abroad. We are going to see more toying with National Socialist ideas, party totalitarianism, the formation of SS and SA units[28] and similar things, economic planning and corporate systems, which will jeopardize the peace, order, credit and security of the country." Bethlen had clearly broken with the government and the governing party, and with his part in the Gömbös experiment, which consisted of "toying" with party totalitarianism. István Bethlen might be expelled personally from Hungarian politics, but his position expressed the views of the whole conservative landowning and capitalist bloc, and contained a message for the opposition as well.

Bethlen's intervention introduced the election campaign, in which the Gömbösites clearly expressed their support for the principles of dictatorship coupled with social and welfare reforms. Gömbös announced that he had no use for carping political parties, and he would liquidate socialism "with the weapons of justice and life." The elections themselves took place on March 31–April 7, amidst intimidation of opposition voters, arrests, bribery, forgery, and so on. At Endrőd, the gendarmerie fired into the crowd at a Smallholders' Party rally, killing six people. In the end, the National Unity Party obtained 170 seats out of the 245, and 25 seats went to the second-placed Independent Smallholders. But the merciless government terror applied against Smallholder candidates meant that there could never again be any word of cooperation with their party, which became an implacable enemy of the government.

The election victory was predictable, bearing in mind the electoral system. The Bethlen group in Parliament went down to 30–40 members, which left several decisive figures out in the cold, such as István Rubinek, Ferenc Keresztes-Fischer, Gedeon Ráday, Iván Rakovszky and Lajos Walko. There were 98 new National Unity Party members of Parliament, drawn mainly from the "old vanguard" of former commandos, ÉME activists, MOVE members, National Unity Party organizers, and non-serving military officers. One of the newcomers was Kálmán Rátz, later a founder of the Arrow-Cross Party, Mátyás Matolcsy, a leader of the Arrow-Cross front at one time, and Ferenc Rajniss, who became a minister in the 1945 Arrow-Cross government. If 1920 had been the year of the "booted" and 1922 that of the Bethlenite advance, 1935 was the year when the far-right "middle" entered Parliament. That year and those general elections also marked a caesura in Hungarian power relations between the two world wars. Thereafter that stratum was to obtain ever more posts in public administration, so that it became impossible by the means available to squeeze it back or remove it from politics again.

Gömbös might well imagine after the great electoral victory that he could start on his avalanche of reforms. The four-year plan of action produced on the basis of the national plan covered every portfolio and almost every aspect of life. Some proposals really addressed vital problems, and there were even cases where opposition votes were also cast for them. But the peace did not last long: organization of a single-party system restarted behind the scenes. This time the government made no secret of its intention to introduce a bill on interest representation that would place the legislature itself on a corporate basis, like the Italian system.[29] Corporate chambers were to have dealt with all the labor and welfare matters, under executives appointed for five years by the government. But opposition to introducing dictatorship was voiced in the lower house by Eckhardt and in the upper house by Count Gyula Károlyi, with Ministry of the Interior observers reporting Károlyi's opinion as being representative of the aristocracy and big business. The objections were supported by a joint memorandum from the National Association of Industrialists, National Hungarian Farming Association, and Association of Savings Unions and Banks[30] stating that the country had no need of compulsory corporate membership or joint employer–employee associations. The same view was held in their own way by the left-wing parties, and underlined by the Social Democratic Party with industrial action on a scale long not seen. (There were 50 strikes in 1935, involving 17,000 workers, as opposed to 20 in 1932, involving 5,000 workers.) Furthermore the flow of temporary interest in the Gömbös program by the leading intelligentsia, especially writers, ebbed again. The "New Intellectual Front" formed by the populist writers began to break up over the elections and the government proposals that followed them, and disintegrated totally as it became clear that the enticing plans for reform were either empty words or had ulterior motives. There was a revival of legitimism, too. This did not become a decisively influential trend, but it helped to turn intellectual opinion against the efforts to impose dictatorship.[31]

At the turn of 1935–1936, the bourgeois opposition formed a united front with the single purpose of defending constitutionalism from dictatorship. While the bourgeois opposition was voicing this in Parliament, the group of opponents of Gömbös in the National Unity Party were busy sabotaging the organization of a single-party system. Factions formed within the governing party to express dissatisfaction with what the government was doing. Even the minister of the interior, Miklós Kozma, disagreed with Gömbös's principles of party organization, while some of the high sheriffs did all that they could to obstruct the plan. So the government was obliged simply to "forget" the proposal. Nor was the situation improved by the very modest plan for agricultural settlement, under which a mere 400,000 *hold* (228,000 ha) were to be redistributed over 25 years, with 30 percent of the purchase price to be paid down and security to be given that the future owner possessed the tools for tilling the soil. This was hardly a promising prospect for the million people applying for land. Meanwhile, the numerically weak but strongly anti-Semitic wing of the far right had declared that Gömbös was betraying his original principles. So despite his great electoral victory, Gömbös was not in an enviable position. Having begun well (up to the end of 1934), he was now isolated from most of Hungarian society. Miklós Horthy had less and less faith in him and those around the regent were increasingly critical of Gömbös or thought that he should be dismissed. According to a memorandum of Horthy's, he had already decided to have him resign "in a friendly way," and all that dissuaded him was probably the fact that the prime minister became seriously ill. The position and behavior of the regent throughout the Gömbös period is extremely difficult to follow and cannot be interpreted accurately. Nor are the motives behind his measures known.

The prime minister's national plan of action had been read hopefully, not just by those around him, and his new style had won the sympathy of many. Yet from the first serious signs of his kidney trouble at the end of March 1936 until his death on October 6, 1936, in a German clinic, he lived out his life in the political wilderness. The country's affairs were managed (apart from a short interlude in August) by Kálmán Darányi, whom Horthy was known to favor as Gömbös's successor.

Gömbös's four years in office showed that the political system devised by Bethlen was still very strong. It was so strong, in fact, that no external pressure from the opposition could attack it effectively, and although the political antagonisms increased, it remained strong enough to resist the attempts to transform it made by another very committed and dynamic prime minister. An important part in the proceedings was certainly played by those to whom the regent was inclined to listen at various times. These are known only in broad terms. The "captains" had mostly departed from Buda Castle, and it seems to have been more important to Horthy at that time to know the opinions of the great landowners and big business. These were strong opponents of Gömbös's experiment. The great landowners were motivated in this both by their conservative legal inclinations, and by their distaste for the abolition of entail, prescribed in the government's legislative plans, as the land question immediately aroused their defensive instincts.[32] But the conduct of Hungarian big business was exceptional, as this was the stratum that would have benefited from elimination of the labor unions and setting up a corporate system. In both Italy and Germany, that was the main reason why most big business people were prepared to support the appointment of Mussolini and Hitler respectively. It is hard to imagine that Hungarian big business opposed the installation of a corporate system simply on constitutional grounds or out of sympathy with the unions. It was presumably because they assumed from the history of Nazi dictatorship in Germany that anything becomes possible once a dictatorship is installed and there is nothing left to protect the country's citizens. Germany in the autumn of 1935 was passing its first anti-Jewish legislation;[33] Hungary's big business community, most of them Jewish, could not be sure that Gömbös's concessions would survive long under a similar Hungarian dictatorship.

Gömbös's experiment also showed the difficulty (for the time being) of getting large numbers in Hungarian society to support a radical swing to the right. The relative success with the National Unity Party was attributed even by the organizers to desires for greater or lesser financial advantage, or to the way in which everything could be fixed with the help of the public administration, even a victory for the governing party in each general election. But the actual decisions were made elsewhere and by others, who did not include the new elite emerging in Gömbös's reorganized army. Ferenc Szálasi had founded his first party, the Party of National Will[34] (March 1935–April 1937) and some other little Nazi-style parties existed, but there was still no radical right-wing mass movement capable of influencing Hungary's affairs.

Gyula Gömbös failed to achieve his main objectives. He pushed through a few proposals, some of them fortunate, and bequeathed a legislature reorganized on "gentlemanly" fascist lines, and an army and public administration spiked with several dozen radical right-wingers. But two years of rising popularity did not translate into the kind of respect that Bethlen had won, and he was followed by successive fragile prime ministers.

Notes

1. I say presumably as Gömbös never stated his views coherently. Nor is his national plan of action much help, as it dealt mainly with practicalities.
2. István Friedrich, Károly Huszár and Sándor Simonyi-Semadam.
3. Mussolini's father was a blacksmith and his mother a teacher. Hitler's father was a senior customs officer, with social status and pay roughly corresponding to those of a civil school director.
4. *Öncélú.*
5. Imrédy was still considered to be more of an Anglophile than a right-winger at this time. Hóman was known as an excellent historian.
6. This was still not fashionable. Hitler began to introduce it, but Mussolini did not follow his example.
7. Bethlen had sent out a ministry delegation, which returned home with a huge quantity of material in 1927. This would have been available to him.
8. His mother was ethnically German.
9. This served as a pretext in 1941 for deporting about 15,000 Jews to the Kamenets Podolsk region of Ukraine, where most of them were massacred by a German commando unit.
10. German evidence confirms this for ÉME, but there are signs that the contacts were wider.

11. Józef Piłsudski had behind him important sections of the army, with which he made his "march on Warsaw." There were long years of military dictatorship behind the political power of António de Oliveira Salazar. The army also backed the Baltic dictators and Balkan royal dictators.

12. Gömbös, like Bethlen, was convinced that the *Anschluss* was inevitable, and he thought that Germany might be induced to pay for Hungary's concurrence with it, although it was not his intention to provoke the German government by raising tensions over the Austrian issue. During his talks, he acted firmly in Rome to ensure that this could be avoided.

13. The mutual reproaches continued for months, one target being the Hungarian minister in Berlin. One especially insulting gesture was made by Hermann Goering in November 1934, when he crossed Hungary by plane but met with no Hungarians at all during a stopover in Budaörs.

14. Before the Abyssinian campaign, Hungarian staff analysts were expecting Italian influence in the Danube Basin to be shaken by the absence of the army, with Germany taking advantage of this.

15. The expression "axis" was used by Gömbös, and earlier still by Bethlen.

16. The attempt to murder the king was organized by the Croatian far-right organization *Ustaše*. Louis Barthou was wounded by a stray police bullet and the ensuing panic prevented him from receiving medical treatment in time to save his life.

17. Mussolini's reflections on the map suggest that it distinguished on ethnic grounds between areas with a Hungarian majority and those with a mixed population, probably with an eye to proposing plebiscites in the latter.

18. In any case, the change may have been only a tactical move by the Foreign Ministry and Gömbös, adjusted to the current diplomatic conditions.

19. German friendship with Romania and Yugoslavia posed similar concerns for Bulgaria and Italy to those that it did for Hungary. Italy, with its African demands and aspirations, had no objection to Nazi leadership in the Mediterranean, and indeed supported it in principle, but it was not yet in a position to contribute to it.

20. There are signs that the Foreign Ministry had learned of some major *Ustaše* plan and wished to dissociate itself from this by removing the bases.

21. The French government was on its way to agreeing with Italy on several questions and establishing cooperation of the "Latin Sisters," while Berlin did not want to turn either the French or the Yugoslavs against Germany.

22. According to the Foreign Ministry plan, Gömbös would tell Mussolini that Hungary was proposing a full enquiry into the question in Geneva. What Gömbös said instead was that some people were advising this. This should all be seen in relation to the Hungarian government's possession of a mass of material on the Italian ties of the *Ustaše*.

23. Kozma was certainly the best educated of the original Gömbösite group, with political acumen and flexibility as well. Also important is the way in which his links with groups in Hungarian society and politics (closing and distancing) affected his work at the head of the two main channels of communication (MTI and the radio). Kozma joined the government early in 1935, but soon turned against Gömbös's efforts at state centralization.

24. Accounts of the meeting differ widely. Zilahy presented it as almost idyllic and successful; others stressed the confusion, even tension present in the conversation.

25. *Társadalmi Egyesületek Szervezete (TESZ)*.

26. There Eckhardt accomplished little, for reasons that are not wholly clear.

27. The practice of allowing a landowner to set a future order of inheritance, to prevent the estate from leaving the family, became known in Hungary in the seventeenth century. Rights of entail were approved by the king. The government proposed to make such estates partly or wholly divisible or alienable.

28. The *Schutzstaffeln* and *Sturmabteilung* of Nazi Germany.

29. The Italian system, already in place, meant essentially that in any dispute between the two sides of the corporate organizations—that of the employers and that of the employees—the deciding factor was played by the representation of the state, and this representation in most cases preferred the employer. This same organization nominated the lists of those who were to be elected as legislators. Only the Fascist Grand Council had the right to amend it.

30. *Takarékpénztárak és Bankok Egyesülete (TÉBE)*.

31. The most sophisticated voice in this regard was Sándor Pethő's. He combined the idea of monarchy as the embodiment of legality with self-defense against dictatorship.

32. Hitler showed some insight into this in 1928, when he revised the section on land policy in his party's program so that it applied only to Jewish-owned estates.
33. The first debate on these racially based laws was held at the Nuremberg party event of 1935, but the meeting did not decide which of the variants to adopt. Hitler then chose the one that was enacted by the Reichstag.
34. *Nemzet Akaratának Pártja.*

2. An Armaments Program under Kálmán Darányi

Kálmán Darányi had been standing in for Gömbös for several months, and his appointment as prime minister brought political reassurance and hopes of a return to normal. Darányi, an affluent landowner and former high sheriff, had experience in public administration and then as head of government. He seemed to embody calm and reliability. His introductory speech in Parliament suggested that without more ado he would return the ship of state to its familiar calm waters. He represented continuity but dissociated himself from the moves towards dictatorship. He removed from the governing party the group trying to reorganize it (Béla Márton and many associates) and restored earlier procedures in party activity.

The temporary calm was helped by the fact that Hitler refrained from further "weekend surprises" after March 1936,[1] and there was relative tranquility in international affairs, except for the Spanish Civil War, which was going on at some distance from Hungary. But beneath the peaceful surface, at home and abroad, there were great changes taking place, with far-reaching consequences. Germany began in the autumn of 1936 to implement military preparations for war (the second four-year plan), and early in November 1937, Hitler decided on his first two big moves: *Anschluss* with Austria and dismemberment of Czechoslovakia.[2]

Hungary, meanwhile, was undergoing major social developments: the appearance of the military elite as a power factor, stronger parliamentary pressure from the far right, which had gained seats in the last elections, and headway made by extra-parliamentary far-right groups. None of these could be blamed directly on the government, but its impotence against them led many people to see it as incompetent and, not without reason, as too ready to bargain. The prime minister failed to defend his minister of the interior of a few months, Miklós Kozma, who had to resign and opined that nobody could stir up public hysteria like Darányi, the man who proclaimed calm.

There was certainly no shortage of hysteria. The paid officials squeezed out of the National Party of Unity went about activating far-right groups, and the rumor spread that MOVE was planning a coup. The gossip also spoke of German figures being behind it, and this seemed to be supported by a change of German envoy in Budapest.[3] The far-right parties gained strength, especially the Party of National Will, whose founder and leader, Ferenc Szálasi, visited Germany. There he presumably received plenty of advice on how to develop his organization and propaganda, and almost certainly obtained some financial support, without which his party's great campaign in the second half of 1937 could hardly be imagined.[4]

As for the governing party, it could hardly be called that in a strict sense, as many of its members of Parliament represented the far right and only backed government policy sporadically if at all. That was an inevitable consequence of Gömbös's elections in 1935, and the developmental principles and personnel changes in the army soon gave command to a group advocating military dictatorship and full foreign policy commitment.[5] The regent could still dismiss these demands easily, but thenceforth he had to reckon with the military elite as a pressurizing force, or at least as a group with strong pressurizing tendencies.

Public nervousness was exacerbated by proliferating strikes, especially the strike of Pécs miners, which led to violent clashes and deaths. There was also organization in the intelligentsia, with debates about what constituted the Hungarian community and about history and the road to follow—in other words, really about politics and the right political orientation. Many who had paid no heed to politics, seldom read a newspaper, and listened only to popular music on the radio now began to argue in every corner of the country and to follow Hungarian and international political events. The public had become politicized, which meant that any imminent election was going to attract a high turnout.[6]

What lay behind this feverish, agitated mood? It cannot be explained adequately in terms of changes in the economy or standards of living. The Depression had lifted from the Hungarian economy, and some signs of improvement and recovery were apparent. Industrial recovery did not lead automatically to higher wages, which explains the strikes, but not the clear shift to the right in other parts of society (even in sections of the working class). It seems clear that a movement to the right on a societal scale began in 1937 and was strongest in 1938–1939, after which it eased and showed signs of decline.

Apart from the social issues mentioned several times, the explanation presumably concerned mainly the political and intellectual milieu. This was a political system in which the governing party could control the majority of the electorate by administrative means, but whole social groups remained largely unrepresented. They saw the maneuvers by which the governing party in 1935 ensured that the Smallholders, representing the rural voters, received minimal representation in Parliament, without the landowners in the governing party making any real compromise on the land question. Nor was there separate representation for the bourgeoisie, the bourgeois intelligentsia, or the petite bourgeoisie, as seen before. Their interests were represented by the traditional parliamentary parties rhetorically, but not in practice. Legal and illegal restrictions, incidentally, left it impossible to establish how many Social Democratic voters there would be if this party's supporters were able to express their views and the party itself to organize freely. One great impetus behind the social movements of 1937–1939 certainly came from groups who had livelihood grievances but were squeezed out of politics, seeking ways of expressing their views after all. Since the old structure gave them no chance of doing so, they hoped to find ways in the new parties and movements. That may at least partly explain why extremist parties and movements in the provinces contained members of all these strata: petit-bourgeois, intellectuals, peasants and workers.

This was made all the easier because most of the far-right radical groups came forward with a strong welfare policy and laid
great emphasis on representing "the people," especially the poor. It
has been seen that this was by no means a Hungarian invention, as
social promises were integral to early fascism as well,[7] and the Nazi
propagandists before the party came to power likewise came up
with welfare plans and proposals, in contradiction to Hitler.[8] This
strand only had to be adapted, which is what happened in slogan
terms, although in a rather cautious, muted way. But it was not hard
for the groups concerned to be persuaded that the existing government and system did nothing for them, and what official representatives they had were useless at promoting their interests.

One driving force for the far right was the national criterion on
the new international stage created by Germany's foreign policy
successes. There is no way to establish how deeply Hungarian society felt the breakneck succession of events. But it can safely be
assumed that no class or stratum was left unaffected: Hungary's
present grievances were ceaselessly reiterated in official and unofficial propaganda, and there was a mental scar left by a line of
injustices running back several centuries. The national principle
took various forms under various conditions, but those conditions
never failed to emphasize the fact that there was an inseparable link
between national interest and the welfare and very existence of the
individual. This was a period when it was easy to cite national criteria anywhere in the world, but easier than ever in Hungary, where
the idea rested on long, cogent, deeply felt traditions.[9]

Trianon had made the territorial question central to the idea of
nation, and there was not a party or school of thought that was able
to ignore it in that period. They differed only in the scale of the cor-
rection that they envisaged and the path that they proposed to take
towards it. In government policy, the concept of "optimal" revision
that developed towards the end of the 1920s gave way in the
Gömbös period to a formula of revision on a tripartite ethnic basis.

The Gömbös government refused to abandon this idea, despite all German objections and inducements to do so, believing that German reluctance could be offset to some extent by putative Italian support. Not even the global weakening of Italian influence made this entirely unrealistic in relation to Yugoslavia up to 1937, as the wish to dismember Yugoslavia was a hardline position in Italian foreign policy.[10] It soon emerged how little basis there was for expecting Italian support and counteraction. It will be seen shortly that the Hungarian government was faced in the autumn of 1937 with a question for which it was unprepared, although it had long been expecting it. The dilemma recurred in the summer of 1938, in a way far more dramatic in its form and outcome.

The idea of national indemnity had been handled very gingerly by Hungarian governments so far, including the Darányi government. It wanted to obtain it without one-sided commitments or major conflicts, not least because the country was quite unprepared for war. But that approach provoked impetuous criticism of the government, from groups ranging from the far right to the governing party's right wing, including unconditionally pro-German groups in the national socialist parties, and the military elite, dazzled by German victories and successes in military organization. Those heterogeneous groups agreed in seeing the government as incompetent in handling the territorial question and in calling for immediate and complete alignment with German policy.

However, they were opposed strongly by much of the economic elite and a sizable proportion of the upper middle classes, just as they had been under the Gömbös government. These strata found close or more distant allies on the left, and from time to time, among Catholic strands of opinion. So the political elite—although actually indifferent in the matter, due to or irrespective of Darányi—became hysterical. Respect for the governing party and the government was shaken. Disregarding outward signs and the widely held official image, it is questionable also what changes began in the regent's reputation in those years, as anti-Horthy leaflets started to appear from the far right and he and his family were denounced in officers' circles.[11]

So Darányi, having represented and emanated calm, found himself in the midst of a hornets' nest. He lacked the prestige or talent to consolidate the situation. The government tried to smooth matters over by implementing or continuing social measures accepted earlier by Gömbös and by introducing amendments to the constitution. Bills were introduced to widen the powers of the upper house and of the regent, and to reform the franchise. Increasing the powers of the upper house was intended mainly to curb the influence of the far right: it had not been radicalized like the lower house and was protected from being so by its legally defined composition. Now the upper house was to gain a virtual power of veto, as no bill could come before the regent without its endorsement, and where the upper and lower houses voted differently, the matter had to be decided by a secret vote in a joint session. After all that, the regent was to be able to return twice to the legislature for reconsideration any legislation of which he disapproved. It is hard to imagine more forceful curbs and control than that. Yet subsequent events would show that fatal decisions could be taken irrespective of Parliament and outside it, at least amidst restrictions of another kind on parliamentary activity.

The bill on the upper house aroused little controversy, but one term in the bill widening the regent's powers caused sharp debate about the law of succession, since many saw the bill as an attempt to establish a Horthy dynasty, which may not have been far from the truth. The idea was opposed not only by legitimists, but by some monarchists who sought to keep a free hand in the matter, and by left-wingers advocating some system of presidents elected at regular intervals. Further repugnance arose out of legends about Horthy's elder son, István, who was said to be a skirt-chaser and fond of the bottle, which even sympathizers failed to deny with enough vigor and authority.[12] Whatever the truth was, the rumors damaged István Horthy's reputation and chances and caused difficulties in getting the bill passed. In the end, the opposition laid aside their concerns, mainly because it seemed advisable in anxious and uncertain times to ensure continuity in the head of state; in this at least they were absolutely right, for no move of any kind was made in 1920 to restrict the regent's period of office or regulate succession to it. This could have been justified at the time, when the institution was assumed to be temporary and the monarchy was being retained in theory, in the hope of an eventual solution. But 17 years had passed with no hope of filling the throne or any other possible solution emerging.[13] It was time to act, and giving the right of succession to the regent was the only move that could be envisaged.

The franchise bill introduced early in 1938 had been drafted in the Gömbös period, but received its final form under Darányi. Its two prominent features were that it abolished open voting, while narrowing the franchise. According to the calculations known, some 250,000–300,000 people (potentially or actually) lost the right to vote.[14] The act differed mainly in requiring six years' local residence instead of two and setting the minimum voting age at 26 or 30, for a list or an individual seat respectively. There had been debate on the matter over several years, in which the Social Democrats (and the far right, incidentally) sought universal franchise and the conservatives attacked the principle of secret voting. In the end, a majority emerged on this question as well. The conservatives reluctantly accepted the franchise restrictions as sufficient to ensure that neither the left nor the right could pose a serious danger to political stability, while the left coaxed itself into thinking that secrecy would be an initial step towards eventual universal franchise. Both sides were deeply mistaken.

What has been said so far shows clearly that the country contained a large number of groups, schools and individuals who opposed the efforts of the far right for various reasons and were prepared to combat it. But the divisions between these groups were too deep to allow them to cooperate. The divisions concerned, for instance, the form of state (succession of a Habsburg, free choice of king, or republic), religious affiliations (Catholic, Reformed, atheist), suspicion of communists, and treatment of the national question in principle and practice, to name only the main ones. There was also a sharp division over the land question. This was seen as a matter of life and death by the conservative great landowners, who would not and could not yield an inch over their social principles, dating back a thousand years, their way of life and their principles of state.

Despite every effort of the Social Democratic Party and the presence in it of some open-minded thinkers,[15] it was unable to escape from the specters of the past, the perils of the present and the fear of losing legality. There was no escape from its ideological (social and political) quarantine. Meanwhile, the Communist Party had descended into deep crisis, at a time when the 1935 congress of the Comintern had set it the task of organizing a popular front against fascism. Its previous leadership, based in Moscow, had been dismissed in favor of a new group based in Prague, but this had no contact with the members in Hungary, not least because Moscow had dissolved the domestic leadership as well, and thus an almost completely fresh start had to be made. Thereafter, the activists of the Hungarian Party of Communists gathered more often in Spain than in Hungary.[16] Practically nobody was in touch with those in Budapest who actually set about renewal and formation of a broad popular front, still under conditions of illegality. Not even the leaders of the Social Democrats were, even though the party was divided into factions, yet nobody could argue seriously, after the experiences of 1919, for linking up with the communists. Eventually the party got as far as opening up its mass organizations to communists, mainly to young people.[17] No move towards an agreement between the two parties was made, for fear that this would endanger the Social Democrats' status of legality. Nor was there much chance of institutionalized Social Democratic–bourgeois liberal cooperation developing, partly because the Social Democrats justifiably did not consider the latter to be an effective force, and partly because the liberals feared that the Social Democrats would become infected with left-wing ideas.

There were similarly stubborn differences between the conservatives opposed to fascist dictatorship and the Social Democratic–liberal bourgeois camp, involving interests and perceptions of interest, and mutual antipathy and distrust. Such traditions dating back several decades could not be overcome all of a sudden. The gulf between employee and employer, landlord and peasant, gentleman and "non-gentleman" gaped socially as well as politically. It was a decisive feature of mentality and culture that not even the most impartial political leader could overcome. This feature, incidentally, gave greater scope to the far right, especially the Arrow-Cross Party, in that their leaders set out to address all strata of society and give the impression that they alone could transcend the conditions and began a force for national integration.

The conditions in politics and public life left little scope for the initiatives by writers, which began with the *népi* writers mentioned earlier. The distinguishing mark of this school was the fact that its members clearly entered the political arena, even though the members of the group differed widely in their political beliefs. The group included writers and poets of varying talent (Gyula Illyés, László Németh, Péter Veres and István Sinka) and scholarly men (Imre Kovács and Ferenc Erdei) who devoted themselves primarily to sociographic writings. It has been seen that some of them noticed Gömbös's plans for reform, although the episode did not last long. On seeing the organization under way on the far right, many others were induced to build lines of defense. This led to the publication on March 15, 1938, of a program of 12 points, covering land reform and also assertions against big business, while on

the question of territorial revision they essentially supported an ethnic basis, which meant self-determination based on plebiscite.

The rural radicalism of the group known as the March Front
seemed so dangerous to the government that it acted almost at once
to ban its journal *Válasz*. (Proceedings were taken against Illyés,
Géza Féja and Imre Kovács.) Yet the writers' remarks had no effect
on the parties. The Smallholders saw no need for a competitor, and
the Social Democrats were still indifferent to the peasantry's problems, despite the 1930 agricultural program, and nursed some anti-
intellectual resentment, which probably had to do with the social
insensitivity found in much of the intelligentsia. The conservatives
found the 12 points sufficiently alarming to endorse the government's action against the group, while the liberal bourgeois and
intellectual camp met the initiative with litigation and anger.
Culturally, the 1930s were marked by a *népi–urbánus* ("popular/
urban") divide. Despite all the ramifications and fine detail, this
boiled down to urban, Western European, and partly Jewish (or presumably Jewish-influenced) literature being opposed by another
strand that rated itself as the one true indigenous culture, drawn
from the Hungarian people. This underlying *népi* stance influenced
how Hungarian history was interpreted (*kuruc* versus *labanc*),[18]
what "Hungarian" was considered to mean, how the Jewish question was perceived, and so on. But the *népi* writers themselves were
not unanimous about these details, which soon caused the group to
break up. Early in 1939, some of them (Erdei, Péter Veres, and so
on) would establish the National Peasants' Party and others (Illyés
and Németh) would continue the struggle as individuals, but some
drew close to the far right. Many others became thoroughly isolated.

This was the seething political and intellectual stage on which
a hesitant Darányi government stood, initially with some success,
and faced two successive challenges. The first was Germany's
diplomatic and military plans for Austria, the second a strident
advance by the Szálasi camp.

Despite denials by historians, one reason why Darányi fell is still thought to be the fact that he committed himself to Hitler over Czechoslovakia. This view is unsupported by published sources, where it appears that no changes in the earlier underlying principles of foreign policy were made in government circles before the autumn of 1938. This is corroborated by the fact that the post of foreign minister was still held by Kálmán Kánya,[19] who was not known to shift his position easily, and also by Darányi's decided efforts to better Anglo-Hungarian relations and consolidate those with France, and finally by several months of fine tactical efforts to shake the unity of the Little Entente. These need not be considered in detail. But it must be seen that there would have been no sense in such efforts if the heads of Hungarian diplomacy had had the faintest idea of Germany's imminent plans. The Hungarian government would never have continued to bargain with the Little Entente if it had seen the least chance of Germany making an early move against Czechoslovakia, the country that Hungary sought to isolate, or expected that it could approach or force to agree to some form of revision, in 1938. Such efforts against the Little Entente would have been superfluous if the Czechoslovak question had been elucidated by the Germans in 1937 or if some encouraging conclusions could have been drawn at that time.

But these matters were far from clarified when a Hungarian government delegation under Darányi held talks in Berlin in November 1937. In fact, by contrast with the erroneous assumption just mentioned, the Czechoslovak question was not essentially discussed at all. The Germans were primarily concerned with making sure that the Hungarian government was not under some kind of obligation to protect Austria's independence. In fact it wanted to squeeze out a statement raising no objection to the *Anschluss*, regardless of how it was carried out. This statement was freely given, as the Hungarian Foreign Ministry had considered for years that the *Anschluss* was inevitable. Hungary's representatives may have defended the Austrian government from German accusations, but they stated that Hungary had no commitments over the Austrian issue. The conclusion that could be drawn from this multiple mention of the Austrian question, always from the same direction, was that the *Anschluss* would soon be on the agenda, but none of the talks pointed to the Germans wanting to attack Czechoslovakia in the foreseeable future. Goering was primarily concerned with convincing Foreign Minister Kánya that Hungary had to reach agreement with Yugoslavia, because that was the only way to forestall support for Prague in a case of Hungarian–Czechoslovak conflict. The Czechoslovak question itself was only touched upon in outline, almost theoretically and incidentally. According to Kánya's notes, Goering described the partition of Czechoslovakia as inevitable, but he added that this could only happen within the framework of "a larger war." Still less plain was Hitler's comment on the matter. All that he did was to recommend the Hungarian government not to "dissipate its policy in various directions," but to concentrate its efforts against Czechoslovakia. That was nothing new, as Nazi circles and German Foreign Ministry officials had been saying the same for years.[20]

There was no "agreement in principle" in November 1937 between the Darányi government and the Germans over a joint military move against Czechoslovakia. In fact no pact of any kind was reached, and the Hungarian delegation was not informed of Germany's plan. Only one statement of importance to Hungary was heard. The foreign minister replied to Hitler that Hungary would follow precisely the policy desired, and the Germans need lose no sleep over the articles about revision that appeared in the newspapers. This airily appended comment by Kánya consigned revision almost to parentheses. That, if you like, was the "agreement in principle." But it is probable that Kánya attached no practical importance to this off-the-cuff remark, intended simply as momentary reassurance for Hitler. He was more concerned to convey the impression that the Germans need have no fear of any unguarded saber-rattling or conflict provocation by Hungary. That is supported by the following sentence in the minutes taken by Otto Meissner, head of the Presidential Chancellery: "At the end of the conference, Kánya emphasized again the point that despite various rumors, Hungary did not in the least intend to assert its revision demands by force of arms and thereby precipitate war in Europe." This sentence supports what has been said: that Czechoslovakia did not constitute in any sense an object of Hungarian–German agreement in November 1937, and still less was there any commitment by Hungary to attack Czechoslovakia. So the bargaining and wrangling with the Little Entente continued.

Piecing the Berlin talks together also sheds new light on the subsequent history of the Darányi government. Darányi can no longer be accused of making excessive unilateral commitments to Germany—he had undertaken practically nothing. Those viewing the remarks about the *Anschluss* as such might note at most that Bethlen's idea of "sending in a bill" had been dropped, but it is unlikely that anybody could think seriously and rationally of billing the Germans in 1937.

What Budapest learnt above all in Berlin was the unexpected knowledge that the *Anschluss* was approaching, which would create a new geopolitical situation. Germany as an immediate neighbor would gain great influence in politics, and its absorption of the Austrian market would have economic effects as well. The direct German pressure would be joined by stronger activity by the far-right groups that Germany encouraged and supported.

There was not long to wait for the latter, which began before the *Anschluss*. Szálasi was serving ten months in prison, but his adjutants and supporters flooded Budapest on New Year's Day with leaflets headed "1938. Szálasi!" Far-right parties big and small held rallies and marches, and became increasingly strident and demanding. The government decided to dissolve the Hungarian National

Socialist Party and Party of National Will, but the prime minister thought it better to negotiate with them. He sought to take the wind out of their sails by reaching some kind of pact with Szálasi, as Bethlen had once with Károly Peyer. The first such tactic was to couple the ban on Szálasi's party with permission for a new Hungarist Movement to be established, which everybody knew to be the old Arrow-Cross Party under a new name. Then in a clearly unthinking move, Darányi contacted Szálasi through intermediaries and agreed that as long as the new Hungarist Movement abided by the constitution, the government would guarantee it seven seats in Parliament, including one for Szálasi himself.[21] The Arrow-Cross gladly accepted the gift and announced that they would confine themselves to constitutional means in their struggle. (Szálasi would have known that Hitler did the same on his release from prison in 1925.)

Szálasi was public enemy No. 1 among opponents of dictatorship, although it is hard to say why, as his party had yet to achieve real success. Perhaps it was the aversion to him in both the conservative and the left-wing camps, and even among the general public, who saw him as abnormal yet effective, and so as more dangerous than others.[22] The Arrow-Cross, at the peak of its influence, may have had 300,000–400,000 followers, as Szálasi claimed, but it certainly took 20 percent of votes cast (about half a million out of 2.5 million) in the 1939 elections, although the proportion of firm opponents was certainly high among the 80 percent who did not vote for it. This applied even to the right wing of the National Unity Party, who would hear nothing of keeping company with Szálasi, let alone cooperating with him. One factor apart from personal reasons may have been the fact that the Szálasi group had recruited further down the social scale than "middle-class" careerists thought wise. As for the epithets applied to Szálasi by the general public, they ranged widely, from "Mr. Punch"[23] to "syphilitic madman."

This widespread phobia against Szálasi seems to have been an important factor in Darányi's political demise. Neither the opposition nor the conservative wing of the governing party, nor even its right wing, could forgive him for treating with Szálasi, and so the prime minister remained practically without support. But it is harder to understand why three months should have gone by (the notorious pact was made sometime in February 1938) before Horthy's reproaches prompted Darányi to resign. One consideration may have been the fact that the regent wanted certain matters concluded before a change of government. Nor can it be ruled out that it was a while before the regent felt any firm desire to see Darányi removed, or that some further problem arose of which we know nothing. Whatever the case, Horthy waited for the announcement of the military program, for the turbulence after the *Anschluss* to die down, and for the law on the Jews to be presented to Parliament, before dismissing his prime minister at last.

It has been widely assumed by Hungarian historians that there was a link between announcement of the process of military development known as the Győr program and commitments against Czechoslovakia purportedly made in November 1937. Yet attempts in military circles to promote military development had been going on for some time, and the program was agreed upon in principle before Darányi's visit to Germany. The Berlin talks could not have done more than hasten its implementation by making Hitler's plan for the *Anschluss* more specific. Little is known of the history and condition of the army in that period, but it can be said that there was still hardly any army to talk of. Hungary's embryonic national defense force had faced three relatively large and well-equipped armies. Austria was also weak militarily, but now there was expected on the Austrian frontier an ostensibly friendly power with the biggest, best-equipped, and most modern army in Europe. And all the signs pointed to imminent international turmoil, meaning that the military program seemed apposite, and nobody at the time raised any objection in principle.

This activated people in military circles, or rather, they were the ones who brought it up, unsurprisingly, as concern for the army's condition and development is among the duties of its commanders. But the Hungarian staff went much further. One group of military elite had raised the matter of expanding and modernizing the army earlier and begun a resolute campaign to achieve it. Jenő Rátz, chief of General Staff since September 1936, drew up a plan in 1937 based on spending 1,700,000 *pengő*, which Minister of Defense Vilmos Rőder considered to be exorbitant. Stronger objections still came from Minister of Finance Tihamér Fabinyi and the big business group. There ensued a long period of wrangling, punctuated by staff memoranda. The General Staff began to play politics, with Rátz in one submission advocating land reform, a restructured distribution of national income, and an end to the "preponderance" of Jews, as spiritual preparations for war. Another group even sought to tie the demand for rearmament to a complete state and political overhaul. General Károly Soós submitted to Horthy a memorandum of demands by a far-right group of staff officers. Darányi was accused of ignoring Jewish influence and left-wing Marxist agitation, while denying the far right its freedom to organize. The memorandum proposed suspending constitutional activity and instituting temporary dictatorship by the regent, and looked for measures to restrict the Jews' economic and intellectual influence. This was the first serious sign that the desirable harmony was lacking between the regent and the army High Command and that Horthy's views and political behavior failed to meet elite military expectations. Soós and those for whom he spoke should have known well that Horthy would not grant the kind of dictatorship that they sought.

Finally, Darányi's March 5 Győr program, passed later by Parliament, earmarked 600 million *pengő* for direct military expenditure and 400 more for infrastructural investment, to be carried out over five years. In the end it started in 1939 and took only two years. Greater sums than planned were spent, but World War II experience would show that even these were too little to bring the army and its equipment up to date. The military program began to bring appreciable industrial expansion in 1939, along with initially mild inflation that soon accelerated. (The issue of banknotes doubled between 1938 and 1941 and grew fivefold by 1943.)

There was still no sign then that Horthy was thinking seriously of dismissing Darányi, but the prime minister tendered his resignation on March 9, only a few days after his Győr speech. His intention was simply to replace a few ministers, and the regent allowed him to do so. Apart from some alterations of no political importance, there were two essential changes in the new Darányi cabinet. The finance portfolio went to Lajos Reményi-Schneller, a well-known figure on the far right who was highly pro-German, and Béla Imrédy was appointed "economics minister without portfolio," in which capacity he worked out the detailed financial plans for the military program and prepared the first law on the Jews.

The swing to the right in the new government was sharply apparent when the *Wehrmacht* marched into Austria on March 12–13 and Hitler declared an annexation that everybody knew was in fact an occupation.[24] The so-called Agrarian Group in the governing party turned to the prime minister, calling for a strong statement of dissociation by the party from the far right, especially the Arrow-Cross. Then the regent, for the first time in his life, made a radio announcement on April 3, to quell the anxiety caused by the *Anschluss*,[25] and to condemn far-right incitement. Horthy announced that he was ending political agitation in the army. He failed to do so, but the speech brought some reassurance nevertheless.

By this time the prime minister's position was looking very unstable, but Darányi was still able to present the first law on the Jews to a meeting of the National Unity Party and on April 8 to the lower house of Parliament. There is no known sign or evidence of German inducement to do this, nor even any indication that the

Germans raised the matter, but such a possibility cannot be excluded. It might seem that there would have been consultation with Italian government personnel, as Italy also passed a law on the Jews in 1938, but Italy's ideas were still embryonic when the Hungarian bill was put forward and no documentation of such talks has been found.[26] It can be concluded from our present knowledge that this was an autonomous move by the Hungarian government, probably guided by some idea of keeping ahead of matters—taking the wind out of the sails of the far right—rather than having to face much more ruthless proposals and motives in the future. There were certainly several initiatory documents before the government by early 1938: not only the military memoranda mentioned earlier, but a 1937 one from Béla Imrédy in 1937, when still president of the National Bank, considering how young Hungarians might be given more scope in the country's economy and intellectual life at the expense of the Jews. So it was not fortuitous that Darányi charged Imrédy with drafting the bill.

The government presumably expected that restrictions on Jewish participation would reassure and calm the restless groups in the middle classes, as the law promised better prospects for them in certain professions and types of employment. That was not to be the case. The bill that became law after Darányi's fall defined "Jew" in denominational terms. It did not consider those baptized before 1919 as Jews. Furthermore it set at 20 percent the quota for Jews in the press, in the chambers of lawyers, doctors, and engineers, and in corporate employment outside public service. The law in itself was neither strict nor racial in basis. But it involved discrimination, provided a precedent for further legal restrictions, and offered an immediate basis for anti-Jewish measures that were illegal in a strict sense, but now rendered permissible in spirit. Above all, it made it clear that Jews were "not Hungarians." The Hungarian state had definitively abandoned the idea of ever integrating the Jews.

Many people were aware of the grave legal and ethical conse-quences of the law and how it was judged internationally, and many of them reacted accordingly. There were some who realized its social consequences as well. Not long after the bill was announced, 59 writers, scholars, and artists issued a proclamation about the imminent infringement of human rights. They included the com-posers Béla Bartók and Zoltán Kodály, the painter István Csók, the writers Aladár Schöpflin, Lajos Zilahy, József Darvas and Géza Féja, and many others.

Horthy's radio speech on April 3 opened the last act of the Darányi administration. He had probably decided to make the change by then and was waiting only for a favorable moment for holding discussions about it. His task was made easier as the Bethlen group and the Smallholders had both made moves against Darányi, and 60 members of the upper house were preparing a vote of no confidence, which they only ceased to do when it became clear that the prime minister's fate was sealed in any case.

The regent called the prime minister in on May 10 and over-whelmed him with reproaches, whereupon Darányi tendered his resignation. The news was made public on May 13, along with the fact that the regent had chosen Béla Imrédy to succeed him in the premiership.

Notes

1. Hitler had regularly timed his dangerous measures for Saturday or Sunday to prevent absent politicians from reacting immediately.
2. There were hitches. Minister of War Werner von Blomberg, Foreign Minister Konstantin von Neurath and General Werner Fritsch, com-mander-in-chief of the land forces, all dismissed the plan as rash and premature. All three had to be dispensed with before Hitler could proceed.
3. Otto Erdmannsdorff replaced Hans Georg Mackensen, who became state secretary at the Foreign Ministry, then ambassador in Rome.

4. Little or nothing is known of the party's finances, but Szálasi may have received big business support as well. No modern mass party could have been instituted and mobilized in this way without spending major sums. Nazi centers in Austria are known to have given major support later.
5. They included Jenő Rátz, Károly Soós and Henrik Werth.
6. It is reckoned that about 90 percent of the electorate voted in the 1939 general elections.
7. When he began to organize, Mussolini retained most of the ideas of socialist transformation. Indeed some were lifted out of their context and espoused throughout.
8. This was mainly due to the so-called Nazi left wing led by the Strasser brothers, before the group was expelled by Hitler.
9. However, the average person was even less able to gauge the consequences of satisfying national demands than the elites were.
10. The Italian government changed its Yugoslav policy in 1937, hoping to counteract German influence with a Hungarian–Yugoslav–Italian bloc. After further vacillation, Mussolini began in 1940 to contemplate an attack on Yugoslavia as part of his "parallel war" policy, but dropped the idea in the face of strong German protests. Then he was again prompted by Germany to push for Hungarian–Yugoslav "reconciliation."
11. The regent was attacked mainly through his family members and his circle. It was alleged that his wife was of Jewish origin, that his elder son was an alcoholic, and that his younger son was abnormal.
12. Defenders of István Horthy conceded there were grounds for some of the charges in his conduct as a young man, but said that he had sobered up by then.
13. There were whispers at this time about Otto, son of Charles IV, who was a young man by then, but he lacked close connections with any appreciable political group in the country and nothing came of it.
14. This meant the number of extra people who could have voted if the old law had remained in force.
15. Such as Illés Mónus and Anna Kéthly of the younger generation.
16. The police tried to prevent people leaving for Spain, but the number of Hungarian volunteers fighting on the Republican side there exceeded 1,000, a high proportion of them presumably being exiles.
17. There were communists active in the trade unions and in the National Youth Committee (*Országos Ifjúsági Bizottság, OIB*).

18. *Kuruc* was a term for the armed anti-Habsburg rebels in Royal Hungary in 1671–1711. *Labanc* was a derogatory term for government supporters in the latter part of that period. The terms were revived in the nineteenth century as political labels.

19. Kánya had started his career in Vienna and originally had excellent German connections, and thus he was long thought in Western Europe to be Germany's man in Budapest. But in the 1930s he became a curb on German relations, not a force behind them, as the Germans soon realized.

20. German foreign policy and Hitler himself were probably counting on longer-term cooperation with Yugoslavia, whose conduct while the *Anschluss* occurred was especially important. So it was also important that Belgrade should not be irritated by Hungary's policy.

21. The parties often changed their names, but none so often as the Arrow-Cross

22. Szálasi was never declared clinically unstable (for if so he could not have been sentenced to death for his crimes), but his statements and behavior point to an abnormal, paranoid personality.

23. *Paprikajancsi.*

24. The reason for the invasion was precisely the fact that Hitler feared the outcome of an independence referendum called by the Austrian chancellor.

25. Disquiet was increased when the German government only confirmed its recognition of the Austro-Hungarian border after several Hungarian requests, well after it had done so for Italy, Yugoslavia and Switzerland. The reason for the omission is not known.

26. Mussolini was still denying in February that his government had anything of the kind in mind. The Jewish question was then studied by a body of scientists, whose manifesto did not appear until July. Then the Fascist Grand Council joined in and the law was passed in the autumn of 1938.

3. Béla Imrédy and Territorial Revision

Béla Imrédy, who succeeded as Hungary's head of government, was an excellent, highly qualified financier of ascetic appearance.[1] Politically, however, this "banking boy" was less of a manager than a fanatical careerist.[2] But unlike other great careerists in that period, he had a poor ability to analyze situations and lacked strong tactical, manipulating instincts.

Some studies have suggested that there was a radical change in Imrédy's life and political career early in September, after some months of presenting himself as a respectable, reliable prime minister. But this assumption of a trauma raises some questions. There is doubt about the depth of the change, or, to put it another way, about the relations between continuity and change, and about the point when the latter occurred. It seems likely that the change in domestic policy was not drastic, and it is almost certain that it occurred not in September, but after the Munich conference, during October and November. There certainly were domestic political consequences of that reassessment in foreign policy, but Imrédy's convictions had deeper and more permanent roots as well.

Those who drew from Imrédy's continued international financial ties general conclusions about an Anglophile policy and consequent respect for constitutionality seem to have been mistaken from the outset. It was mentioned earlier that Imrédy's anti-Semitism had materialized in 1937, when he acted as an initiator and drafter of policy. As prime minister, he was mainly occupied in May–September 1938 with continuing the program of social legislation, bringing in measures to preserve public order, and curbing Arrow-Cross rowdyism. Meanwhile, the period was dominated in Budapest by the 34th International Eucharistic Congress and the Year of St. Stephen,[3] with the celebrations culminating on his feast day in August.

The social measures were by no means at odds with the principles that Imrédy later revealed. They were integral to them, and to the concept of a far right-wing single-party system. The measures to preserve order—tougher political sentencing and Ministry of the Interior permits for new associations and parties—were aimed mainly at the Arrow-Cross and other national socialist organizations, but remained an essential part of Imrédy's later policies. Neither then nor later did he want to be subordinate to the Arrow-Cross or ally himself with them. (He later made concessions in this regard.) His idea was to break up the Arrow-Cross party and win over its members or some of them. Two other measures—his ban on public employees joining extremist parties (including both the Arrow-Cross and the Social Democrats) and his press law—hit both left and right, which again tied in closely with his plans, which he later articulated more clearly. The last measure brought in censorship and the closure of 400 newspapers of varying importance.

None of these moves aroused antipathy among conservatives. Nor was much protest at the pressure on the Arrow-Cross heard in Parliament, from the far-right benches of the governing party, where the prime minister's view of this was largely shared, and the aim was for far-right interests to be asserted in Parliament, not a free hand given to the Arrow-Cross. There was relative quiet from the left, pleased to see the Arrow-Cross curbed and perhaps hoping that it implied a general rejection and restriction of the far right.

Any suspicion of Imrédy's plans was masked for the time being by the great celebrations, which also held the prime minister back from provoking strong political debates. Imrédy received his appointment on May 13, 1938, and the Eucharistic Congress (a solemn international Catholic assembly to celebrate the sacrament) opened on May 25[4] in the presence of numerous clerical and lay dignitaries. Pope Pius XI was represented by Cardinal Eugenio Pacelli.[5] The event was an opportunity to enhance the reputation of the country, and to bring the Catholic prime minister to the fore, as no occasion was given for the Protestant head of state to take part. Hungary presented itself as a reliable, faithful Catholic country, although its Parliament was debating and accepting the first law on the Jews at that time. Here it has to be noted that the Pope's was the one voice heard to criticize Italy's similar law on the Jews introduced a few days later, although the voice was not a loud one; no such gesture came from the Catholic Church in Hungary.

The act on "ensuring more effectively the balance of social and economic life" was not opposed in the lower house only by the left-wing opposition (Károly Rassay, Gyula Peidl and Anna Kéthly) and the Jewish members. Statements against it were also heard from some liberal aristocrats (György Apponyi and György Széchenyi) and also from the legitimist Gusztáv Gratz. The opponents in the upper house included István Bethlen, Gyula Kornis and the Evangelical Bishop Sándor Raffay. The act did not provoke much resistance among Jews, who saw it in many cases as the least of evils and trusted that matters would end there, as leading figures in the Hungarian state had said. In fact the Imrédy government began revising the act almost immediately, as the prime minister did not consider it to be effective enough.

A further distraction from the country's domestic political tensions and curb on the prime minister's radical plans was provided by the ceremonies to mark the 900th anniversary of the death of Stephen, Hungary's founder saint-king, with a large part reserved for the hierarchy of the Catholic Church. This received strong recompense from the two religious events, after almost two decades of failing to be reconciled to the Reformed head of state and successive Reformed prime ministers. Given an atmosphere of peace, order and devotion, it seemed sacrilegious to suspect that the practicing Catholic prime minister could be considering any kind of coup. The scene and mood in Budapest in the spring and summer of 1938 were such as the historian Gyula Szekfű might have ordered to confirm the views that he had developed of "Hungarian neo-Baroque." But that neo-Baroque had already been abandoned by many in Parliament and the extra-parliamentary far right. Nevertheless, the celebrations were undisturbed by any militant marches or breaches of the peace by men wearing uniforms, badges or armbands. It was the calm before the storm in Budapest.

There were extreme right-wing views of many kinds in Hungary, of which Imrédy's were among those compatible with religious conviction. It was rare for such a wide range of far-right views as Hungary's to develop.[6] The 1930s in Hungary had seen a revival of the commandos—MOVE and ÉME men—of whom some sought to foment a secret military conspiracy. It has also been seen that some of the military elite sought military dictatorship. Parties were formed after the Italian or the National Socialist pattern, with great social variation among their leaders, some being aristocrats, some active or retired army officers, and some intellectuals. People who had risen from below were only found in the second and third ranks.

But the numerous significant far-right attempts in the country arose for the time being not as actions by movements or parties, but as measures introduced by the governing party. By spreading and reorganizing the one unified state party, Gömbös wanted to achieve a great national unity, into which the various insignificant little extremist parties would be absorbed. His ideas focused on the Italian Fascist structure of state,[7] and his planned corporate system was aligned to this, while his social basis lay in the "middle" middle class. The signs seem to indicate that Kálmán Darányi had no rounded concept, and despite the shift to the right at the end of his administration, his deeds were almost certainly done out of political opportunism, not principle. The case was quite different with Imrédy, who seems to have had decided goals, but it remained unknown and unclear for him how to approach them. His concept resembled Gömbös's, but it was not identical to it.

Like Gömbös, Imrédy wanted one great party to embrace the nation, rather as António Salazar in Portugal and Engelbert Dollfuss in Austria did. This he saw as the starting point for a broad program of welfare measures and for the corporatism that he associated with it, although his plan began differently from Gömbös's. The idea of social welfare as needful protection for society from extremes was linked with the papal bulls *Rerum novarum...* of 1891 and *Quadragesimo anno...* of 1931, which fitted well with Imrédy's Catholicism. As with Salazar, Othmar Spann, and his successor Dollfuss, Imrédy tied this to corporate ideas that harmonized with his religious beliefs. That was not so with the Jewish question. The prime minister's anti-Semitism seemed initially to be associated closely with efforts to cure the ills of Hungarian society: some relegation of religious Jews so as to open up the way for larger numbers of Hungarians. But rapid radicalization ensued, to an extent that ought normally to have caused Imrédy a crisis of conscience, as his beliefs could no longer be reconciled with the Vatican's position or the spirit of Catholicism in general.[8]

Before Imrédy could make much of a start on his party organizing or the rest of his program, he had some duties to perform abroad. It was proper for him to present himself in Rome and Berlin. The German government had been pressing for the latter for some time. The Hungarian delegation returned from Italy with the impression that Italian support had weakened, not strengthened. Mussolini and Foreign Minister Ciano clearly had a serious interest only in the prospect of rapprochement and agreement with Yugoslavia and in having Hungary accomplish the same.[9] But the Hungarian government was still not prepared to go along with that without receiving something substantial in exchange.

A government delegation led by the prime minister arrived in Germany on August 22, on the same day that agreement was reached at Bled between Hungary and the Little Entente countries, whereby Hungary would renounce the use of force against its neighbors in return for recognition of its equal right to rearm. Hungary made ratification conditional on separate agreements with each country on measures to improve conditions for its respective Hungarian minority, which left Hungary's hands fairly free.

But the real nature of the pact made after months of careful diplomacy, was not immediately apparent. Still less was Hungary's secret aim: not reconciliation, as some have thought, but continued efforts to drive a wedge into the Little Entente in some way, which was seen as the first and foremost condition for every subsequent Hungarian move. This was not appreciated by the international or the Hungarian left-wing press, which saw Bled as a stabilizing factor. Nor did the Germans grasp it, or seem as if they had. The talks with Germany went off at an unfortunate tangent, with unpleasant questions or even accusations heard, as the Hungarian team, especially Foreign Minister Kálmán Kánya, tried to ignore Bled or play it down.

The atmosphere became tenser still when Germany announced its imminent action against Czechoslovakia and expected the Hungarian government to offer to participate straight away. It seemed highly important to Germany's politicians and military commanders in 1938 that Poland and Hungary should participate actively in the moves against Czechoslovakia, because this concerned a military attack, with no prospect of a negotiated solution on the horizon.[10] Instead of acquiescence, the Germans heard from the Hungarians the view that their participation (and actually the strike itself) was not timely, partly because of the risk of French and Russian intervention,[11] partly because Hungary had no guarantee that Yugoslavia and Romania would not attack from behind, and finally because the army was still unprepared for combat.

This was the first reaction to the German proposal, and the response was uniform, from the regent to the foreign minister. That behavior obviously matched the spirit of the foreign policy hitherto. The Hungarians seem to have been expecting a further lengthy period of preparations. Just as their delegation had been unprepared for the imminence of the *Anschluss* in November 1937, so it was caught unawares now by the Czechoslovak affair. Had that not been so, there would have been no point in negotiating with the Little Entente or signing the Bled agreement, a Hungarian masterstroke that was now seen as quite unnecessary, when it was no longer a matter of isolating Czechoslovakia, but of conniving in a military attack on it. Hitler had full confidence that neither France nor Russia, nor Britain either, would make a move over Czechoslovakia. As for Yugoslavia, the Hungarians, Hitler had been advising for years, only had to make a gesture to ensure neutrality, the required gesture being recognition of Yugoslavia's borders.

Although the Germans delivered all the planned pageantry of the visit, from the parade of ships at Kiel to the grand receptions, the atmosphere became increasingly tense, even frosty. The Hungarian delegation probably held consultations during the visit and reassessed the situation in the light of new information. It is hard to imagine that Kánya (with whom Hitler was so angry that he would not talk to him) had not consulted his prime minister before requesting another meeting with Foreign Minister Ribbentrop without consulting his prime minister and issuing a statement in a quite new tone. During the events of the 25th, Kánya announced, at least according to the German minutes, that Hungary stood better militarily than he had suggested before, and so it could take part in the action on October 1. This was a huge concession, resulting from a swift review of the situation and an intention of retaining German goodwill. The announcement appears to mark a radical change in the Hungarian position, and if it really was, it should have elicited cries of joy from the Germans. But nothing of the kind ensued. The Nazi anger against Kánya was not assuaged in the least. The minutes say that Ribbentrop did not even react to the crucial Hungarian announcement. The Germans continued to take offense to the end and could not reproach the Hungarians enough with their cowardice and egoism. On top of it all, the Hungarian government, at further negotiations in September, picked up its argument where it had left it off on August 22–24. In the light of all this, it must be assumed that something is missing from the Weizsäcker minutes, probably the conditions that Kánya attached to Hungarian participation in the attack on Czechoslovakia. Without some such event, the story makes no sense, and neither do the developments that followed this series of negotiations. Whatever the case, the Germans concluded the talks by stating that the Hungarians were seeking to revise their borders without making any sacrifice, or as one or other of them put it, they wanted to sit down to the meal without helping to cook it. That was a message that Hungarian politicians would have plenty of chances to hear in the future.

The prime minister did not abandon Hungary's caution in foreign policy, as will be seen from the talks in September. But he began to forsake the wait-and-see line in domestic policy. He found posts for several people close to him personally and started a publicity campaign for the program that he had announced earlier, which incidentally contained popular, acceptable items in the main. Only after a speech in Kaposvár on September 4 did the general public begin to sense that Imrédy might have a still hidden agenda. He could not be said to have laid his cards on the table in Kaposvár, but he divulged an ambition to carry out a "miraculous revolution," in which he would delve beneath the surface to the roots. The foreign influence on this statement—from Italy and Germany—can probably be sensed only insofar as the "great achievements" seen there gave grounds for Imrédy's conviction, his faith in himself and his concept, by seeming to show that he was following the right road. He may also have been encouraged by them to speed up implementation of his plans, but little more can be said, not least because Imrédy was an intellectual, demanding of himself that he integrate his views at any time into the intellectual capital that he had built up.

However, there are technical and political conditions required before a specific plan can be carried out, and the prime minister had to wait for some to be met. The technical conditions were under way, in terms of legislation, and of bypassing political parties and the parliamentary system with a suitable mass movement. But he could hardly expect requisite political conditions to emerge from the existing framework.

There matters stalled for a time, as the Czechoslovak question reached an acute stage in which it had to take priority. After the meeting between the British prime minister, Neville Chamberlain, and Hitler at Berchtesgaden on September 17, the Hungarian government intimated through several channels that it sought for the Hungarians there the same concessions that Germany had won by international agreement for the German-speaking Sudetenland of Czechoslovakia. On September 20, Imrédy set out for Germany again, accompanied by Kánya, to clarify Hungary's demands and chances of success. However, Hitler proposed that while he was still negotiating sporadically with the British prime minister, Hungary should attack Czechoslovakia, giving the *Wehrmacht* an excuse and occasion to intervene. He did not conceal the fact that such a scenario would lead to the complete breakup of Czechoslovakia, so that Hungary might obtain the whole of the northern territory that it had lost: Slovakia and Subcarpathia (Kárpátalja and Podkarpatská Rus). Despite that enticement, Imrédy refused. With British, French and Russian behavior still uncertain and its southern and eastern borders still unsecured, Hungary would not take a risk in which there was not even a guarantee that Germany would not leave it in the lurch, to be tried alone for breaching the peace. In other words, Imrédy refused to perform a diplomatic *volte-face* even on his second visit to Germany towards the end of September. There is still no way of telling how much the foreign minister had to do with that and how much the prime minister, but the latter was the one who negotiated with Hitler, who still refused to speak to Kánya.

However, the Hungarian side undertook to put immediate diplomatic pressure on Prague, which it did, making known in Prague, London, Rome and Berlin its claim for the return of Hungarian-inhabited territories, which also showed that despite Hitler's offer, the Hungarian government was keeping to an ethnic revision. (This would soon change.) Hungary's stock in Berlin stood extremely low when the Munich conference began on September 29, which might explain why Hitler did not press for examination or immediate recognition of the Hungarian and Polish claims.[12] This is worth noting, because satisfaction of the Polish and Hungarian claims was certainly in Hitler's interests, as they would have served to weaken the country that he was setting out to fragment. The powers meeting in Munich accepted the Polish and Hungarian claims in principle and designated bilateral negotiations as the method of resolving them, stating that if these had not yielded results within three months, the question would be reconsidered by the representatives of the Four (the United Kingdom, France, Germany and Italy).

The bilateral negotiations naturally reached deadlock, as the Hungarian government insisted on the return of all territory with a majority of Hungarian inhabitants, and the opposite side rejected this. (The maximum Slovak offer was the whole of Csallóköz island.)[13] The French and British governments were not in any hurry to take part in further fragmentation of Czechoslovakia, and Hitler did not insist on their cooperation, and so Berlin and Rome eventually performed the next task under the Munich agreement as the outcome of further Hungarian moves.

But before that happened, the Hungarian government had virtually to plead in Rome, and still more in Berlin. That was about when Imrédy really revised his foreign policy line and demands. He concluded that Germany had become the decisive factor in European events, even if it was not quite sovereign, and if the Hungarian government failed to support Germany's ideas faithfully, it would suffer serious losses and fail to attain its goals. Caution hitherto had meant being satisfied with a partial ethnic solution, instead of Hungary receiving back the whole of Slovakia and Subcarpathia. The combination of German superiority and the Western democracies' weakness at Munich was probably what convinced Imrédy that democracy was more senile and weakened than he had presumed. This strengthened his centralist, étatist intentions, and among others, he could now see foreign policy reasons for expunging liberal and Jewish influence for the sake of the cause, and even such wily old conservatives as Kálmán Kánya. The events to do with Czechoslovakia made these steps look urgent: there was a danger that Hungary might lose all chances of territorial revision by showing indecision about Germany's political demands.

Influenced by Munich, Imrédy became thoroughly radical and also changed gear. He presumably learnt a lesson from the political failure of Gömbös to establish the necessary basis of support for himself. Imrédy did not want to experiment with reorganizing the governing party. Instead he began to attack the existing political structures openly. On October 4, he surprised the government by announcing that he wanted to introduce a general enabling bill in Parliament, allowing government by decree and short-circuiting the parliamentary system. The prime minister's proposal made plain his long-term plans, previously revealed only in hints and leaks. The idea of a general enabling act lent credit to the notion or even confirmed that Imrédy wanted to wind up the parliamentary system and establish a single great organizing force or movement that would embrace the "national" forces—in practice all right-wing forces—in a new party. The constitutional forces made an immediate move. Pál Teleki and Ferenc Keresztes-Fischer protested against Imrédy's proposal immediately at the government meeting, and Teleki raised the alarm with the regent and the conservative group. The resistance began immediately, with the liberals, Smallholders and Social Democrats being joined also by the *Magyar Nemzet*, Sándor Pethő's legitimist paper.

The first sign of foreign policy change came after the Slovak–Hungarian talks had failed, when Imrédy dispatched Darányi to Berlin to seek German help in settling matters, unskilled though he was in diplomatic negotiations. Hitler, at a meeting on October 14, listed several times his reasons for displeasure with the Hungarian government, especially Kánya's behavior. He then stressed repeatedly his view that he did not think the four-power international solution a good one, and ended by his almost throwaway resolve to call for the maximum Czech and minimum Hungarian offers. Then came some blackmail. He demanded of Darányi a statement that Hungary would "henceforth adhere more closely to the Rome–Berlin axis" and asked in a friendly way why Hungary was still a member of the League of Nations. Darányi replied that the government could probably manage a withdrawal, and then, obviously in the light of instructions from Imrédy, he enquired whether it would not be desirable for Hungary to join the anti-Comintern pact. Based on these pleasant prospects, the Führer ordered his foreign minister to inform the Czechs that Germany would guarantee their borders only if a "fair border" were ensured for the Hungarians.

Based on that contract of purchase and sale, German–Italian mediation began, leading to what was termed "arbitration," although the German and Italian governments took part in it almost exclusively, with Ciano arguing with Ribbentrop on behalf of the Hungarians, while the directly interested parties merely peddled their causes or their complaints. Hungary had Italian intervention to thank for the return of Kassa (Košice), Munkács (Mukachevo) and Ungvár (Uzhhorod), while Ribbentrop's objections prevented Pozsony (Bratislava) and Nyitra (Nitra) from being added.[14] The results of the Italian–German deliberations were announced in the Belvedere Palace in Vienna on November 2. Under the First Vienna Award, Hungary regained along the border a 12,400 sq. km band of territory with 1.1 million inhabitants, of whom about 86 percent were Hungarian. Not one Great Power raised any objection to the First Vienna Award, which followed the ethnic divide fairly accurately.

The first great peaceful return of territory, followed by a ceremonial entry of the regent and the Hungarian army, produced
euphoria in wide sections of the Hungarian population, but reactions in the political sphere were more restrained. The left wing had
long espoused the ethnic principle and was quite satisfied with the
government's performance, but Imrédy's own supporters and the
rest of the far right remained dissatisfied. They reproached the government mainly for failing to regain Subcarpathia, and some of the
conservatives agreed with them. It was obviously not possible to
justify a revanchist demand for Subcarpathia on ethnic grounds, but
importance was attached to ownership of it for an assortment of
reasons. Some simply wanted to increase the spoils. For Imrédy it
meant regaining some of the face lost at Munich. The Foreign
Ministry was interested in Subcarpathia on geopolitical and associated foreign policy grounds. There were at least as many in the
Foreign Ministry who feared the prospect of unbridled German
power as there were who looked forward to further German cooperation in revising Hungary's borders. But Germany's apparent policy line and the present constellation of events seemed to leave little
prospect of the latter, while overwhelming German hegemony was
a reality. The faint initial effort to counteract that brought a cautious
reaction from Italy as well. This was the sense behind Rome's
efforts for a time to recommend agreement with Yugoslavia to the
Hungarian government, and for a short while, the Italians toyed
with the idea of extending the cooperation to Poland. That produced
a joint Hungarian–Italian interest in restoring a common
Hungarian–Polish border in Subcarpathia and brought hope of
Italian support for Hungarian action there.

The revisionist success fell far short of what the prime minister needed for his schemes to undermine the constitution. He was
obliged to withdraw his proposal for a general enabling act. But he
does not seem to have learnt from this. He announced at a meeting
of the National Unity Party on November 15 that he wanted to

tighten up the parliamentary standing orders and the law on the Jews that had only just been passed, and that he would start to form a great national right-wing movement that would cover the political spectrum and include all the political parties of the right. The opponents of dictatorship immediately forgot any revisionist merit that the prime minister had won and lined up against Imrédy. This led to a further meeting of the governing party on November 22, where 54 members of Parliament announced that they were leaving the party and were joined in doing so by another eight.[15] That lost Imrédy his parliamentary majority, and on the following day the government was voted down by 115 to 94.

This appeared to show that the legal foundations of parliamentarianism in Hungary were still in existence and viable, but the events that immediately followed the vote showed otherwise. Constitutionally, the regent should have dismissed Imrédy immediately. Instead, he failed to reply to the prime minister's offer of resignation, and then, after long negotiations, persuaded him to stay. Meanwhile, there were demonstrations in support of Imrédy. The regent's actions gave the impression that he had bowed to these, which made a further dent in his reputation.

But there was more to it than the issues of constitutional law and system of government just described. Kánya, the foreign minister, had also tendered his resignation, and whether he stayed or went represented under the circumstances a foreign policy decision for the country and the government to make. Kánya's remaining would mean greater caution and abandoning the strong commitment to Germany that Darányi had more or less promised. It seems, furthermore, that Imrédy's remaining and Kánya's departure were two sides of the same coin. So it can be seen as catastrophic that the need for action against the prime minister was the only common ground found among those opposed to Imrédy. They could not lay aside their differences to the extent necessary for a parliamentary majority behind a coalition government that excluded the far right.

On the other hand, the anti-dictatorship camp was unnerved by the prime minister's survival, which turned their attention also to unconstitutional, extra-parliamentary, politically questionable means of attaining their goals. So Imrédy stayed and Kánya went. The latter was soon succeeded by István Csáky, as Imrédy wished, which brought about a sharp change of foreign policy.

Csáky probably did not like the Nazis at all, but his hasty, unreliable, almost clinically irritable temperament led to a succession of mistakes. Kánya's resignation was made public on November 29 and Csáky was appointed by the regent only on December 10, which showed that there had been problems with finding a successor.[16] The choice could hardly have been worse. Ciano's first impression was of a "conceited little man" who was physically and morally weak, but constantly struck a heroic pose. The Hungarian ambassador in Rome, Frigyes Villani, described him as a man with no scruples "governed by unbalanced, unlimited ambitions." There are no good opinions of Csáky to be found anywhere, in fact. The baneful results of the change of foreign minister began to be felt in January 1939. There cannot be any doubt that Csáky's "line" conformed basically with Imrédy's position and the conclusions that he drew from the "solution" to the Czech crisis and the Western behavior over it. Those were, essentially, that if the democracies were not obstructing Germany's demands, Hungary could and should follow the Germans, which would entail little risk, and would mean that the country would do better than it could by pondering, procrastinating and exercising caution.

During a visit to Berlin on January 16, 1939, Csáky made some unilateral concessions that committed Hungary deeply, but obtained nothing in exchange, not even a promise on Subcarpathia. Csáky promised that Hungary would join the anti-Comintern pact. (This had been announced earlier, but the signing took place only on February 4, 1939. It led to Hungarian–Soviet diplomatic relations being broken off.) He also pledged that Hungary would leave the League of Nations. (It did so in May 1939.)[17] He offered to place economic relations on a basis more favorable to the German side, dangled the prospect of a Hungarian "arms rush," himself raised the Jewish question, and showed willingness to accord "appropriate" treatment to Hungary's German ethnic minority. None of these concessions changed the German government's resolve to cool Hungary's ambitions in Subcarpathia and fend off any initiatives on it. This had been the German position since the autumn of 1938, and like it or not, Ciano had had to endorse it as well, and thus the Hungarian preparations, the organization of irregular forces, and other preparations for an entry into Subcarpathia proved to be futile.[18] What prompted Germany's attitude was resentment by the Nazi leaders at the way in which Hungary had behaved over the Czech crisis. They wanted to chastise Budapest for this, and there was also a more rational desire not to see the imminent German action in Czechoslovakia confused by any Hungarian hastiness or even military action. However, they did not reveal anything of their plans to Csáky in January 1939. Hitler declared at the talks on January 16 that they had to seek "a territorial solution" to the Czech question, and this called for very good military preparation as well, but he did not reveal that the German army had already devised a plan of attack. When Csáky asked about this, coming straight to the point, Ribbentrop gave an evasive answer. Ribbentrop also emphasized the point that there were negotiations in progress with Czechoslovakia and not a single shot should be fired. This, incidentally, was not exceptional behavior by the Germans. Hitler and the German government were not in the habit of reconciling their ideas even with their Axis partner, Italy, let alone with Hungary. In fact it can be stated that no German measure was ever squared with a partner country in time for the latter to react or prepare for it. But when the question of Subcarpathia was resolved quite without warning for Hungary in March 1939, Imrédy could not reap any benefit, as he had been ousted from politics by then.

The disorganization in the opposition was such that the pre-
siding board of the National Unity Party agreed eventually on
December 13 to Imrédy's ideas, which paved the way for the formation of the Hungarian Life Movement.[19] The inauguration took
place in the Vigadó in Budapest on January 6, 1939. The emblem
chosen for of the movement, a golden figure of a miraculous stag
of legend, was an attractive one, and the founders reflected in their
dress not only the ceremonious occasion, but the character of their
social strata: not "gala" Hungarian dress or a military look, but
somber, sober, simple Hungarian attire with black frogging. There
were big draperies and standard-bearers. It was hard to say what the
decorations were trying to imitate, or to discern from Imrédy's
inaugural speech where the movement wanted to go. It was clear
only that the prime minister had a more urgent need than ever for a
movement because it had turned out that he had no party. But if
anybody had thought about the nature of the political base and how
finite it was numerically, they would not even have given Imrédy as
much chance as Gömbös had had a few years earlier. Then there
had still been no Arrow-Cross to mobilize the middle classes (and
others), but by 1938 that party was well on its way to gaining a high
proportion of such people, and had been successful with just the
groups prepared to take a step to the right. But in the very middle
of the middle, where Imrédy could operate, he had little chance of
freeing or utilizing new forces. He was joined only by two tiny
Nazi-type parties led by Sándor Festetics and Fidél Pálffy, which
had no appreciable influence.

The great utterances about development, racial protection and
"one will" to guide the nation were scarcely heeded, and Imrédy
could only fall back on Gömbös's course of using the public administration for his movement.

The main outcome of the formation of the Hungarian Life
Movement was to revive the temporarily discouraged constitutional
group. Its resolve to oust Imrédy was intensified by a hand-grenade

attack made by an Arrow-Cross group on the Dohány utca Synagogue in Budapest on February 3, 1939. Then there was the news of a further law against the Jews that would affect the professions and industry and commerce, and was opposed not only by Jewish big business, but by many Hungarian conservatives and legitimists. The landowners and the Catholic hierarchy also opposed the government's planned land reform, which looked as if it would be more radical than any before.

The prime minister, once almost universally popular, was being attacked from all sides by the beginning of 1939. Strong attacks on the government were heard on January 10, 1939, at a dinner held by some of the opposition (defectors from the National Unity Party, Smallholders and members of the Christian parties), and a steering committee was set up. This met two days later to launch the campaign against Imrédy. A memorandum was swiftly produced, and the group fabricated a great dispute in Parliament on February 13, designed to provoke another vote of no confidence. This was frustrated when the speaker unexpectedly closed the debate, but the government had been within a hair's breath of being voted down again.

Finally, Imrédy was ousted without the need for a vote. There had been rumors for some time that the prime minister's ancestry was not entirely "Aryan." This Imrédy denied, either out of ignorance of his own descent, or confidence that nobody would trace his family far enough. He was mistaken. An aide to the liberal party leader Károly Rassay managed to identify one of Imrédy's great-grandfathers as a Jew. A copy of the document was shown to the regent, who had it checked and then summoned the prime minister, calling on him to resign within 48 hours. This timetable again showed the weakness of Hungary's parliamentary system, and it shed an unfortunate light on the opposition group concerned—one of several that opposed further measures against the Jews. There was something very dubious about opposing discrimination on the one hand while stooping to exploit it on the other. The gambit was superfluous in any case, as Imrédy's political fate was sealed by that time. Yet the constitutional group attained its purpose and the question of government had to be rethought.

Notes

1. His banking connections meant that his appointment was greeted with relief in London and unease in Berlin.
2. His contemporaries were fond of comparing him to Savonarola.
3. Hungary's first king died in 1038 and was canonized in 1083.
4. The originally French initiative became international in 1881 and was held biennially from 1922. It was decided in 1936 to make the next venue Budapest, where preparations began straight away. One factor behind Imrédy's appointment was the desire to have a Catholic head of government for the great Catholic celebration.
5. He was elected pope as Pius XII on March 2, 1939.
6. There was a choice of far-right bodies almost everywhere, but before the far right could gain power, one group had to integrate or outstrip the others, without which there was no fascist or Nazi-type break-through.
7. A delegation to study this was sent out by Bethlen and returned with large amounts of material, although this was mainly consigned to the archives.
8. It must be added that the weak resistance of the Catholic Church to racial anti-Semitism could in no wise excuse an initiative like Imrédy's.
9. Italy's policy towards Yugoslavia in 1937–1941 did more than fluc-tuate. It underwent changes so strong and sudden that they became hard to follow. Yugoslavia came into question as an Italian ally against German advances in the Balkans, but Italy still toyed with notions of attacking and dismembering the country. At this point, the former was to the fore, and could, incidentally, be reconciled with German ideas at that time.
10. It presented itself to Hitler as a strike, not a possibility.
11. Grounds for this in principle were provided by the Franco-Soviet and Czechoslovak–Soviet agreements of 1935.

12. Here the draft was not prepared in advance and the Germans themselves were probably unsure how far they wanted to fulfill such demands.
13. The island is known as Žitný ostrov in Slovak. The negotiating partner was not the Czechoslovak government, but a delegation from Slovakia, which had just gained internal autonomy.
14. German opposition to the transfer of Pozsony suggests that the notion had already been raised in Germany of creating an independent Slovak state, for which it would have been hard to find another capital. But despite the Munich conference, Hitler never for a moment abandoned the idea of dismembering Czechoslovakia completely.
15. It should be noted that Teleki disagreed with this defection, fearing that it would lead to chaos, and he was right in that to some extent.
16. These occurred even though Kánya himself proposed Csáky, whose damaging characteristics he had failed to notice.
17. The Italians had been trying to convince the Hungarian government to do this since 1936, but Kánya had resisted the demand.
18. Preparations began immediately after the First Vienna Award. The task of raising commando forces was taken on by Miklós Kozma at the request of the government. His "Ragged Guard" was formed, but German and Italian protests prevented it from ever being deployed.
19. *Magyar Élet Mozgalom (MÉM)*.

4. The Economy and Society in the 1930s

Most economic gains of the 1920s were lost again in the Depression. Some industries underwent a decline greater than their rise had been, with the consequent accompanying symptoms, of which some details have already been given. All that needs to be recalled here is the fact that the mounting sales problems in agriculture caused not only a decline in grain output and livestock, but also a dramatic technical decline, for instance in the use of tractors and artificial fertilizers, and that in industry, the volume and value of production plunged. For a time it was not possible to offset this by developing foreign trade, as all Hungary's big customers had to cut their imports.

Normalization of the economy began in 1934: as the world-wide recession was reversed, grain prices began to rise. This was also helped through a trade-friendly financial policy by the government and because the German market reopened to Hungarian agricultural goods for the first time since the war. So by 1934, the changes in Germany were decisively influencing the specific ways in which Hungary was recovering from the Depression.

The recovery was accompanied by new monetary and foreign exchange policies that would eventually lead to economic catastrophe. Successive Hungarian governments remained cautious about putting exchange rates and foreign exchange controls to major use in handling the recession, although it was clear that overvaluation of the Hungarian currency was impeding recovery, increasing the trade deficit, adversely affecting domestic prices, and so contributing to unemployment. Meanwhile, the German National Socialist government was making unabashed use of such methods. There was no alternative to the German market for Hungary's agricultural goods, which meant that Hungary and its economy were slowly being lured into a trap.

Germany began in 1934 to make clearing or compensation-trading agreements with several countries. Among these was a compensation-trading agreement with Hungary, although this too has often been called a clearing agreement. What the German–Hungarian agreement meant was that the Germans would buy Hungary's agricultural produce at preferential rates, higher than world market prices, but the Hungarian government agreed to accept payment for them in non-convertible German marks or in industrial goods. This bargain was helped by the fact that Hungary's exports elsewhere were disturbed by the high *pengő* exchange rate, which the government offset with a complex system of surcharges that amounted to a system of export premiums. After all, the convertible currency and foreign exchange to cover imports of raw materials had to be obtained from somewhere. Up to 1939, the National Bank of Hungary and the government insisted that although they were obliged to make concessions to the Germans, they would retain their own decision-making and policy-making capability in other trade relations. But that meant having as many convertible currency relations as possible and minimizing the clearing and compensation-trading agreements reached. This effort met with little success. Clearing and compensation-trading agreements accounted for 66 percent of trade turnover in 1932, but 75 percent by 1935.

Béla Imrédy, as the new president of the National Bank of Hungary in 1935, set out to increase convertible exports and reduce exports to Germany. This plan presupposed rationalizing the premium system and identifying new markets, in which there was little success despite the premiums. The premiums were set at new levels of 50–54 percent for countries possessing convertible currency and 41 percent for those with a clearing agreement, while the rates for Germany and Italy were left open for the time being. However, the demand for convertible currency began to increase further in 1937, as the rate of repayment of earlier debt was agreed upon at international negotiations and such repayment could be made only in convertible currency. In December 1935, the National Bank of Hungary had devalued the German mark in relation to all other currencies. The technical solution used was to raise the premium for convertible currencies to several times the 18 percent premium applied by Hungary to Germany. This Berlin swallowed almost without a word, partly because it was dependent on Hungarian agricultural supplies, and partly because it was still being allowed to pay for the agricultural imports in non-convertible marks or in barter goods, which it could not do in its trade relations with other countries.

The Győr program of investment for the next five years, unveiled by the Darányi government in 1938, managed to produce some economic recovery in the form of rising industrial output and rising consumption, for which more imports of raw materials were required. The necessary goods were arriving from Germany more sparingly and the Hungarian government had to turn to convertible currency markets. Relations with Germany were unsatisfactory in other regards as well, as the Germans had, after the *Anschluss*, abolished the transit concession awarded by the Austrians, and the same thing happened with the Czechs and the Poles in 1939. This all led the National Bank of Hungary to devalue the German mark again, by about 11 percent, in September 1939.

This relative Hungarian independence steadily came to an end as the war progressed. The Germans set mark exchange rates in the occupied countries at whatever rates they wanted. In fact it was up to them whether the national currency could still be used as a means of payment at all, while the small states allied with Germany came under increasing pressure. This pressure increased in Hungary's case because the Germans had obtained the Austrian and Czech markets. Discussion about the mark exchange rate began in Budapest at the end of September 1939, with Lipót Baranyai, the National Bank of Hungary president, still resisting the German demands. This resistance was broken automatically by the success of the *Wehrmacht* in Western Europe in 1940, which blocked access to convertible currency markets. Hungary was entirely at the mercy of the Germans.

The Nazi idea was basically to give the German economy hegemony over the whole area ruled by the Germans and demote the other countries to the position of suppliers. The consequent *Grossraumwirtschaft* would have the mark as its leading currency, with a multinational, centralized clearing system in Berlin. For this, the Germans wanted to revalue the mark, to price it not more than 20 percent less than the US dollar and bring it to parity soon after. This financial solution was taken to be a precondition for the *Grossraum* economy, but the motive was also that revaluing the mark would reduce the volume of compensatory goods to be shipped to other countries, including Hungary. Hungary's negotiators put up bitter resistance, but there was no hope of success after August 1941, when the dollar and pound sterling ceased to be traded in Hungary. The imposed agreement revalued the mark and devalued the *pengő*. By that time, about 70 percent of trade was with Germany and only a tiny fraction with Switzerland and Sweden, the two remaining convertible currency markets. Furthermore, Germany's deliveries and payments fell increasingly far behind Hungary's deliveries, meaning that Germany built up its debt to Hungary.

Hungary's industrial output began to rise steeply after 1934, when the Depression was over. The estimates of annual growth up to 1938 give an aggregate within the range of 6–13 percent, with 13 percent very probably an exaggeration. Two foreign scholars agree on an annual increment of 1.7 percent, making a five-year aggregate of 8.5 percent, which can be accepted as a median. Adding the increases in the post-war period and in the five years after the Depression gives a combined increment of 20–20.5 percent. This is somewhat lower than the performance in the period of Dualism, considerably lower than inter-war figures for the German, British and French economies, similar to those of Austria and Czechoslovakia, and higher than those of Poland, Portugal, Romania and Yugoslavia. Hungary's relative position had worsened since the pre-war period, but it had not dropped out of the European field. Its position can be seen as creditable for a country on the losing side in the war, which had lost vast amounts of territory, raw materials and infrastructure, and remained isolated for several years. 1939 brought a surge of industrial expansion directly tied to the war. This needs separate consideration, not least because it was associated with mounting inflation and indebtedness.

Industry, transportation and commerce were the growth areas in the second half of the 1930s, as they had been in the second half of the 1920s, which meant that agriculture was only the second-largest contributor to national income by the end of the decade. An important factor for heavy industry was the discovery of gas and oil fields at Bükkszék, Lispe and elsewhere. To exploit the Lispe deposits, the Hungarian–American Oil Industry Co. Ltd.[1] was formed, and was able to cover 50 percent of the country's oil needs in 1939. The Germans soon noticed this resource and tried to utilize it for themselves and later expropriate it. The output of natural gas increased rapidly (about fivefold between 1931 and 1939), which attracted the chemical industry. The production of the Hungária Artificial Fertilizer Factory[2] allowed the utilization of artificial fertilizers in Hungarian agriculture to increase again. Meanwhile, bauxite mines opened in several places and the first aluminum smelter went into production in Csepel in 1935. A majority of the stock in some of the bauxite mines was bought by German interests, and so much of the bauxite was delivered there as well for refining.

One billion *pengő*'s worth of modernization covering 10 percent of the Hungarian State Railways network began in 1938, as part of the five-year investment program. Sizable sums were also spent on expanding and modernizing the free port at Csepel and other infrastructural investments, but about 60 percent went on expanding the arms industry. Production began of Hungarian tanks, semi-heavy weaponry, and vehicle tires, and the output of aircraft parts was increased. The investment program led to a change in the statutes of the National Bank of Hungary, abandoning the gold standard and allowing banknotes to be printed as required. This caused the money supply to increase from 466 million to 863 million *pengő* in one year, and rise to almost 2,000 million in 1941, which went beyond any exchange rate adjustment and precipitated rapid inflation.

Another growth area in the second half of the 1930s was that of textiles, not just to meet increasing demand for military uniforms, but to produce fine textiles as well. Products of the Goldberger factory met with success at the 1937 World Exposition in Paris. Mechanical engineering, which had weakened in the 1920s, began to recover. There were good performances especially in tractors, and diesel and electric motors, and the industry's output by value in 1938 was 28 percent higher than in 1913. The expansion in artificial fertilizers, rubber tires and pharmaceuticals benefited the chemical industry. Electronics gained a place on the world market and 75 percent of the radio sets produced went abroad. Although the food industry as a whole stagnated, the canning industry doubled its output and broke onto world markets with Globus-brand products. In fact canning exports increased twelve times over in just a few years, but as Hungary entered the war, exports declined and the significance of the home market increased again. (The biggest customer for canned tomatoes had been the United Kingdom, where sales ceased after war broke out.)

In agriculture, the production area of wheat finally began to decline in favor of corn, potatoes, sugar beet, and so on. Vegetable and fruit production also expanded. The volume of fruit grown increased, and some of it was exported, fresh or in processed form.

Different districts specialized in different fruits, according to the nature of the land: Szabolcs for apples, Kecskemét for apricots, Szatmár for plums, and so forth. Apples were only distilled for liquor on a domestic basis, but the apricot *pálinka* of Kecskemét and the plum spirit of Szatmár became renowned, one admirer of the former being the Prince of Wales, who visited the country. A lot of fresh fruit was exported in that period, with the Nagykőrös district to the fore. There was plenty of vegetable canning as well. Peppers and onions maintained their positions, but the biggest crop was tomatoes, followed by green peas. Hungary in that period was Europe's fourth-largest wine producer. About 90 percent of the annual production of 3–4 million hectoliters was drunk at home, but the best wines of the Tokaj region were exported all over the world. Hungarians were drinking an average of 40 liters of wine each a year, which was probably a European record, although far less beer was drunk than by Germans or Czechs, and a smaller quantity of spirits than by the British or French.

Much attention focused on the land question in the 1930s, a prominent feature of Gömbös's program. There were long debates on land distribution and the relative merits of large and small land-holdings. Trends in the 1930s showed plainly what could have been deduced earlier: large estates had an advantage in fodder grain, corn and livestock, offset by the advantage of smaller holdings in vegetables, fruit and poultry. Whatever the case, there were plenty of advocates of a healthier, more beneficial distribution of land, to various extents and in various forms. Gömbös's 1936 Settlement Act was a disappointment: the mountain had labored and brought forth a mouse. The law called for 420 million ha to be redistributed as tenancies (150,000 *hold*—85,500 ha) and 35,000 freehold small-holdings. This was to be carried out over 25 years, which meant that only 15–16 million ha were involved each year. Not even that pace was managed initially, as only 80 *hold* (46 ha) were redistributed in the first year. This increased in five years to an average of almost 230,000 *hold* (131,000 ha) a year, with 2,500 households receiving a smallholding or a tenancy. The second law on Jews in 1939 obliged about 5,000 Jewish landowners to hand in about 400,000 *hold* (228,000 ha), which provided the basis for an act on small tenancies passed in that year and redistribution of another 100,000 *hold* (57,000 ha), under a plan to be implemented over ten years.

This did nothing for the structure of land ownership other than leave it more fragmented. The only modernization in agriculture was the significant change in product structure. Yields increased over two decades to about 6.5 percent higher than they had averaged before the war, which was an advance, but a much slower one than in the West. The deterioration in livestock farming remained, with the national herds in 1938 still about 15 percent lower than they had been in 1911.

Electrification was resumed in 1935, and 36 percent of the country's communities (71 percent of the population) had electric light by 1939. Supplies of gas spread in the cities, along with the use of gas heaters and cookers, as well as electric water heaters in bathrooms. There was a rapid increase in motorization in the same period, but motorcycles remained the dominant form, as private automobiles and trucks were still only being produced in short runs. Nevertheless, imports increased the number of vehicles in urban areas, although there were still only two private cars per thousand population, which meant that Hungary was ahead only of the Balkan countries and Eastern Europe. There were 3,083 trucks on the road in 1938, 1,217 of them made in Hungary. Aviation was still in its infancy. There were scheduled flights from Budapest to Vienna and to Belgrade, but only a few thousand passengers a year were carried. Planes landed at Budaörs or Mátyásföld, but it had been decided in 1938 to build a new airport at Ferihegy, and work on it soon began. There were regular flights during the war years to other Hungarian cities with airports. These were used by officials and cost the price of a first-class Hungarian State Railways ticket for the same journey. The volume of postal business was increasing rapidly. There were almost 150,000 telephone subscribers in 1940 and some half a million radio subscribers.

Economic recovery and industrial growth were much helped by special state subsidies to some industries. Hungary did not follow the Keynesian model that was gaining ground in Western Europe. The Hungarian state almost exclusively supported small businesses, not employment or consumption. The industries selected were the ones that were holding their ground best throughout the world and had suffered least during the Depression. They included electric power generation, the radio industry, bauxite mining and aluminum making, and the hydrocarbon program. German capital also appeared in Hungarian industry in 1935, initially in heavy industry, arms manufacture, transportation, bauxite mining and, to a lesser extent, the oil industry.

The real spur to growth was the program for military development. Large state financing in 1939–1940 brought a leap in industrial production, and unemployment practically ceased. The main reason for the growth was a jump in the proportion of industry in national income, from 30 to 36 percent from 1938, while that of agriculture sank from 42 to 40 and then to 37 percent, with the tendency still speeding up. But the industry that overtook agriculture was heavily slanted towards arms manufacture, and the army was an important factor in securing employment. Furthermore, Hungary's Czech and Austrian interests had passed into German hands and the arms industry was taking a high share of German investment in Hungary. (Some 20 percent of arms manufacturing was in German hands.)

These economic factors contributed to making Hungary's policy of friendship with Germany relatively popular, with few people pointing to the dangers of dependence and unilateral reliance. As life grew easier, clearly as a result of the new policy towards

Germany, it provided cogent arguments for seeing such a policy as useful or at least for not opposing a pro-German policy. Combined with this was the conviction that German assistance or *de facto* action was the main requirement for Hungary to regain territory and raw materials, and a bigger home market. This precluded for a long time any effective antidote to the orientation towards Germany.

The social changes of the 1930s were shown in sharp relief only in the leading political stratum. There was not a single aristocrat in Gömbös's government. The cabinet consisted mainly of figures and experts close to the prime minister who belonged to or had reached the upper middle class. No aristocrat apart from Teleki was to hold the premiership again, and aristocratic ministers would appear only sporadically. But although Gömbös was anti-aristocratic and clashed with some of the aristocracy, landed estates retained weight as a political and social factor, and in fact, gained more weight as big business began to be relegated. Once Hitler had come to power, it was out of the question for a Jewish expert to negotiate with the Germans on financial or economic relations, and not even the Hungarian government availed itself of such expertise. But for a time, the leading big business group—through Bethlen and associates, the National Bank of Hungary, and connections with the regent—still exerted indirect influence and kept its economic positions until the German occupation.

Politics was invaded, however, by the group of right-wing high-ranking officers of the army whom Gömbös had promoted to high positions. They made use of the regent's particular interest in the army and began to exert pressure as a political force at the end of the 1930s.

There were no great shifts in the social structure. The number of non-urban inhabitants did not fall, but the ratio of urban to non-urban shifted in favor of the former. Change in income relations came primarily from the program that commenced in 1938. Pay rises still exceeded the rate of inflation for a while and urban unemployment ceased, while tensions over the shortage of rural work were reduced.

The decade brought a number of new welfare measures, but the government also abolished or reduced other social services. At the beginning of 1933, the Gömbös government introduced an insurance measure for war wounded, war widows and war orphans, setting the benefit to be paid and seeing to medical care and places in children's homes and homes for the disabled. On the other hand, the government abolished the Ministry of Labor and Welfare, and split its tasks among six other ministries, claiming that this would spread social sensitivity to them all. But the real purpose was surely expressed in the foundation of the National Social Policy Council,[3] under the aegis of the prime minister, so that he could follow the welfare and social policy issues with a view to centralizing them within the state. This was augmented by an act already passed in 1932 that ended social insurance arbitration, which many people rightly felt was an attack on the autonomy of the interest-representing organizations. Meanwhile, the government steadily reduced the services provided by the insurance association. Sickness and maternity benefits were reduced, various charges were introduced, and the provision of certain more expensive drugs and medical appliances was withdrawn.

Early in 1935, Gömbös sent a draft proposal to several bodies, including the leaders of the Social Democratic Party, for compulsory chamber membership, stating that the chambers would have sole jurisdiction in labor arbitration, payment of benefits, and collective agreements, and that their leaders for the first five years would be appointed by the government. The draft was made public by the prime minister in Szeged on March 17. Although the idea had already been leaked and aroused considerable opposition in various circles, it was put to a practical test at the elections due to be held in the two big insurance associations. At MABI, the association for private employees, which had overtaken OTI in the early

1930s, in terms of the extent and standard of its services, the winner by a big margin was the Democratic Bloc, which convinced the right wing that it had to pay much more attention to the elections at OTI. Nevertheless, the National Bloc won only 22.6 percent of the votes and the Trade Union Council 71.8 percent. That result could be taken as a vote against the interest-representation system, as the labor unions could not have gained so many votes without some support from the urban petite bourgeoisie.

Among the first measures taken by the Darányi government was that of pushing through legislation giving full insurance rights to farm stewards, as the 1938 act on compulsory old age insurance for agricultural workers prescribed. This entitlement to an old age pension (of 60 *pengő* a year) and a mortality grant (of 30 *pengő*) applied to every male agricultural employee over the age of 18, on reaching the age of 65 or on dying, whichever was sooner. The welfare legislation was continued under Béla Imrédy, who introduced a bill calling for a child allowance for those working in industry, commerce and mining—the first time that such a benefit had been proposed in Hungary, and a scheme that proved to be a significant step towards the protection of children. Then came an order from the Ministry of the Interior raising the sum paid as pregnancy and maternity benefit, while OTI in that year began to provide holidays for young workers aged 14–18.

While Pál Teleki was prime minister, an order appeared establishing the National People's and Family Protection Fund,[4] primarily to protect large families. Its tasks included extending credit for the purchase of small plots of land and for housing, and as a result, some 12,000 modern houses were built in the early 1940s, mainly in villages as blocks. The government of László Bárdossy that followed Teleki's death confined its welfare measures to raising sick pay, accident benefits and old age pensions, but this was simply designed to offset the scale of inflation, as were the moves to raise wages and officials' salaries.

The health of the public improved substantially in the second half of the 1920s and in the 1930s. The mortality rate declined by 4 percent. The number of deaths from lung disease declined from 3.05 per thousand in 1920 to 1.52 per thousand in 1936. Trained physicians increased in numbers by 250 percent. The number of hospital beds rose from 26,451 in 1921 to 48,000 in 1936 and more than 66,000 in 1943.

Notes

1. *Magyar-Amerikai Olajipari Rt. (MAORT).*
2. *Hungária Műtrágyagyár.*
3. *Országos Társadalompolitikai Tanács.*
4. *Országos Nép- és Családvédelmi Alap (ONCSA).*

5. Education

Public education seems at first sight to have changed hardly at all. Bálint Hóman, who held the portfolio in 1932–1938 and, after a short break, in 1939–1942, continued Klebelsberg's school-building program, although with less money to spend, and hardly altered the system that he had established. Looking more closely, however, there were marked changes in the educational principles applied in schools. These were summed up and projected onto every school subject in an elementary school "curriculum" published in 1941. There had been enraged attacks on Klebelsberg for his "liberal individualistic policy." Hóman focused instead on a collective education of the nation. He also felt that there were too many universities and colleges and that the proportions between the different types of school were wrong. He tried to rationalize matters by merging economics into the Budapest Technical University and also integrating the forestry faculty at Sopron and the agriculture and veterinary medicine schools, under an act passed in 1934. This did not change the internal structures of the facilities, cause operative problems in the umbrella university, or reduce funding or enrollment.

The minister also turned to rationalizing the system of secondary education, which was complex and not entirely logical. In support of the bill that he introduced in the spring of 1934, he argued that middle schools should not be marked by a bias towards the humanities or the natural sciences, but have a general national character, so that the "national subjects" (Hungarian, history, geography, ethnography and religion) should have priority. This, he claimed, would also meet the requirements of national education and character development. Hóman had the same purpose in mind when he introduced class teachers' lessons and paid great attention to physical education. These criteria were applied in the curricula, which increased the number of lessons for the humanities and decreased it for the natural sciences. There was a conspicuous reduction in the number of mathematics lessons. Language teaching lost ground at every level, especially the teaching of Greek and Latin. But this structure was only compulsory in the state gymnasia. Church schools had to send in their own plans for ministerial approval. As the Ministry of Religion and Public Education had no wish to quarrel with any of the major churches, there were cases of church schools following a curriculum that differed from the state one in many regards, although the general opinion was that the church schools were of a much higher standard than the state ones.

Although the minister took steps to decrease the variety in the types of middle school, he himself increased that variety by introducing in 1938 what were known as economic middle schools, which offered a school-leaving certificate, but pointed students towards business rather than university. He also turned the teachers' training schools into what were known as lyceums, from which students could move on to a teachers' training academy. These two new types of school were certainly a response to the changing demands of the period, allowing students to leave school with a certificate of which they could make use later in life.

Hóman continued the development of elementary schools started by his predecessor, overseeing the building of 2,000 new schools by 1940. That was a lower rate of increase than under Klebelsberg, but it certainly helped to ease the problems, even if many of the people's (elementary) schools still had beaten mud or mud-brick walls, earth floors and a thatched roof.

What Hóman advanced as the universities' tasks of educating the nation was applied in every segment of education. The whole of education had to serve the development of national character, or, as he put it, "The young people emerging from school must be able to stand their ground in the great battle of world views." For similar reasons, he laid great emphasis on the Levente youth movement and its semi-military training. The number of students in secondary education increased during his period as minister, but university enrollment declined.

The system of views during the short period when Pál Teleki took over the Ministry of Religion and Public Education differed only from Hóman's in attaching great significance (as Klebelsberg had done) to elite university training. Teleki also endorsed selection in middle schools, arguing that great care needed to be taken to identify talent, and that everything should be done to ensure that exceptional young people received the best further educational opportunities at home and abroad. Citing St. Stephen of Hungary, Teleki emphasized cultural equality, and in 1938, when he became minister, he described wise adaptation to Europe as a condition for the state's survival

When Hóman returned to the portfolio in 1939, he submitted a bill on a gradual transition to eight years of elementary education in people's schools. This was passed by Parliament but hardly implemented, because of the war.

After the territorial revision in Transylvania, the Ministry of Religion and Public Education began moving back the university that had been transferred from Kolozsvár (Cluj) to Szeged, while taking steps to give Szeged a university of its own. The minister also announced that each university would be given a specialist profile, with Budapest remaining as the only general university of sciences. This involved closing the arts faculty at Pécs, the law faculty at Szeged and the natural science departments at Debrecen. There were now five universities in the country, but there was a full range of university education available in Budapest.

Education policy in the 1930s was coupled with a more thorough and obvious program of "Hungarianization," affecting uniforms, inscriptions, badges and school ceremonies.

6. Political Schools of Thought, 1919–1945

The Great War and Trianon caused a break in political thinking and the content and style of public utterance. Contributions on the latter began to come from wider sections of society and to be debated on several levels. Political debate took place in the traditional way in Parliament, but on a higher plane in periodicals, old and new, and at discussions and conferences called by associations or ministries. Views also clashed in the daily papers, of course. (The radio repeated the government's position in the main, but it did not engage directly in politics before 1939.)

It is also worth noting that Parliament, in various ways, represented much broader and more socially articulate strata than it had before the war. It was not simply that 6 percent of the adult population was represented in the old legislature, 40 percent in the first post-war National Assembly, 28 percent in the next, and similar proportions in subsequent parliaments. There was also a broader social spectrum among the elected members. The broad electorate for the first post-war parliament resulted from the electoral law passed by the Friedrich government and drafted under Mihály Károlyi. The franchise was narrowed again under Bethlen, but a more serious setback was the fact that the secret ballot gave way to a system of open voting in most constituencies. Such a low proportion of eligible voters was far from usual anywhere in Europe at that time and still less in Western Europe. Only about 20 percent of voters, in Budapest and cities with municipal rights, could vote secretly, and the system was all but unique in Europe in this regard as well. The secret ballot returned under new legislation presented by Darányi and passed in 1938, but at the expense of further restrictions on suffrage.

The social structure of the members had altered radically since the war. The aristocratic character of Parliament had almost vanished. The proportion of aristocrats in the House of Representatives

322

was increased somewhat in the three general elections under Bethlen, especially in 1931, but it fell again in 1935 and in 1939. Starting in 1922, the proportion of aristocratic members was 8–10 percent during the period. Meanwhile, the proportion of landowners with medium-sized estates (the "gentry") also declined. They were the other big losers in the first National Assembly, with 25 percent. Although they gained ground in the Bethlen-period elections, they fell below 30 percent again in the last two elections of the period. The main gains in the first National Assembly were made by the smallholder class, which made up about half of the house that convened in 1920. Most of the other half of the seats were won by the broad-based Christian National Unity Party, which had the broadest social mix among its supporters. Anybody from an aristocrat to an urban petit-bourgeois might vote for the party, for want of alternatives. After Bethlen's group had managed to fragment and then absorb both these parties, the Smallholders' Party disappeared for a good while, and representation of the upper middle class increased, alongside that of the gentry. That was mainly why the governing party (the Unity Party, National Unity Party, and then Party of Hungarian Life) managed after 1922 to gain an absolute majority (58, 69, 64, 69 and 73 percent in successive elections). The Christian Farming and Social Party,[1] left out of the National Unity Party, managed to obtain parliamentary seats and seats in the cabinet (for József Vass and Sándor Ernszt) until 1931.

The opposition parties and independent candidates won 20–30 percent of the seats. The Hungarian Social Democratic Party, which appeared in 1922, began in the 1930s to target in principle not just the urban working class, but the agricultural proletariat, artisans and traders, the growing numbers of clerical staff, and, rather later, many of the professions (teaching, medical, engineering, and so on). This change of course obviously necessitated a Social Democratic proposal on land reform, which appeared in 1931. But the party bore a burden of past uncertainty coupled with waning support and organizational shortcomings. Far from embracing new sections of society as the program envisaged, it lost ground among the urban proletariat to right-wing and even far-right parties in the 1930s. Its 25 parliamentary seats in 1922 became 14 in 1926 and 1931, 11 in 1935, and 5 in 1939.

Representation of the rural smallholders declined sharply in the latter half of the Bethlen period, but revived in the 1930s. What was known at that time as the Independent Smallholders' Party was reorganized in 1930 and gained 11 seats in Parliament in the following year. This became 23 seats in 1935 and 14 in 1939. The party's support was concentrated among the rural (and not always just the rural) intelligentsia and the wealthier stratum of peasant farmers, but according to its program, it represented the peasantry generally, and joined several other parties in calling for a transformation of land ownership. Its arguments were dominated initially by criteria of saving the nation, associated with Tibor Eckhardt, including a land reform to be carried out at the expense of Jewish owners, but that changed after Eckhardt left the country and influence passed to the writer and Reformed Church minister Péter Veres and to Ferenc Nagy, a respected farmer.

Various "remnant" liberal groups gained 2–6 percent of the poll. Their support showed a similar tendency to decline to that of the Social Democrats. This seems to confirm the idea that as middle-class representatives who had high hopes of Nazi German policies crowded into Parliament, so the left wing tended to be squeezed. The effectiveness of the liberal and bourgeois radical trends was reduced after the death of Vilmos Vázsonyi in 1926, which left only Károly Rassay (and possibly Rezső Rupert) to represent liberal principles at any high level. The great representative of the bourgeois left, Oszkár Jászi, was living abroad.

The government and the governing party were attacked by nobody from the right initially, and then from 1923 only by the Racial Protection Party that Gömbös had founded, which initially had seven members of Parliament and latterly four. Its leader disbanded the tiny organization in 1928. Two former members, Eckhardt and Endre Bajcsy-Zsilinszky, set about founding new parties, but Bajcsy-Zsilinszky gave up the idea and joined the Smallholders. But the far right revived during the Depression. There was a proliferation of fascist or Nazi-type parties in the 1930s, although none of them fitted their patterns entirely. The one that became most influential was the Party of National Will[2] founded by Ferenc Szálasi in 1935, which changed its name several times but became known colloquially as the Arrow-Cross. Szálasi's party and the other far-right parties around him had great success in the 1939 general elections, when they won a total of 49 seats (31 of them for the Arrow-Cross). According to opinion at the time, the far right could attribute this to the petit-bourgeois, so-called *lumpen*, or more elegantly marginal strata in urban society, but this seems to have been a one-sided view. The far right won a sizable share of the vote in working-class urban districts and among the very poor in the agricultural population. The Arrow-Cross was highly successful, for instance, in Zala and Szabolcs, Hungary's two poorest counties.

The governing party, with its comfortable majority, acted throughout as an umbrella party, although it sometimes had trouble maintaining cohesion, and groups broke away from it occasionally. Bethlen managed to balance the industrial/mercantile interests with the agricultural ones up to about 1930, but had trouble doing so in his last two years. He then took part as leader of the Unity Party in turning out the government of Gyula Károlyi. Gyula Gömbös, endorsed as prime minister by the National Unity Party, soon resigned from it, went with his supporters into opposition, and finally withdrew formally from politics and accepted a seat in the upper house offered by the regent. Subsequent prime ministers encountered right-wing opposition within their governing party, and offsetting it, opposition from the other side, often known within the party as the "left wing," although it was hardly that, as the groups within it included some expressly conservative figures.

The efforts of the liberals and Social Democrats, and after 1935 of the Smallholders, were often augmented by the conservative opposition, against the moves towards dictatorship and the domination of a pro-German policy. So the antipathy and opposition to the dangerous tendencies stretched from the left wing even into the government benches. The right-wing pressure on the government from the governing party became especially strong after the 1939 elections, by which time great changes had occurred in the structure of the party, due to an influx of impatient middle-class elements, whose pro-German and anti-Semitic aspirations were nourished by the successive German successes and even military victories. Pál Teleki was pushed into sharp debates with his predecessor, Béla Imrédy, who still belonged to the party. Imrédy demanded several times that Hungary should transform itself according to the German–Italian pattern that accorded with the spirit of the times and that it should turn to a clearly pro-German foreign policy. The antagonism worsened to a point where Imrédy resigned from the party in October 1940 and established the Hungarian Renewal Party with his friends. But only 17 members followed him, and thus there remained within the government party in Parliament a good number of members who agreed with Imrédy but were not prepared to break with the authorities for opportunistic reasons.

This was a material expression of the fact that new currents of political ideology had arrived. The changes can be summarized as follows. The earlier conservative liberalism had given way to a conservatism whose every strand had turned against liberalism, or at least against liberal economic policy. This was probably because the system that conservative liberalism represented had itself disappeared, meaning that the old policy no longer seemed viable. Some old liberals had become neo-liberals or social liberals, but their presence in the legislature became minimal. There were also attempts to set up a far-right grouping or party, but these had not made any headway in society until one far-right group made a firm start in 1919–1921, and after a pause, extended its influence strongly in the 1930s. Another feature was the ground gained by social democratic ideas, despite the animosity aroused by involvement in the Hungarian Soviet Republic, but the Social Democratic Party's success in the 1920s gave way to a steady decline in the 1930s. The communists scraped through the period as an illegal party, but the party's very existence was a novelty. Even when the sporadic contacts between home communists and émigrés in the Soviet Union dwindled to nothing, the tiny movement still had a great system of state looming over it. That and memories of Béla Kun's regime cast a long political shadow, especially during World War II.

There was also a change in the subject matter of political discourse. The concept of nation, present in Hungarian politics for centuries, would undergo alteration periodically. This had been defined by two contexts in the Dualist period: conflicts in Vienna–Budapest relations, usually over pan-Imperial concerns, and the issue of nations and national groups native to Hungary, which the political class proved itself to be largely incapable of resolving. After the war, there was no Dualist system of power any more and no large groups in the population that belonged to other nations. The largest community were the German-speakers, who only began to cause problems in the mid-1930s and then mainly because of manipulation by German Nazism. The question of the Hungarian nation became centered on the trauma of Trianon, its causes and the responsibility for it, and the general problem of national survival.

The subject matter was joined by some further questions not considered in the recent past. One was the form of state and the question of the empty throne. One small group saw Charles's abdication letter just as a transitional measure to do with exercise of kingly functions, and called themselves Carlists, or after the ex-king's death, legitimists. The leaders of the group were not all aristocrats.

Alongside Count Gyula Andrássy and his aristocratic associates were figures such as István Rakovszky, Gusztáv Gratz, Albin Lingauer, and some high-ranking army officers such as Antal Lehár. There was some initial support for legitimism from church leaders as well. This school of thought remained alive in some form throughout the period, although some advocates of restoring the monarchy in the second half of the 1930s were concerned with finding shelter from German Nazism, not just with constitutional considerations. Republicanism had never put down deep roots in Hungary, and its popularity had been undermined by the ill-fated attempt of Mihály Károlyi, but it retained some support.

Most people in politics called themselves monarchists, but now that Hungary had regained its sovereignty they wanted a free choice of king—not a Habsburg or a foreigner, but a Hungarian king. The problem was that they failed to agree on a candidate. The vast majority resigned themselves to the current situation of having a regent as head of state, but the subject kept returning and remained an irritant because the matter of succession had not been resolved. The right of free election of a king was raised by the Smallholders, who initially gained a parliamentary majority and mainly expressed their antipathy to the Habsburgs. The Habsburgs were also rejected by the Szeged group surrounding Miklós Horthy, who argued that Charles had forfeited his moral right to the Hungarian throne by his weakness. Another group, headed by Bethlen, rejected a restoration on the grounds of rationality, a stance backed by feelings that Austria would inevitably be annexed by Germany, coupled with the idea that under current international conditions Charles (or his son Otto) could not ascend the throne unless the Austro-Hungarian union were reinstated.

Almost all took the view initially that the regency was a temporary institution, and that is what the law stated as well. Accordingly, the regent could only return an act to the legislature for reconsideration once, after which he had to promulgate it. He could suspend the House for up to 30 days and dissolve it if it proved to be persistently inoperable. So the basic law of 1920 put strong curbs on the regent's powers and Horthy made only a faint impression on politics in the 1920s. Bethlen probably did not confine himself to putting legislation to the regent and discussed with him every major step that the government took, but the prime minister, not the regent, remained the dominant figure in the system of state of the 1920s. The regent's powers became much stronger in the 1930s, however. The person of Miklós Horthy became the deciding factor and the main point of reference for the system, except to the extremists and the legitimists. In 1933, he received the right to suspend the legislature for long periods, and in 1937 Parliament repealed provision that allowed the head of state to be called to account, and granted him a right of veto if he had twice sent a bill back to the House for reconsideration. The compulsory period of publication was increased and the regent gained the right to appoint his successor. The last provision in particular offers grounds for saying that the regency was no longer a provisional form of state. It had taken root because a decisive step had been taken to ensure its continuity, although the formal status of the country as a kingdom was retained. Parliament had accepted the institution of deputy regent in 1939 and elected Horthy's son István to that post, meaning that the regency took on a dynastic character. Implementation was prevented only by the fatal accident that befell István, which left the question of the form of the state open again in the final years of the system. That openness increased the scope for the far right, calling out for a leader, and undermined among wide circles of the public the high prestige previously enjoyed by the regent.

Another new element to enter political discourse was the broad subject matter of the economy, which had been discussed hitherto only in terms of affairs within the Empire. Despite occasional tugs of war, there had been no trouble in the Dualist period about admitting alongside the dominant landowning sector the development of the modern branches of the economy: large-scale industry, banking, wholesaling, and so on. In fact landowners had shown willing to accept the Jewish leaders in such fields and draw them into the elite, in a process that essentially encompassed the so-called emancipation of the Jews. After the war, the matter of the economy, which had to be reorganized and placed on its own two feet, led to this relationship being questioned, as interest representation became decisively one of livelihood. It can be understood on that basis how politics became filled with reports, proposals and debates on the state of the economy and what was to be done about it, embracing all branches of the economy, but with especially great emphasis on agriculture. The debates flared up initially over customs tariff law, and then became constant during the Great Depression, centering on broad, committed protection of agricultural interests. When the agricultural problems appeared to have been solved in the mid-1930s, the far right, representing the middle classes, launched a general attack on all the Jews' positions. They attacked the banking system and the cartels (with which people clearly associated the Jews), and also brought up the question of overrepresentation of the Jews in some professions—the law and medicine—and in the media, the film industry, the theater, and so on.

The main division on economic issues was between advocates of pan-European (Western European) integration and those with an "independent" conception, referred to later as "self-purposed."[3] The government was attacked from the liberal side for needless intervention and from the other for neglecting the state's responsibilities. After the "self-purposed" concept had succumbed in practice to mounting dependence on the Germans, the far right argued ever more urgently for integration into the German *Grossraumwirtschaft*. That was done, for example, by Béla Imrédy, who wanted above all to retain the basis for Hungary's successes in the modern branches of the economy. That was also proclaimed by former Gömbös supporter Béla Béldi of the Arrow-Cross, but he was prepared to sacrifice industry and see the country agricultural again.

One side of the economic debate concerned welfare, later a separate subject, partly because social problems became a matter of international concern that the League of Nations could not ignore, but also for reasons specific to Hungary. Despite all the denunciations of the Hungarian Soviet Republic, it had made a surprising number of politicians aware of the social dangers inherent in ignoring and neglecting the welfare of the lower strata of society, especially the urban working class. Another group of economic questions that became distinct concerned "the village"—because of its abject poverty, and because some politicians and intellectuals saw the peasantry as the guarantee of the survival of the Hungarian community (or race).

Looking at the subject matter of political discourse chronologically, questions of money, loans, tariffs and trade dominated in the 1920s, while preference in the 1930s went to the land, the village and the peasantry. In both cases there was a dominant foreign policy background that also featured in political exchanges. The discussions on the agrarian question that dominated political life in the 1930s extended to every detail. But the governing party and those around it largely lost interest in the matter in the second half of the decade, leaving it to the attentions of the Smallholders, the far right and the so-called *népi* writers. The economists engaged in agricultural relations put the efficiency and livelihood aspects to the fore. The sociologists examined the causes of rural poverty and its dangerous social effects. The *népi* writers, apart from sociographic activities, showed great sensitivity to the human and the national aspects.

The attribute *népi* (to do with the people) denoted, incidentally, a very loose group of young writers keen to dissociate themselves from a non-*népi*, urban literature seen as alien to a true, "deep," Hungarian mentality. The Hungarians and their values and history were the subject in the 1930s of a general debate over principles, in which László Németh and Gyula Szekfű were the central figures. The *népi* writers saw the people of the village as the one true medium of these values, and they based on them a vision of a pure, *népi* Hungary, from which all silt would be removed. They attacked all the bargaining and compromises and the "greater Hungarian" solution, and rejected foreign influences. The one who formulated this was László Németh, who became engaged in sharp debate on the matter with the historian Gyula Szekfű.

Szekfű's work *Three Generations*[4] appeared in 1920 and its expanded edition in 1934,[5] followed a year later by the first volume of his *Hungarian History*, discussing the eighteenth and nineteenth centuries with a look at the twentieth as well.[6] Szekfű's critique of capitalism and liberalism and Jewish penetration, along with the general anti-Semitic strand in the works mentioned, fitted well with several other currents of thinking, and so it became the decisive basis of reference not just in government circles, but in other spheres. But the recognition that Szekfű gave to the great Hungarian ability to compromise, the "greater Hungarian" (all-embracing) solution and the positive aspects of Habsburg rule brought him into conflict with the *népi* writers , especially László Németh. Thereafter, there was conflict and bitter struggles not only between "deep" and "diluted" Hungarians, but between "lesser" and "greater" ones.[7] It was not acknowledged that the fate of the Hungarian nation would probably have been much worse had it not been for compromises and "greater Hungarians," or that no compromises would have been made without the struggles and sacrifices of combatant "lesser Hungarians."

The *népi* writers divided into many political strands and came from a variety of initial intellectual bases. One of the influences was certainly Dezső Szabó, an anti-urban, anti-Semitic figure, given to praising the Eastern ties of the Hungarians, while dismissing the general literary achievement of the West and of some sympathizers with the "East" who had a strong element of the Reformed Church in their thinking, such as Sándor Karácsony. Thus the *népi* writers also became in several senses participants in the East–West debate, as the subject of the pro-Western culture tied in with the question of broader orientation. Although religious matters did not come to the fore, the *népi* writers were mainly Protestant in their thinking, and it was not by chance that they gathered twice at the premises of the *Soli Deo Gloria* Reformed Youth Federation at Balatonszárszó to debate the problems facing the country. *Soli Deo Gloria* was established in 1928 and several youth rallies were held on the site that it had bought at Balatonszárszó, sometimes with celebrated speakers. One member society was the Márton Kabay Circle,[8] which later took part in the resistance.

The gathering at Balatonszárszó at the end of June and the beginning of July 1942 was attended mainly by Reformed intellectuals, and resulted in an anti-German intellectual grouping. The next conference in August 1943 attracted an exceptionally wide public. The youth organization was joined there by most of the *népi* group, representatives of the Smallholders' and Peasant Parties, and by Ferenc Erdei of the Marxist left wing. Most of the participants expressed optimism about the future, since they felt almost sure that the Anglo-Saxon powers would liberate the country. They could not know that Franklin D. Roosevelt and Winston Churchill were at that very time agreeing in Quebec to make the next great assault in northern France and embark on other campaigns only when a superfluity of forces appeared on the French front. The only pessimistic statement at Balatonszárszó was made by László Németh, for which he received bitter reproaches. He was attacked still more when his somber 1943 prediction came true.

Some of the *népi* group made an approach to the far right, but others such as Géza Féja, Gyula Illyés and Imre Kovács took part in the anti-German March Front, where some young communists also appeared. There had also been several *népi* writers to be seen when the National Peasant Party had been founded in 1939. This party joined the Hungarian Front in 1944 and was represented in the Interim National Assembly.

However, the "urban" thinkers also inhabited a highly hetero-geneous world. Their works appeared throughout the period, but it is not possible to analyze them in terms of politics and worldview, as they never made a concerted political appearance. Although there were forums for the urban, pro-Western currents of opinion—publishers, periodicals and papers—their influence steadily decreased. The liberal newspaper *Világ* was wound up in 1926, in the Bethlen period. Later, more than 400 larger or smaller publications fell victim to the laws on the Jews, to political manipulations, and to rationalizations with the paper shortage as a pretext. The victims included the bourgeois radical periodical *Századunk* and the social democratic *Szocializmus*, and the two most popular daily papers: *Az Est* and *Pesti Napló*. Although big business managed to launch the *Magyar Nemzet* in 1938, which acted as a spokesman for independent anti-German thinking, the most influential organ was *Új Nemzedék*, edited by István Milotay of the far right. Then came the extreme irredentist and anti-Semitic weekly *Magyar Futár*, alongside the Hungarian version of *Signal*, issued by the Germans. The culture known as "urban" suffered greatly under the laws on the Jews, as the work of Jewish authors could no longer appear, nor Jewish composers' works be heard, nor Jewish actors be seen in the theaters. Among those affected by the purge were the famous playwright Ferenc Molnár, the popular writer Jenő Heltai, the composer Pál Ábrahám, the outstanding actor Gyula Kabos, and many others. Finally, at the climax of Jewish persecution in 1945, several famous creative figures were murdered, including writers Miklós Radnóti and Antal Szerb.

Amidst the cacophony of debate, some undoubtedly modern representatives of culture who were not *népi*, not Jewish, but nevertheless producers of peak Hungarian cultural achievements, became homeless, so to speak. Some of them tried to retreat into an ivory tower, such as Mihály Babits, or committed suicide, such as Attila József, or chose to emigrate, such as the greatest Hungarian composer of the period, Béla Bartók.

The foreign policy question behind the disputes was not openly debated for some time, as the legislature accepted the prime minister's view that any debate would damage the country's interests. But it remained pending. The goals of Bethlen's government from the outset included wide revision of the peace treaty—removing the financial obligations and military restrictions, and eventually, revising the country's borders. But Bethlen did not see any of these as feasible except in pan-European terms. The first two required the cooperation of the Western European powers, which is why he emphasized the point that Hungary's policy had to regain its foreign policy dimension and Hungarian prosperity was conceivable only in a European context. He linked territorial revision with a return of German power, weight and pressure, but he did not expect that weight to become dominant, in Hungary or in Europe. His idea, spread privately among politicians, was endorsed by a wide majority.

But foreign policy in the later 1930s came out in the open. A growing body of opinion expressed with growing stridency the belief that Hungary's place was beside a victorious Germany and any other approach would be an attack on the national interest. There was very little counterweight to that growing belief, as the left had weakened in Parliament, and as no interest was being shown or could be realistically expected from the Western European powers. Western Europe had been unable to take part in resolving the problems of the agricultural states of Central Europe and the Balkans, then acknowledged the *Anschluss* silently, assisted at Munich in reducing the size of Czechoslovakia, stood by helplessly when Czechoslovakia was occupied and dissected, and did nothing to defend Poland beyond declaring war. German power seemed unstoppable for a time. Expectations of the West picked up again in 1942–1943 after the United States entered the war, but eventually proved to be illusory from the point of view of saving Central Europe.

One new topic of political debate typical of the times was sovereignty and self-rehabilitation, provoked by Gömbös and discussed already. This extended beyond the tariff debate mentioned before to the question of the state's role in managing the economy, to which were added the great conferences on social and educational matters. The demands for a great role to be played by the state came mainly from the spokesmen for strata that felt that they were losing out due to the loans taken out, the tariff regulations, or the general monetary and interest policies of the government and National Bank. Government policy was also attacked by the advocates of orthodox liberal economic outlook, who thought that the Hungarian economy would suffer damage if the state intervened too deeply or frequently in its affairs. The government was reproached from almost all sides for the mounting taxation. It became fashionable towards the end of the 1920s to criticize the so-called "unproductive" expenditures of the government.

Intellectual developments in Western Europe and Hungary's own experiences alike gave encouragement to the idea that the economy had become a global economy, in which nation states, especially such small states as Hungary, were incapable of solving the problems internally. This spatial idea of the economy temporarily gave rise in the early 1930s to a new direction and outlook in foreign policy as well. Plans and proposals were aimed at regional, even continental, solutions. Such modern ideas did not simply emanate from highly qualified economists or public figures who had considered matters deeply. Great attention was also paid in Hungary's pro-government press to French Prime Minister Aristide Briand's plan for uniting Europe economically, with famous politicians such as Pál Teleki and Gusztáv Gratz speaking up for the idea of union. Bethlen, after he had ceased to be prime minister, also spoke positively of the idea of European economic union, provided that the political issues involved could be settled. But such ideas made no more sense by the mid-1930s. Government circles were concerned by then to preserve as much of the country's sovereignty as possible, in economic and financial matters, and in foreign affairs. That increasingly hopeless objective was decisive to government policy up to 1938, and then also, after a brief interlude under Imrédy, up to 1941.

Meanwhile, the regime's original "counter-revolutionary" definition of itself lost its meaning as well. Some of the communist leaders paid for the 1919 experiment with their lives; others, along with some social democrats, fled abroad or were exchanged by the Hungarian government for army officers who had been taken prisoner-of-war in Soviet Russia. The second- or third-ranking communists were never able to rally more than a couple of thousand people, except in the final stage of the war, when quite a lot of communist young people followed the banner, with the primary aim of being part of a broader political framework (a people's front) to struggle against the Germans. By that time the prospect was opening up of victory and a consequent great transformation. Since the social democratic leaders of the Hungarian Soviet Republic also left the country, those who remained were previous outsiders, of whom Károly Peyer and Gyula Peidl were the decisive figures initially. They were express believers in bourgeois democracy and a parliamentary system, who lined up behind an ethnic solution to the national question. It has already been seen that the Hungarian Social Democratic Party later, after Illés Mónus, Anna Kéthly, and other younger members set the course for the party, formally revising the program in terms of its direct purpose (bourgeois democracy) and its aim of widening its support, and raising the issue of European union.

So the regime was not threatened by revolution or even the left wing. The growing danger in the final Horthy years came from the far right, because of the 1939 election breakthrough, and because the far right was joined by some highly educated people with good debating and writing skills, which had not happened in Hungary

before. Imrédy was a superb financial expert and a good debater,
and István Milotay and Ferenc Rajniss were journalists of a high
standard. Among the other eminent right-wingers were Bálint
Hóman, Elemér Mályusz, also a historian, and Ferenc Orsós, a
pathologist and academician. When Alfred Rosenberg, head of the
German Foreign Bureau, wanted to convoke an international conference on race in 1943, Hungary was the one country where the
official making preliminary enquiries could find suitable "experts."
(The idea was dropped, however.) But another side of the picture
was the fact that many eminent people moved across during the war
to join the opponents of dictatorship and the German alliance,
including Gyula Szekfű, Gusztáv Gratz and Endre Bajcsy-
Zsilinszky.

Although the police and government realized that there was
much more to fear from far-right upheaval than from the left, that
fact did not stop conspicuous action and reprisals being taken
against the left from time to time, while the response to the other
extreme was more moderate. This had more to do with realities than
with attitudes. The same approach as the one that the police were
taking could be seen in censorship, bans on newspapers, and the
handling of street protests and demonstrations. Even the regent stated privately the principle that guns had to be turned on all subver-
sives—joyfully on the left and sorrowfully on the right—although
the label "revolutionary" in the earlier sense hardly applied to the
far right.

The description "Christian national" gained real acceptance in
the 1930s as an emblem, because the concepts of "Christian" and
of "national" were flexible enough to embrace many interpretations. "Christian" could imply universalism and adherence to
European civilization. To Catholics it implied legitimism and the
value of Habsburg rule, while to adherents of the Reformed Church
it suggested a spirit of resistance and an Eastern orientation, the
need to look to the East. The Catholic Christian viewpoint could

include intolerance of liberalism and anti-Semitism, but accompanied by social demands, as with Ottokár Prohászka, or a tone of understanding and cooperation in approaching social problems, as with Sándor Giessvein. Christian principles could also be employed pragmatically, as József Vass managed on social issues as minister. Gyula Kornis gave the Christian idea a diehard conservative slant by protesting against all modernization. Christian socialism also spread in the 1930s, albeit in several versions.

After a time, the Christian idea in the regime began to be interpreted by the high clergy to include support for the regime in return for support for the church by the regime. The high clergy would defend their position and their flocks even against the intentions of the state, but they would not go further than that. This was the position that the Catholic Church took on the Jewish question as well, defending the converts but not the others.

This also meant that church leaders gave no support to the various Catholic-inclined political parties that appeared or to the Christian socialist movements. Christian socialism had antecedents in Hungary and gained momentum with the encyclical *Quadragesimo anno* issued by Pope Pius XI in 1931, but several variants appeared. Radicals sought far-reaching transformation and thorough land reform, while others drew up milder demands that they hoped were more attainable. A few took to the idea of a corporate type of organization and others were dissuaded from this only by the fear that it would lead to Italian-type fascism, as was suspected, then confirmed in the plans of Gyula Gömbös. Some Christian socialists and other political Catholics could place German Nazism among the changing political systems, but most, at least initially, saw its teachings as incompatible with the foundations of Catholicism and Christianity in general.

Finally, many used "Christian" to mean Gentile. Some attacked the Jews for religious reasons, stressing their "pagan" outlook and the recurrent charge of murdering Christ. Others used

"Christian" as a code word, especially in the years when open abuse of Jews was still taboo—which was not the case by the mid-1930s.

Similarly flexible use could be made of the word "national." Hardly anybody failed to identify with it or to want to further national interests—not even communists in the final years, when the struggle against fascism was a national slogan. The persistent issue was how to define the national criterion. National interest could mean democratization at one end and dictatorship at the other, while the government in the middle saw it as avoiding any extremes. The national interest could be formulated as ethnically based revision, optimal revision, or total, "everything back" revision, and again there was wide variation. Acceptance of the ethnic criterion was not confined to the left. It had conservative advocates too, including Gyula Gömbös, as has been seen. Finally, the concept of national interest was polarized between believers in unconditional incorporation into the sphere of the nation and the introduction of dictatorship, and those fleeing before German pressure, even members of various resistance organizations.

The whole period was prone to Hungarian-style window-dressing, especially the 1930s. School uniforms, gala adult attire, and the formal dress of ministers had to be Hungarian in character. Celebrations brought out the more or less traditional formal wear known as the *díszmagyar*, and the *párta* hairstyle, *pruszlik* bodice, and red boots for girls, all figments of fancy. Popular songs might usurp the role of true folk songs, as the true folk music collected by Bartók and Kodály had yet to reach the schools or the public.

This effort to Hungarianize marked one side of daily life. There were also growing efforts undertaken to distract people and public tastes with films, radio broadcasts and books made available at cut prices or on credit. What people received from newspapers, the radio, the motion pictures, and the books that they bought ranged from shoddy goods and political demagoguery to works of a high standard. Readers could buy penny booklets of stories by Conan Doyle and others, or subscribe to the complete works of Ferenc Móra, Kálmán Mikszáth or Géza Gárdonyi, or the long series of works by Transylvanian Hungarian authors published by the Transylvanian Arts Guild.[9] The motion pictures produced and shown ranged from masterpieces to the silliest stories. Radio likewise broadcast a music repertory ranging from hit songs, through Gypsy music and jazz, to opera, and the same applied to other types of program, although the medium was useful in making important specialist and medical knowledge generally known.

Life in the second half of the 1930s seemed to become more colorful. Relatively few people noticed the gathering clouds. As millions took hikes and excursions in the hills, frequented the urban lidos that were opening, enjoyed vacations, or looked forward to owning a motorcycle or even an automobile, those in military circles were drawing up wartime scenarios and plans that also belonged to the intellectual milieu of the period.

Notes

1. *Keresztény Gazdasági és Szociális Párt.*
2. *Nemzeti Akarat Pártja.*
3. *Öncélú.*
4. *Három nemzedék: Egy hanyatló kor története* (Three Generations: History of a Waning Age), Budapest: Élet, 1920.
5. *Három nemzedék és ami utána következett* (Three Generations and What Came After), Budapest: Királyi Magyar Egyetemi Nyomda, 1934.
6. Gyula Szekfű and Bálint Hóman, *Magyar Történet.* I (Hungarian History I), Budapest: Királyi Magyar Egyetemi Nyomda, 1935.
7. Known in Hungarian as *mély-/hígmagyar* and *kis-/nagymagyar.*
8. Named for Márton Kabai (c. 1650–post-1715), a Reformed minister taken prisoner in the war of independence, who ended his life in the galleys.
9. *Erdélyi Szépműves Céh.*

7. Pál Teleki's Attempt at Peaceful Revision and Subsequent Death

"Count Teleki," according to an unsigned German report, "is not a politician, not even an economic expert, simply a gray, stuffy old man." Teleki was indeed no politician or economic expert, but he was not "stuffy" either, nor gray. He was cultivated in a broad and colorful way, and his professional, scholarly expertise, along with his knowledge of geography, allowed him at this time to weigh up much more thoroughly and soberly than the Hungarian elites did what forces were affecting the world, how they might develop, and what Hungary's prospects were. He wrote in 1931, "We have not much time." In 1939, he knew there was none. That knowledge, sadly, left him sensitive, uncertain and mentally unbalanced to a degree that even his religious convictions could not control in the end.

Teleki was deeply pessimistic by 1939. He realized with bitterness that the Western powers had not acted when they might have done to maintain peace in Europe by reconsidering the conditions that were untenable. He had little zest for the premiership, but he agreed to take it because he still kept a faint hope of achieving more for Hungary, within the international grouping dominated by Germany and thanks to German pressure, but by independent Hungarian action. He wanted to gain the compensation for Hungary that the Western powers had failed to provide, but without attracting their condemnation, let alone coming into conflict with them. That result was something that he could expect only of himself.

But there was little hope. Teleki's minimal chances were undermined when he could hardly find a domestic partner for his foreign policy. The General Staff were against the idea. The regent would not allow him to touch the army and was himself being influenced at that time by the military.[1] Most of the governing party was demanding further territorial successes without questioning the price. Pressure from the Arrow-Cross was increasing, and the prime minister could not trust several members of his own government. He managed to exchange several of them for his own men, for various reasons and pretexts, but he did not touch Reményi-Schneller or Csáky.[2] Hungary began to succumb to power-political chaos, in which the prime minister was far from capable of asserting his own views and will. There was just one circumstance in his favor. At least the conservative group did not attack him and tended to support him, although its influence in the lower house soon ended and all that he gained in foreign policy was a few cooperative envoys. Criticism from the left was also muted, but the left soon became insignificant in Parliament as well.

The crucial issue was how to rate Germany and its presumed successes. Some of the political world (Arrow-Cross, supporters of Imrédy, and a group of army officers) had utter faith in almost unlimited German successes, which they anticipated without scruple, with complete satisfaction. Another group predicted almost total German success but feared for Hungary's sovereignty and national interests, and was already objecting to German intervention in Hungarian economic affairs and the question of the German minority. Finally, there was a politically variegated group mainly of intellectuals and analysts, hardly discernible in public life, which ruled out the possibility of German victory or was quite skeptical about it. One such was the "gray" Teleki, with his temperamental abhorrence of the Nazis, and knowledge of the overlapping interests and potentials of the British Empire and of the United States, which suggested that there was no chance of durable or permanent German victory. There was hardly anybody with whom he could discuss these convictions and fears, as the other "pessimists" did not belong to the same circles or to groups with influence. Teleki could only rely on a few of his own men. He did not even have close ties with the Bethlen group. He gathered confidential associates who trusted in the possibility of a non-dictatorial, corporate state structure, who like him believed that there was a chance of relying on German power for an independent policy of territorial revision, and were anti-Semitic in a biological sense. Yet Teleki was not a Nazi-type anti-Semite, as he could not reconcile murder with his religious feelings or authentic Christian spirituality.

The prime minister's position and actions were hindered by not daring to change his foreign minister for fear of offending the Germans. Knowing Csáky and his staff, he devised a separate foreign policy of his own, which he tried to pursue through trusted envoys and others, private correspondence and personal talks. It is hard to speak at all of "Hungarian foreign policy" at that time. Teleki sent letters with his own men or couriers of other countries, and devised devious means to bypass the foreign minister and negotiate unbeknownst to him. Even the prime minister himself had several foreign policy "lines"—one for the public, one for the government and one for his intimates—not to mention the fact that he put on another face and made pronouncements in Rome that were different from the ones that he made in Berlin (as did Csáky). It was all a painful reminder of the fallibility and vulnerability of a prime minister and his whole country.

Nevertheless, the new government set to work. Teleki told a governing party meeting on February 22, 1939, that there was no further need for the Hungarian Life Movement initiated by Imrédy, as the party saw its goals as its own. This was emphasized when the National Unity Party renamed itself the Party of Hungarian Life.[3] The movement remained for a short time, until Imrédy disbanded it as insignificant and began to organize a new party.

When Hitler told Csáky in January that he did not see the Czech question as closed, the Foreign Ministry began to make moves on Subcarpathia, and the Germans were not entirely dismissive this time. This time the Hungarian government had an inkling of the German preparations and announced that if the rest of Czechoslovakia were to be occupied by the Germans, the

Hungarian army would advance into Subcarpathia, even if Berlin opposed this. There was no question of that. Two days later, Hitler informed the Hungarian envoy Döme Sztójay that the solution of the Czech question was at hand. Germany recognized Slovakia as a separate state, but would not make an announcement about Subcarpathia for 24 hours. So the Hungarian government had a day to resolve matters. There was nobody to reject this gift presented on a plate. Subcarpathia wanted independence, but its voice was unheeded in Berlin or Budapest. The *Wehrmacht* set out on March 15 and entered Prague. At almost the same time (according to some reports a little earlier) Hungarian units were deployed, and they had taken possession of the whole territory by March 18.

This move is hard to qualify. The Hungarian occupation attracted hardly any of the world's attention, which was focused on Prague, not Ungvár (Uzhhorod), but the occupation was clearly unilateral and forcible in nature. Nor could it be justified on ethnic grounds: only 40,000 of the 600,000 inhabitants in 12,000 sq. km of annexed territory were Hungarians. (Teleki tried to allay this by promising the area territorial autonomy, but that did not prove to be realistic under wartime conditions.)[4] But the annexation produced a Polish–Hungarian border, the value of which had just been much enhanced, although the Germans had already begun their propaganda war against the Poles, and the importance of that Polish–Hungarian point of contact was negated in a few days and turned into a problem, as Hungary became a potential route for entering Poland. But in any case, Budapest must have been somewhat relieved that the move created little stir in Western Europe and the powers swallowed the annexation of Subcarpathia quite easily. The new revision was important because Hungarian had regained in the northeast a short length of its natural and credibly defensible border, a strategically significant area that had been repossessed by military forces from Hungary and nowhere else.

The latest success in revising the country's border calmed the right wing of the Party of Hungarian Life, and more trouble was caused for a while by the advance of the Arrow-Cross. It was no secret in government circles on the eve of the elections that the Arrow-Cross had German support that allowed them to conduct an exceptional campaign. Teleki, on the other hand, had no way of amending the accepted electoral law. He could only trust again in the public administration, but that was not by any means as effective as it had been. More specifically, it was not really effective against the Arrow-Cross. This in some places was presumably because some public officials connived with the Arrow-Cross. Yet that same public administration was excelling itself at the same time in squeezing out Smallholders, Social Democrats or other left-wingers. None of this favored Teleki's line of policy.

The various conservatively inclined organizations in which the churches and Teleki himself were influential did not have broad support. One was the Scout movement, in which only the leaders counted in electoral terms, of course. Another was *Actio Catholica*—less influential in Hungary than in Italy.[5] Then there was the National Corps of Catholic Agricultural Young Men's Societies and its female equivalent,[6] the Reformed Church's *Soli Deo Gloria*, mentioned earlier, and some other larger and smaller associations. These amounted to nothing compared with the radical right wing, and consisted mainly of young people without voting rights. The far right, meanwhile, gained new strength in March 1939 from legislation on compulsory military training and requisite alteration of the Levente organization. This military training for boys aged 12–18 replicated the Italian and German systems. It was not in itself fatal politically, but it certainly gave further influence to extreme right-wingers.

The first domestic move was to debate the second law on the Jews drafted and tabled by Imrédy on December 23, 1938. The main differences from the first were that it classed the Jews as a separate race (the threshold was one Jewish parent or two grand-parents), and drastically cut the quotas and extended the quota system. There was a changeover in financial and industrial circles, to the benefit of the Hungarian middle class, with 23,000–24,000 dismissals in manufacturing alone. Although Horthy in his memo forcing Imrédy to resign (on February 14) made the remarkable claim that the law had been tabled without his prior knowledge or consent, there is no sign of Horthy or the new government doing anything to tone it down.

This was not to be expected of Teleki, who was convinced that the Jews constituted a separate "biological and mental" race that had to be restricted. As a member of the Imrédy government, he had in fact taken a more radical position than the prime minister himself. Teleki's anti-Semitism rested on ideas of his own, independent of the racial theory of the Nazis, and his conclusions were different as well. He certainly wanted to curb Jewish influence, but he had no murderous intentions. During his introductory speech in the lower house, he argued for tightening the law against the Jews by saying that "Eastern" conditions prevailed in Hungary in relation to the Jews in Hungary, while the treatment of them was "Western," which had to be stopped, as it caused untold harm to the Hungarians.

In the debate in the lower house that began two days later, on February 24, many arguments against the bill were heard, but the vast majority of members supported it. That was not the case in the upper house, where amendments were proposed mainly by church representatives, some of which were passed. These mainly served to protect Jews who had converted to Christianity and extended the sphere of those not covered by the law. Finally, the previous quota of 20 percent was reduced to 6 percent (12 percent in some professions) and a "closure of accounts" placed on all industrial, financial and commercial companies.[7] The proportion of Jews in most of the occupations concerned was over 6 percent and the livelihood of many people was affected. The conclusions on how the law applied in practice have been very varied. Some have seen the Hungarian laws on the Jews simply as pieces of paper, with hardly any practical effect. Others seem to think that the implementation was much harsher than the law itself, thanks to human malice, envy and self-interest. For instance, they began to apply the 6 percent university quota in middle schools as well, or began to segregate Jewish pupils. The first view does not even fit the facts if the effects of later measures are deducted, and the second is too much of a generalization for conditions in 1939–1941. Jews in Hungary suffered plenty of grave wrongs in those two years, but their situation was still enviable compared with that of their counterparts in Nazi-ruled areas.[8]

Meanwhile, there was a swift succession of important foreign events to which the government had to react. The German occupation of the Memel could be left unremarked; even Franco's victory in Madrid and the end of the Spanish Civil War did not affect Hungary directly.[9] That was not the case with the Italian occupation of Albania, which began on April 7, as King Zog and his Hungarian consort Geraldine Apponyi had to flee the country, and the question arose as to whether the Italians were using Albania as a military springboard, as they had been in virtual control in any case.[10] However, the Hungarian government decided to ignore this act as well, for the sake of Italian friendship. But it could not do the same with events in Poland. On March 21, Foreign Minister Ribbentrop put a third proposal to the Polish government on settling the so-called Danzig question to Germany's satisfaction, and it was rejected on the 26th. The West, increasingly uncertain since the German entry into Prague, decided to take a stronger stand, and announced on the 31st an Anglo-French guarantee to protect Poland's independence.[11]

Foreign Minister Csáky, in a climate of now open international crisis, announced that Hungary was withdrawing from the League of Nations, and Teleki made official visits to Rome (April

18–22) and Berlin (April 29–May 1). The surviving documents of the visits present a very taciturn Teleki, who made no statements of any substance. He did not even open his mouth, according to Ciano.[12] The Italians, weighing every possibility, explained that if Yugoslavia should break up, contrary to their wishes, they would consider Croatia to be in their sphere of interest. Since nobody was denying or casting doubt on that from the German side, it can be described as a shared illusion that both Hungary and Italy would have some three years at their disposal before a major conflict was likely to break out. Although there were several complaints from the Hungarian side about the behavior of the new Slovak state towards its Hungarian minority and Hungary itself, which the Italians saw as a sign that the Hungarian government would seek further concessions with Axis help, Teleki and Csáky stated that they would do nothing against Slovakia without German approval.

Teleki hardly said a word during his "negotiations" with Hitler, allowing him to rant on for hours, as was his wont. However, it would have been a bold conclusion to draw from the harangue that the attack on Poland was just a question of diplomatic preparations, and still bolder to assume that the preparations had begun in Moscow.[13] It would have needed a very close acquaintance with Hitler to have understood the import of such a remark as that the Polish question certainly had to be solved "one way or the other," or to notice how often Hitler was returning in his harangue to Russia. Hitler, incidentally, expressed hope that the disputes with Poland could be settled, allowing everybody "a breather." The Hungarian negotiators presumably believed Hitler, because they immediately offered to mediate between Berlin and Warsaw, which the Germans refused, initially with despair and later quite roughly.[14]

The discussions with Ribbentrop were no more informative. The German foreign minister emphasized his point that Poland did not present a problem to Germany militarily (any more than France or Britain did), but he too left open the possibility of agreement. On the other hand, he returned several times to the problem of

minorities, in practice Hungary's German minority, demanding
greater rights for them. Foreign Minister Csáky triumphantly displayed a telegram from the new leader of the *Volksbund der
Deutschen in Ungarn*, containing warm greetings to the Hungarian
government for authorizing its foundation.

Here let us pause for a moment to consider the nature and role
of the *Volksbund*, in the light of the ample facts and data discovered
so far. Some have assumed that the moral rehabilitation of the
Volksbund follows directly from the fact that the post-1945 German
deportations were indispensable and senseless in legal and human
terms. This is obviously not a tenable position on a theoretical
plane, as one mistaken or criminal act cannot wipe out another. As
for the practical activity of the *Volksbund*, it can be conceded that
many who joined were well-intentioned people defending their situation or very existence (mainly later), and it can also be assumed
that "collective" judgment cannot be passed directly on the members. Yet organizationally, it was certainly a Nazi tool and plaything
used to harass and blackmail the Hungarian state. The heads of the
Volksbund connived with the Nazis, and some were not far from the
idea (which occurred to Hitler as well) that it should take over, from
the Gypsy-related Hungarians, the leadership of the Danubian
lands, including Hungary, within the framework of the German
Reich. On the other hand, the *Volksbund* members recalled what
Hitler had said in his great speech in the Reichstag in the autumn of
1939, when he remembered the great deportation and transportation
campaigns planned with the approval of Stalin. That was already
something that the Germans of Hungary, including the most
devoted members of the *Volksbund*, would not wish, and hence this
likewise provides no grounds for saying that some of them chose
"rule" and others "fidelity." (Here there were other, emotional and
financial motives at work as well.)

To return to Teleki's first visit to Berlin, the merit of it can be
summed up by saying that the utterances of the Nazi leaders might

raise many suspicions, but nothing was clarified and no major question advanced. The Hungarian prime minister stated, amid the toasts and statements, what Axis friendship required, but committed himself to nothing.

The general elections held at Whitsuntide, on May 28–29, ensured the governing party an absolute majority as usual (201 seats), but the Bethlen group had entirely vanished from the parliamentary group, and many "moderate" members who had won seats in 1935 were missing as well. Representation of the haute bourgeoisie and the great landowners was entirely lacking. Only 29 of the 170 members elected under governing party colors in 1935 were reelected. About half of the Hungarian Party of Life group consisted of extreme right-wingers. Bethlen was right in saying that this 50 percent was on flirting terms with the extra-party extreme right wing, with which there was also connivance in Parliament. For the great winner by the elections was Szálasi's party,[15] calling itself the Arrow-Cross Party at the time (as it had done since March 15, 1939), and in its wake, the lower house had been joined by three smaller national socialist parties and some non-party persons close to them. The Arrow-Cross, with its 29 seats, became the second-biggest group in Parliament, to which could be added the 20 seats won by other parties of the Arrow-Cross type (the United Hungarian National Socialist Party, the National Front, the racial protectors, and so on).[16] The 49 seats that they occupied compared with 24 for the Smallholder–Social Democrat–bourgeois opposition. That election amounted to a political earthquake.

Big business in Bethlen's time performed its function as one of the three pillars of power indirectly, and asserted its economic interests in the main. In 1939 there began the process of squeezing out big business from power—through the second law on the Jews and through the election results. This was offset partly by higher arms production and the need to keep the economy operating.

The bigger losers in the elections were the left-wing opposition and the Christian camp. Further research is needed into why the Smallholders and the Social Democrats collapsed. The Smallholders managed to retain only 14 of their 26 seats and the Social Democrats won 5 instead of 11. The Hungarian Party of Life used its tried methods so successfully against the Smallholders that the leader of the latter, Tibor Eckhardt, failed to get into Parliament. The Social Democrats suffered catastrophic defeats in the seats that had been thought to be safe—several in Budapest and large provincial cities. The party's newspaper, *Népszava*, ascribed this to "working-class strata still unaware politically," who had fallen victim to demagoguery. But the paper failed to explain why this had happened. The Christian party more or less destroyed itself by splitting just before the elections, so that two of the new little parties failed to gain seats, and the one that managed to ride the storm could only manage three. The new Parliament bore little similarity to the old, whose framework Bethlen had established so carefully. The whole system was collapsing. Since the method remained the same as it had been, it might be said that the "owner" was shelling it with his own guns: the aversion to reform, the manipulation of the electoral system, and the inability to open out were taking their toll.

The government could have been voted down in theory at any time. German observers were convinced that Hungarian domestic politics were explosive, and that the "solution" to this could only be a full breakthrough by the far right or military dictatorship. That did not happen, however, partly because of Teleki's great caution, and partly because the coopted members of Parliament from the newly recovered territories were still mainly loyal to the government, and finally because the Arrow-Cross-type parties could only manage to cooperate or flirt occasionally among themselves or with the extreme right-wingers of the Hungarian Party of Life. No permanent alliance of these parties and groups could be formed.

In foreign policy, Budapest suffered from a shortage of information almost equivalent to the one that it had in 1918, despite feverish diplomatic activity. Only through signs and rumors was it discovered what Germany was planning or deciding. If Rome was appealed to for extra information, it was often vague or fabricated, for two reasons: the Italians themselves were not receiving credible information in good time either, and almost too obviously by this time, they too were often unwilling to brief the "unreliable" Hungarians. An important factor in the second was Ciano. He had formed a low opinion of the Hungarian foreign minister,[17] and his orientation towards Germany had not been seriously shaken. Nevertheless, the quite unexpected news of the German–Soviet talks reached Budapest somehow, and made it clear at least that military action against Poland was inevitable. (In any case, that would probably have been the conclusion from the signs so far.) Hardly anything is known about the reactions to this news in Hungary. It can only be assumed that most camps and political groups were disorientated by it—the right and far right because it could not be squared with earlier propaganda, and the government because it contradicted the previous demands of the German government, to which Hungary had acceded by joining the anti-Comintern pact. There were the broken diplomatic relations and consequences of this, while German–Soviet pact was obviously aimed against Poland and the Baltic states, which Germany and the Soviet Union would divide between themselves. Furthermore, the Hungarian state had always officially followed an anti-Soviet and anti-Bolshevik line.

The first perceptible reaction came when government circles voiced fears of possible Russian demands and intrigues, and of pan-Slavism. Feelings seem to have been calmed quite quickly, and the outlines of a new possibility were seen. But before that possibility could be explored, the Polish question had to be considered. It is not known exactly what persuaded Teleki to address two letters each to Hitler and Mussolini on July 24, emphasizing the point that Hungary was a staunch friend to the Axis, but did not wish to take part in the campaign against Poland. In the letter emphasizing friendship, joint Hungarian–German–Italian talks were proposed to discuss the problems, and although there was no specific mention of this, the prime desire was probably to discuss territorial revision in Transylvania. The second letter laconically stated Hungary's reservations on the Polish question. This was presumably the most important message in Teleki's eyes, but it remains unclear why he felt the need to state it. Nobody had approached the Hungarian government about participation beforehand.[18] The German–Soviet pact had not been concluded. The letter caused untold (and at the time unnecessary) indignation in Berlin, in which Rome was obliged to join, although Mussolini and Ciano actually wanted to stay out of Poland as well. The basis for the letter in Teleki's eyes may have been the German propaganda against the Poles, and he seems to have read something further into those signs.

The Hungarian government cited several times the idea of "national honor" as the basis for its procedure, but the real reason may have been that Teleki wanted at all costs to keep the country out of any war. Here he was well able to do so because he had public opinion behind him, while the far right, confused by the way in which Germany was palling up with the Soviet Union, had no prescription of its own. Isolated and without a friendly neighbor as they were, the Hungarians had traditionally and instinctively supported the Poles, associating them, for instance, with the officers and men who had fought beside them against Vienna in 1848–1849. That sentimental tie continued throughout the war and even later (as in 1956, for instance), and although rationally unclear, it was strong enough to prevent either Hitler or the Arrow-Cross from breaking it. The Polish crisis proved that public opinion in Hungary could have an influence in exceptional cases. The government would have risked all its popularity if it had tried to give active support to the German campaign against Poland. (A similar, if perhaps less intense, public sentiment in favor of the Finns appeared during the Finno-Soviet war.)

The Teleki government, apart from dissociating itself from the German–Soviet war against Poland, rejected the German request on September 10 to allow reinforcements for the Polish front to pass through Hungarian territory, and responded to a similar request from the Slovak government with outright threats.[19] The faith of Germany's political and military leaders had been shaken during the Czech crisis. It now became the decisive view that such representatives of the traditional Hungarian ruling class as Horthy, Teleki and Bethlen saw the Germans as milch-cows, and had no desire to repay in any way the favors that Germany did them (or sacrifices made for them, as Hitler put it.) No account was taken of the gestures that Hungary made (withdrawing from the League of Nations, authorizing the foundation of the *Volksbund*, showing willingness to meet economic demands, reconciling military plans, and so on), but their grievances were stored up and exaggerated. The latter were crowned by the appearance in Pécs in five successive editions of a lengthy pamphlet by Iván Lajos, which assembled data to show that there was no prospect of German victory.[20] Later, the Germans were outraged when the Hungarian border was opened for Polish refugees, Polish soldiers and civilians were kept in hiding, and several other favors done by the Hungarian state.

Despite the pro-Axis statements of Teleki and Csáky, many of them made simply to hide the truth, Hungarian–German relations were clearly bad in the autumn and winter of 1939. There was no improvement in 1940 either. Spring began in foreign policy with a request from the German military High Command for safe passage across Hungary for their troops. It was explained that the Soviet Union would soon demand Bessarabia back from Romania and a German military force would be sent to protect the Romanian oilfields. There was panic in Budapest because Romania had an

Anglo-French guarantee at that time. Another factor in assessing the situation is the fact that Teleki's relations in Rome had been deepening to some extent. He went to Rome again on March 23 for a few days, and seeing Italian receptiveness to him, laid aside his reserve. While playing golf, he told Ciano that 95 percent of Hungary's population loathed the Germans (which was not true). More importantly, he said that Hungary's aim was to keep out of the conflict and he hoped that Italy would agree. On another occasion, the prime minister said that he did not want to annex to Hungary a large alien minority, which would be dangerous for the country. However, Teleki had a more notable argument to put forward about Romania, which neither Ciano nor Ribbentrop noticed. Teleki explained that Hungary did not want to move against Romania because it did not wish to be responsible, even indirectly, for opening a gate to the West for Russia. Teleki thereby made it known that if Hungary wished to do this it could. In fact the High Command had worked out in 1939 a plan for destabilizing and overrunning Romania, and in principle, it was only waiting for the requisite moment to apply it. Teleki revealed that Romania, surrounded by the Soviet Union and Germany, was in a position of defeat, a hopeless situation that Hungary wished to use against it. He added that Hungary might also work together with the Soviet Union, but it would not do so if the other side were prepared to help. Teleki's remarks were a call to the Axis powers for support for territorial revision in Transylvania.[21] This was not the prime minister's only explanation of this kind.

This concept was contradicted by the German request mentioned already, which offered Hungary no kind of compensation, in line with the prevailing German mood at the time. Some German historians have called the rumor that spread all over Europe in early 1940 of German units being sent to Romania an example of deliberately misleading German propaganda, designed to distract attention from the Western campaign that was actually being prepared.

But it is not certain that this was so. It certainly did not look like it from Budapest. Teleki drew strength out of panic. He sought a way out by alternating between capitulation and resistance, both equally unfortunate types of behavior. As he saw it, failing to meet the German request would bring a threat of occupation, while meeting it without compensation would mean that he could never look public opinion or his own reflection in the eye again. He made concrete during those days a plan that he had been nursing since January for the diplomatic and financial conditions required for establishing a government abroad. Teleki managed to send $5 million to the Washington mission through financiers.[22] He sent another trusted associate, Lipót Baranyai, to Rome, where he explained this dilemma to Mussolini and Ciano on April 8, adding that the Hungarian government was inclined towards resisting the Germans, which would result in occupation… "but," Ciano quoted him as saying, "they would prepare for a future revival." If the Italian documents can be trusted, the Duce was not impressed by that, and advised Teleki's envoy to do the Germans' bidding, emphasizing the point that Italy stood on Germany's side. About the same time, Tibor Eckhardt moved abroad by agreement with the government and the regent. Initially, he drew attention to himself with anti-German statements, but he also began secret talks in London and Washington. Eckhardt settled in the United States and continued to gather useful information to send home, about the likely direction of future American and Allied policy and requirements of Hungary.

The threat over Romania ceased after the *Wehrmacht* commenced its operations in Western Europe. Again Hungary was given no advance warning. Teleki ordered the distributed money to be returned home and continued the art of groping in the half-darkness, this time with some success. The German army was occupied in Western Europe and Romania had lost all its allies and support. There was no Czechoslovakia or Poland any more. Russia was positively hostile, and it was only a matter of time before it presented its demands in Bucharest. The Soviet state was generally known to have acknowledged some of its territorial losses after the revolution, but never in the cases of Bessarabia and Bukovina. Yugoslavia was still there in theory and might stand by Romania in memory of the Little Entente, but that could no longer be a rational expectation.

In May 1940, the Hungarian government began a systematic campaign to regain Transylvania, and there is every sign that the second Vienna Award would never have taken place otherwise. The government used not only diplomacy but military pressure, giving the impression that it would not shrink from a military solution either. It was not impossible that with Romania under Soviet, Bulgarian and Hungarian pressure, Budapest seriously considered this, ruling out the possibility that Romania would turn its back on the Soviet Union and deploy most of its troops against Hungary, and assuming that Yugoslavia would not attack Hungary from behind. The Soviet Union issued an ultimatum to Romania on June 26, and from then on, the Transylvanian question became one of great urgency and daily interest. But the military option seems not to have been chosen, despite the threats and maneuvers, as the best time for the campaign—as Red Army units marched into the territories ceded by Romania—was ignored.

Hitler had had quite enough of the Hungarians after Czechoslovakia and Poland, and for a time he refused imperiously to talk with any Hungarian representatives. Finally, he showed willingness to "dispense justice." After several postponements, he eventually received Teleki on July 11, partly to ward off any separate measures, and partly to show grace by making moves towards border revision in Transylvania. It is not absolutely certain what Hitler's motives were. He had not yet decided on his next military move (to attack Britain, the British Empire or the Soviet Union) and the German army did not know at that juncture what its next assignment would be. Perhaps the "Führer and chancellor" was already thinking of the more distant future, when his long-cherished plan to move against the East would require the use of Hungarian territory—and it would be better if this were granted voluntarily, rather than taken by force. But it is possible that he simply wanted to avoid an unnecessary conflict in a sphere in which he had an interest, while showing the "unreliable" Hungarians and the Romanians who was boss. Nor can the possibility be entirely excluded that Hitler wanted to exclude finally any chance of the Hungarian–Soviet cooperation that was always being denied in Budapest. Whatever the case, he made a promise to Teleki during the discussion that he would call on the Kingdom of Romania to examine the Hungarian demands and meet Hungary's rightful claims.

Hitler kept his promise, and a quite isolated Romanian government was forced to start negotiations. But like the Slovak–Hungarian talks, they did not lead to agreement. The Romanian government understandably wanted to minimize the territory and population that it was handing over, but what the Hungarian goal was is not quite clear. Teleki certainly wanted to regain the Székely Country, but he was not keen on corridor solutions. The two sides were so far apart that there was no prospect of bilateral agreement in any case. A new Hungarian ploy began so that the government could avoid calling on the Germans to mediate. Teleki wanted to show by this that Hungary was not competing for Nazi favors. Instead he brought up the military solution again, which attracted rather less attention in the wide world than the Hungarian government assumed. So eventually, the question was decided by a German–Italian arbitration tribunal again. The arbitrators summoned the representatives of the Hungarian and Romanian parties to Vienna, where they played a rather smaller part than at the first Vienna Award, but they had to declare in advance that they would abide by the tribunal's decision.

The arbitration tribunal announced its decision on August 30, 1940, splitting Transylvania in two.[23] Hungary gained 43,104 sq.

km with 2.4 million inhabitants, of whom 51.4 percent were
Hungarian: there were thus over a million non-Hungarians among
them. Over 400,000 Hungarians remained in Romanian territory.
This award reflected the ethnic multiplicity of the area, which
meant that it was impossible to draw a fair border, but it was capable, whether Hitler wanted it or not, of sowing even more dissension, anger, hatred and rivalry between the two countries. The
beneficiaries were certainly the Nazis.

Hardly had Miklós Horthy entered Kolozsvár on a white
horse, or the Hungarians finished rejoicing at the return of long-
desired places, before news came of mutual atrocities: Romanian
inhabitants on one side and Hungarian ones on the other being
importuned, molested and persecuted. There was little improvement in these dire conditions before the end of the war, and they
were accompanied by constant intrigues by both governments.
Victory in the ghastly contest to win the favor of the Nazis that
went on until the autumn of 1944 certainly went, incidentally, to
Marshal Ion Victor Antonescu against the Hungarians, as they
fussed, maneuvered, and fled into clumsy, easily exposed revolt.

Despite unpleasant side-effects, Teleki had scored a huge success with the second Vienna Award. But his frame of mind failed to
improve. He was clearly depressed after his triumph, if witnesses
can be believed. Some put this down to gaining less in Transylvania
than he wanted, but the depressive bout is more likely to have come
from not making the territorial revision alone and having to pay the
Nazis' price, without having requested their "good services." He
had to be "grateful" for an unrequested favor.

The huge change in the political climate is apparent. Darányi
had fallen simply for consorting with Szálasi's representatives.
Now, with Arrow-Cross prominent in the lower house, it seemed
almost natural for the party's leader, Ferenc Szálasi, to benefit from
an amnesty, and shortly afterwards, to be received by the prime
minister, who promised to obtain him an audience with the regent.
However, the Horthy–Szálasi meeting would never take place,

probably because Horthy was set firmly against it. The great expansion of the Arrow-Cross Party took place, incidentally, when its members simply mentioned the "leader," who was out of action in prison. Party organization during what was the party's most successful period was handled by Kálmán Hubay. Szálasi, after his release, managed to broker a merger of three Arrow-Cross-inclined parties, but peace did not last long. The Pálffy group soon split off, and a group of Szálasi's own party, headed by László Baky, left to join Imrédy's group. Then, as Szálasi himself concluded, the party began steadily to lose its attraction and support, so that by October 1941, it was down to about 10–15 percent of what it had been. But that could not be predicted in September 1940, of course.

The Arrow-Cross Party was a threat to the state insofar as it enjoyed German recognition and support, which varied and never exceeded certain bounds until the autumn of 1944. The reservations of Nazi observers and others had to do with Szálasi's character, behavior and remarks that sometimes conflicted with the German demand for superiority. They were also connected with the economic need felt for an "orderly" country, and the military requirement of considering the army commander-in-chief—for, whatever that job description might mean in practice, Horthy was seen as the point of reference by at least some senior officers. In the light of all this, the Germans became more interested in the now expressly far-right grouping that Imrédy was leading. Szálasi also began to be very cautious in January 1941. Hitler had bowed to Antonescu and sacrificed the Romanian Iron Guard, which the Germans had been supporting, allowing the Romanian army to mow down or arrest the Iron Guard members before the eyes of German troops stationed there. Only the leaders were taken to Germany, where they were then kept under strict guard in a camp. Szálasi had no wish to suffer the same fate, and that dictated his behavior up to September 1944, although that caution may have been one reason why his party waned.

Béla Imrédy—the ex-premier thrown out of office, thwarted in his ambitions, and deeply wounded in his feelings—had now shifted towards Nazism, encouraged by a purported discovery by German racial researchers that the "charge" against him of having a Jewish grandparent was unfounded. What they actually discovered is uncertain, however. When Imrédy opposed German expropriation of the Weiss–Chorin assets in 1944, the racial researchers announced a further discovery that the Hungarians had been right about Imrédy's ancestry after all.

In October 1940, Imrédy set up his own Party of Hungarian Renewal, causing the most rejoicing among the Germans. Imrédy appointed as "deputy leaders" Jenő Rátz, who had been his army chief of staff, and Andor Jaross, one of the coopted members of Parliament from Upper Hungary, that is, the regained area of Slovakia.[24] The split in the governing party had symbolic importance, but it made little difference to voting strengths in Parliament, as only 17 members followed Imrédy out, far fewer than he had expected. Thereafter, the struggles within the far right were about whether Szálasi and his Arrow-Cross could harness the Party of Hungarian Renewal, or whether the cleverer and more experienced Imrédy could subordinate the Arrow-Cross to him. The go-between was Jenő Ruszkay, but he could do little with the two obstinate and power-hungry men.

Romania sank into domestic crisis after meeting the Soviet ultimatum on Bessarabia and Bukovina, the Bulgarian demands in Dobrudja, and the second Vienna Award. This led to dictatorship by Antonescu, whose pro-German government requested a German guarantee and renewed an earlier request for German protection of Romanian oil wells. Berlin was happy to respond by sending so-called training troops to Romania, in what was clearly an amicable occupation of the country. But access to Romania was difficult without sending the troops across Hungary, and a further request to do this arrived in Budapest. The matter did not look too troublesome in terms of international law, as there had been a request from Romania for the troops, but the passage across Hungary was not without risks. The government agreed in return for receiving half of Transylvania, whereupon a warning came from the Foreign Office in London. If German troops were permitted to pass across to a country classed as a British ally, Britain would break off diplomatic relations, or even declare war.

The Hungarian government made a further commitment to the German bloc by signing a document of accession to the German–Italian–Japanese Tripartite Agreement on November 20.[25] Signatory governments, including the Hungarian one, salved their consciences by saying that the agreement committed them only to giving military support to another signatory in the case of attack, and it might be assumed that no such attack would occur. But regardless of the wording, joining the German–Italian–Japanese grouping inevitably set the country against the Anglo-Saxon world.

By this time, Hungary had lost all space for independent maneuver. Of the Western powers, Britain was still on its feet, but it was quite alone and the German *Luftwaffe* was making daily attempts to break its resistance and force its government into making peace. Although the United States was known to be supporting Britain in every possible way, President Franklin D. Roosevelt was a long distance away, whereas Hitler was on the doorstep. The Polish defenses had long collapsed and Mussolini had proved himself to be faithful to Germany. People were not aware in Hungary of what troubles there were in that relationship, but if they had known it would have made no difference. Teleki by now was fighting a rearguard action, whether he knew it or not.

The only direction left in which Hungary might have promoted other relations was with the Soviet Union, which was also a German ally at that time. After a fruitless attempt in the 1920s, Hungary had established diplomatic relations with the Soviets in 1934, but they were broken again by Moscow when Hungary signed the anti-Comintern pact. The German–Soviet pact had placed matters in a new light. Foreign Minister Vyacheslav Molotov now had no objection to reopening the missions and resuming relations as if nothing had happened. Negotiations began on trade matters, on the release of the communist Mátyás Rákosi, who was in prison in Hungary, and on the return of Hungarian military banners captured by the Russian army in 1849. Rákosi was indeed released to the Soviet Union, and the Russians returned 56 banners on March 20, 1941, to József Kristóffy, the Hungarian envoy in Moscow, and Major General Gábor Faragho, the military attaché. These were shipped back to Budapest under military guard and placed in the Museum of Military History. By that time, Berlin had already decided that the Soviet Union would be the next direction of attack for the *Wehrmacht*, and military preparations were under way.

Hungary's foreign policy suffered a catastrophe with Mussolini's so-called plan for parallel war and its failure.[26] The first stage was an attack on Greece on October 28, 1940. The Italian defeat at Greek hands placed much more emphasis on the Yugoslav question. Hitler soon saw that the outcome in Greece meant that he had come to Italy's aid, and it was not immaterial how Yugoslavia would react to that. The Germans, incidentally, had been pointing out to the Hungarian government for many years the importance of reaching agreement with Yugoslavia, but now it was more urgent still, and the effort was understandably supported by Italy as well. It gained further significance in the late autumn of 1940, when Hitler decided on the directions of possible German military policy, rejecting any landing in Britain or formation of a broad system of alliances against the British Empire in favor of an attack to the East. That meant setting in order the Balkans and the whole "intermediate area."

Teleki had been dealing with the Yugoslav question ever since his appointment. A reliable associate, Miklós Kozma, had been sent to Belgrade in the spring of 1939 to put out peace feelers, but the Yugoslav government showed little enthusiasm for the small territorial adjustments proposed as a condition for friendship. So the prime minister presumably had to swallow hard when Yugoslav–Hungarian relations were settled on German and Italian advice without any Hungarian conditions being met. The treaty of eternal friendship signed in Belgrade on December 12 meant in practice that Hungary had abandoned all aspirations to revise its border with Yugoslavia. Whether this was in the hope of obtaining "more room for maneuver" has not been verified, but it seems unlikely. On the other hand, the agreement slotted well into Germany's policy of securing Yugoslavia as an ally, or at least as a benevolent neutral country. This Hitler tried to promote also by diplomatic means. He managed to persuade Bulgaria to accede to the Tripartite Agreement. The Yugoslavs resigned themselves to the same move after long hesitation, and actually signed it on March 25, 1941, but when the signatory prime minister arrived back in Belgrade, he found that a coup led by the Air Force general Dusan Simović had installed a new government. Simović refused to recognize the signature, appealed for British protection of his country, and even established relations with the Soviet Union. Hitler decided on the same day to attack, occupy and dismember Yugoslavia.

Yugoslavia could have been approached across Austria (in other words, directly from Germany), but Hitler knew that Hungary, regardless of its treaty of friendship, had territorial demands on Yugoslavia. He insisted that some of the attacking forces approach through Hungary, and that the Hungarian army take part in the campaign as well. The German Foreign Ministry made this demand on the same day and informing the Hungarian envoy. The message was addressed to Horthy, who on the following day, March 28, held a select meeting that Teleki and Foreign Minister László Bárdossy attended. It was decided to meet the German demand with certain reservations. The exchange of letters between Hitler and Horthy was noted at the next meeting of the government, where the prime minister expressed his concerns. Teleki's hesitant, uncertain nature was again displayed during those days. He announced to the Council of Ministers that he was resigning, thereby signifying *de facto* that he disagreed with the decision on Yugoslavia, but he immediately withdrew his resignation again at the ministers' request. The question was finally decided at a meeting of the High Defense Council on April 1.

Teleki devised an artful way of minimizing Hungary's responsibility for the decision in the eyes of the Western powers, but in the meantime the Hungarian and German military commanders were agreeing on their cooperation down to the finest detail. Teleki then tried to gain acceptance in London and Washington for a formula in which Hungary was not moving against Yugoslavia, with which it had signed a treaty only days before, because that country had ceased to exist by the time that the Hungarian move took place. (Hungary's campaign would be delayed compared with Germany's for just that reason.) Furthermore, Hungary was not going to carry out a real military campaign, but simply advance into Hungarian-inhabited districts to protect the population there. The Foreign Ministry sent off the telegrams about this on March 30 and received a reply from London on April 2. Apparently the arrival of that telegram was the moment at which Pál Teleki decided to take his own life.

But the background to the telegram from London is rather uncertain. Envoy György Barczay, in his memoirs, recalls in detail the letter that Teleki wrote to him on March 12, which caused him to wait on the Foreign Office. There he spoke with Anthony Eden, who essentially had the same to say about Hungary as had been said by the British in the autumn of 1940.[27] However, he cannot identify the day on which the discussion took place, and so there is no way to tell if the Yugoslav question could have been raised at all. It could certainly not have been raised on the basis of Teleki's letter of early March, because no such question existed until March 27 and Teleki did not even mention Yugoslavia in his letter. Nor does Barczay state that he met somebody again afterwards. So what did he do? Very probably, he repeated what he had heard before, applying the British position of principle to the now specific Yugoslav case. This assumption is supported by the wording of one sentence in his telegram as well: "The strong emphasis on special Hungarian motives expressed by your Excellency in the above telegram will hardly be understood here…" If the envoy had already put forward these points to the British, he would hardly have referred to the want of understanding in the future tense. But the envoy was essentially right in saying that Teleki's Hungarian formula stood little chance of being understood. However, Teleki knew the general British view well. He could have drawn the same conclusion for himself, and if he was astounded by Barczay's telegram, then that says more about Teleki's state of mind than about the contents of the telegram.

Teleki made his confession during the night and visited his dying wife in her sanatorium—something that a man is hardly likely to do without good reason. He must have gone to see her to say farewell. In the morning, he was found dead in his apartment in the prime minister's offices in the Sándor Palace, with a bullet through his skull. Teleki had sunk under the weight of responsibility. As he wrote in his parting note to Horthy, he felt guilty of "breaking his word," damaging the nation's pride, and "robbing a corpse." Despite his crisis of conscience, Teleki would probably not have taken the ultimate step if he too had written off in his thoughts the Western powers and in principle the democracies, as Hitler, Mussolini, and many leading Hungarians had done, and if he had believed as blithely as they did in German victory. But he did not do the first and he was far from sure about the second. In fact, he felt sure that there was no prospect of German victory. That appears in his briefing to the London and Washington envoys about a month earlier, where he called "staying out" the main strand of Hungary policy, and argued that the outcome of the war was "doubtful" and likely to lead to total or "not quite total" defeat for Germany. What is more, the prime minister had to realize that he had nobody to turn to on this. Horthy agreed to the German request in return for further promises of territory. The chiefs of staff supported it wholeheartedly, and most of the cabinet was in favor. The majority of Parliament would never have forgiven him for missing the chance of further territorial gains.

It seems that the main motive behind Teleki's suicide should be sought in the German defeat that he foresaw, coupled with his mental state and the fact that his wife was dying. His state of mind was exacerbated by the domestic political situation, which had left him nowhere to go. The death of Teleki breached the last barrier that was preventing Hungary from falling into the Nazi trap. The Catholic Church agreed that the suicidal prime minister could be buried with church rites, and thereby unwittingly stoked rumors that Pál Teleki had not taken his own life at all, but been murdered.[28]

Notes

1. News spread in the early 1920s that Horthy was impressionable. More research is needed, but it can be said that he was seemingly influenced on many questions but implacable on others. The latter included the idea or conviction that he developed about the relation between himself and the army.
2. This was because of German sensitivities, as Reményi-Schneller was one of their most important confidants. Dismissing Csáky would have caused immediate suspicion in Berlin. However, Teleki should probably have risked the second in the interests of his own policy, at least replacing the unreliable Csáky with an ostensibly neutral, balanced career diplomat.
3. *Magyar Élet Pártja.*

4. It was opposed first of all by the army. Teleki had to withdraw the plans that he had detailed from the agenda.

5. It began to operate in Hungary in 1932.

6. KALOT and KALÁSZ.

7. The first law had applied only to state-owned corporations.

8. The first massive wave of Jewish persecution began in Polish territories in 1939. The second began in 1941.

9. The government recognized and established diplomatic relations with the new regime.

10. It was assumed that Albania would be a military base for future Italian military action in the Balkans.

11. This formula left room for negotiation, as it did not include a guarantee of Poland's territorial integrity.

12. Csáky, on the other hand, said, *inter alia*, that Hitler was mad, as he had established with his own eyes. This was still the golden age of the German–Italian relationship, with the two dictators in full personal sympathy with each other, and so Csáky's comment outraged not only Mussolini, but even the cynical Ciano.

13. Our knowledge of those negotiations is incomplete, but Stalin and Hitler had certainly made the first gestures by then and had started talking about economic matters.

14. The episode shows that German organizations and personages disagreed on the Polish question. Csáky noted how Goering had expressly requested such a move, but Ribbentrop decisively rejected it.

15. Szálasi himself was serving a prison sentence at the time and so did not gain a seat.

16. *Egyesült Magyar Nemzeti Szocialista Párt*; National Front. These usually worked together but not always. There were cases where one or other party dissociated itself from the Arrow-Cross and support for the government.

17. Ciano's role was ambivalent not only in his own country, but also from the Hungarian point of view. He generally agreed with the Hungarian criticisms of the Germans, but at least in 1938–1940 he decided every question in the Germans' favor when he negotiated with them. He then tried to assert his own convictions (if he had any) through certain details and obscure political combinations.

18. The known documents do not even include a notification to the Hungarian government of the impending attack.

19. The German foreign minister brusquely rebuked the Hungarian government, but also forbade the Slovaks to take any step against Hungary without Berlin's approval.

20. *Németország háborús esélyei a német szakirodalom tükrében* (Germany's War Chances in the Light of German Specialist Literature), Pécs, 1939. The government banned the brochure on German insistence, but helped its author to go abroad.

21. During the visit, Teleki enquired about Ciano's knowledge of bridge, saying that they had to think of the time when they would meet in Dachau. This showed that Teleki knew about the German concentration camps, but had no idea how they operated.

22. The money was to be banked by János Pelényi, the Hungarian envoy in Washington DC, and Teleki's instructions listed the people who could make use of the sum.

23. Hungary's interests were again upheld by Ciano against the hesitant Ribbentrop.

24. Jaross had been "government commissioner for Upper Hungary," but was dismissed by Teleki on the grounds that the task was over.

25. The agreement was signed on September 27.

26. This meant that the Italian army would act in parallel with the Germans but not together. German potential and friendship was to lead to Italian rule in the Mediterranean (including a significant part of North Africa), and to Italian dominance in the Balkans. The concept foundered on the Italian defeats in Greece and North Africa.

27. According to Gyula Juhász, Barczay spoke with Alexander Cadogan, the permanent undersecretary. Juhász is probably right, as he relied on British records, whereas Barczay wrote from memory. The two accounts of the discussion agree.

28. These assumptions involve an intricate scenario that seems impossible and superfluous. There was no motive for Germany to murder Teleki once Hungary had agreed to give the *Wehrmacht* passage and join in the attack on Yugoslavia. Nor did the very varied arsenal of Nazi methods otherwise include the assassination of individual politicians.

8. The Economy and Society
in the Period of Territorial Revision and War

The territorial changes of 1938–1941 greatly increased Hungary's population and caused major movements of people. A population of 8,688,312 in 1930 had become 14,683,323 by 1941, and its density decreased, as the areas gained were more lightly populated. By the end of the war, 64,000 public employees had moved into the reannexed territories, while 90,000 Slovaks had fled from Upper Hungary, some 200,000 Romanians from North Transylvania, and 21,000 Serbs from the South Country (Vojvodina), and 190,000 Hungarians had left Romanian-ruled South Transylvania, for North Transylvania or for the Trianon territory. There were smaller refugee movements in collapsing Yugoslavia, mainly Croatia (about 1,500). Another movement involved settling about 18,000 ethnic Hungarians (Székely and Csángó) from Bukovina in the South Country, mainly in homes and on land abandoned by Serbs.

Territorially speaking, the country had almost doubled in size, from 93,000 sq. km to 171,000 sq. km, by 1941. Many areas of historical Hungary rich in mineral resources and other valuable industrial raw materials still remained outside the borders, but there was a considerable gain. Imports of timber and salt became superfluous. North Transylvania had valuable gold, silver, copper and lead mines, and some minor coal mines, although the major coal mines and mineral workings remained in Romania, along with the oil and gas fields. So too did the major industrial installations of South Transylvania, while the North had only small-scale or insignificant manufacturing firms, apart from a few processors of timber and food. The main raw materials to be found in the reannexed North were timber and iron ore.

The area of farmland increased in absolute terms from 13,142,000 sq. km to 21,987,000 sq. km, but the proportion of the total declined from 70.73 to 62.85 percent, mainly to the detriment

of arable land (down from 60.4 to 50.74 percent). Valuable agricultural land was gained in the Csallóköz (Žitný ostrov) and Bácska
(Bačka) districts. Elsewhere the arable land was less fertile.
Subcarpathia, North Transylvania and the strip of Upper Hungary
were not self-sufficient in grain or meat, although they were rich in
meadow and good-quality pasture, with relatively greater herds of
cattle and sheep than Trianon Hungary. These were expressly agricultural areas, however, and far from self-sufficient in manufacturing. Bácska, as the most valuable grain-producing area of historical
Hungary, could have supplied the needs of the areas that suffered
from shortages, but for a May 1941 agreement to supply all the
Bácska grain surplus to the Germans (and to a lesser extent the
Italians.)

Most of the public greeted the increase in the country's territory and economic wealth with great joy. Few appreciated the price
paid or projected it forward. The war was felt little in Hungary
before 1941, except as a factor behind the economic growth that
started with the Győr program of 1938. Industrial growth in 1939
was almost 24 percent, including 53.2 percent for engineering,
which was more than the aggregate increase of the previous 20
years. Such expansion was unprecedented in Hungarian industrial
history. There was a corresponding increase in export volume from
362,400 tons in 1938 to 1,026,000 tons in 1942. But the figures disguised wasteful exploitation of resources that would cause rapid
falls in production and exports later.

Trading had become almost unidirectional. Apart from the two
Axis powers, Hungary could only trade with neutral European
countries (Sweden, Switzerland and Turkey), whose demand for
Hungarian goods was minimal. After the *Anschluss*, 66 percent of
Hungary's exports went to Germany, which took more than was
actually produced in 1939 and 1940. In 1942, German orders
amounted to 92 percent of exports. This domination would have
been oppressive in any case, even if the Germans had paid their

bills. In fact, accumulated German debt to Hungary was far from negligible, and its effect extended from trade into public finance, where it exacerbated an already desperate situation. The German debt rose year by year after 1941 (from 140 million marks to 1,035 and then 1,500 million), and reached 4,765 million *pengő* by 1944. The Germans offset 35 million *pengő* of that in 1943 by returning Hungarian securities in German hands, but it was only a symbolic gesture amounting to 1 percent of the debt. As the Germans scoured the country for raw materials and industrial capacity, German politicians spoke of compulsory sacrifices, and their so-called economic experts and Hungarian followers emphasized how Hungary should be satisfied with the role of an agricultural country, turning itself into one gigantic cannery.

The budget deficit was not all due to German non-payment. Mounting military spending and arms orders could not be funded out of revenues. Successive state loans were raised and inflation became chronic. National income in 1944 was four times that of 1938–1939, but the proportion of expenditure rose from 33.1 percent to 71.7 percent. State debt in 1943 was about 6.9 billion *pengő* and rose to incalculable heights in 1944.

As for agricultural status within the Nazi *Grossraumwirtschaft*, the logic of war called for the opposite: as fast an industrial development as possible. The main investments were in bauxite mining and aluminum processing. Most of the bauxite was shipped to Germany, but Hungarian aluminum production increased several times over. Alumina production rose from 10,000 tons to 40,000, and aluminum output from 1,310 tons to 9,870, through major capacity increases at the Mosonmagyaróvár Alumina Factory and the aluminum smelters at Csepel and Felsőgalla. A whole new combine was built at Ajka. Even these could not meet the wartime demand, and a new high-capacity Danube Valley Alumina Factory[1] was started, but never completed. The war also promoted oil production in Hungary, with the

Germans taking 43 percent of the output in 1943 and 77 percent in 1944.

The impetus for industry came from iron and steel. The increase in military consumption was covered partly from regained iron ore deposits and partly from the cessation of exports. The big ironworks (Weiss Manfréd, MÁVAG, Győr Wagon, Hunters' Ammunition, Láng Engineering, and so on) responded to huge state orders for everything from ammunition to helmets and tanks by expanding capacity and workforce enormously. The Hungarian orders were paid out of the budget. The 1 billion *pengő* of investment in 1938 became 4.5 billion by 1942, of which 2.3 billion had already been spent by the end of 1941. German orders also increased, as Germany sought to decentralize production, in order to keep it away from the increasingly effective Allied bombing raids. Most of the German commission work concerned aircraft production. Hungary had been making small numbers of aircraft at Csepel and Győr before 1938, but the big factories were built during the war. The Danube Aircraft Factory[2] built fuselages and engines, and the aircraft division of Győr Wagon[3] built fuselages as well. Manufacture of various Messerschmidt types began in 1943. The state's role in this is clear from the fact that Győr Wagon's order book, worth about 13.6 million *pengő* in 1938, leaped up year after year to reach 430 million in 1942–1943, while the average workforce rose from 1,272 to 12,000. There were similar changes in the figures for other big arms manufacturers.

While the arms industry flourished, consumer goods were in dire straits, mainly for want of raw materials. Most affected was the rapidly expanding textile industry, as it received only a fraction of its required cotton imports (1,660 tons out of 30,000 in 1942). Attempts were made to use flax and hemp flock and artificial fibers as substitutes. Although domestic wool was available, it was mixed with artificial fibers. The leather industry suffered a shortage of cow hide, and so only army boots were made out of leather, and civilians had to make do with soles made of wood or rubber and uppers made of pigskin. Soon there was no more good-quality rubber for soles either, as it was taken for tires on military vehicles. In food processing, the canneries did well on military orders. Chemicals also developed, but feedstock problems caused some sections to plunge into decline. Artificial fertilizer production, for instance, peaked at 102,000 tons in 1941, only to fall to 27,000 tons in 1942 and just 14,600 tons in 1943. The Győr program meant big construction orders up to 1941 (for infrastructural and military installations) and then a drastic decline due to curbs on energy and raw materials.

All in all, Hungary's industrial capacity and output grew rapidly from 1938 to 1943—the high point, with a production increase of 38 percent over 1938. Thereafter, capacity could be increased no further, and the persecution of the Jews in 1944 brought about an economic and social crisis, while the air raids did huge damage to human lives and to industry and the infrastructure. In September 1944, the country became a battle zone.

The huge investments and orders were far from covered by state revenues. State debt rose and inflation accelerated. Overspending could be expected to have catastrophic results even if it was possible to dream of "ultimate" victory, but the front situation in 1943 made that look out of the question.

The Győr program had not reckoned with the way in which the foreseeable and now pressing needs of war called for a program of agricultural development. Some preliminary efforts had been made, but the sudden increase in needs meant that the work of the Ministry of Agriculture and its experts had to be speeded up. It has been seen that agriculture had performed poorly in Trianon Hungary, and in the recovered territories it was even more backward and its yields even lower. The Ministry of Agriculture under Dániel Bánffy submitted to Parliament at the end of 1941 a ten-year development plan for the whole sector and connected activity, budgeted to cost 1 million *pengő*. It included education, experimentation, soil improvement, consolidation of land holdings, irrigation, establishment of model farms, processing, and improvement of the sales chain, in other words all the positive proposals ever made. The Ministry presumably intended this seriously, as work on the irrigation system for the plan had started before the bill was presented. This involved irrigating 200,000 *hold* (114,000 ha) of the Great Plain and constructing a navigable 100-kilometer Eastern Main Canal. That is as far as the grand program for agriculture ever got, for want of funds to finance it.

After Hungary entered the war, the state began the compulsory purchase of ever-larger quantities of a widening range of agricultural products, for central distribution. There was a swift succession of regulations to cover rationing of foodstuffs with coupons. The obligation to sell to the state was joined in 1942 by a measure setting the amount to be sold at 50 kg of grain equivalent for each unit of land valued at 1 gold crown, 20–22 percent of it in grain and fat, and the rest in any other produce. The state then began to interfere in production itself, designating certain industrial crops, such as flax, hemp, sunflower, tobacco, rape and sugar beet, followed later by soybeans. This slewed the growing structure towards industrial crops.

The rationing system introduced in 1941 was extended gradually to all foodstuffs and most articles in general use. It started with bread and flour coupons and went on to sugar, meat, fats, milk and dairy products. Appropriate coupons had to be presented in restaurants as well. The system allowed for extra rations for those doing heavy manual labor, for pregnant women, and so on, but the rations in every category were steadily reduced. Rationing of consumer goods such as clothes, shoes, detergents and soap soon followed, and there were curbs on electricity, gas, and water consumption. Serving meat was forbidden on certain days of the week. Daily life soon became a tortuous affair, compounded after the German occupation by regular Allied air raids.

The territorial revisions altered the structure of society. What had been an almost pure nation state came to include sizable ethnic minorities again: 13.5 percent in Upper Hungary, 87.3 percent in Subcarpathia, 48.6 percent in North Transylvania, and 36.6 percent in the South Country were not ethnic Hungarians, but Slovaks, Ruthenians, Romanians, Serbs or Croats. (The proportion of non-Hungarians nationally rose to 22–25 percent.) These sizable communities in the reoccupied territories either greeted the Hungarian army and ensuing officials with hostility, or soon turned against a regime that promised them no good. Teleki was aware of these tensions and devised a scheme for the autonomy of Subcarpathia, where the native Hungarian population was small, and submitted it to Parliament on August 5, 1939, but it met with military opposition and had to be withdrawn. He tried to lessen the anomalies in North Transylvania by himself taking on the post of government commissioner, but that did not do much good either and the atrocities continued. The situation was even worse in the South Country, where the Hungarian army encountered partisan units in the early days, and about 150,000 Serbs who had settled since December 31, 1918, were deported. (They were partly replaced by Székely or Csángó Hungarians from Bukovina and Moldavia.) As before, the Hungarian state stood helpless before the national question, without any plans or techniques. This left a great deal of scope for carpet-baggers and careerists in the newly acquired territories. The efficiency of the Hungarian civil administration that took over from the military was far below the average for the rest of the country. The harm was not confined to the minorities; the local Hungarians were soon disillusioned by it as well.

The structure of religious affiliations also changed. The proportion of Roman Catholics declined from 66 percent to 55 percent, while that of Greek Catholics jumped to 10 percent. The Reformed Church accounted for 19 percent, the Evangelicals (Lutherans) for 5 percent, and the Orthodox Churches for 3.8 percent. There was also a shift in the urban/rural ratio, as the acquired territories were

more agricultural than Trianon Hungary. The latter took all the
investment in response to the wartime economic growth. Nothing
of any note was developed in the new territories, where people
hardly discerned anything of the temporary boom.

The boom for the population as a whole lasted until 1941, after
which it was hidden by the multiplicity of everyday problems.
There had already been challenges, but they had lasted a relatively
short time and there was still nothing to fear from the peacetime
enlistments of men into the army. The year 1941 marked the beginning of the war for the Hungarians, with its especially cruel and
tragic phase taking place in 1943–1945. Irrespective of the size of
the Hungarian forces on the eastern front, the High Command
sought the highest level of military readiness, and called up the age
cohorts in succession for military training, so that in the end there
were almost a million men under arms. Most of these were peasants, as the workers and engineers in industry could hardly be
spared, and the public administration, health service and education
sectors could contribute little. The call-up of the male population
caused increasing disturbance in agriculture. Everybody knew that
you could be wounded, killed or taken prisoner on the eastern front.
Families often received news of heroic deaths or were informed
that a soldier—a husband, a son or a grandson—was missing. Some
of the injured arrived home again, many of them to face lifelong
handicaps. The remnants of the Second Army were in such a state
that the authorities hardly wanted to let them home, lest their tales
of their ghastly experiences cause tension behind the lines.

The confusion in society was exacerbated by the laws and regulations on the Jews. Jews and non-Jews alike had to learn that this
was now a country whose citizens differed in their rights, or where
citizens who qualified as Jews had no rights at all. A succession of
laws left ever more Jews and their families destitute, as they lost
their jobs, chamber memberships and trading licenses, were forbidden to publish, exhibit or act, had their trading licenses withdrawn

or had their property confiscated. The National Defense Act of 1939 established labor service, into which were enlisted those not qualified to bear arms on some grounds. Among the grounds cited were origin, and moral or political objections, which showed that those to be enlisted in the labor service would mainly be Jews, members of ethnic minorities, and left-wingers. However, Jews were not explicitly barred from armed service until the act of 1942, which stated that they could only be called up for labor service. Unarmed labor servicemen sent to the front were given mortally dangerous tasks such as mine clearance, and treated so badly that Minister of Defense Vilmos Nagy, who had contrived to visit a labor service unit during a tour of the front, swore to improve their conditions. He had little success. The inaccurate figures available suggest that some 25,000–50,000 men died in labor service.

There was further social confusion as people classed as Jews sought ways to protect themselves through flight, while others fished in muddy waters trying to turn their plight to their advantage. There was trouble in the churches as Jews rushed to protect themselves through baptism, although the clergy, Catholic or Reformed, were aware that the converts were not sincere in their beliefs, but just seeking refuge. The Catholic Church was fairly liberal about baptizing converts, but the Reformed Church was more rigorous. Meanwhile, Jewish artisans and traders sought "straw men"— dummy non-Jewish partners—in whose name the business could continue and who charged highly for the service. This all caused moral depravation, which increased under the German occupation.

As Jewish authors, artists and performers vanished, Nazi films began to replace Western ones, and the radio was full of news from the front and bellicose military music. There was a fashion for "remote marriage," often never consummated as the men at the front were killed in battle. The intellectual, cultural and associated moral decline that had begun in 1938–1939 culminated during the occupation. Only right-wing and far-right papers and publications remained by 1944. With the deportation of the Jews came vultures to seize their possessions, in ostensibly legal ways and simply by looting.

The war gradually robbed people of their pleasures. Life became filled increasingly with cares and suffering. There was no longer any sense in saving or making big purchases, as the army would requisition cars, motorcycles, carts or horses, and the Arrow-Cross confiscated radios. By this time families had themselves as well as their young men at the front to worry about, as their homes and possessions were in danger. Because of the air raids, anybody who could left the cities and the areas around railway junctions, and those who remained did not stray far from an air raid shelter. Life had become paralyzed.

Notes

1. *Dunavölgyi Timföldgyár.*
2. *Duna Repülőgépgyár.*
3. *Győri Vagongyár Repülőgépipari Üzem.*

6. WARFARE RETURNS

1. Hungary's Entry into the War

It was a mistake to appoint László Bárdossy as foreign minister,[1] but it was an even graver one to let him run the country in perilous times. This was a task for which his qualifications and capabilities might have been adequate in peacetime, but not in the political conditions of Hungary in 1941, least of all after a lifetime as a Foreign Ministry official.[2] Bárdossy had no political experience, no political support of his own, nor even a group around him. He stood almost alone, and tried to make up for that partly by behaving simply as an executive, and partly by interfering in an arbitrary fashion.

On the Yugoslav question, he simply carried out what had been prepared under the Teleki government. He waited for Yugoslavia to be broken up by the *Wehrmacht* and the Croatian state to be declared on April 10, while confirming accurately with the Germans what territory the Hungarian army was to occupy. The army then occupied these areas—the Bácska (Bačka), the Danube–Dráva triangle, the Muravidék (Pomurje) and the Muraköz (Međimurje)—on April 11. Hitler had made mention at the beginning of the crisis of some kind of "Croatian–Hungarian" cooperation, but Horthy had rejected the idea. Somewhat later debate arose over the status of the Yugoslav Banate, which Hitler had promised to Hungary, but he backed down on that in the face of Romania's chagrin, and thought it best to keep the disputed area under German occupation. The Muraköz was later claimed by Croatia under Ante Pavelić, but there Hitler ruled in Hungary's favor. As a result of the military campaign, considered at the time to be a territorial revision, Hungary gained over 11,000 sq. km and 1 million inhabitants, of whom only 40 percent were Hungarians.

With that, Hungary gained its greatest extent since Trianon. The extra territory obviously increased the country's military potential, raw material resources and economy, but it also exacerbated problems in the annexed areas, such as the revival of the minority question, the general lack of preparation and the capital shortage.

The South Country was occupied without major military incidents, with just a few paramilitary detachments opposing quite modest Hungarian forces. But dissatisfaction spread rapidly, mainly because the government expelled some 150,000 non-Hungarians who had settled there since December 31, 1918. The resulting partisan activity caught the army unprepared.

The General Staff—Henrik Werth had replaced Jenő Rátz as chief in 1938—operated as a pressure group. Werth's excellent links with the German military gave him faster access to information than the Foreign Ministry or the government had. He knew at the beginning of May of the German plan for an eastern offensive and recommended to the government on the 6th that it should offer Hungary's forces for an attack on the Soviet Union. This proposal was rejected by the Council of Ministers on June 15, but the matter remained open and unavoidable thereafter, as Werth made sure that it stayed on the agenda, and he seems to have been the main influence on the decision-making process. One argument that he advanced concerned territorial matters. Romania, he said, would undoubtedly want to take part, and this would place Hungary at a disadvantage, perhaps jeopardizing its territorial gains. He also mentioned with less emphasis the demands to be made for taking part in the anti-Bolshevik struggle. Werth was the one to elicit the German statement that the *Wehrmacht* would be glad to see Hungarian participation if the government ostensibly offered it voluntarily. The chief of General Staff had only to put the question to hear the desired answer and pass it on to the government and to Horthy.[3]

But the final decision to join the war was prompted by the mysterious bombing incident at Kassa (Košice). It is not worth surveying here all the conflicting reports, statements and denials, as they provide no clear evidence from which a firm conclusion can be drawn, but there is one thing that is known for sure worth mentioning. An exactly equivalent provocation from the air preceded the Finnish declaration of war on the Soviet Union on June 25, 1941, not illogically in view of the Soviet losses in the Winter War of 1939–1940. But the conclusion to be drawn from a real concurrence between the two incidents would have to be that the Soviet Air Command was making some kind of sport out of seeing how many neighboring countries could be provoked into entering the war against the Soviet Union, which is absurd, to say the least. Although there is no excluding the possibility that some kind of Soviet mistake was made at Kassa, there is a likelier assumption on the *cui prodest* principle that the impetus behind the provocations came from military circles intent on pushing Hungary into the war. The likeliest explanation is that certain local and German personages were involved.

Border incidents and similar provocations often supply an excuse for war, as psychological resonators, but only occasional provocations out of the many lead to actual conflict. With the Kassa incident, it would have been possible to accept the reports stating that the planes were not Soviet, or to take the Soviet denial at face value. But these reports were not known to the regent or members of the government, as nobody told them of them.[4] The prime minister had been convinced by Werth and his "military" argument. Bárdossy shared the view that entry into the war was necessary and inevitable. Rather than pursuing the political debate further, he intervened arbitrarily in the decision-making after hearing the reports.[5] The strongest factor was probably a succession of announcements by Italy, Romania, Slovakia and Finland that they would join the German campaign, leading to fears of isolation that

would put Hungary's territorial gains at risk. The military and political leaders, still convinced of German victory, took the country
into war to protect or build on the territorial gains, not with any
desire to overthrow Bolshevism. Among the concrete evidence of
this is the way in which the politicians and the chiefs of staff who
succeeded Werth sought to minimize the part that Hungary played
in the Russian campaigns. Only later, as the prospect of German
defeat loomed, was fear of Bolshevism the factor that kept the
country in the war, along with fear of German occupation.

It is time to approach a question that still engrosses
Hungarians today. What would have happened if Hungary had not
joined the war? The political defenders of the war argue that there
would have been immediate or imminent occupation and more
bloodshed than actually occurred. The question is academic, of
course, as there was no political force in Hungary to push for such
a policy, but it can be seen as a theoretical alternative. First of all,
it can be stated confidently that no German occupation would have
occurred in 1941. Hitler and the Armed Forces High Command
(OKW) had been convinced that the German army could complete
the eastern campaign in five or six months, but it was clear by 1942
that any such *Blitzkrieg* was unrealistic. German pressure was
stepped up. When German intelligence indicated in the spring of
1943 that Hungary was seeking a way out of the war, the German
Army Command was ordered by Hitler to devise another plan for
occupying Hungary, although this was not carried out, probably
because of events in Italy. Thereafter, it was only a matter of when
the occupation would occur, and the Hungarian government and
army should have considered that. If the Germans had carried out
in the autumn of 1943 the plan that they had devised, it would have
advanced the date when the Allies began to bombard Hungarian
targets, and allowed the Nazis to exterminate every single Jew and
spread havoc among opposing conservatives and left-wingers. But
there is very little likelihood that German occupation would have

brought much greater loss of life on the front. After all, it was Hitler's unshakable conviction that arms should not be placed in the hands of inimical peoples, who were not to be credited however much they pleaded or swore.[6] This remained his belief, and he allowed only his most faithful followers in occupied countries to raise small units of volunteers and send them to war.[7] So there were no Czech, Polish or Serb units on the eastern front, and the French and Belgians could only send insignificant bands of volunteers. After the tide turned in Italy and German forces moved in, the Germans disarmed the Italian army and interned its soldiers. The same procedure featured in the plans for Hungary. So if the Germans had arrived earlier, bomb damage and the number of racial and political victims would have been greater, but military losses would have been smaller. However, that no longer applied in 1944.

On June 26, Bárdossy told the Council of Ministers that the regent had decided to declare war on the Soviet Union over the Kassa bombing. Note was taken of this without debate. He then made the announcement to the Soviet envoy, and units of the Hungarian army crossed the border on the following day. Some 90,000 men of the Carpathian Group[8] rapidly reached the River Dnester with hardly any resistance and then divided the group into two. The Rapid Deployment Force continued the advance while the other units performed occupation tasks in Ukraine.

According to the database of the aliens' office (KEOKH) and the Ministry of the Interior, it was agreed at the same time with the prime minister's approval that Jews from the northeastern territories, Subcarpathia and Northern Transylvania would be deported to Ukraine. Some 15,000 people were rounded up according to lists and sent by train to Kőrösmező (Jasinya), whence they were taken by various means of transportation to the Kamenets Podolsky district and released. Nothing could be done with this mass of people bringing minimal means of subsistence, and eventually the problem was "solved" by an *Einsatzgruppe*, which rounded up the Jews and massacred them *tout court*, leaving the bodies in a heap.[9] A small, unknown number of the deportees managed to escape, having set off back home and received some help on the way from local people and railway workers.

The persecution of the Jews in 1941 did not remain on the level of individual atrocities. The third law on the Jews was conceived in terms of "racial protection." The government had been under constant pressure in this regard since the second law had been proclaimed, from the Arrow-Cross, the extreme right-wingers in Imrédy's circle, the right wing of the governing party, and even some members of the government itself. The main objections were that many people had been able to evade the second law, above all the very rich, and that it had made too many exceptions in the first place (for converts to Christianity, half-Jews and mixed marriages). The prospect of amending it had not been ruled out by Teleki, but the drafting and submission to Parliament came in Bárdossy's time, in June 1941. The fourth section of the Act on Augmenting and Amending the Marriage Act forbade marriage between Jews and non-Jews on grounds of protecting the purity of the Hungarian race. During the debate in the lower house it was mainly the Catholic clergy, irrespective of party, that spoke against the bill, along with Károly Rassay on behalf of the left-wing opposition. The opposition was much more vehement in the upper house, a bastion of conservatism, where two high church dignitaries—the Catholic prince-primate, Cardinal Jusztinian Serédi, and the Reformed Church moderator, Bishop László Ravasz—were joined in leading the opposition by Gyula Károlyi and István Bethlen. The debate, of a theological nature, ended with the upper house rejecting the bill in that form, and the appointment of a joint committee of the two houses to devise a compromise. This Catholic–conservative opposition moderated the measure but could not prevent the principle of racial discrimination from being placed on the statute book. The act, after several amendments, was proclaimed on August 8.

In terms of its ideological-intellectual underpinning, Act XV/1941 followed the German legislation of 1935—known as the "Nuremberg law"—closely enough, since it forbade not only marriage (with a few exceptions made under certain circumstances of birth, upbringing and nationality) but also extramarital intimacy between Jews and non-Jews, just as the German act did. The practical effects of that side were few, in fact, as Hungarian Jews seldom married outside their community and there were not a large number of mixed marriages. The act's significance mainly lay in the fact that it demonstrated that the Hungarian state had ended its longstanding efforts at assimilation in favor of segregation, ostracism and stigmatization, and declared the Jews plainly to be inferior. This was compounded by the 1942 amendment on labor service, whereby it was the only service that Jews could do; Jewish males who had enlisted in the army were deprived of the right to bear arms. Jews on labor service were available for duty at home or abroad or even at the front, but could not hold rank or bear arms.

As for Hungarian service at the front, Werth was always trying to increase it and Horthy and the government to reduce or abolish it. The regent, fed up with a chief of General Staff who wanted to move Hungary's entire armed strength to the front, replaced Werth with Ferenc Szombathelyi, previously commander of the Carpathian Group. He and Bárdossy traveled together on September 7 to German headquarters, to seek German consent for withdrawing the Hungarian forces. They did not succeed, but they were allowed to recall one rapid deployment corps, and the remaining troops at the front were given occupation tasks. Service at the front, incidentally, had shed light on several shortcomings of the Hungarian army. It had insufficient transport. The cycle units could not operate effectively over such a large area, as soldiers were exhausted by traveling enormous distances over poor roads before reaching their stations. The small tanks and fighter planes obtained from Italy were unreliable. Replacement of them from German and to some extent Hungarian sources came only later, and then slowly, in inadequate quantities, and after delays.

German commanders had realized by the autumn of 1941 that the original plan would not work, as confirmed by events around Moscow—the resistance and Soviet counterattack. This would be a long war, not a *Blitzkrieg*. Doubts about German victory were even expressed by Szombathelyi as chief of General Staff, but there still seemed to be several possible outcomes to the war, perhaps even a compromise peace in the East. These were the conditions as the Germans began to coerce the Hungarian government and army into making bigger sacrifices for final victory.

Bárdossy then made a second arbitrary move by declaring war on the United States, under German pressure, but without consultation at home with the government or with the regent. The reasoning behind his decision started with the Japanese attack on the US fleet at Pearl Harbor on December 7, to which the United States responded by declaring war. Hitler had wanted Japan to attack the Soviet Union, but still decided to enter the war against America and put pressure on his allies to do likewise.[10] Bárdossy first informed the US envoy in Budapest that Hungary was solidly behind the Tripartite Agreement signatories, and then altered this to say that his statement amounted to a declaration of war,[11] which was confirmed on December 13 in an official communiqué. The British government had put off declaring war on Hungary, perhaps because Prime Minister Churchill saw Teleki's suicide as an anti-war protest, but eventually did so on December 7. Hungary was now at war with much of the world—the Soviet Union, United Kingdom and United States—yet had only a few thousand soldiers in the occupation zone. This was a situation that the Germans would clearly not tolerate much longer.

Nor did they. General Wilhelm Keitel, head of the OKW, Foreign Minister Ribbentrop, and Hitler himself pressed Hungary to send a sizable contingent to the eastern front. After long negotiations, they ensured that a start was made to assembling the Second Hungarian Army of some 200,000 men, who began to be sent to the Don in April 1942.[12]

Everything appeared to be stable in the "hinterland," although all kinds of changes had begun. The wartime boom expanded until there was nothing that industry or agriculture could produce that would not sell, but the rise in standards of living faltered and a period of restrictions began. There were quite regular pay rises, but they failed to compensate for the privations. The public still felt little of the human effects of war. (There was little loss of life in the Carpathian Group.) The rationing system was still fairly lenient, but it was slowly extended to every major type of goods, while legal rations were reduced. Hungarian consumers received the rations due to them right up to the collapse of the state, so that they neither starved nor came to depend on the black market. To that extent at least, the public administration kept going. Also on the dark side of the wartime boom was creeping inflation, which began in a mild form in 1938 and steadily accelerated and became more conspicuous. Facilitation of daily life up to 1941 was still stronger than deterioration, but big problems with supplies, procurement, working hours, discipline at work, and so on, appeared in 1942.

January 1942 brought one of the gravest incidents in the wartime history of the army and gendarmerie. It began as an attempt to clear Zsablya (Žabalj), Újvidék (Novi Sad) and district in the South Country of partisan forces, and degenerated into a mindless bloodbath that cost about 5,000 lives, most of them Jews, although some Serbs and Hungarians were also murdered. The army made strong initial efforts to cover up the incident, and it was not investigated properly at the time. Those questioned later made statements or depositions that suited their own interests, so that the true story of the Újvidék massacre remains unknown. For instance, it cannot be established how the blame should be apportioned between the various officers in the field. However, the responsibility for the stain on the army over Újvidék undoubtedly belonged to its commanders, as the men would certainly not have become embroiled in such thing without an order or other encouragement (such as the influence of alcohol).

Both the conservative and the left-wing opposition in the lower house were depleted, and opposition political activity moved outside Parliament. One sign of this came on September 28, 1941: two leading Smallholders, Ferenc Nagy and Béla Kovács, formed the Hungarian Peasant Federation,[13] which bypassed parties and Parliament in a successful move to mobilize the peasantry. On October 6, 1941, liberals and Social Democrats organized a com-memoration of the the martyred prime minister of 1848, Lajos Batthyány, followed on November 20 by a demonstration at the graves of Kossuth and the nineteenth-century radical Mihály Táncsics. The Social Democratic paper *Népszava* published a spe-cial Christmas number in which articles by Endre Bajcsy-Zsilinszky, Gyula Szekfű and Marcell Benedek appeared beside contributions from Social Democrats and communists. In February 1942, the Hungarian Historical Memorial Committee was formed, mainly by left-wing anti-German figures concerned for Hungary's independence, but it crossed the familiar party lines. It contained communists at one extreme; however, at the other, Szekfű was among the organizers, editing a volume by committee members entitled *On Petőfi's Road*.[14]

Conservatives squeezed out of the legislature joined likemind-ed members of the upper house in a group around Horthy. The regent began to practice "personal" politics, giving rise to a small, trusted group dubbed the Castle Clique by the Arrow-Cross and others on the far right. This gained another side in January 1942, when Bethlen began to give dinners and private receptions attend-ed regularly or occasionally by people ranging from legitimists (Antal Sigray), through liberals (Rassay and others), to Small-holders (Zoltán Tildy) and Social Democrats (Árpád Szakasits). This was a further sign that the system of state and normal regent/Parliament and regent/government relations were break-ing down. The Castle Clique had two aims: to see Horthy's elder son István elected deputy regent, and to replace Bárdossy with a reliable, acceptable prime minister. The two were connected as the prime minister was impeding the election of Horthy's son.

Although the regent already had a right to appoint his successor, he did not wish to exercise it, as his preferred candidate was his own son. This complicated matters somewhat, especially as the prime minister was no admirer of István Horthy. All factions on the far right self-evidently opposed and attacked the proposal, pointing to the young Horthy's "Anglomania" and ties of friendship with Jewish big business. He was accepted only with difficulty by the legitimists, as it was easy to assume that there were dynastic aspirations behind the proposal, and the left also had to swallow their reservations before they could vote for him. Eventually, common sense prevailed in most camps. The regent was in his 74th year and it would cause immeasurable problems and upheaval if he died without a successor. Though Hitler saw István Horthy as a worse Anglophile and pro-Jew than his father, there was little to be gained by attacking a war hero. He thought it better to laugh the matter off by saying that the regent had "cooked the books" well. In the event, István Horthy's election on February 16, 1942, solved nothing, as he died in an air crash at the front on August 20. This, like most Hungarian disasters, became a subject of rumor and speculation. The Arrow-Cross put it about that he had been drunk at the controls, while the anti-Germans suspected a German hand in the matter. Neither supposition can be confirmed, of course.

After his son's successful election by acclaim, Horthy at last took his friends' advice and dismissed Bárdossy, who had circumvented him on several important issues and proved disloyal over the deputy regency. Bárdossy was called upon to resign on March 7, 1942.

Notes

1. On February 4, 1941, after István Csáky's early death on January 27.
2. He headed the Press Department at the Foreign Ministry, then served as counselor at the London Legation, before heading the Bucharest mission.
3. The importance of this lay in the fact that the German side did not ask officially for Hungarian collaboration. Werth's question was answered as desired by a German officer stationed in Budapest, but the government rightly doubted the authenticity of this, until Werth could extract a statement from Colonel General Franz Halder, the chief of General Staff.
4. One informant thought that the planes had an explicitly "Axis" look, another called them unidentifiable, and a third said that they were certainly Soviet. Later explanations included the possibility of a Slovak or Romanian hand in the matter, although no reason could be given why it would have served the interests of either.
5. He was not legally obliged to seek parliamentary approval for this, and if he had, it would simply have taken up time, as it is hard to imagine a lower house with that composition ever rejecting the proposal.
6. There were several debates about this among the Germans, as the *Wehrmacht* and some of the Nazi leaders argued for rationalizing occupation policy to reduce resistance and for utilizing all available military "material," but Hitler gave no ground.
7. This happened with the French and Walloon volunteer legions, but they were insignificant in size. Hitler finally allowed Soviet prisoners to form units in 1944 (the Vlaslov Brigade and the Cossack units), but most of these were intended for minor, auxiliary tasks.
8. Earlier estimates of 45,000 have been upped to 90,000 by military historians.
9. It was probably *Einsatzgruppe* C. The news went round that a Hungarian engineer unit had assisted in the massacre, and Gyula Kádár recalls in a memoir a photograph shown to him, in which a young Hungarian ensign was seen smoking a cigarette by the grave. See Gyula Kádár, *A Ludovikától Sopronkőhidáig* (From the Ludovika to Sopronkőhida), Budapest: Magvető Kiadó, Vol. II, p. 509.

10. Several German attempts had been made to persuade Japan to attack the Soviets, but when these were refused, Hitler saw it as an advantage that the Japanese were at least tying down some US military potential.

11. It emerged between the two statements that Berlin was not satisfied with the initial formula, and Germany's other allies (including Italy) were following its example.

12. Hitler altered the plan of operations for 1942. He expected a decisive breakthrough to the south, with the oilfields as the main target. However, he broadened the southern front so much that the plan can be seen as exaggerated and impracticable from the outset.

13. *Magyar Parasztszövetség.*

14. *Petőfi útján*, Budapest: Horizont Kiadás, n. d. [1942]. Sándor Petőfi was an influential poet and key figure of the 1848 Revolution, who died in a battle in 1849.

2. A Hesitant Ally: The Government of Miklós Kállay

Pál Teleki had already sought to be a "servant of two masters," but this pendulum approach became linked in the public mind with Miklós Kállay, not him. Teleki, after all, had failed to apply his ideas. The question was whether Kállay could do better under the worse conditions of 1942, by which time the task was to bail Hungary out of the war, not keep it out in the first place. Teleki, caught between a rock and a hard place, chose suicide. Kállay hesitated for about a year before plumping for the goal of withdrawing from the war. This obviously meant that he had to be devious in his statements and remarks, to disguise what he was really doing. He saw the task as important enough to make him stick to it and resist urges to flee abroad.

"I realized that I could never say another open, honest word," Kállay wrote in his memoirs about a discussion with the leaders of what was ostensibly his own party, the Party of Hungarian Life, a few days after his appointment and before his official introduction to Parliament.[1] The meeting had been held because Kállay had resigned as minister of agriculture and left the then National Unity Party during the Bethlen rebellion against Gömbös in early 1935. He had then withdrawn from politics, which meant by now that many leaders did not even know him. Everybody linked him with the conservative group, but his relative "innocence" at that time made it hard to attack him, despite the suspicions of him among the far right and in Berlin.[2]

Kállay's impressions of that meeting matched the immediate situation and his prime ministerial prospects. The memoirs show him as reticent not only before the public, but also at an otherwise confidential meeting of the Foreign Affairs Committee of the lower house. Nor could he put the plans that he devised in 1943 before most of his General Staff. There was only one cabinet member, Minister of the Interior Ferenc Keresztes-Fischer, with whom he could share some of his concerns and plans, and for a good while he dared not give detailed information to the regent, to protect him as head of state. Kállay pursued an almost one-man policy in the second year of his premiership. He sought secret supporters and supportive groups through his personal connections and friendships, and even supportive political parties, with the remarkable exception of the governing party. The parliamentary regime was maintained, but almost everything took place behind its back, which meant, paradoxically, that the far right could use it as a propaganda weapon, while the prime minister conducted his secret campaigns in its corridors. It was as if he were trying to dance while bound hand and foot.

There has been no understanding, let alone appreciation, in Anglo-Saxon countries of what Kállay's government was trying to do, because it has seemed absurd to those used to democracy. Again it cannot be accused of dictatorship or absolutism. Kállay's, like Teleki's, was a weak and rootless cabinet, without hope of consolidation within the domestic or current international system.

Kállay himself (and some later admirers) tried to present his two years in government as a continuum, emphasizing the way in which the failures of the Axis powers in late 1942 and early 1943 brought at most some shifts of policy emphasis. This interpretation is hard to square with certain facts or with logic. Nor is it clear why this fiction had to be maintained at all costs. As his memoirs emphasize continuity, there is no way of telling from it what criteria were really guiding him during 1942. One must certainly have been the international military and diplomatic course of events. General Staff analyses show that faith in German victory began to falter in the autumn of 1941, giving way in 1942 to grave doubts, or even dismissal of the possibility of full victory, but that was far from the same as predicting total German defeat. There had been no important turns of events on any front.[3] Kállay wrote that Mussolini had high hopes in the spring of 1943 that Hitler would talk the

Soviets into agreement and end the war in the east,[4] but oddly, he did not comment on that. So there is no knowing if news of Soviet peace feelers ever reached Budapest, but either way, common sense would suggest this possibility, even if Hitler's habits were ignored or insufficiently known.[5]

The uncertain, undecided situation is reflected in Kállay's caution in his public statements in 1942, coupled with hesitant moves towards making contact with the West, although these went no further at the time. The prime minister spoke of "self-aimed" Hungarian policy, as Gömbös had done, but he meant something different by it. For Gömbös it had meant cutting Western ties and reducing dependence on Germany. Now the prime minister was allowing himself to be blackmailed by the right wing of the Party of Hungarian Life, perhaps partly because he was still unfamiliar with the political ground and lacking in the invisible contacts with associates and groups that he would build up in future months. Kállay himself admitted that he was blackmailed over the Jewish question. He justified the bill for compensated expropriation of Jewish landed property by saying that the right-wing party leaders had made support or at least toleration for this a condition for their support at his initial talks with them. This was probably the case, for Kállay wrote that he was convinced that the question of great estates had to be tackled at some stage and the terms of the legislation had to be extended to non-Jewish landowners. This helps to explain how he could convince some prominent Jews that the act was in their favor rather than against them. It was passed by Parliament largely without debate and proclaimed on September 6. It meant that Jews could not acquire landed property or realty in general, and realty in their possession had to be transferred to the state in return for partial compensation.[6]

But similar practicalities could not be used to justify downgrading the classification of the Israelite religion from "admitted" to "recognized,"[7] or passing the measure on compulsory labor service. Hitherto, only those Jews called up into the army had been assigned to labor service. Now it was to be all male Jews aged 18–48.[8] These moves were probably prompted by much broader considerations. Both the government and the regent were prepared to go a long way on the Jewish question, but neither wanted to follow the Nazi "final solution." It is not possible to say how much of a role was played in their case by the kind of anti-Semitism that called for restriction of the Jews, and how much of a consideration it was to appease the Germans without actually fulfilling their demands. Their emphasis, as against the German demands, was on the Hungarian economy not being viable without Jewish capital and having a need for labor, which meant Jewish labor servicemen.

The Jewish question in Hungary certainly took on a very different complexion. Hungarian Jews and Hungarian politicians alike knew that the Jews had been deported from Germany *en masse*, and processes of gathering and confining them in ghettos and transporting them away were under way in neighboring countries.[9] This prompted more and more Jewish refugees to hide in Hungary, with no fear so far that the government would extradite them.[10] Any "solution" other than Nazi practice, even one by which the government restricted the lives or took away the rights of Jews, seemed preferable and acceptable. There is also no doubt that huge pressure was placed on the Hungarian government once the Nazis had decided to exterminate the Jews of Europe, whom they estimated as numbering 30 million.[11] Successive calls came in the second half of 1942 for the government to require Jews to wear a yellow star, to begin isolating them in ghettos, and to provide 300,000 to the *Reich* for work in Ukraine.[12] Kállay, remembering the measures that he had already taken, sought to show "goodwill" in his treatment of Jews and make up for his earlier acts, so to speak, by failing to meet the German demands. He refused to hand Jews over to Germany, on the grounds that the Hungarian economy had need of their labor, seeking to back that argument up by making labor service general.

While the labor service tortured or caused the deaths of masses of Jewish men, the Nazis were quite unmoved by Kállay's arguments.

The prime minister wrote nothing in his memoirs on being blackmailed over his treatment of left-wingers. Yet that was the field where Kállay's policy underwent a major 180-degree turn. He had hardly taken office before 400 left-wingers (mainly Social Democrats) had been rounded up and sent off to the front for labor service. In April, the police began several months of house raids to arrest communist cadres and leaders, and other left-wingers.[13] That behavior ceased in the spring of 1943, when the prime minister began to make approaches to the left wing. Meanwhile, there was a favorable change in the composition of the government when Károly Bartha was replaced as minister of defense by Vilmos Nagybaconi Nagy.[14]

The German–Italian–Japanese threesome visibly weakened between the two phases. Italian and German units suffered serious losses in North Africa, where the British and Americans made a successful landing on the northwest coast on November 8. Elimination of the *Afrikakorps* was only a matter of time. In June 1942, American forces began to gain the upper hand in the Pacific. As for the eastern front, the most important one for Hungary, the German plan for a great summer offensive in 1942 could not be completed. It was to support that summer campaign as a second line of defense that Hungary's Second Army had been sent off in April. Instead, about 200,000 officers and men found themselves, as winter set in, on the Don Bend south of Voronezh, along a 200-kilometer stretch of front line, trying to perform a military task that several factors rendered impossible. Firstly, they could not take control of the entire line, because the Soviets had managed to retain a few bases on the Hungarians' side of the Don. The army had already suffered serious losses in the unsuccessful struggle to take these bases. Secondly, the stretch of front line would have been too long even for a well-equipped army of that size, but the Second

Army was neither well equipped nor well supplied. The Germans had failed to provide the promised heavy artillery units, and so it could not defend itself. And they had been expecting a summer campaign, meaning that they were not equipped for winter. It turned out that many of the weapons were useless in a heavy frost as well.

Gusztáv Jány, the commander of the Second Army, certainly knew that his men could not escape a catastrophe if the Soviets attacked, and he gave the necessary danger signals. It was not Jány's fault that he received no substantive response from the Hungarian General Staff, Horthy as commander-in-chief, or ultimately, the requisite German Commands. But, in clear possession of the facts, he was to blame for issuing an order to resist to the last and sticking by that to the bitter end, although he was not alone in making such demands on his men. Hitler and Stalin did likewise,[15] but it still cannot be taken as a general requirement of military conduct. The catastrophe began promptly on January 12, 1943, as the Soviets broke out first from Uriv and then from their other bridgehead at Shchuche. There was no assistance to be had. The Italian units on the Hungarians' left had already been dispersed and fragmented. The German corps on the right made no move. The Second Army broke up within a week and most of it had left the front by the 24th. The Third Division held out longest, but it was doomed by the end of January.[16] Jány's verdict in an order of the 24th, "The Second Hungarian Army has lost its honor,"[17] allowed Hitler to blame the Voronezh disaster on the Hungarian army, and further eroded fighting morale. Witnesses and analysts report that the Hungarian troops behaved respectably and dutifully, although nobody could have accused them of eagerness to take control of the winding River Don, so far from home. Nor were they prepared to advance meekly to a certain, and militarily senseless, death.[18] It is hard to say how far the Hungarian soldiers were affected by fear of Bolshevism, but there are many signs that they held low opinions of the Soviet system, although they did not identify it with "Ivan," the ordinary Russian soldier, or with the general population.

In the end there were almost 150,000 Hungarian dead, wounded, imprisoned and missing on the Don (including some 40,000 dead and 60,000 prisoners), and several hundred thousand labor servicemen met the same fate. Those fleeing the battlefield later regrouped. Some returned home, and others continued to serve in the Soviet Union, but only on occupation, railway security and anti-partisan duties. Notes and memoirs suggest that the last were taken lightly by the Hungarian units. Local deals were done with Ukrainian national partisans, and it seems as if a general, high-level agreement may have been reached between the two sides to keep out of each other's way.

The Nazi leaders tried in 1943 to persuade the Hungarian government to send occupation forces to Serbia, to relieve German Balkan forces. This was seized upon by Lajos Csatay, who had taken over from Vilmos Nagy as minister of defense, as it might then have been possible to avoid sending more troops to the eastern front. Kállay, however, would not hear of the bargain, He did not want to see Hungary's reputation in Serbia ruined further than it had been by the 1941 occupation and massacre at Újvidék, or destroy the relationship built up with the commander of the Serb Četnik resistance forces, Draža Mihailović. Most of all, Kállay did not want the Hungarian army to clash with the Allied forces that were expected to land in the Balkans. According to Kállay, the Četnik were receiving clothing and medical supplies from Hungary. Interestingly, when Kállay met Mussolini in Rome in April 1943, he reproached him with assisting Tito's partisans, not Mihailović's, although in fact the Italians were the latter's main supporters.

Another move presumably connected with policy on Serbia came when Kállay, having consulted the regent and the chief of General Staff, ordered a new inquiry into the Újvidék massacre,

after Bajcsy-Zsilinszky tabled a parliamentary question at the end
of 1942. This time it was conducted as properly as conditions
allowed, beginning with military court proceedings. The principal
accused did not wait for the verdict and went into hiding. They
were then helped to escape by the SS and enlisted in the German
army.[19]

Although Voronezh and the Don debacle were only knock-on
effects of the great German defeat at Stalingrad, they marked a
turning point in Hungarian politics, affecting the thinking and
activity of the prime minister, and of a broad group of politically
active people. Without that defeat, there would hardly have been a
policy at all. It was becoming apparent that Germany could not win
the war, and Hungary's participation was raising the number of victims without altering the outcome. It was emerging by then that the
future victorious Allied powers would call the defeated countries to
account for everything. It was impossible to have the same outlook
after Stalingrad and Voronezh as before.

Kállay displayed a sense of reality in drawing fundamental
conclusions from the radical change in conditions. No further measures were taken against the Jews. The new minister of defense,
Vilmos Nagy, made efforts to normalize and humanize conditions
for labor servicemen that continued under his successor, Lajos
Csatay. Raids and arrests of left-wingers also ceased. Censorship
was imposed on the Arrow-Cross and far right for the first time.
Kállay contacted Western Allies through the Hungarian missions in
every neutral country or sent out special envoys for the purpose. He
forged relations with the anti-German conservatives and all parties
and groups pressing for an end to the war.

The main idea held by the prime minister and most other
Hungarian politicians about how the war would go from there was
that the Anglo-Saxons had every reason to want to keep the Red
Army out of the heart of Europe, after it had defeated the *Wehrmacht*. So they expected the second front in the south, logically in

the Balkans,[20] or the Italian campaign to be speeded up and extended towards Austria and Hungary, using extra forces. That was no senseless prediction at the time, as the decision on the second front had not been made, and the British prime minister was thinking about how the West might contain the Soviets. So he did propose a Balkan landing, and later, reinforcement of the Allied forces in Italy for a powerful strike northward. The main strategic issues of the war were an issue between the British and the Americans from the outset. Churchill consistently favored attacking via the "soft underbelly of Europe," but the Americans thought otherwise. Nor was the question quite resolved militarily when, to Stalin's delight, northern France was chosen for the second front—at the August 1943 meeting of Churchill and Roosevelt in Quebec and at the Teheran Conference in late November. What could be done in Italy still depended on how available troops were deployed. The later neglect of the Italian front can be put down partly to military considerations, but the main factor was the political will of Roosevelt. His main aim in Europe, probably rightly, was for the Allies to gain as much territory as possible in Western Europe, including Germany itself. He was also keen for Soviet aid in the Far East against Japan, and did not think it a high price to pay if the Soviet zone of influence were to be extended. It is not known how clear the president was about future consequences of that policy.

Certainly Kállay's diplomatic soundings were made exclusively to the Western allies. The initial assumption was that Hungary would be occupied by Anglo-Saxon forces. This changed later into the Western arrival on Hungarian soil preceding or coinciding with that of the Russians, but certainly not coming long after. The government policy of procrastination was justified, because a Hungarian attempt at a bailout would leave no alternative to German occupation. There were no Western or Eastern Allied forces within reach in 1943. Kállay avoided contact with the Soviets in the hope of avoiding Russian occupation, but if he had put out feelers to Moscow as well, it would have made no difference militarily, as the front was so far away. There is no denying that Kállay's policy included designs to save the country's system, but it is another matter to say what he and his closest conservative group understood by "system." He could hardly have meant retention of existing property relations or the existing (perhaps previous, peacetime) political system if he wanted to rely on the Western democracies, which is what he chose to do, for want of an alternative. The relations built up by Kállay in 1943 and his statements on them show that he understood that Hungary had to embrace democracy. We know from Bethlen that Kállay still wanted to avoid or limit severely any opening up to the left, but it is hardly possible to gauge how far his thinking went in this direction. He certainly did not want to admit any possibility of a Bolshevik solution.

The relations that Kállay desired meant initiating talks with Allied diplomats in all neutral countries, through locally stationed diplomats or through special envoys. The succession began with a mission by Albert Szentgyörgyi, the Nobel Prize-winning biology professor, who ran straight into the arms of a double agent. Thereafter the Hungarian moves were watched keenly by German intelligence, so that all of them were eventually revealed to the German secret service. Based on that, Hitler heaped reproaches on the Hungarian government in April 1943 and demanded a change of prime minister.

The most important contact was made by László Veress, a relatively low-ranking Foreign Ministry official, at a trade fair in Istanbul. Veress, with the help of the consul-general, managed to contact a counselor at the British mission. This happened in August, after the Sicily landings and the ousting of Mussolini, when there was a glimmer of hope that Western forces might soon approach Hungary through Italy. The British government reacted quite quickly, handing Veress conditions for a separate armistice on September 9. This meant reducing military and financial support for Germany

and reorganizing the Army Command to make it suitable for carrying out the change of sides. The switch was to occur only once the
Allies had reached the country's borders, and the armistice was not
to be advertised beforehand. This text shows how realistically
British Foreign Office officials saw the situation, and although they
held to the principle of "unconditional surrender," they did not
advance any impossible demands. It is reasonable to assume that
both Budapest and London thought at that time that it was feasible
for the Allies to reach Hungary's borders. In that case, it also has to
be assumed that they had still to learn of the agreement of Churchill
and Roosevelt in Quebec. The Istanbul contact led to regular radio
contact with the British.[21] Another contact made in Switzerland led
the Americans in early 1944 to parachute three officers into
Hungary, but they walked straight into the arms of the occupying
German forces.[22]

The regular Nazi intelligence reports on most of the talks initiated by Kállay were one reason why Hitler wanted urgent talks
with the regent. Horthy was treated to one of Hitler's famous bursts
of rage on April 16–17. There Hitler had three objectives: the dismissal of Kállay, "solution" of the Jewish question, and increased
Hungarian military participation on the eastern front. He read out a
list of Kállay's sins, but Horthy refused to accept it as authentic and
defended his prime minister. The regent's reply to Hitler's charge
that Hungary was a safe haven for Jews was that he had done his
best to curb and restrict the Jews, but he could not "knock their
brains out." (He presumably knew that this was just what Hitler
wanted, but the latter had refrained as usual from saying so in so
many words.) Hitler abused the Hungarian soldiers at Voronezh for
cowardly conduct, while Horthy defended the army. So the
Klessheim talks were unsuccessful for the Germans on every count.
Budapest, on the other hand, had to realize that the die had been
cast. Little imagination was needed to appreciate that the logistical
department of the Army High Command (OKH) had begun working on plans to occupy Hungary.

In fact, all that had prevented the Germans from carrying out the occupation already were some other difficulties: the dispersal of the Italian–German forces in North Africa in May, the Allied landings in Sicily in July, and the fall of Mussolini on July 25. Meanwhile, the Soviets were preparing a summer offensive, but the eastern front was still far enough away for settlement of the Hungarian question to be postponed. It is worth noting that the situation for the Germans would have been unchanged if Hungary had not formally been a combatant.

It was no secret to military experts or informed lay people in the spring and summer of 1943 that the Germans were losing or had lost the war. On the other hand, the worse the Germans stood on the eastern front, the greater the danger that they might occupy Hungary. The military leadership had to draw conclusions from all this. Ferenc Szombathelyi seems to have taken a realistic view. His two aims were to avoid German occupation and to prevent the Red Army from appearing in the country. He saw procrastination as the only way to prevent both. He wanted to strengthen the borders and keep the available Hungarian military potential in reserve for holding up the Russians until the Western Allies appeared in the region. So it followed logically that he ignored the repeated German demands, but the other side of the coin was the fact that he did not replace the troops serving in Ukraine with fresh ones. There were several difficulties with this concept. Firstly, Szombathelyi had no plan of action for a possible German occupation. Secondly, he could not guarantee that the Red Army would appear precisely where the border could be reinforced, in the Carpathians, and not along the more or less defenseless southern border. The argument was weak as well. It was assumed that Hungary could do nothing to defend itself against the Germans, but it was necessary to imagine that it could do just that, at least for some time, against the Red Army, which already had an obvious advantage over the *Wehrmacht*, as Szombathelyi had also recognized. Added to all this was another problem. Hungary had the potential to raise an army of a million men, yet it had on the eastern front, or behind it, a mere 30,000–40,000 serving. It is hard to imagine that this had escaped the notice of the Germans.

An unexpectedly promising situation for Hungary came about at the end of July and the beginning of August, but whether it could be exploited depended on the Italian government and military authorities. There were relatively few German forces in Italy at the time when Mussolini fell and the Badoglio government was appointed. If the Italian army had turned against it, in cooperation with the Allied forces behind it, there would have been some hope of success. But the new government declared that the war would continue and did not sign the armistice until September 3. During that period of waiting, it had emerged that the Allies at that time, during the month of August, were in no position to deploy troops to support an Italian change of sides. This was in line with the Quebec agreement mentioned earlier. Once the armistice had been announced by the British on September 8, a headlong advance southward began. The *Wehrmacht* managed to occupy the country right down to Naples with hardly a shot being fired, and to disarm hundreds of thousands of Italian soldiers on the peninsula and in the Italian zone of occupation in the Balkans.

Meanwhile, the "sins" of the Hungarian government and prime minister were multiplying further in German eyes. Kállay set about preparing his bailout policy, a task made easier because many of the political elite also saw German defeat as inevitable. The need to escape from the war and prepare for the period after German defeat was felt not only by him and his government, but by the conservative and legitimist group, most of the senior officers, and the leaders of the Smallholders' Party and Social Democratic Party. This increased Kállay's scope, although it has to be admitted that these groups did not agree on means and methods. Several notes and memoranda appeared,[23] but unfortunately none of them was translated into a government plan of action. Some people, such as

Endre Bajcsy-Zsilinszky, were even prepared to risk German occupation in the interests of the future. Most, including the prime minister, were paralyzed by the idea. Those who feared Nazi occupation most were the Jewish politicians and Social Democrats directly threatened by it. The most interesting position was taken by Horthy, who accepted the need to bail out, but whose sense of honor led him to argue that comrades in arms could not be stabbed in the back, as he announced even to Hitler, who had misled and cheated Horthy several times. As for the intransigent radicalism of Kossuth Radio in Moscow and of left-wing Hungarian émigrés (even broadcasting on some Western stations), calling on the "people" to turn out their "treacherous" government and turn their weapons on their base oppressors, it lacked realism or knowledge of the Hungarian political equation.

Some new party groupings arose despite the differences of opinion. In August 1943, the Smallholders and the Social Democrats formed an alliance. In the autumn, Bethlen established the Democratic Bourgeois Alliance. The latter, however, was not prepared to talk with the communists (known as the Peace Party at the time) and attached conditions to cooperating with the Social Democrats, with the result that a united anti-German bloc failed to emerge. A bigger problem was the fact that the army had no military plan in the event of a German occupation and Kállay had no political one. If there had been such a plan, he might have attempted to align the disparate forces around him, for they were in basic agreement.

However, the wait-and-see tactics were rendered very questionable by the Teheran Conference of the Allies on November 28–December 1. There the three leaders decided that the second front should be opened in Western Europe, which meant almost certainly that Hungary would be taken by the Red Army, which had been inflicting huge human, material and territorial losses on the *Wehrmacht* during the year. But this possibility was not an immediate one either, as it would be another nine months before the Soviet forces reached Hungary, although the change of sides by the Romanians meant that they gained vast territories without firing a shot. However, there was an immediate danger of the Germans taking possession of strategic areas of major importance to them. Hungary, like the occupied parts of Italy, was seen simply as the foreground of Germany's internal lines of defense. They could not allow a zone of prime importance for the east and the Balkans to undergo any kind of upheaval, or to see the "Italian treachery" repeated. Furthermore, the Western Allies put up a number of smokescreens designed to mislead the Germans about the site of the landings. One of these was a rumor that they would take place in the Balkans. This was not believed by the German leaders, but for want of credible information from their own intelligence, they could not exclude any possibility. The rumor also misled many gullible Hungarian dreamers.

The plan of occupation, codenamed Margareta, had been ready for some time and simply needed dusting off. That was where matters stood in Berlin when the regent received an invitation from Hitler on March 17, 1944, to discuss the military situation. Some members of the Hungarian political leadership smelled a rat, not least because there had been reports for several days of German infiltration into the border guard, the railway security forces, the police and the army, and other strange events, on which the government and the regent had allowed themselves to be reassured by German explanations. Szombathelyi thought that there really would be a discussion of military matters at Klessheim, and thought it better if Horthy had his help in the bargaining. So he came out in favor of Horthy making the journey. The question was finally decided by Horthy himself. He probably shared Mussolini's illusion that he was the exceptional one who could exert influence through Hitler's regard for him. Horthy did not know that the Führer actually despised and loathed him. He despised him as a representative of the *ancient régime*, as an exploiter of the people, and as a man incapable of putting a respectable army into the field. He loathed him for his gentlemanly appearance, Anglophile sentiments and sympathy for the Jews.

Historians have clarified the course of that second meeting between Hitler and Horthy at Klessheim, as far as the available records allow. Horthy initially protested vehemently against the entry of the *Wehrmacht*, turning his back on Hitler, and intending to leave the venue as well. Somewhat later, having considered matters and taken advice from his entourage, he decided after all to sign the prepared document, thereby giving his sanction to the occupation, but by remaining at his post, he helped to ensure that it went ahead without resistance. He also extracted a promise from Hitler that the German troops' stay in Hungary would be temporary. Horthy subsequent justification of his decision was firstly the fact that the Germans had threatened that if they met with resistance they would send in Romanian and Slovak troops, and secondly his assumption that even under such conditions he could better protect the country's interests than if he left it entirely to the tyranny of the Germans and the Arrow-Cross. However, the personal alternative for Horthy at that time, if he had shown further resistance, would have been immediate arrest and transfer to a concentration camp.

There were positive and negative sides to this decision of the regent's, which will be considered further. It is enough here to mention the one consequence that it had that caused the Germans to alter their plans. The occupying *Wehrmacht* and SS troops had been ordered originally to confine Hungarian units to barracks and disarm them, select the most useful among them, and send the bulk off to labor service or forced labor. That was what had been done with the Italian army.[24] Hitler was induced to change his mind on March 26 by Horthy's "consideration" and some German comments that Hungarian soldiers were better used as cannon fodder than as labor.[25] The two consequences of this were that it became impossible to avoid making further Hungarian units available, which meant additional loss of life, but Horthy retained a military force at his disposal, for use at the appropriate moment. The latter was the most promising side of the regent's decision, and might have justified it if he had actually made good use of it.

Notes

1. Kállay had become minister of agriculture in 1932, working mainly on the land reform bill and later the irrigation plan.
2. He was not invited to Berlin for some time, and his one audience with Hitler was a formality. After a while, the German envoy hardly had contacts with him.
3. The air and sea battle of Midway on June 4–7, 1942, showed US potential steadily overtaking Japanese, but it was a sign at most, not an omen.
4. Mussolini thought that agreement could be reached with Stalin on a territorial basis, thereby giving the Axis, particularly Italy, greater chances against the Anglo-Saxons. But the proposals were dismissed outright by Hitler, although the idea of compromise in the east was also supported by Japan, and even some Nazi leaders, such as Goering and Ribbentrop.
5. The reports were widespread and it is hard to imagine that they did not reach Budapest. No documentary evidence has been found, but there are reliable reports of three approaches by Moscow in mid-1943.
6. Act XV/1942.
7. From *bevett* to *elismert*. Act VIII/1942 set aside an act of 1895 granting a classification that entitled it to state subsidy, which was now withdrawn.
8. Minister of Defense's Order No. 69059/1942.
9. However, these processes had not assumed the scale in either Slovakia or Romania that they would in Hungary in 1944.
10. There were also large numbers of Polish, French and Belgian refugees.
11. The extermination campaign began in Poland in 1939 and on Soviet territory in 1941, but the ultimate decision on a global "final solution" came early in 1942.

12. The initial demands came as "friendly advice" through Döme Sztójay, envoy in Berlin, but eventually there were official demands as well.
13. Among the victims were Zoltán Schönherz and Ferenc Rózsa.
14. When the far right wanted to attack the minister in a parliamentary question, Kállay dismissed Nagy rather than defending him; however, Kállay asked the regent to suspend the session to prevent the question being put.
15. Hitler's stance caused the disaster at Stalingrad, of which the Hungarian–Italian–Romanian debacle along the Don was only a consequence.
16. The divisional commander, Marcell Stomm, announced that he could not issue a sensible command and ordered all to save themselves as best they could. He was soon taken prisoner by the Soviets.
17. He tried to correct the insulting order on his return home, but that could no longer have any effect.
18. The many documents and eyewitness accounts of the chaotic retreat concur in stating that many losses were due to brutal and uncomradely conduct by German officers.
19. Ferenc Feketehalmy-Czeidner, József Grassy and others joined the Waffen SS. They returned to Hungary at the time of the occupation, when the proceedings against them were dropped and they were readmitted into the Hungarian army.
20. What Churchill meant by the Balkans was not Yugoslavia, as the Hungarians thought, but Turkey and the eastern Mediterranean.
21. Veress himself brought the transceiver home.
22. The action was initiated by Secretary of State Allen Dulles and endorsed by the High Command as "Mission Sparrow."
23. From the Smallholders and the Hungarian Social Democratic Party, and from Bethlen and Bajcsy-Zsilinszky.
24. The selected soldiers were assigned to units in Germany. Mussolini wanted these back after the puppet Salò Republic had been set up, but the Germans refused to return them or any of those on forced labor.
25. The confinement to barracks then ceased.

7. OCCUPATION AND ATTEMPT TO GAIN FREEDOM

1. Occupied Hungary

German occupation forces overran Hungary under cover of darkness on March 18–19, 1944, taking over transport and telecommunication centers and sealing off barracks.[1] The chief of General Staff, on his way back to Hungary by train, gave an order forbidding resistance, and no shots were fired. The Germans purposely delayed the regent's train; things were all over by the time that it reached Budapest.[2] On the same train sat Edmund Veesenmayer, bearing a recall for the German envoy and his own appointment as minister and plenipotentiary. Veesenmayer had spent some time in the country earlier and was seen as a Hungarian specialist. His position precisely matched the system set up by the Germans in several other occupied countries.[3] It was his decision to try to bring more cunning and political sense to the task than most of his counterparts did.

The *Wehrmacht* was accompanied not just by Veesenmayer and the SS, but by the *Gestapo* and the SD.[4] They clearly had a prepared list of most of the persons to arrest, which must have been compiled by Hungarian collaborators and spies. The German police and intelligence arrived almost instantly at the homes of left-wingers and anti-Germans, including conservative and legitimist leaders (Gusztáv Gratz, György Apponyi and Antal Sigray), Smallholders (Endre Bajcsy-Zsilinszky and Ferenc Nagy), numerous Social Democrats (Károly Peyer, György Marosán, and so on) and anti-German businessmen (Ferenc Chorin, Lipót Baranyay, and many others). Some went into hiding, such as Miklós Kállay and István Bethlen, who had adventurous escapes from the parties sent to arrest them.[5] It took longer before the seat of military resistance was tracked down by the *Gestapo*, which eventually eliminated most of the anti-German core in the General Staff.[6] This sharply decreased the scope for the regent and any chance for Hungary to change sides. The Germans also secured the dismissal of Colonel General Ferenc Szombathelyi as chief of General Staff[7] in favor of Colonel General János Vörös, whom the Germans saw as reliable.

But the regent did manage to prevent the post of prime minister from going to Béla Imrédy, for whom the Germans were pressing.[8] It might be said that the outlooks and sympathies of Döme Sztójay, the regent's choice, were no better than Imrédy's, but Horthy seems to have had luck or foresight. Imrédy, after all, had some political support and might have widened it considerably with the Germans behind him. Sztójay had nothing of the kind. He had been an eagerly pro-German envoy in Berlin for many years, which meant that the Germans could not easily have opposed him, but nothing more. There was no reason to fear that Sztójay could gather domestic forces to do much further damage at home.

The German occupation and the presence of the *Gestapo* themselves brought about a fundamental change in domestic relations. Thereafter, if the regent wanted to do something, he had no trustworthy associates on whom he could count on in the government. The parties with whom he had been in touch no longer existed legally, and their leaders were in prison or in concentration camps. The same could be said of the party officials with whom he had cooperated up to now. They had been arrested, or at least excluded from the leadership. That left him a choice of two courses. He could resign from the game (setting his Klessheim decision at naught), or he could settle for sitting the matter out. Now it was the government, not the prime minister, who applied a one-man policy. But Horthy would have had to be a genius for that policy to succeed, and geniuses, of course, need luck on their side as well.

The power system that Bethlen had founded was in ruins by this time. The laws on the Jews had knocked out the big business group, whose members were lucky if the state could protect their lives; their influence was confined to occasional agreements on this with bodies in authority. Their approach, like that of almost every representative of the Jews, had been to accept all constraints and humiliations for fear of the worst—the German occupation—and to cling to a desperate hope that their lives and those of most of the Jewish community could be saved, however much else they might lose. Of that there was no prospect after March 19, 1944. None of the earlier members of Parliament who had represented the professional standards of the upper middle class remained in the political arena. The new arrivals were joining the far right to attack the vestiges of the old system, not to defend it. The upper middle-class anti-German liberals and conservatives operated as a now illegal opposition or kept their heads down. The army, on the other hand, increasingly gained exceptional importance, although it was an army that could not have been called united or disciplined for a long time, if it ever could have been so called. Many authors have stated that Horthy failed to notice that process and believed blindly, up to the last minute, that he could trust the army. But that is hard to credit, and the regent's practical moves do not bear it out in general. Horthy, in fact, was the one who sought to dismiss from proximity to decision-making all officers whom he deemed untrustworthy and who discussed his decisions exclusively with those whom he saw as most reliable. Horthy sometimes erred in his assessments of people, but he did so quite rarely. He presumably trusted the bulk of the army to obey the orders that he issued through reliable commanders, which was probably a realistic assumption. It will be seen that there were many other causes behind the failure of the action on October 15, apart from obvious treachery by certain officers. Taking all this together points to the conclusion that the "system" as such no longer functioned; the operation of state was as chaotic as it had been initially, after the Great War.

Divorced from his contacts, devoid of powers, and hemmed in by an alien army, the regent could only gather round him a few reliable cronies and wait for the outcome. He watched idly as a major new Hungarian force—the 180,000-strong First Army—set off for the front and the Germans set about despoiling the land without inhibition or hindrance. The Hungarian state met unlimited German demands (where production was still possible), while the German side practically ceased to pay. Full removal of Jews and dispersal of their wealth began. In line with German demands and on orders from SD *Obersturmbandführer* Adolf Eichmann, the government placed Jews in ghettos and deported most of them. First the Jews were ordered to wear the yellow star of David (on March 29), then ghettos were set up in larger cities (from April 26), and finally successive deportation of Hungary's Jews began in the eastern parts of the country (from March 15). The majority of those deported perished.[9] According to a report by Veesenmayer on July 9, 437,402 Jews had been sent out by that time, about 300,000 of them from the reannexed territories. The main destination from Hungary was Auschwitz, but some Jews were sent to Dachau, Mauthausen, and other camps as well.[10] There were over 200,000 Jews registered in Budapest, and the Germans, assisted by the state secretaries at the Ministry of the Interior—László Baky and László Endre—and the gendarmerie, had prepared a veritable campaign to round them up into railway freight cars as well.

The confinement of the Jews in ghettos and deportation of them certainly did not provoke public resistance on a society-wide scale. Some groups and persons did what they could, but there were too few of them for a full-scale rescue operation. One reason may have been the absence of any organization among the Hungarian public in those weeks and months that could have attempted resistance, as the opposition parties and trade unions were all illegal by that time. Sometimes a newspaper can play an organizing role in resistance, but the anti-German opposition had no newspaper by then and most of its leading lights had been arrested. In any case, most Hungarians were struggling to stay alive, having been abandoned as the Jews had, even if the danger that they faced was not equal. But a real assessment of what happened must include the fact that most of the public assumed that the oft-repeated Nazi promises were false, and they had no idea what fate actually awaited the deported Jews. For many, the suspicions were enough to generate sympathy for the Jews, which widened the gulf between most of the population and the ostensible German ally. The absence of resistance did not mean that Hungarians other than the Arrow-Cross and other extreme right-wingers agreed with the gendarmerie and police actions provoked and committed by the Nazis or with the extermination of the Jews.

By this time, the left-wing parties had been banned and the unions placed under surveillance, while the government consisted of extreme right-wing persons who were committed to the Germans. Horthy had not prevented Imrédy from joining the government later, as overall minister for the economy, with the one task of fulfilling the German demands. The government agreed on April 14 that young indigenous Germans should be drafted into the Waffen SS, although this had remarkably slim results, in spite of being compulsory (about 42,000 had been enlisted by mid-August), and a further wave of conscription ensued. Meanwhile the Allies began air raids on Budapest and other major cities.[11]

Historians largely agree that Horthy eventually stopped the death march of the Jews in July 1944, after various foreign and domestic protests, thereby ensuring that many of the Budapest Jews survived. (It will be seen later that the Arrow-Cross later managed to murder about half of them after all.) There can be no doubt that the warnings played a part in Horthy's decision, but they do not explain well the events of June–October, in which Horthy was the main inspiration and played the main part. His idleness for about three months is usually explained by historians as an effect of shock, to which is sometimes added the remark that the regent had little objection anyway to the mass of "insignificant Jews" being removed from the country. Thus he intervened only when it was the turn of higher, richer groups concentrated in Budapest and their friends. There would certainly have been a strong mental shock to the regent from the national and personal humiliation that he had suffered in March, and it can be assumed also that he had less interest in the fate of the provincial Jews than he had in that of the Budapest Jews. But it is worth weighing further points, above all the fact that the political sweep undertaken on March 19 would have given time in which the regent might have worked out where, if anywhere, and to whom, if anybody, he could turn, under German pressure and conditions of occupation, if he wanted to do something on his own. Other motivating factors will be mentioned later.

Veesenmayer first reported in June that cooperation was not as smooth as it had been initially, but he thought that the problems could still be handled and did not seek military reinforcements.[12] The basis of the report was the fact that Horthy began at that time to raise objections to German expectations and demands, and even to voice demands of his own. He wanted László Baky and László Endre removed from the government, and he urgently requested the withdrawal of German forces, notably the *Gestapo*, from the country—as Hitler had promised him. Then in June he placed difficulties in the way of dispersing Jews seeking asylum in churches around Pest. Horthy having decided to prevent the deportation of Budapest Jews, he failed to prevent Baky from ordering up gendarmerie units, presumably to carry out the large-scale action against the Jews of the capital,[13] but he managed to order the gendarmes back with the aid of reliable army units, and the Germans could not load the Jews up without them. Horthy thought initially that he could install a government made up entirely of military officers and officials without German resistance, and he might have succeeded if his list had not consisted entirely of names that were suspect in the eyes of the Nazis. So Horthy's plan for a government reshuffle met with a huge German outcry. Hitler uttered threats again, but this time he failed to rein Horthy in.

After almost three months of inaction, the regent's behavior changed radically in mid-June. This change almost coincided with the Allied Normandy landings on June 6, which meant that the number of troops occupying Hungary had to be reduced significantly, to about 80,000. Another factor, besides the opening of the second front, was a rapid deterioration in the German situation in the east. The Soviet army units were fast approaching the northeastern Carpathians. Horthy could rely on not inconsiderable Hungarian forces. The First Army mentioned earlier was deployed in Ukraine, where it had seen action, but without suffering sizable losses. (It can be estimated from military historical sources that the figure was 17,000–18,000, including the missing, the prisoners and the wounded.) The commanders of the army had been Géza Lakatos, then Károly Beregfy, and finally Béla Dálnoki Miklós, an officer whom Horthy considered to be loyal to him. The Second Army was also reviving, commanded by Lajos Veress, another general loyal to the regent. He had advanced into Transylvania, where one task would be to push into southern Transylvania and secure the southern line of the Carpathians. The Third Army, with the lowest strength of the three, was stationed between the two, but its commander, Lieutenant General József Heszlényi, was not an officer on whom Horthy could rely.

As the regent became more active and occupation forces were cut because of the Normandy landings, various resistance groups and organizations began to liven up—a sign that the country was reviving again. This meant that the regent had not only some reliable army officers, but political partners, who would be essential after the military change of sides. In May, the Hungarian Front, covering Social Democrats and communists, as well as legitimists, Smallholders and members of the National Peasant Party, was set up to begin organizing national resistance. The Front formed an executive committee to coordinate its work, while the "Peace Party" (a sobriquet of the Communist Party) organized armed detachments. That led to the organization of some partisan groups in the capital and to blowing up the statue of Gyula Gömbös on October 6. Some other smaller resistance groups were also set up under the wing of the Hungarian Front, but it is often observed that the scale of resistance was tiny compared with northern Italy, France and elsewhere. Summing up the experiences of World War II, it must be seen that, except in Yugoslavia, it took quite a time to develop resistance in countries occupied by Germany. Resistance in the Western European countries dated back to May–June 1940 and in Italy to September 1943, whereas the illegal forces in Hungary had only a couple of months, and fewer of the wooded and mountainous areas that were used by partisan movements in other countries.

The Germans' problems in Hungary were increased and their position weakened when one of their actions caused dissension among their supporters. The SS wanted to expropriate the vast assets of the Manfréd Weiss and Ferenc Chorin concerns,[14] and to make matters easier by short-circuiting the Hungarian state, it offered 32 members of the two families a free passage out of Hungary. But this did not simply affect two families and a sizable fortune. It twisted much of Hungary's industrial and financial potential out of Hungarian hands. People would do anything for the lives of themselves and their families, it seems, even sacrifice a business empire built up over generations. But hard as the Germans tried to prove otherwise, it also meant that the bastion of the Hungarian economy had passed into Nazi hands. And the ill-disguised robbery seemed too much of a sacrifice to friendship even to some faithful German and Nazi supporters. Among the opponents was

Béla Imrédy, who was so obstructive that his ministry was abolished and Nazi race experts began to suggest again that he might be one eighth Jewish by descent. One result was that Veesenmayer had to expunge any idea that Imrédy would be coming to power, which gave greater weight to the possibility of Ferenc Szálasi taking power. Meanwhile the diehard anti-Semites in Hungary reproached the Germans for sacrificing their racial principles by making exceptions for the Weiss and Chorin families.

Notes

1. Several reports in the next few days told of discontent at the confinement to barracks, which the Germans feared could lead to disturbances in an otherwise smooth occupation.
2. The prime minister and some other ministers had hoped for a signal from the regent or the chief of General Staff authorizing resistance.
3. *Gesandter I. Klasse zum Bevollmächtigten des Großdeutschen Reichs in Ungarn.* Three systems of occupation were employed: military administration; dispatch of a Reich minister under whom a previous or newly appointed government would perform the administrative tasks and carry out German instructions; installation of a puppet government with relatively greater freedom of action.
4. The *Schutzstaffeln* ("defense guard"—a vast organization with its own fighting forces or Waffen SS), the *Geheime Staatspolizei* ("secret state police"), and the *Sicherheitsdienst* ("security service"), respectively.
5. Both escaped through the tunnel systems under the Buda Castle District. Kállay received temporary asylum with his family in the Turkish Embassy, but surrendered when the Germans seriously threatened the Turkish envoy. He was then sent to a concentration camp. Bethlen hid with relatives and friends until the Soviet army arrived.
6. Among them István Újszászy and Gyula Kádár, who were working within the General Staff on the bailout attempt.
7. He was arrested after the Arrow-Cross took power.
8. Securing Imrédy's appointment was one of the instructions that Veesenmayer had received.

9. Smaller groups had been deported in April, but deportation on a mass scale began on May 15.
10. The other camps offered the main hope of survival. Returning alive from Auschwitz was little short of a miracle.
11. This could have been done earlier from Italian bases, but the Allies had refrained. Under the Kállay government, incidentally, Hungarian anti-aircraft defense did not attack Allied planes flying over the country.
12. The German plenipotentiary, known for his refinement and his independence of political mind, made a bad mistake when he thought that the regent could be manipulated at will. That he never managed to do.
13. Horthy countered Baky's move to bring gendarmes up to Budapest by alleging that they were being deployed for a coup. This Baky vigorously denied, but the truth of the matter has never been clarified.
14. As a state within the Nazi state, the SS grabbed huge assets, companies and estates all over the occupied zones.

2. Bailout or Switching Sides?

At this time if at any it was possible to talk of a "Castle clique" and a "bailout office" in its midst, but with the difference that apart from a few army officers, it consisted almost exclusively of the Horthy family and a few remaining friends, including for a while Bethlen, who was still in hiding.[1] The main motivating force was Miklós Horthy, Jr., who tried to build up relations in every conceivable direction and mediate between these and his father. He had contacts with the Hungarian Front parties and even Tito's partisans in Yugoslavia. He was helped in this underground activity by the regent's wife and his brother's widow. There had never before been any such an attempt as the one that Horthy was preparing.[2] The weakness in the plan was the fact that Horthy had very few high-ranking officers on whom he could rely. (It turned out later that some of these were less than steadfast, while others were clumsy and unable to bear the heavy responsibility.) Furthermore, the country was riddled with collaborators and informers, with the result that the German secret service heard about almost every move.

And the Germans still had a card that they had not played, for their March seizure of power had been carried out without the Arrow-Cross. It had been felt that without this all too willful party, with its confused ideas about Nazism, it would be easier to shelter behind a subservient regent, whereas they knew that they would never have gained his consent to having the Arrow-Cross imposed on him. Szálasi, deeply offended, tried initially to meet with Horthy, to work out a peaceable way in which he could creep into power, but the regent had other matters on his mind. Veesenmayer and other German figures, on the other hand, soon discovered the Arrow-Cross camp as a last refuge if they encountered official difficulties and troubles.

There was extreme tension in Budapest after a well-prepared coup in Bucharest on August 23, conducted by King Michael, with enthusiastic support from the army for the plan to reacquire northern Transylvania, lost to Hungary in the Second Vienna Award. It is unclear why the move took the Germans by surprise.[3] The none too considerable German forces in Romania hardly managed to escape, and when an attempt was made to bombard Bucharest, the government replied by declaring war. The Red Army was able to march into Romania without resistance, which left Hungary's eastern flank undefended. Hungary's Second and Third Armies attempted preventive attacks in southern Transylvania, but were thwarted after some initial success. Soviet troops broke through to the north from Brassó (Brașov) at the beginning of September. Colonel General Veress switched to defense, and then gave the order to retreat on October 8. (He was arrested for this by the Germans on October 16.) The Third Army initially occupied Arad and Temesvár (Timișoara), but then succumbed to combined Romanian–Soviet attack. The two cities were abandoned on September 22, and Soviet troops crossed the 1938 border of Hungary (near Battonya and Csanádpalota) two days later, robbing the careful fortification of the northern line of the Carpathians (three parallel lines of defense) of its significance.

Hungary's military position had become untenable. Furthermore, the Red Army marched unimpeded into Bulgaria as well on September 9, and Mannerheim, the Finnish commander-in-chief, requested an armistice, which was signed in Moscow on September 19. The regent understood that the last moment for action had come. Earlier anxiety about his own future was assuaged by the Romanian and Finnish armistice agreements, according to which not a hair on the head of the Romanian king or the Finnish commander-in-chief was to be touched. By this time, Horthy was in his 77th year, and suffered more still from the weight of military defeat and the loss of his children.[4] Several people who held talks with him in that period said later that Horthy had had trouble attending to what they were saying: there was something wrong with his concentration, he would repeat himself, and so on.[5] It seems likely that he was receptive to facts and figures only over a limited spectrum of ideas. He was concentrating on the armistice and preparing for it with all his energy, to the detriment of other, incidental things.

By June and July, Horthy saw as the main requirement for an armistice a new, reliable—or more reliable—government. He tried first with a military-type government, but backed down in the face of firm German opposition. He was probably influenced by the Romanian bailout in deciding to change governments without asking the Germans first. He had told Géza Lakatos on several occasions that he would be his candidate for prime minister, and he managed to persuade the hesitant colonel general to accept the post. Horthy did not hide from Lakatos his aim of restoring the country's sovereignty and bailing out of the war. The new government took over on August 29, to great German indignation, with Colonel General Lajos Csatay as minister of defense and Lieutenant General Gusztáv Hennyey as foreign minister, both of whom were keen to see the war end as soon as possible.[6]

After long vacillations, Horthy eventually accepted that no armistice or bailout was possible without making contact with the Russians. But he immediately ran up against an obstacle. It turned out that he had not chosen his prime minister well, although it is difficult to say who would have been better. The new government suited the regent in several ways, but it failed on the most important question. On the positive side, it banned the remaining political parties (all on the far right, as Sztójay had already banned those on the left), and released several hundred prisoners and internees (including Bajcsy-Zsilinszky and several dozen Social Democrats). It dismissed a succession of pro-Nazi county lieutenants, lifted measures against the Jews, and ended the activity of Adolf Eichmann in Hungary. But Lakatos, as a soldier bound by the ethics of an officer and a gentleman, yet in spite of his military training, was a man of compromise, who sought to avoid a decision in any difficult situation. In that, incidentally, he was the opposite of Horthy, the elderly regent, who had managed to overcome his past and outgrow all his previous anxieties. He no longer wanted to part with Hitler in a comradely fashion, because he saw that there was no time left for that, and he was even prepared to countenance "Muscovite leadership."[7] The one principle of honor that he retained forbade him to attack his former ally from behind without warning, but he expected the warning to prompt the Germans to march out of the country, as they had out of Finland. Horthy essentially realized that the Western Allies would not arrive in the region, neither ahead of the Red Army nor later.

On September 7, Horthy convened the Crown Council and announced his intention of seeking an armistice. But his soldier-prime minister found this move "unconstitutional" and advised that it be put before Parliament. This proposal was grotesque to say the least, as all political parties had been banned. The astonished regent rejected it decisively, but as none of the other ministers proved any braver or cleverer than Lakatos, and Reményi-Schneller expressly opposed Horthy's proposal, the scene was repeated on the following day in the meeting of the Council of Ministers. Eventually a compromise was reached whereby there would be a further appeal to the Germans for reinforcements to guard the Hungarian borders, and if these were not received, an armistice would be requested. Horthy drew the conclusion from the whole palaver that the government would have to be excluded from subsequent moves and he would have to act by himself.

And so it happened. A small delegation under Colonel General Gábor Faragho, a former military attaché in Moscow, set out on September 28, crossed the front without mishap, and arrived in Moscow on October 1. Despite a warm, even friendly reception, the negotiations only limped along, for several reasons. One was the technical problem of communicating with Budapest. Another was the Hungarians' insistence on a "Finnish formula"—the bailout was not to entail war against Germany. Horthy hoped that if this could be ensured, the Germans would simply abandon Hungary and leave, as they had done in the case of Finland.[8] It was a foolish hope, one that failed to consider differences of geographical position and importance to Germany's lines of defense. Nor was the foreign commissar, Vyacheslav Molotov, going to budge on the matter.[9] Finally, the regent apparently had at the back of his mind, as he gave his signature to the preliminary armistice agreement, the idea that he could somehow get around that paragraph. If Lieutenant General Béla Aggteleky's memoirs are to be believed, Horthy was still trying to avoid stabbing his former ally in the back even in the final hours. However, Lieutenant General Antal Vattay, who headed the regent's military bureau, remembered otherwise. For it is hard to imagine militarily that Hungary could become a no-man's land between the two sides, able to preserve its neutrality, and it is hard to find any practical argument to support the idea that the Germans would simply stand aside and watch peaceably as their most important piece of defensive territory slipped over to the other side.

On October 10, Horthy gave his authorization and the preliminary armistice was signed on the following day in the Kremlin. It stated that the Hungarian forces would withdraw to the country's 1937 borders and the country's army would join in the fight for liberation. There was silence on the question of Transylvania. This caused disillusionment, as the Romanian armistice had contained a clause that left a glimmer of hope. The Vienna Award had been declared invalid, but it had been specified in parentheses that this applied to "the larger part" of Transylvania, leaving the possibility that Hungary would be allowed to retain the smaller part. That hope was dispelled by the text of the Hungarian armistice, but the Soviets did promise to fulfill the military requests in connection with the *renversement des alliances*. Meanwhile the Red Army continued its military operations in Hungary, pushing forward into the trans-Tisza region and reaching the River Tisza near Szolnok. The Second Ukrainian Front under Rodion Yakovlevich Malinovsky advanced on Debrecen, where there were devastating tank battles around the city on October 10–22.

In other words, the country was under dual occupation at the end of September and beginning of October 1944. The larger part of the territory was held by the retreating Germans and the smaller by the advancing Soviets. Organized evacuation and voluntary flight from the trans-Tisza region began in September. The area was abandoned by large numbers of business corporations, institutions and public offices, which tried to reorganize themselves in Budapest or Transdanubia.[10] Some of the retreating German units plundered, usually in an organized way, while some of the Soviet units did the same, but in a disorganized fashion. The Germans would dismantle factories, blow up bridges, and drive off farm animals. The "Russkies" sought drink, collected wristwatches, and raped women. The behavior of Soviet soldiers clearly depended on the attitude and strictness of the commanding officer. It was hardly possible to use the roads, which were jammed with various military convoys as well as refugees, with jeeps, cars, trucks, carts, barrows and droves of animals in confusion. Public administration broke down over wide areas, along with the system of food rationing. All that hundreds of thousands of people could hope was that their hoards of food would last until the nightmare was over.

There were two people who were making preparations in Budapest that night: Regent Miklós Horthy and Reich Minister Plenipotentiary Edmund Veesenmayer. Horthy relied principally on his senior officers: Béla Miklós, commander of the First Army, Lajos Veress, commander of the Second, and Szilárd Bakay, commander of the Budapest garrison. Then on October 8, the Germans removed Bakay simply by attacking him in the street and carrying him off. His replacement, Béla Aggteleky, was also reliable, but he did not have Bakay's abilities. Quite what the chief of General Staff, János Vörös, was doing during these days is unclear. Some have it that he had withdrawn himself from the scheme, while others say that Horthy had never initiated him into the plans, which was the main reason why the action failed. The chief of General

Staff was certainly not where he ought to have been, and that is why he failed to take action.

Horthy strove otherwise to make circumspect and thorough preparations, checking his plans with the military commanders concerned and agreeing on a day when the move was to be made—probably October 20 originally, not October 15. They would then receive a coded message reading "My order of March 1, 1920, is to be carried out." This meant for Vattay that hostilities against the Russians had to cease, and contact had to be made with the Soviet Command, in order to turn against the Germans in consort with the Soviets. Colonel General Veress added that the First and Second Armies should move towards the Tisza, link up in the Szatmárnémeti (Satu Mare) district, and then turn against the Germans by agreement with the Russians. The evidence of Lieutenant General Vattay and Colonel General Veress means that from October 11 onwards Horthy's idea was not just armistice and bailout, but a switch of sides, so that his action would include attacking the *Wehrmacht*. That is confirmed by a meeting with representatives of the Hungarian Front, set up for Horthy by his son Miklós, at which he presented his decision and agreed to cooperate with the Front. Furthermore, the regent allegedly promised weapons to arm the workers,[11] which again signified that he was expecting a fight.

Historians have dealt often and thoroughly with the question of why this order failed to reach its destination. The picture presented after this examination suggests partly that there was almost incomprehensible confusion, and partly that there was betrayal on the one side and weakness and incapacity on the other. But it seems that the chaos and failure were caused above all because the action had to be brought forward by five days, which did not leave any time for Horthy to have further discussions, or rather any time for anybody to adapt to the unexpected change.

What probably forced the time change was the fact that the regent got wind of the German–Arrow-Cross coup and wanted to forestall it. One consequence was that the units to defend Budapest could not arrive by the earlier date. Meanwhile a meeting arranged at Szatmárnémeti between the two army commanders and the chief of General Staff failed to occur, for unexplained reasons. Vörös failed to appear, which meant that the two commanders did not agree on the events of the following day, and knew nothing of the change in schedule.[12] Thereafter there were two decisive factors behind events: the activity of the General Staff (especially Vörös), and the decision made on their own responsibility by the two commanders, who had remained without orders. Soldiers, incidentally, are not trained or usually expected to make such decisions.

The determinant on October 15 was the fact that the Germans and Arrow-Cross were preparing a coup, while the Russians demanded in ultimatum form that the measures in the preliminary armistice be carried out,[13] Budapest was still undefended, and the commanders of the two great armies had still not received their instructions. By this time, there was only a faint hope of success, if Horthy let himself be persuaded to travel to the First Army at Huszt and give supplementary orders for its defense.[14] Another faint hope might have come if the Soviet Command had broken its promise to the Hungarians, and instead of ordering a cease-fire against the Hungarians advancing on Budapest had applied greater pressure on the Germans. The regent saw Budapest as some kind of fortress, whose commander could not abandon it, and thus his code of honor prevented him from seizing his last chance and escaping from the trap. But the Soviet Command kept its promise. It gave free passage to the Hungarian units, which could not possibly have reached Budapest in time.

After the appointment of the Lakatos government, Veesenmayer had concluded that he could not be fastidious any longer. He could only save the day (and his own skin)[15] if he relied on the Arrow-Cross to stabilize the situation. Szálasi was in hiding, afraid of arrest if he defied the ban on political parties. So the Germans had first contacted his representative, Emil Kovarcz,

commander-in-chief of the "Hungarist Forces," who set himself up
in a villa provided by the SS in the Pasarét district and began to
organize illegally. He created a chain of Arrow-Cross party workers and activists to spread warnings, prepared in sealed envelopes
the orders to be sent to public utilities, the radio, the post office, and
so on, when the time came, and built up a large cache of weaponry,
with the help of sympathetic army officers. The Arrow-Cross found
two senior officers willing to cooperate—Colonel General Károly
Beregfy, and Colonel Lajos Nádas of the General Staff, who played
an important part in sabotaging the change of sides[16]—and suitably
high-ranking liaisons in the gendarmerie and the police.

The Germans finally sat down to negotiate with Szálasi himself. One condition that he made before doing anything was that he
should receive full and exclusive recognition from Hitler. So
Veesenmayer was obliged to contact Hitler to discuss the situation
in Hungary. Approval for the planned Arrow-Cross coup was
received at the end of September, and Szálasi was reassured that he
was the one leader in Hungary to have Hitler's approval, and his
loyalty and respect for the regent vanished instantly. Szálasi was
the first one to suggest that Horthy might be blackmailed through
his affection for his family.

The Germans then brought new forces into the country, ostensibly to assist the Hungarian army, but they were deployed around
Budapest, not sent to the front. There also arrived a special force
under Otto Skorzeny, who had been involved in rescuing Mussolini
in 1943.[17] Early on the morning of October 15, the Germans, on
orders from Colonel General Heinz Guderian, classified Hungary
as a war zone and assumed the right of command. About that time,
the younger Horthy received a false message that an envoy from
Tito was awaiting him in the office of Félix Bornemissza, his usual
liaison. There he was surprised by the Germans, who burst into the
room, arrested them both, and carried each of them off rolled up in
a carpet. Kovarcz had no knowledge of these moves, but soon
began ordering alerts of his own.

A little after eleven o'clock, Horthy told a meeting of the Crown Council that he was requesting an armistice in view of the military situation. He probably wanted to avoid another constitutional debate by referring to the armistice in the future, instead of the past, or perhaps to leave a slight chance open for talks with the Germans leading (as he envisaged) to the withdrawal of German forces. Horthy's proposal was backed by János Vörös, who favored an armistice. But Prime Minister Lakatos, still unsatisfied, staged another constitutional scene by resigning with his government, although the regent persuaded him to head the "new" government. Horthy's disenchantment with his prime minister is apparent in the fact that he did not initiate him into the armistice or side-changing plan, but simply forced them upon him.

Meanwhile Rudolf Rahn, German envoy in Salo,[18] arrived with a message from Hitler, but their talk did not prevent Horthy from nodding to his daughter-in-law, so sending off a prepared proclamation to the radio. Although Horthy was still trying to persuade Rahn of the need for the German troops to withdraw peaceably, it was clear that he no longer attached much significance to this or much hope of it happening.

The regent's statement, broadcast at about one o'clock, emphasized the fact that Germany had lost the war and a nation could not sacrifice itself on the altar of alliance. Much of the proclamation was devoted to listing German crimes against Hungary and its obligations as an ally, from the occupation and waves of arrests to "administration of the Jewish question in the known way, contrary to the demands of humanity," the kidnapping of Bakay, and the most recently planned coup. The vital passage ran as follows: "I have therefore informed the representative here of the German Reich that we are concluding a provisional armistice with our foes up to now, and ceasing all hostilities against them… I have ordered the heads of the army accordingly, and the commanders appointed by me are obliged to obey, in line with the oath of the forces and the military order issued at the same time."

Everything suggests that Horthy's proclamation was received with delight by the vast majority of the population, but they did not know that there were two big problems. One was that the provisional armistice was already signed, not due to be signed in the future. The other was that the requisite order to the heads of the army had not been given. The regent was still disguising the fact that the provisional armistice was signed, and that was a serious mistake in terms of orienting his commanders. The phrase about the armistice could hardly have derived from a misunderstanding or have been an error. It is much more likely that this, like the submission to the government and the proposal to Rahn, sought to provide further scope in principle for bargaining with the Germans. For the latter were, as we have seen and will see further, uncertain in their actions. It was far from immaterial to them whether they faced a *fait accompli* or a probable scenario.

That did not apply, of course, to those still committed to cooperation with the Germans and trusting in ultimate German victory. Such faith can hardly be explained rationally in highly trained officers and generals. Nor does "Swabian" origin help to clarify matters. Recent discoveries show that Hungarians of German origin were not so strongly represented in the officer elite as was previously thought, and in any case, that stance was as unintelligible in the German officer corps as in the Hungarian one. Even in a country ostensibly imbued with fear of the Bolsheviks, the behavior of the key officers in these critical hours still cannot be explained satisfactorily. The Soviet forces were already fighting in the heart of the country (the tank battle for Debrecen was taking place) and a few hours' drive from the capital. No trained army officer could seriously imagine that the inexorably advancing Soviet war machine could be halted on the plains of Hungary, of all places, or that it would take only the removal of "traitors," coupled with guts and pluck, to do so. No such officer could suppose that the *Wehrmacht*, after two years of retreat and attacked on two sides, could gain a foothold anywhere. Although the Germans had begun aiming their V1 flying bombs on London in June 1944, and many Germans from Hitler downwards were advertising the imminent arrival of a miracle weapon, it had to be seen that neither the V1 nor the more efficient V2 missile introduced in September had changed the course of the war. For Hungarian officers to put their faith in those or in another weapon still at the laboratory stage was hardly a normal approach to war. All in all, it can be assumed that the impetus behind the betrayal should be sought in the field of officer training or among those with personal motives. Personal motives can be interpreted to include previous participation in crimes against humanity, for which many officers, gendarmes and police had good reason to fear the Russians and the Allies in general. These would cover crimes against the partisans, the labor service and the Jews in general. Such psychological motives might provide grounds for some officers to lose touch with reality, overlook their professional knowledge, and continue, quite ludicrously in the end, to risk themselves on the Nazi side in the hope of a miracle.

It is another matter to say why the advocates of switching sides—the officers and generals intent on ending the war on realistic grounds—failed to carry it out. The main cause, mentioned earlier, was incomplete preparation for the operation, whose date had been advanced. To this can be traced many other contributors, such as the uncertainty, contradictory moves and orders, tardiness, and indecision shown. Additional factors, again mentioned before, were that most people were unaware that the provisional armistice had been signed, and that the traitors were unable to prevent the prepared coded order from being cabled.

The plan to switch sides might have been saved if Chief of General Staff Vörös, First Army Commander Miklós, and Second Army Commander Veress had been on top of the situation, which was not true in any of their cases. Vörös was not at his post at the critical time,[19] which gave the traitors time to organize and strike back. When he finally appeared, he had to argue with his own underlings, notably Lajos Nádas, before issuing a war order that called for resistance to all attackers but still referred to continuing the hostilities against Soviet forces. Veress, obviously awaiting an order, did not move immediately and was arrested by the Germans on October 16 for something else.[20] The most extraordinary behavior was shown by Béla Dálnoki Miklós. His actions can be called logical up to the point where he agreed with his subordinate chief of staff, Kálmán Kéri, that Kéri would cross the lines and negotiate with the Russians, for that was certainly needed if there was to be a change of sides. But it is quite impossible to understand why he decided at the last minute, on the 16th, to abandon his army and accompany Kéri. The situation was made worse when the officer who was asked to deputize for Veress vehemently declined. If Miklós thought that he could return to his army after all this, he was deluding himself. According to Kéri, there was no discussion of the matter between the two of them, and Miklós failed to brief him on previous agreements. The story is noticeably incomplete and hard to envisage. The result was that a small part of the First Army changed sides, but most of it was scooped up by the Arrow-Cross.

Add to all this the fact that Aggteleky, commander of the Budapest garrison, was arrested by his own officers, while the river guard, the gendarmerie and the police lined up against Horthy, and it becomes clear that the attempt to change sides would have failed even if the Germans and the Arrow-Cross had stood aside. The army failed by itself, or more precisely due to the incompetence of one part and the clumsiness and treachery of the other. Only the Castle and Horthy stood in the way on October 16. Some of the senior officers in Horthy's army betrayed him and some served him badly. He controlled nothing any more. When the Germans, at Szálasi's instigation, began to blackmail him with his son's life, he could choose only between making a heroic gesture or trying to save his only surviving child and himself. It is not possible to say how far he believed in Veesenmayer's promise of "princely treatment" in a distant part of the Reich.

Horthy rejected the German offer for the first time on the night of October 15–16: he refused to withdraw his proclamation or to resign. Then two men in particular—Antal Vattay, head of the regent's military bureau, and Géza Lakatos, his prime minister—set about persuading him to change his view. Then Vattay wrongly told Lakatos that the regent had changed his mind, and Lakatos, without checking, immediately informed Gerhart Feine, counselor at the German Embassy, that Horthy would withdraw his proclamation, hand over power to the persons whom the Germans recommended, and place himself and his family under the protection of the German Reich. At dawn on the 16th, Feine asked for the defense of the Castle to cease and Lakatos gave orders accordingly to Lieutenant Károly Lázár, the appointed commander. When Skorzeny's men turned up a little later, there was still some scattered resistance, as the order had not reached all the defensive positions, but before firing could break out, Veesenmayer appeared in the palace and requested Horthy to accompany him to SS headquarters, as there was likely to be fighting. At that point, the regent realized that he was under arrest. Horthy gave way in two stages to the blackmail to which he was subjected, with the full cooperation of Lakatos. On the afternoon of the 16th, at SS headquarters, he signed a document saying that he withdrew his proclamation of the previous day and called on the army to keep fighting. He was allowed in return to go back to the Castle to pack.[21] There he was approached again by Veesenmayer, accompanied by Lakatos, with a paper stating that he would resign and hand over power to Szálasi. The plenipotentiary gave "his word of honor" that his son would be released if he was prepared to do this last favor for the Reich. Horthy, now an old man quite without hope, signed the paper, but he maintained for the rest of his life that a signature obtained under such conditions was not a signature.

The regent and his family, under strong German guard, were placed on a train at Budapest Kelenföld station and sent to a hunting lodge in Bavaria,[22] where they lived under Nazi supervision until the Allies arrived.[23] But the younger Horthy was not allowed to join them. He awaited liberation in a cell in Mauthausen concentration camp. The regent's signature was not enough to persuade the Nazis to keep Veesenmayer's word of honor.

However, that signature was enough to allow Szálasi and his followers to take power with a semblance of legality.

Notes

1. If reports can be believed, even the timid, retiring Mrs. Horthy played an active part in the family conspiracy.
2. The Finnish commander-in-chief, Marshal Carl Gustaf Mannerheim, was recommending a rapid end to the war and an armistice in 1943, but he bowed to the head of state's contrary opinion. He then took Finland out of the war in September 1944 with the backing of practically the whole army. Italy, despite Allied backing, could only get as far as dismissing Mussolini; a military change of sides could not be managed.
3. One subjective factor may have been Hitler's absolute trust in Marshal Ion Antonescu, prompting German intelligence to pay less heed in Romania than in Hungary. But the Germans may simply have been late because they did not think the young king capable of such a move.
4. Horthy lost both his son István and his daughters Magdolna and Paula.
5. Several people added that the regent would agree with the one who had spoken last, but that was probably true only verbally. Most of Horthy's decisions seem to have been taken in a thoroughly sovereign fashion.
6. There had been a previous parley with the Germans, as Veesenmayer wanted to salvage what was possible. The only concession made to him was that Reményi-Schneller would remain in the government.
7. The phrase had been used by Miklós Kállay when refusing to appeal to Moscow for an armistice.

8. According to the Finns, however, the withdrawal was accompanied by robbery and plunder.
9. It is not known why the Soviet leadership made an exception for Finland.
10. For the officials involved, failure to obey the evacuation orders or sabotage of them meant that they would no longer receive their salaries.
11. Despite notes to the contrary, the matter had significance. Part of the Social Democratic Party network had survived in illegality and amounted to several tens of thousands of Budapest workers. Together with the communists, the Demény group, according to present knowledge, could mobilize about 2,000 people.
12. Nor is it certain that Vörös knew of the time change when he altered his program, or that he even knew of the whole idea. Horthy only made the decision during the morning of the 14th, while Vörös was traveling to Székesfehérvár.
13. The demand reached the regent's office on the afternoon of October 14.
14. The chief of General Staff was certainly right in trying to persuade him to do so.
15. Hitler would not hesitate to blame him for the whole position in Hungary.
16. In Vörös's absence, he stopped orders from the Castle from being forwarded to the front and ordered the fighting to continue. When the chief of General Staff reappeared, Vörös took issue with him and managed to have subsequent orders altered.
17. Skorzeny, as on other occasions, used the Nazi-favored pseudonym Wolf.
18. The seat of Mussolini's puppet government in northern Italy.
19. The reason for this is unknown.
20. The reason was his order to retreat on October 8.
21. Here he was apparently greeted by the sight of indescribable plundering and destruction by the commandos who had occupied the Castle.
22. To Hirschberg, near Weilheim.
23. The Allies did not return Horthy to the Hungarian authorities, which they might have done easily as his extradition was not opposed by the Russians.

8. TWO OCCUPIERS, TWO GOVERNMENTS

The Arrow-Cross Party was a product of Hungarian society, but Szálasi's rule was not. Support for the party and its leader had fallen dramatically since its peak in 1938–1939. By the autumn of 1944, it found little sympathy anywhere outside its own fairly numerous, well-organized body of activists. It is not right to say that this guard consisted entirely of marginal or hooligan elements, for the Arrow-Cross and its supporters included many army officers, some of high rank, and some well-educated members of the intelligentsia, although the backbone was made up of marginalized younger people from petit-bourgeois families. Yet Arrow-Cross rule did not express the will of society or of any section of it. Szálasi could never have come to power without Hitler and Veesenmayer.

The task that the Germans set the Arrow-Cross was circumscribed by the military situation that had caused it to be summoned in the first place. It had to provide the scope for the *Wehrmacht* to conduct German resistance on Hungary's remaining area and offer up what financial and human resources remained in the Hungarian economy. This Szálasi knew in one sense but not in another. He was not in a clinical sense declared insane in his later trial, but he was not "normal" in an ordinary sense either. He displayed tunnel vision and fanaticism: his assumptions, ideology and goals were impervious to reality and quite divorced from it. On one level he grasped what the Germans intended, but on another he thought that the situation favored his ultimate goals, despite all the evidence to the contrary. These goals he pursued through fire and water, first in Budapest, then on the western borders, and finally from his asylum in Austria. He would have been prepared to advance his ultimate purpose even by deporting the entire Hungarian population to the Reich. He still stood by his beliefs when he was tried before the people's court. The factors behind this behavior were "lust for power" and fanatical devotion to his own system of views and ideology.

The ideology itself can be seen as a variant of Nazism. His racial theory was absolute in relation to the Jews, but relative in relation to the other national communities "dwelling in the great Hungarist house." Szálasi envisaged only that the Hungarians would have the leading role in this community. He attached significance not only to ties of blood, but also to "roots," meaning ties of place among the inhabitants. These "roots" provided the basis on which Hungary could claim its historical lands, or even territory beyond them. He and the Arrow-Cross still expected National Socialism and its leader to conduct a great reorganization, retaining what was by that time blind trust in a miracle. Szálasi had been troubled for years about what he reproachfully called German "imperialism," which certainly could not be reconciled with his plans, but this seems to have concerned him less in 1944. The Germans similarly had laid aside their reservations about Szálasi's outsized Hungarian "self-esteem" and "imperialism" and no longer attached any importance to it.

As for Szálasi's latter-day supporters, they fall broadly into two groups. The majority was made up of ordinary people, many of them young, whose lack of education and political experience left them open to infection by the Arrow-Cross slogans and by the chance of wielding power, with all its alluring financial and moral side-effects. Property, income, a shop or a workshop could be obtained, mainly at the expense of the Jews. Appointments and decorations could be gained—and, once in possession of such power, there was no obstacle to people revenging themselves on their enemies or indulging their sadistic inclinations. These were the rank-and-file Arrow-Cross. The others—leading Arrow-Cross and those who served them—were mainly people no longer able to change sides, who may have thought that the game was up in their sober moments. They were fleeing from their fate.

Szálasi first appeared before the public with a radio statement on the evening of October 15. (A unit of Kovarcz's men had taken over the undefended radio building in the afternoon.) His "order of the day for the armed nation" announced his assumption of power, to which he had been forced by the "self-seeking cronyism" in the Castle. He called people to the final battle, which meant bringing up every force for a "certain victory." Yet the pledges of that victory were frail. Germany was waging a bitter war on two fronts and retreating on both, Japan was losing successive occupied bases in a merciless war of the islands, and Italy was divided and mainly conquered, its northern parts ostensibly ruled by Mussolini, now a caricature of his old self and wholly dependent on German weapons. Szálasi was clearly unperturbed by these conditions as he emerged from hiding and took the helm late on the evening of the 15th.

The composition of the "government of national cohesion" was discussed between Szálasi and Veesenmayer. In addition to the Arrow-Cross leaders, there were places for Lajos Reményi-Schneller, Colonel General Károly Beregfy and Ferenc Rajniss. The lower house of Parliament was quickly summoned and a modest 55 members appeared to vote on the proposed powers of the "national leader." Szálasi took an oath on November 4, before the "national assembly," the government and his party associates—on the Hungarian constitution, which he had just flouted with his alien-assisted coup. He assumed the powers of the regent, becoming commander-in-chief of the army as well as head of state and government. From his titles, it seems that he must have imagined himself a lesser version of Hitler.

The national leader ordered total mobilization on October 18 and then set up a National Reckoning Bench.[1] He also proclaimed the principle of corporate reorganization of the economy, but no start could be made on implementing it. Persecution of left-wingers and ostensible anti-nationals resumed, and new plans were made for annihilating the Jews of Budapest. An order appeared on November 3 nationalizing all Jewish property, which led in practice to a free-for-all among the Arrow-Cross and other people with no scruples. Arrow-Cross groups took to rounding up Jews and herding them down to the Danube, where hundreds of them were shot and dumped in the river. One larger group (of about 50,000 people) was sent off towards Germany on foot, for want of transport to take them. A section of Budapest's 6th District was marked out for a ghetto, where the Jews began to be moved at the beginning of December, on the assumption that deportation of the Jews crowded into there could also be arranged. The ghetto area was relatively small, and so other houses were also marked with a yellow star as being set aside for Jews. Tens of thousands of people crowded into these closed areas, while others—an estimated 30,000—went into hiding with well-intentioned Christians or various social and church organizations. A further number of about 100,000 Jews were murdered under Szálasi's rule, but the Arrow-Cross did not have time to finish its baneful work, although the hunt was not entirely abandoned even during the siege of Budapest.

Help in saving Jews came from the Swedish Embassy (due to Raoul Wallenberg) and the Vatican Mission (where Angelo Rotta was papal nuncio), religious orders such as *Soli Deo Gloria* and the Institute of the Good Shepherd, several other religious and lay organizations (including Zionists), some Hungarian church dignitaries, army officers, and so on.

The whole country had become an area of military operations by the end of October, and the capital city began to be evacuated. Transdanubia, especially the west of it, became unbearably crowded with official staff, soldiers and civilian refugees. There was no space and there were no supplies for this extra population. The apparatus of state that was still operating and every means of transport were directed to the one purpose of shifting out remaining munitions and other assets for the final struggle by the *Wehrmacht*. Total mobilization meant that absolutely everybody—men and women, children and elderly—was used to dig fortifications and organize and operate air defenses. Two SS divisions of young Hungarians (known as *Hunyadi* and *Hungária*) could still be organized with German cooperation, and Beregfy, as minister of defense and commander-in-chief, sent off major Hungarian army units to Austria and then to Germany. (However, these no longer took part in the hostilities in most cases.) At the beginning of November, new headquarters in western Hungary were designated for the main government and state organizations, and a start was made on moving them there. Parliament moved to Sopron and the "leader's" office to Kőszeg. Further orders were issued from there, but they were implemented to an ever smaller territory as the Soviet army advanced. Some Arrow-Cross units and organizations remained behind in Budapest, continuing to hunt out resistance fighters, people giving asylum to Jews, Jews themselves, left-wingers, draft-dodgers, those concealing goods that should have been delivered for central distribution, and so on.

After the Arrow-Cross came to power, activity was resumed by several anti-German groups whose members had spent some months in hiding or been released from prison or internment by the Lakatos government. Endre Bajcsy-Zsilinszky set up the Liberation Committee of the Hungarian National Uprising[2] and its military body, to prepare for an armed uprising. The purpose was to open a corridor out of Budapest for the Russians, thus avoiding a long and destructive siege. They made contact with worker resistance people and with the command of a division stationed on the edge of the city. However, the Arrow-Cross police managed to plant an agent in the organization and arrest the entire leadership on November 22. Lieutenant General János Kiss, Colonel Jenő Nagy and Captain Vilmos Tartsay were executed in Budapest on December 8, and

Bajcsy-Zsilinszky at Sopronkőhida on December 24. Several other officers also started to organize, which brought into being several small partisan groups and the Buda Volunteer Regiment. The most important of these groups operated under the auspices of the Auxiliary Force[3] and had contacts with further groups. Sporadic armed resistance was led in some cases by émigré communists sent back from the Soviet Union (such as Gyula Uszta in Subcarpathia and Sándor Nógrádi around Salgótarján) and in some cases by communists within the country. The Hungarian Communist Anti-Nazi Committee[4] formed in the Borsod industrial area. A group led by Pál Demény in Budapest, in collaboration with the Peace Party, conducted several successful acts of sabotage. (The Demény group was independent both of Moscow and of the Muscovite communist leadership at home.)[5]

Ultimately, what can be said about Hungarian resistance? It seems not to have been nearly as trivial as people thought for a long while. Nor is there evidence for saying that the resisters were almost all communists. There is no denying the latter's presence or importance in the resistance, but account must be taken of all who resisted continuation of the Nazi war in any way. There were those who helped to save people or Hungarian goods, obstructed the dismantling and shipment of factories, sabotaged deliveries intended for Austria, hid Jews and those escaping enlistment, or joined military ventures. Much light has been shed recently on such activities, but the explorations are not over, and it is still not possible to estimate the number of resisters—intellectual, humanitarian and military. The trifling effect of the Hungarian resistance seems to have come not from low participation, but from poor communications between groups and individuals, impeded by lack of time, ideological prejudices and the specific conditions of the time.

The organization and operation of Arrow-Cross power coincided with a process of organization that began on the Great Plain under the auspices of the Soviet occupation authorities. Here the main impetus came from the Hungarian returnees from exile, who appeared in Szeged in October, before moving to Debrecen to build their own party and revive others. The Smallholders', Social Democratic and Peasant Parties were quite quick to appear, but they lacked leaders, who were either in Budapest or in confinement. The Hungarian Communist Party,[6] on the other hand, already had a chosen leadership, although none of the communist leaders inside the country was able to appear. János Kádár was in hiding and László Rajk in the hands of the Arrow-Cross. But that did not bother Ernő Gerő, József Révai, and the others. In any case, the parties that would be decisive to the events of the next few years were quick to appear. They were soon joined by the Citizens' Democratic Party.[7]

The Soviet commands did not impose a military administration. They aimed to restore as soon as possible the old frameworks of public administration and leave the old leaders in charge, where they had not fled, or make rapid appointments of new people who seemed to be suitable. National committees appeared across the Soviet occupation zone, although those organizing them soon found that they were given disappointingly little to do. That was not the case with the land claim committees that sprang up in the rapidly expanding zone and began immediately to register claimants. Great hopes were aroused in the countryside. Most of the landowners had departed along with the old police and gendarmerie.

The siege of Budapest was still in the future, and Szálasi had only just begun to operate from Kőszeg, when communist emissaries started appearing in all the larger liberated cities to organize election rallies and have the crowds that gathered elect representatives after the methods of indirect democracy. The results were haphazard and disproportionate, but on December 21, 230 such representatives came together in Debrecen to form a Provisional National Assembly, which elected a provisional government list on the following day. This coalition government set about establishing new institutions of state, dissolving parties and organizations considered to be fascist or right-wing, drawing up blacklists of books and publications, and forming political screening committees. Preparations were also begun for land reform legislation.

The government's main tasks were to sign the armistice (on January 20, 1945), provide for the occupying army, make contributions to the hostilities against the Germans in line with the armistice, and carry out the behests of the Allied Control Commission.[8] The Allied Control Commission was chaired by Marshal Kliment Yefremovich Voroshilov. The British and American representatives only arrived in Hungary somewhat later, and their activity remained limited. While Szálasi and his regime were pushing many units of the Hungarian army across the western border into Austria and Germany, two divisions set up in the Soviet zone followed the same route somewhat later, arriving in Austria in May, but they, like their compatriots on the other side, did not take part in the fighting. Regret over this has been voiced by some historians, as something that robbed the Hungarians of the glory of fighting against Nazism. While this can be conceded, it was still very lucky that they did not. For the units transported out by the Arrow-Cross had arrived on Austrian and German soil only a couple of weeks before the newly formed army units, and might easily have fired on each other. Meanwhile the occupiers were rounding up large contingents of prisoners of war and civilians treated as such and sending them off to the Soviet Union to work on reconstruction projects.[9] By the time that the whole country was occupied, the number deported had reached 170,000–180,000, no small proportion of them women.

Budapest became trapped between the two sides during the autumn. The Soviets completed their encirclement on December 25. From the German point of view, the only sense in defending the Hungarian capital was to slow the advance of Soviet forces into Austria.[10] Colonel General Hans Friessner, commander-in-chief of the German forces in Hungary, put SS General Karl

Pfeffer-Wildenbruch in command in Budapest, with Lieutenant Colonel Usdau Lindenau as his chief of staff. The 50,000–60,000 Hungarian troops were under the direct command of Iván Hindy, but subordinate to the Germans. The inhabitants of the city spent most of Christmas in shelters, cellars and other relatively protected corners, with stores of food, medicines, candles and lamps, wondering how they could obtain water and dig latrines.[11]

The German commanders knew that they had been given an insoluble task, because a great city cannot be defended with tanks and cavalry. On December 27, they recommended that the city be evacuated, thinking that they could break out on the western side, but Hitler, as usual, forbade a retreat. Not much later, some independent military action to save Budapest was organized. Units were sent for the purpose from the Tata district towards the capital, early in January. Hitler was also the obstacle to the Soviet initiative, when an appeal was made on December 29 for the Germans and Hungarians to hand over the city in exchange for concessions.[12] So a siege of almost six weeks began. The forces of Marshal Rodion Yakovlevich Malinovsky advanced through the city block by block and house by house. When the Germans withdrew their last units from Pest on January 17, Malinovsky thought that the liberation of Buda could be accomplished in a few days. In fact the fighting in Buda lasted until February 12.

At the last moment, on February 11, Pfeffer-Wildenbruch decided to disobey Hitler's orders and try to break out of Buda, or rather Buda Castle, the only part of the city still in their hands. An attempt at escape in a northwesterly direction was to be made with the surviving Hungarian and German forces. He signaled his decision and then destroyed his radio so as not to receive a countermanding order. The escape was to be through the sewage system, but the plan was betrayed to the Russians, who were waiting near the Bólyai barracks. There was a massacre and the few survivors were captured.

Deathly white faces appeared from the cellars of Buda in the next few days, to search, like the people of Pest before them, for any small things of value to be found in the rubble, to seek food, and to try to restore a semblance of normality. But that was not the end either. Hitler still carried out a campaign on Hungarian soil codenamed Spring Awakening, in the Balaton region, causing the destruction of much of Székesfehérvár and great suffering in the communities around the lake. Then Hitler defended Vienna. A quite strong German counterattack on March 6–17 held down large Soviet forces, but it could not prevent the Russians from crossing the Hungarian–Austrian border early in April. The last Hungarian villages were captured between April 4 and 14.

The war had ended for Hungary. Once those able and willing to return home had done so, the loss of life within the Trianon borders was estimated to be between half a million and one million people. (None of the figures making up the total are accurate, and so there is no point in attempting a closer estimate.) There were no Danube bridges left. Almost half the railway track was unusable and the Germans had carried away most of the rolling stock. Between 40 and 50 percent of the industrial capacity had been destroyed. Szálasi and his men had stolen the gold reserves. Much of the housing was ruined and uninhabitable. Urban transport had stopped and the Budapest utilities were not working. There were no food stocks, and most of the farmland had not been tilled in 1944. The country that came out of the war was bombed out and shot to pieces, and its economic assets could be written off.

History seldom offers clear "beginnings" or "ends," but this was certainly an end of something—not just of the war, but of the Hungarian state that had slowly risen from post-war inferno and consolidated itself, only to be wrecked again by the Depression and shattered by the chaos and destruction of World War II. It had taken some ten years for financial and military controls to end and Hungary to build up its sovereignty. Then sovereignty had been lost again, at first bit by bit, then at breakneck speed after 1941, until the country was finally occupied first by one power and then by another. The country and its leaders and people had played a very small part, if any, in precipitating the Great War. The Great Depression had been an external factor, and World War II broke out independently of Hungary. But the decision-makers at various times seem often to have made only sparing use of the conditions and opportunities available. They were not capable, in the 1918 period of bourgeois democracy, of harnessing the forces of society to consolidate the system. The new group headed by Bethlen did the most to restore the economy, modernize education, and resolve social problems, but it failed to resolve the land problem, abandoned the principle of national integration, and strongly restricted the parliamentary system, or made it subservient to the public administration. This ruled out alternation in political power and coalition solutions, an omission that later wreaked havoc on the system. A solution to the Depression was not sought through a consensus, or expansion of the market, and there was no real impetus given to the economy before rearmament began.

Finally, the government, influenced and pressurized by the somewhat anachronistic Hungarian elites, above all the army commanders, went in for joining Germany's war in the hope of regaining territory. They went in for the war for reasons of territorial revision, but they failed to bail out of it in time for fear of German occupation, of Bolshevism, and of the long shadow cast by their own past, in the case of the Arrow-Cross and other extreme right-wingers and their supporters. Yet there was certainly no way that Hungary could have kept out of the great storm. It had to face the alternatives of joining the war on Germany's side or undergoing German occupation, if not in 1941, then in 1943 or, as happened, 1944. The leaders made their decision in 1941, but in 1943 they faced another choice: to continue the war, or to bail out and face occupation. But by 1943 there was no longer any real alternative to occupation or anywhere to run. The decision might be (or could rationally be) postponed. But in the autumn of 1944, the main conditions appeared on the front, and the time had come. It was a matter of urgency to act. This was recognized by Horthy, the officers supporting him, and the conservative, Smallholder, bourgeois liberal and Social Democratic politicians as well, but they failed to carry out their plans, for want of time, and through bad preparation, haste and fear of taking responsibility. Horthy's signature to his resignation, appointing Szálasi as his successor, has importance primarily in personal and moral terms.

It is hard to say what the country lost by the failure of October 1944 or why. The moral damage and loss of self-esteem were certainly great. If the attempt to change sides had succeeded, nobody could have dubbed Hungary the last satellite or fashioned arguments from that against paying the slightest heed to Hungary's ethnic demands in the Paris Peace Treaty of 1947. Stalin had not shown any sympathy for the Hungarians beforehand either, but he would probably have found it harder to push through his intentions if the Hungarian attempt at *renversement* had succeeded. Perhaps there might even have been scope for the traditional Soviet foreign policy line of recognizing Hungary's rights to territorial revision, as there had been in the time of Chicherin and Litvinov, or even Molotov in 1941—the subsequent story of its partial retention or reversal is still not known. Perhaps there would have been some significance attaching to the modest Anglo-Saxon proposals for revision as well. In terms of the division into zones of influence among the Great Powers, post-1945 Hungary suffered the same fate as it would have done however successful a change of sides it had conducted or however strong a resistance to the Germans it had shown. In the event, as the "last satellite" of Germany, it received the same fate that the other countries occupied by Germany suffered in the Soviet zone of influence.

Notes

1. *Nemzeti Számonkérő Szék.*
2. *Magyar Nemzeti Felkelés Felszabadító Bizottsága.*
3. *Kisegítő Karhatalom (KISKA).*
4. *Magyarországi Kommunisták Antináci Komitéja (MOKAN).*
5. The communist émigrés had hardly arrived before Demény was arrested.
6. *Magyar Kommunista Párt.*
7. *Polgári Demokrata Párt.*
8. *Szövetséges Ellenőrző Bizottság (SZEB).*
9. Young men suspected of serving in the SS or joining in the work of the *Volksbund* were sentenced by summary military courts, usually in Baden, Austria, to several years' forced labor and sent to one of the penal camps of the Gulag. It was not taken into consideration that the two Hungarian SS divisions consisted of enlisted men, just like the others.
10. Hitler is unlikely to have felt a moment's concern for the damage to the city. He had always thought it unjust that the Hungarians should have such a lovely capital.
11. The version in which Budapest people spent the days happily celebrating Christmas is based on false information.
12. Two military emissaries, Captain Miklós Steinmetz and Captain Ilya Afanasevich Ostapenko, died in the initiative. Steinmetz's car hit a land mine and Ostapenko came accidentally under Soviet mortar fire.

APPENDIX

Secret Treaty of the Allied and Associated Powers with Romania, August 17, 1916
[Extract. Retranslated from Hungarian]

...

Article 1. France, Great Britain, Italy and Russia guarantee in every regard the territory of the Romanian Kingdom within its present borders.

Article 2. Romania will declare war on Austria-Hungary and commence hostilities according to the methods and conditions laid down in the military agreement of the present treaty. Romania, concurrently with the declaration of war, will sever all economic and commercial relations with the enemies of the Entente Powers.

Article 3. France, Great Britain, Italy and Russia recognize the right of Romania to annex the territories belonging to the Austro-Hungarian Monarchy that are defined in Article 4.

Article 4. The borders of the territories referred to in the previous article are defined as follows:

The frontier begins at the point on the River Prut on the present border that constitutes the border of Romania and Russia near Novoselitza,[1] then follows the present course of the Prut to the border of Galicia, as far as the confluence of the Prut and the River Caremos. From there the line follows first the border between Galicia and Bukovina, then that between Galicia and Hungary, as far as Slog: to an altitude of 1,655 meters. From this high point it follows the watershed of the River Tisza and the River Visó and reaches the Tisza at Trebusa, whence it continues along the right bank of the river

451

to the confluence of the Tisza and the Visó. Hereafter it follows the course of the Tisza right down to a point 4 kilometers below the confluence with the River Szamos, and then—leaving Romania at Vásárosnamény—turns south-southeast and runs to a point 6 kilometers east of Debrecen. Retaining its direction approximately, the frontier continues to a point 3 kilometers below the confluence of the River Körös, the River Fehér-Körös and the River Sebes-Körös, and then goes 3 kilometers further west and makes a curve around the villages of Orosháza and Békéssámson, to reach the Tisza at Algyő. Hereafter it follows the course of the Tisza right down to the confluence with the River Danube and then follows the Danube to the present border of Romania.

...

Article 5. Great Britain, France, Italy and Russia on the one hand and Romania on the other hand undertake that they will not conclude any separate peace or general peace otherwise than conjointly and at one time.

Great Britain, France, Italy and Russia at the same time undertake that they will cause the Austro-Hungarian territory defined in Article 4 of this treaty to be annexed to the Romanian crown as a possession.

Article 6. Romania shall enjoy the same rights as the other contracting parties in preparing the peace, negotiating the same, and in debating all questions relating to the decisions of the peace conference.

Article 7. The Contracting Powers undertake to keep this treaty secret until the conclusion of the general peace.

This treaty has been prepared in five copies in Bucharest
on August 4–17, 1916.   G. Barclay [signature]

                                Saint-Aulaire [signature]

                                        Fasciotti [signature]

                           S. Polevski-Koziell [signature]

                                      Ion I. C. Bratianu[2]

Manifesto of Emperor Charles, October 16, 1918
[Extract]

A start must now be made without delay to rebuilding the country on natural, i.e. reliable, foundations. The desires of the Austrian peoples in this direction must be brought carefully into harmony with each other and then met.

I have decided to perform this task with the free cooperation of my peoples in the spirit of the basic principles that the Allied rulers have adopted in their peace proposal.

Austria—in accordance with the will of its peoples—will become a federal state, in which each people will create its own separate state community on its settlement territory. This will in no wise affect the union of Austria's Polish territories with the independent Polish state. The city and territory of Trieste will receive special status according to the wish of its people.

This new arrangement, which in no wise affects the integrity of the countries of the Hungarian Holy Crown, will ensure the independence of each nation in a separate state.

    …

Charles [signature]
Hussarek [signature][3]

Act I/1920 on Constitutionality, February 29, 1920
[Extracts]

As a reminder to all whom it may concern, the National Assembly[4] of Hungary has passed the following act:

The National Assembly, as the sole legal representative of national sovereignty, establishes that the exercise of royal power ceased on the 13th day of November in the year 1918.[5] It establishes further that the hitherto inalienable and indivisible co-dominion over Hungary and its partner countries and the kingdoms and countries represented in the Austrian Imperial Council has ceased. The National Assembly reserves to itself the task of establishing the consequences of these facts in the period after the conclusion of peace.

It establishes further that the House of Representatives of the Parliament[6] lawfully convened on the 21st day of June in the year 1910 declared itself to be dissolved on the 16th day of November in the year 1918, and its House of Peers at its sitting on the same day took cognizance of this decision and closed its proceedings, since the operation of the National Assembly had ceased. In the light of all these [circumstances], exercise of supreme state power according to the normal forms of the constitution became impossible.

In accordance with the underlying principles of our constitution, the provisional governments established since the 7th day of August in the year 1919 turned to the nation, to elect according to universal suffrage extending also to women and by secret, equal, direct, and compulsory franchise a National Assembly[7] competent to represent its will.

Elections for National Assembly representatives being held thereafter in all parts of the country where hostile occupation did not preclude them,[8] the elected representatives met in Budapest on the 16th day of February in the year 1920 and formed a National Assembly.[9]

The National Assembly so convened hereby adopts the following act:

Chapter One

Measures directed at restoration of constitutionality

§ 1. The National Assembly approves the government orders on whose basis the National Assembly has convened.

§ 2. The National Assembly declares itself the lawful representative of Hungarian state sovereignty, which is authorized according to our constitution to set the subsequent method of exercise of state power.

...

Chapter Two
Powers of the regent

§ 12. The National Assembly, until it has settled finally how the power of the head of state shall be exercised and the office of the head of state is assumed accordingly, shall elect from among the citizens of Hungary by secret ballot a regent for the provisional performance of the tasks of the head of state.

§ 13. The regent is empowered to exercise the constitutional rights of royal power with the following restrictions:

Acts passed by the National Assembly are not subject to assent: the regent will supply them with a promulgation clause and a signature within 60 days. Before issuing the order for promulgation, the regent may return the act once to the National Assembly for reconsideration, giving his reasons for doing so. If the National Assembly leaves the act unchanged, the regent is obliged to promulgate it within 15 days. The regent may not exercise his right of return for reconsideration on acts concerning the question of the form of state and the person of the head of state.

...

The regent may not adjourn the National Assembly,[10] and he may exercise in relation to the National Assembly the royal right to dissolve the Parliament[11] only if the National Assembly[12] becomes durably inoperable despite a message from the regent, and the speaker of the National Assembly is unable to restore operability through the rights accorded to the speaker under the house rules.

...

Previous consent of the National Assembly is needed for a declaration of war, service by the army outside the country, and the conclusion of peace.

The regent shall exert executive power exclusively through the ministry responsible to the National Assembly. All his orders and measures, including his orders to the armed forces, become valid only if they are endorsed by the appropriate responsible minister.[13] However, this does not affect those constitutional rights of the regent in military matters that pertain to the command, leadership and organization of the national army.

He may not grant nobility.

He may not exercise right of patronage.

A general reprieve may only be issued by law.[14]

§ 14. The person of the regent is inviolable, and he enjoys the same penal immunity as the king does under our laws.

The regent may be called to account by the National Assembly in the event of a breach of the constitution or the law.

...

István Rakovszky [signature]
speaker of the National Assembly
Károly Huszár [signature] prime minister
László Kechkemen Petes [signature]
recorder of the National Assembly

Treaty of Peace between the Allied and Associated Powers and Hungary, and Protocol and Declaration, signed at Trianon June 4, 1920 (Act XXXIII/20)[15]

...

PART III.

Section VI

Protection of minorities.

Article 54. Hungary undertakes that the stipulations contained in this Section shall be recognized as fundamental laws, and that no law, regulation or official action shall connect or interfere with these stipulations, and nor shall any law, regulation or official action prevail over them.

Article 55. Hungary undertakes to assure full and complete protection of life and liberty to all inhabitants of Hungary without distinction of birth, nationality, language, race or religion.

All inhabitants of Hungary shall be entitled to the free exercise, whether public or private, of any creed, religion or belief

456

whose practices are not inconsistent with public order or public morals.

Article 56. Hungary admits and declares to be Hungarian nationals *ipso facto* and without the requirement of any formality all persons possessing at the date of the coming into force of the present Treaty rights of citizenship (*pertinenza*) within Hungarian territory who are not nationals of any other state.

Article 57. All persons born in Hungarian territory who are not born nationals of another state shall *ipso facto* become Hungarian nationals.

Article 58. All Hungarian nationals shall be equal before the law and shall enjoy the same civil and political rights without distinction as to race, language or religion.

Difference of religion, creed or confession shall not prejudice any Hungarian national in matters relating to the enjoyment of civil or political rights, such as for instance admission to public employments, functions and honors, or the exercise of professions and industries.

No restriction shall be imposed on the free use by any Hungarian national of any language in private intercourse, in commerce, in religion, in the press or in publications of any kind, or at public meetings.

Notwithstanding any establishment by the Hungarian government of an official language, adequate facilities shall be given to Hungarian nationals of non-Magyar speech for the use of their language, either orally or in writing, before the courts.

Hungarian nationals who belong to racial, religious or linguistic minorities shall enjoy the same treatment and security in law and in fact as the other Hungarian nationals. In particular they shall have an equal right to establish, manage and control at their own expense charitable, religious and social institutions, schools and other educational establishments, with the right to use their own language and to exercise their religion freely therein.[16]

Section VII

Clauses relating to nationality.

Article 61. Every person possessing rights of citizenship (*pertinenza*) in territory that formed part of the territories of the former Austro-Hungarian Monarchy shall obtain *ipso facto*, to the exclusion of Hungarian nationality, the nationality of the state exercising sovereignty over such territory.

Article 62. Notwithstanding the provisions of Article 61, persons who acquired rights of citizenship after January 1, 1910, in territory transferred under the present Treaty to the Serb-Croat-Slovene State, or to the Czecho-Slovak State, will not acquire Serb-Croat-Slovene or Czecho-Slovak nationality without a permit from the Serb-Croat-Slovene State or the Czecho-Slovak State respectively. If the permit referred to in the preceding paragraph is not applied for, or is refused, the persons concerned will obtain *ipso facto* the nationality of the state exercising sovereignty over the territory in which they previously possessed rights of citizenship.

Article 63. Persons over 18 years of age losing their Hungarian nationality and obtaining *ipso facto* a new nationality under Article 61 shall be entitled within a period of one year from the coming into force of the present Treaty to opt for the nationality of the state in which they possessed rights of citizenship before acquiring such rights in the territory transferred.

Option by a husband will cover his wife and option by parents will cover their children under 18 years of age.

Persons who have exercised the above right to opt must within the following 12 months transfer their place of residence to the state for which they have opted.

They will be entitled to retain their immovable property in the territory of the other state where they had their place of residence before exercising their right to opt.

They may carry with them their movable property of every description. No export or import duties may be imposed upon them in connection with the removal of such property.[17]

Article 64. Persons possessing rights of citizenship in territory forming part of the former Austro-Hungarian Monarchy, and differing in race and language from the majority of the population of such territory, shall within 6 months from the coming into force of the present Treaty severally be entitled to opt for Austria, Hungary, Italy, Poland, Romania, the Serb-Croat-Slovene State or the Czecho-Slovak State, if the majority of the population of the state selected is of the same race and language as the person exercising the right to opt. The provisions of Article 63 as to the exercise of the right of option shall apply to the right of option given by this Article.

PART V.
MILITARY, NAVAL AND AIR CLAUSES

...

Section I

Military clauses.

Chapter I

General.

Article 102. Within 3 months of the coming into force of the present Treaty, the military forces of Hungary shall be demobilized to the extent prescribed hereinafter.

Article 103. Universal compulsory military service shall be abolished in Hungary. The Hungarian Army shall in future only be constituted and recruited by means of voluntary enlistment.

Chapter II

Effectives and cadres of the Hungarian army.

Article 104. The total number of military forces in the Hungarian Army shall not exceed 35,000 men, including officers and logistical troops.

...

The Hungarian Army shall be devoted exclusively to the maintenance of order within the territory of Hungary, and to the control of its frontiers.

Article 105. The maximum strength of the staffs and of all formations that Hungary may be permitted to raise are given in the tables annexed to this Section; these figures need not be exactly followed, but must not be exceeded.[18]

All other organizations for the command of troops or for preparation for war are forbidden.

Article 106. All measures of mobilization, or any pertaining to mobilization, are forbidden.

In no case must formations, administrative services or staffs include supplementary cadres.

The carrying out of any preparatory measures with a view to requisitioning animals or other means of military transport is forbidden.

Article 107. The number of gendarmes, customs officers, foresters, members of the local or municipal police, or other similar officials may not exceed the number of men employed in a similar capacity in 1913 within the boundaries of Hungary as fixed by the present Treaty. The Principal Allied and Associated Powers may, however, increase this number should the Commission of Control referred to in Article 137, after examination on the spot, consider it to be insufficient.

The number of these officials shall not be increased in the future except as may be necessary to maintain the same proportion between the number of officials and the total population in the localities or municipalities that employ them.

These officials, as well as officials employed in the railway service, must not be assembled for the purpose of taking part in any military exercises.

Article 108. Every formation of troops not included in the tables annexed to this Section is forbidden. Such other formations as may exist in excess of the 35,000 effectives authorized shall be dissolved within the period laid down by Article 102.

Chapter III
Recruiting and military training.

Article 109. All officers must be commissioned (*officers de carrière*). Officers now serving who are retained in the army must undertake the obligation to serve in it up to the age of 40 years at least. Officers now serving who do not join the new army will be released from all military obligations; they must not take part in any military exercises, whether theoretical or practical.

Officers newly appointed must undertake to serve on the active list for 20 consecutive years at least.

The number of officers discharged for any reason before the expiration of their term of service must not exceed in any year one twentieth of the total of officers provided for in Article 104. If this proportion is unavoidably exceeded, the resulting shortage must not be made good by fresh appointments.

Article 110. The period of enlistment for non-commissioned officers and privates must be a total period of not less than 12 consecutive years, including at least 6 years with the colors.

The proportion of men discharged before the expiration of the period of their enlistment for reasons of health or as a result of disciplinary measures or for any other reasons must not in any year exceed one twentieth of the total strength fixed by Article 104. If this proportion is unavoidably exceeded, the resulting shortage must not be made good by fresh enlistments

Chapter IV
Schools, educational establishments, military clubs and societies.

Article 111. The number of students admitted to attend the courses in military schools shall be strictly in proportion to the vacancies to be filled in the cadres of officers. The students and the cadres shall be included in the effectives fixed by Article 104.

Consequently all military schools not required for this purpose shall be abolished.

Article 112. Educational establishments, other than those referred to in Article III, as well as all sporting and other clubs, must not occupy themselves with any military matters.

Chapter V

Armament, munitions and material.

Article 113. On the expiration of 3 months from the coming into force of the present Treaty, the armament of the Hungarian Army shall not exceed the figures fixed per thousand men in Table No. V annexed to this Section.[19]

Any excess in relation to effectives shall only be used for such replacements as may eventually be necessary.

Article 114. The stock of munitions at the disposal of the Hungarian Army shall not exceed the amounts fixed in Table No. V annexed to this Section.

Within 3 months from the coming into force of the present Treaty the Hungarian government shall deposit any existing surplus of armament and munitions in such places as shall be notified to it by the Principal Allied and Associated Powers.

No other stock, depot or reserve of munitions shall be formed.

Article 115. The manufacture of arms, munitions and war material shall only be carried out in one single factory, which shall be controlled by and belong to the state, and whose output shall be strictly limited to the manufacture of such arms, munitions and war material as is necessary for the military forces and armaments referred to in Articles 104, 107, 113 and 114. The Principal Allied and Associated Powers may, however, authorize such manufacture, for such a period as they may think fit, in one or more other factories to be approved by the Commission of Control referred to in Article 137.[20]

The manufacture of sporting weapons is not forbidden, provided that sporting weapons manufactured in Hungary taking ball cartridges are not of the same caliber as that of military weapons used in any European army.

Within 3 months from the coming into force of the present Treaty, all other establishments for the manufacture, preparation, storage or design of arms, munitions or any other war material shall be closed down or converted to purely commercial uses.

Within the same length of time, all arsenals shall also be closed down, except those to be used as depots for the authorized stocks of munitions, and their staffs discharged.[21]

…

PART IX.

Financial clauses.

Article 180. Subject to such exceptions as the Reparation Commission may make, the first charge upon all the assets and revenues of Hungary shall be the cost of reparation and all other costs arising under the present Treaty or any treaties or agreements supplementary thereto, or under arrangements concluded between Hungary and the Allied and Associated Powers during the Armistice signed on November 3, 1918.

Up to May 1, 1921, the Hungarian government shall not export or dispose of, and shall forbid the export or disposal of, gold without the previous approval of the Allied and Associated Powers acting through the Reparation Commission.

Article 181. There shall be paid by Hungary, subject to the fifth paragraph of this Article, the total cost of all armies of the Allied and Associated governments occupying territory within the boundaries of Hungary as defined by the present Treaty from the date of the signature of the Armistice of November 3, 1918, including the keep of men and beasts, lodging and billeting, pay and allowances, salaries and wages, bedding, heating, lighting, clothing, equipment, harness and saddlery, armament and rolling stock, air services, treatment of the sick and wounded, veterinary and remount services, transport services of all sorts (such as by rail, sea or river, or by motorized lorries), communications and correspondence, and, in general, the cost of all administrative or technical services the working of which is necessary for the training of troops and for keeping their numbers up to strength and preserving their military efficiency.

…

PART X.

Economic clauses.

…

Article 203. Every favor, immunity, or privilege with regard to the importation, exportation or transit of goods granted by Hungary to any Allied or Associated State or to any other foreign country whatsoever shall simultaneously and unconditionally without request and without compensation, be extended to all the Allied and Associated States.

Article 204. By way of exception to the provisions of Article 270, Part XII (Ports, Waterways and Railways), products in transit by the ports that before the war were situated in the territory of the former Austro-Hungarian Monarchy shall, for a period of 3 years from the coming into force of the present Treaty, enjoy on importation into Hungary reductions of duty corresponding to and in proportion to those applied to such products under the Austro-Hungarian Customs Tariff of the year 1906, when imported by such ports.

Article 205. Notwithstanding the provisions of Articles 200 to 203, the Allied and Associated Powers agree that they will not invoke these provisions to secure the advantage of any arrangements that may be made by the Hungarian government with the governments of Austria or of the Czecho-Slovak State for the accord of a special customs regime to certain natural or manufactured products that both originate in and come from those countries, which shall be specified in the arrangements, provided that the duration of these arrangements does not exceed a period of 5 years from the coming into force of the present Treaty.

Act XXV/1920 on Regulations for Enrollment at Institutes of Higher Education, September 26, 1920

§ 1. For the 1920/1921 academic year in the University of Sciences, the Technical University, the Budapest University Faculty of Economic Sciences, and the academies of law, enrollment is confined to individuals who are loyal to the nation and unconditionally trustworthy in moral regards, and in such numbers for which basic education can be provided.

The number of students to be admitted to individual faculties (specialist departments) will be determined by the minister of religious and educational affairs based on the nomination of the faculty (at the technical university, the council) concerned.

Extraordinary students may only be admitted if the quota established according to the previous paragraph has not been filled with regular students, and only within the quota established.

This measure does not apply to those enrolling for state accountancy in the faculties of law and state studies (at the academies of law), but the minister of religious and educational affairs may also set the number of extraordinary students at these.

§ 2. The terms of § 1 do not affect the right of subsequent enrollment for regular students enrolled in previous academic years, or for extraordinary students possessed of a certificate of matriculation and studying in the faculties of humanities (arts, languages and historical studies), mathematics and natural science, and medicine.

§ 3. Those enrolling under the terms of § 1 must request an enrollment permit by submission to the faculty (at the technical university, the council) concerned.

The quota of enrollment permits established according to the terms of § 1 shall be determined finally by a full meeting of the professors of the faculty (at the Technical University, the council).

The grant of a permit shall be determined, apart from the requirements of loyalty to the nation and moral reliability, by the intellectual capacities of the applicants, while attention is also paid to whether the proportions of the young people among the students belonging to the individual races and national groups inhabiting the country match the national proportions of those races and national groups, or make up at least nine tenths of these.[22]

Similarly, only the faculty (at the technical university, the council) concerned in full session may admit those seeking enrollment according to § 2. The rules for the enrollment of these will be established by an order of the minister of religious and educational affairs.

§ 4. This act, which comes into force on the day of its proclamation, will be implemented by the minister of religious and educational affairs.

Government Summary of the Agreement between the Government and the Social Democratic Party, December 21, 1921
[Extract]

The meeting agreed after intensive discussion that:

1. The right of assembly is restored, but meetings may only be held in closed premises; street protest demonstrations are not permitted.
2. The non-political activity of the trade unions described in their statutes may be pursued without hindrance. However, the union of public employees, railway workers and postal workers may not be reinstated.
3. The matter of the General Consumer Cooperative has already been regulated in a separate agreement.
4. Internments will be confined to the minimum, i.e. to terrorists, communist agitators, and other publicly dangerous individuals. Persons falling under the requirement of registration will also be reduced to the minimum.
5. Censorship of the press has already ceased.

6. An amnesty order has been issued for the individuals who committed crimes within or connected with mass movements taking place between October 31, 1918, and March 21, 1919, or covered by § 1 of Order 4039/1919 ME.
7. Expedited judicial proceedings will steadily cease.
8. The exceptional measures will be placed under revision and steadily repealed.
9. The autonomy of workers' insurance will be restored—provided that the Social Democratic working class accepts in theory the principle of triple interest (workers, employees and government).
10. Free movement of mine workers will be allowed; the government commissionership of military supervision of coal will cease.
11. The government will naturally do everything possible to remedy the economic problems; it will also find a suitable form of restricting workers' wages; it may present a parliamentary bill on establishing a conciliation and arbitration tribunal.
12. There will be action to free the blocked deposits of the working class.

In parallel with fulfillment of the wishes of the Social Democratic working class here outlined, the delegates of the working class announce as a consequence of the desires expressed on the government side that:

They consider the interests of the nation and country to be identical with the interests of the working class, so that the working class must struggle and make sacrifices for these. The Social Democratic Party will therefore refrain from all propaganda damaging to Hungary's interests and make active propaganda for Hungary among foreign social democratic party leaderships and governments; it will cooperate with the Royal Hungarian Ministry of Foreign Affairs, break openly with the émigrés, and take up the struggle against them abroad as well. It will deny reports of terror spread about Hungary, and use its influence to ensure that foreigners receive a picture of Hungary that corresponds to the truth. A campaign to this effect will be made in *Népszava* and in the foreign press.

In domestic policy, it is ready to cooperate with the bourgeois classes in the economic field. It will refrain from political strikes, break with the Liberal Bloc, and give no support to bourgeois demagoguery or Octobrist elements. As government opposition, it will struggle with honest weapons, eschew factional demagoguery, and refrain from republican propaganda.

The minutes taken of the meeting have been prepared in two original copies, of which one is to be kept by the minister, and the other is to be handed to the representatives of the Hungarian Social Democratic working class named above.

Dr. Zoltán Bencs, head of department

Italian–Hungarian Treaty of Friendship
Treaty on the Friendship, Arbitration Proceedings and Elected Tribunal between Hungary and Italy, April 5, 1927
[Extract]

Article 1. Constant peace and eternal friendship shall stand between the Kingdom of Hungary and the Kingdom of Italy.

Article 2. The High Contracting Parties undertake to place under conciliation proceedings and before the tribunal proceedings chosen for the question arising all disputed issues of any nature that arise between them and cannot be resolved by diplomatic means within the requisite time.

This provision is not applicable to disputed issues arising from facts that preceded the conclusion of the present treaty and belong to the past.

Issues in dispute for which other valid agreements between the High Contracting Parties prescribe different procedures shall be regulated by the terms of such agreements.

Article 3. Where conciliation does not ensue, either of the High Contracting Parties may desire that the question at issue be placed under elected judicial procedure, provided that the dispute is of a legal nature.

Article 4. The methods of conciliation and elected judicial procedure are stated in the protocol attached to the present treaty.

Article 5. The present treaty shall be ratified and the documents of ratification exchanged in Rome within the shortest possible time.

The treaty shall be valid for a term of 10 years counted from the date of exchange of the documents of ratification. Unless the notice is given by one contracting party more than a year before the term runs out, it shall remain in force for a further 10-year term, and so forth.

In witness of this the persons empowered have signed this treaty.[23]

Dated in Rome this 5th day of April in the year 1927.

Agreements Relating to the Obligations [of Hungary] Resulting from the Treaty of Trianon Paris, April 28, 1930
[Extracts]

AGREEMENT NO. I

Article 1

In complete and final settlement of the charges incumbent on it by virtue of the Treaty of Trianon, of the Armistice of November 3, 1918, and of any Agreements supplementary thereto, without prejudice, however, to the stipulations of Article 2 below, Hungary hereby confirms its obligation to pay the sums specified in the Reparation Commission's decision No. 2797 of February 21, 1924, and undertakes, on account of the special claims that are based on the said Treaty, to make payment of a constant annuity of 13,500,000 gold crowns as from January 1, 1944, and during the years 1944 to 1966 inclusive.

...

Article 4

The payments due after 1944 constitute an unconditional obligation, that is to say, without any right of suspension whatsoever. They shall be made to the Bank for International Settlements, in gold or in currencies equivalent to gold, in two equal installments on January 1 and July 1 of each year, the first installment falling due on January 1, 1944.

...

Article 6

The first charge established by Article 180 of the Treaty of Trianon on all the assets and revenues of Hungary for the cost of reparations and all other costs referred to in the said Article shall definitively cease to have effect as from the date of the coming into force of the present Agreement.

...

Article 9

The Creditor Powers signatory to the present Agreement undertake, as from the date of its coming into force, to cease to apply their right of retention and liquidation of the property, rights and interests that, at the date of the coming into force of the Treaty of Trianon, belonged to nationals of the former Kingdom of Hungary or to companies controlled by them, insofar as such property, rights and interests are not already liquid or liquidated, or have not yet been definitely disposed of.

...

Article 11

The relations between the Reparation Commission and Hungary shall be determined as soon as possible.

The accounts of the Reparation Commission with Hungary shall be considered as finally closed and as no longer being of any effect at the date at which the present Agreement comes into force.

Save as provided for in paragraph 2 of Article 2, the rights and powers conferred on the Reparation Commission shall be transferred as far as is necessary to the Bank for International Settlements.

…

Article 12

Subject to the approval of the Council of the League of Nations, the Committee of Control for Hungary shall cease to exercise its functions as soon as the present Agreement comes into force. The French government, which is entrusted with the duty of receiving the ratifications, is also entrusted with the duty of submitting the necessary request to the Council of the League of Nations.

…[24]

The First Chapter of the National Plan of Action Advertised by Prime Minister Gyula Gömbös October 24, 1932

I. DOMESTIC AND FOREIGN POLICY

1. *The aim of our policy*

The aim of our policy is the reinforcement and prosperity of the Hungarian nation, to ensure the greatest attainable moral and material welfare for every member of the nation.

Since this aim can be attained only within the framework of an independent national state resting on firm foundations and directed by a strong, constitutional, central will, we see it as the direct task of our policy to build up a self-aimed[25] national state.

2. *The task of our foreign policy*

We take it as the task of our foreign policy to secure for the Hungarian national state the role that it merits in terms of the past of our nation, its geographical position, and its historical calling.

3. *Revision, minority rights,*

cooperation between the Danubian states

We will strive by all peaceful means to bring the peace treaties under revision in a spirit of law and justice. We will place emphasis on the full enforcement of minority rights, and we will not rule out cooperation between the Danubian states.

The Program of the March Front
March 15, 1937

WE DEMAND

We live in a critical and decisive period for our people, and we feel that we must declare our faith in our humanity and our Hungarian-ness. This we are impelled to do by the great heritage of March,[26] for every March is the month that calls to action the Hungarian youth of all time. We raise again the misappropriated intellectual heritage of that first March and demand...

1. Democratic transformation of the country.
2. Freedom of thought, speech, the press and assembly.
3. General, equal and secret franchise, without any correctives.
4. , The fullest observance of [the principle of] incompatibility by National Assembly members; may no National Assembly member be allowed to accept membership of a managerial, interest-representing etc. board.
5. Expropriation of landed estates of over 500 *hold* (285 ha).
6. Cessation of the rule of banks, cartels and monopolies, which erodes the Hungarian community.
7. Introduction of a progressive taxation system.
8. Work for all Hungarians desirous of working; introduction of a 40-hour working week for non-manual and manual work alike, an end to job pluralism and mammoth incomes.
9. Establishment of minimum working wages above the minimum for biological subsistence.
10. Freedom for employees to organize in economic regards.
11. Introduction, in the interest of the lower classes of people, of a progressive system of fees in middle schools and higher colleges and of selection by quality.

12. Hungarian revision; respect for the right of self-determination on the question of where the peoples of the Danube Valley should belong. Establishment of the idea of the Danube Valley's self-assertion and confederation against pan-Slav and pan-German imperialist endeavors.

Only in this wise do we see the future of our people secured in this inhuman and un-Hungarian world, and we firmly believe that we will remain true to the spirit of the first March.

Act XV/1938 on More Effective Maintenance of the Balance of Social and Economic Life, May 29, 1938
[Extracts]

§ 1. The Royal Hungarian Ministry is authorized, for 3 months from the promulgation of this act, to take necessary and urgent measures in the form of regulations to ensure more effectively the balance of social and economic life—including measures to overcome professional unemployment—in the fields and by the principles stated in the §'s below, even in cases where the measure would otherwise belong to the domain of the legislature.

§ 2. The Royal Hungarian Ministry is instructed to initiate the foundation of:

a) a press chamber for the publisher and editor of every paper, whether periodical or not, and for the staff in the permanent employ of that paper;

b) a drama and cinema chamber for actors, film actors, film directors, drama and film managers and administrators, and auxiliary artistic staff (choral/orchestral staff) employed in theaters and the film industry.

The tasks of the press chamber and drama and press chamber shall be to meet the demands of national spirit and Christian morality in journalism and press publishing and in drama and cinema respectively, represent the corporate and social interests of chamber members, defend the moral standards and respect of their calling, safeguard their rights connected with the pursuit of their calling, exercise authority over them, [and] take positions and make proposals on issues connected with journalism and press publishing and with drama and cinema respectively.

Only members of the press chamber may serve as temporary or non-temporary publishers, editors or permanent staff members of a periodical or non-periodical paper.

A theater or a company releasing motion pictures by making, leasing or otherwise may only employ a member of the drama and cinema chamber as a director, performer or artistic auxiliary in the employments defined under Point b) of the first paragraph. The minister of religious and cultural affairs may make exceptions to this in the public interest.

§ 3. Only Hungarian citizens may be members of the press chamber or the drama and cinema chamber. The other conditions of membership will be set in the [enabling] order of the Royal Hungarian Ministry.

§ 4. The press chamber and the drama and cinema chamber may admit Jews to membership only in such proportions as do not exceed 20 percent of the total membership of the chamber.

This 20 percent may not be calculated to include:

a) disabled veterans, combat soldiers, or the children or widows of those who died a hero's death;

b) those who were converted before August 1, 1919, to some other recognized religious denomination and have been continually a member of that denomination;

c) such offspring of a parent covered under Point b) who is not a member of the Israelite faith.

...

§ 7. Persons covered by the first paragraph of § 4 may be admitted as members of the lawyers', engineers' or medical chambers in such proportions as do not exceed 20 percent of the total membership of the chamber. Until such time as the proportion of the membership constituted by the other members of the chamber shall exceed 80 percent, persons falling under the first paragraph of § 4 may only constitute up to 5 percent of the newly admitted membership. The minister responsible may make exceptions to this in the public interest.

The second paragraph of § 4 shall be applied to this § accordingly.

§ 8. In a company that falls under Act XXI/1937, where the number of official, commercial assistant and other non-manual jobs is ten or more, persons covered by the first paragraph of § 4 may be employed only in such proportions as do not exceed 20 percent of the total membership of the chamber; the total annual emoluments paid to them on any grounds may not exceed 20 percent of the total annual emoluments paid to all the staff in non-manual occupations on any grounds.

Act IV/1939 on the Expansion of the Jews in Public Life and the Economy, May 5, 1939

§ 1. From the point of view of applying this act, a person is to be regarded as Jewish who has at least one parent or at least two grandparents who were members of the Israelite faith on the coming into force of this act, and all progeny of those listed born after the coming into force of this act.

…

§ 3. No Jew may obtain Hungarian citizenship by naturalization, by marriage, or by legitimacy.

The minister of the interior is authorized to rescind the naturalization (re-naturalization) of Jews who became Hungarian citizens after the 1st day of May in the year 1914 whose conditions in life do not indicate that they should remain in the country. Naturalization (re-naturalization) must be rescinded if the specific conditions in law for naturalization (re-naturalization) do not apply, or if a crime or disciplinary offense was committed for acquisition of Hungarian citizenship through naturalization (re-naturalization), or if the authorities were misled.

Rescission of naturalization (re-naturalization) extends to the cohabiting wife of the naturalized (re-naturalized) person and to minor children under the authority of their parents, if the order does not state otherwise.

Permission for a change of name must also be rescinded along with the rescission of the naturalization (re-naturalization).

§ 4. No Jew may be elected a member of the upper house of Parliament other than pastors called upon to represent the Israelite faith.

A Jew only has a parliamentary, municipal or local franchise and may only be elected a member of Parliament, a municipality or local authority if he/she and his/her parents—and if the parents were born after December 31, 1867, the parents' parents as well—were born in Hungary and if he/she provides trustworthy evidence for the fact that they lived permanently in Hungary and for other legally defined conditions.

A Jew may only be a member of a municipal board[27] through election by all the voters or by virtue of representing a religious denomination. No Jew as chief taxpayer may be a member of a local assembly.[28] No Jew may be registered in the roll of municipal or local chief taxpayers.

If those entered on the parliamentary electoral role are classed as Jews under this act, this must be declared. A Jew may only exercise the right to vote if he/she confirms that he/she is entitled to such a right under § 2.

…

§ 5. No Jew may enter the service of the state, a municipality, a locality, or any other public body, public institute or public utility as an official or an employee. This stipulation applies also to the

physicians contracted or hired temporarily by social security institutions. The president of the insurance institution may terminate the
contractual relations of Jews to the institute with one year's notice.

[Jewish] teachers teaching in middle schools, special middle
schools and elementary schools, and Jewish teachers in elementary
schools, as well as Jewish village (district) clerks, must be retired
by the 1st day of January in the year 1943, and Jewish royal trial
judges and Jewish members of royal prosecution departments by
the 1st day of January in the year 1940, or dismissed from service
with severance pay according to the relevant regulations.

…

§ 9. Jews may only be employed as staff members on periodical or
non-periodical publications according to the rules stated in the regulations on employment in non-manual positions (§ 17).

No Jew may be the responsible editor, publisher, editor-in-
chief or other staff member under any designation on a periodical
paper who determines the intellectual direction of the paper or has
an influence on the editing of the paper in other regards.

…

§ 11. No Jew may be the manager, artistic secretary, scriptwriter,[29]
or otherwise designated employee of a theater who determines the
intellectual or artistic direction of the theater, or has an influence on
the employment of the artistic staff of the theater or otherwise has
an influence on the artistic affairs of the theater.

The provisions in the first paragraph shall be applied appro-
priately to the managers of companies making, distributing and
presenting motion pictures and to artistic directors and executives
performing managerial functions, and to other employees with a
guiding influence on the making, distribution, presentation, and
program compilation of motion pictures.

…

§ 12. No permit to sell goods falling under a state monopoly or
other profitable license likewise dependent on official leave, whose

grant or withholding depends on the free judgment of the authorities, shall be granted to a Jew. Permits (licenses) issued to (acquired by) Jews before this act comes into force shall be withdrawn within 5 years of the act coming into force, as will permits for wholesale and retail trading in tobacco, the sale of small quantities of homemade wine, and licenses to dispense and sell drink in county seats and in large and small communities within 2 years from the act coming into force, and pharmacy licenses within the 5 years commencing 3 years after the act comes into force.

...

§ 14. No industrial license or industrial permit may be issued to a Jew engaged in an industry until the combined number of industrial licenses and permits issued [to Jews] in the community concerned shall fall below 6 percent of the total number of industrial licenses and permits. The minister of trade and transport and the minister of industry may make exceptions in the public interest.

No Jew may receive an industrial permit for an employment bureau or for credit intelligence or credit advice; industrial permits for employment bureaux issued to Jews before the present act comes into force cease on December 31, 1940.

...

§ 16. Without regard for otherwise existing restrictions, Jews may be compelled to hand over all their agricultural property for sale or for smallholdings. This provision shall also apply to agricultural property that a Jew, or any person acting in a case of death, may have transferred to another between the 31st day of December in the year 1937 and the present act coming into force; however, the compulsion to transfer under this provision in the case of property transferred to non-Jews applies only within 3 years of the transfer.

...

§ 17. Outside the public sphere, Jews may only be engaged in industrial (commercial), mining, founding, banking and money-changing firms, private insurance firms, transport firms and agricultural (horticultural, viticultural) concerns, or any other official, clerical or other non-manual posts in other paid employment in such a proportion that the number of Jewish employees at the firm not covered by the first paragraph of § 2 does not exceed 12 percent of those employed at the firm in non-manual capacities, or that the total number of Jewish employees—including those covered by the first paragraph of § 2—does not exceed 15 percent of the employees in non-manual positions.

...

Accession to the Tripartite Agreement
November 20, 1940

The governments of Japan, Germany and Italy on the one hand and the government of Hungary on the other hand agree on the following through their signed representatives:

Article I. Hungary accedes to the Tripartite Agreement between Japan, Germany and Italy signed on the 27th day of September in the year 1940 in Berlin.

Article II. Insofar as the joint specialist committees referred to in Article IV of the Tripartite Agreement discuss such questions as affect the interests of Hungary, the committees must include representatives of Hungary in their deliberations.

Article III. The exact text of the Tripartite Agreement is annexed to this Protocol as an appendix.

This Protocol is prepared in the Hungarian and in the Japanese, German and Italian languages, and each text is to be considered as original. This Protocol comes into force on the day of its signature.

As evidence of this the undersigned, empowered in the right and requisite form by their governments, have signed this Protocol and appended to it their seals.

Prepared in four original copies in Vienna on the 20th day of November in the year 1940, in the XIXth year of Fascist time reckoning and in the 15th year of the Showa period on the 20th day of the 11th month.

S. Kurusu
Von Ribbentrop
Ciano
István Csáky

The Tripartite Agreement
Berlin, September 27, 1940

The governments of Germany, Italy and Japan, considering it as a condition precedent to lasting peace that all nations of the world be given each its own proper place, have decided to stand by and cooperate with one another with regard to their efforts in greater East Asia and regions of Europe respectively, wherein it is their primary purpose to establish and maintain a new order of things calculated to promote the mutual prosperity and welfare of the peoples concerned.

Furthermore, it is the desire of the three governments to extend cooperation to such nations in any other parts of the world as may be inclined to pursue endeavors along lines similar to their own, so that their ultimate aspirations for world peace may thus be realized.

Accordingly, the governments of Germany, Italy and Japan have agreed as follows:

Article 1. Japan recognizes and respects the leadership of Germany and Italy in the establishment of a new order in Europe.

Article 2. Germany and Italy recognize and respect the leadership of Japan in the establishment of a new order in greater East Asia.

Article 3. Germany, Italy and Japan agree to cooperate in their efforts on the aforesaid lines. They further undertake to assist one another by all political, economic and military means when any of the three Contracting Powers is attacked by a power at present not involved in the European war or in the Chinese–Japanese conflict.

Article 4. With a view to implementing the present Agreement, joint technical commissions, the members of which are to be appointed by the respective governments of Germany, Italy and Japan, will meet without delay.

Article 5. Germany, Italy and Japan affirm that the aforesaid terms do not in any way affect the political status that exists at present as between each of the three Contracting Powers and Soviet Russia.

Article 6. The present Agreement shall come into force immediately on signature and shall remain in force for 10 years from the date of its coming into force.

At the proper time before expiration of the said term, the High Contracting Parties shall at the request of any of them enter into negotiations for its renewal.

In faith whereof, the undersigned duly authorized by their respective governments have signed this Agreement and affixed their seals.

Done in triplicate at Berlin on the 27th day of September 1940, in the XVIIIth year of the Fascist Era, which corresponds to the 27th day of the ninth month of the 15th year of Showa.

S. Kurusu
Joachim von Ribbentrop
Ciano

Hungarian–Yugoslav Treaty of Eternal Friendship
December 12, 1940
[Extract]

...

Article 1. Permanent peace and eternal friendship shall subsist between the Kingdom of Hungary and the Kingdom of Yugoslavia.

Article 2. The High Contracting Parties agree to consult on all questions that in their judgment affect their mutual interests.

Article 3. The present Treaty shall be ratified and the confirming documents exchanged in Budapest if possible.

The Treaty will come into force on the day of exchange of the documents of ratification.

In faith whereof the above-named representatives have signed this Treaty and affixed their seals.

Count István Csáky
Al. Cincar-Marković

Memorandum of Henrik Werth, Chief of General Staff, to the Government on the Policy to Pursue, June 14, 1941
[Extracts][30]

...

As I have said in my Memoranda quoted above, we cannot, due to our military policy position, be idle observers of events in the case of a German–Russian war.

It is my firm conviction that Hungary cannot stand by idly in a German–Russian war. We must take part in such a war:

1. because the territorial integrity of our country demands it, as does the safety of our system of state, society and economy,

2. because it is in our prime national concern in the interests of our future to weaken and rid our borders of Russian neighborhood,

3. because our world view resting on a Christian national basis and our position of principle against Bolshevism demands this, in the future as in the past,

4. because politically we have committed ourselves irrevocably to the Axis Powers,

5. because the further national increase depends upon it.

…

We also have an obligation to join the war from our accession to the Axis Powers, but in addition from the fact that we can only hope for further expansion of our country if we remain true to our loyal policy towards the Axis, as a reward for which we are sure to recover the whole of historical Hungary. Competent German circles have always implied this and we can certainly hope for it after the gestures made so far by the Axis Powers. We should join all the more as Romania is already committed to participating in the war. This has been used against us by clever Romanian propaganda. And if we fail to join in, we may not only have to renounce for all time further hopes of [territorial] revision against Romania; we could jeopardize the expansion of our country so far as well.[31]

Act XV/1941 Amending the Law on Marriage
August 8, 1941
[Extracts][32]

IV. Ban on the contracting of marriage between non-Jews and Jews

§ 9. It is forbidden for a non-Jew to contract a marriage with a Jew.

A marriage contracted between a Jewish woman and a non-Jew with foreign citizenship does not fall under the ban proclaimed in this §.

In applying the present §, a Jew is a person two of whose grandparents were born into the Israelite faith, and likewise—irrespective of parentage—one who is a member of the Israelite faith.

Those with two grandparents who were born members of the Israelite faith are not to be considered as Jews if they themselves were born members of the Christian faith and remained so, and if their two parents were members of the Christian faith at the time of their marriage. Such persons are forbidden to marry not only Jews, but such non-Jews who were born with one or two grandparents of the Israelite faith.

The provisions of the last paragraph must also be applied to children born out of wedlock, if the natural father has acknowledged before the registrar or in a sworn deed, or paternity has been established by the courts.

...

V. Penal provisions

...

§ 14. Non-Jewish persons native to Hungary who contract marriage with a Jew, and Jews who contract marriage with a non-Jew native to a foreign country in contravention of the ban stated in § 9 are committing a crime punishable by up to 5 years' imprisonment, loss of office and suspension of political rights. Also punishable are civil officials who know that a hindrance to marriage described in § 9 exists yet commit the offense of conducting such a marriage; this is punishable by up to 3 months in prison.

...

§ 15. An offense punishable by 3 years in prison, loss of office, and suspension of political rights is committed by Jews:

who have extramarital coitus with an honest non-Jewish woman native to Hungary, or

who procure or attempt to procure for themselves or for other Jews an honest non-Jewish woman native to Hungary for the purpose of coitus.

It is a crime punishable by imprisonment for up to 5 years, loss of office and suspension of political rights, if the criminal

1. has committed the act by deceit, force or threat,

2. has committed the act against a dependant, or a person entrusted for the purpose of upbringing, teaching, or supervision,

3. has committed the act when the woman has not completed her 21st year,

4. has committed the act despite having been previously convicted of such an offense and 10 years have not elapsed since completion of the punishment.

…

Act II/1942 on the [Office of] Vice-regent
February 15, 1942
[Extracts]

I. Election of the vice-regent

§ 1. The National Assembly may at the regent's request elect a vice-regent from Hungarian citizens who are of age.

The regent has a right of nomination. The regent may nominate three candidates at most. If the regent exercises his right of nomination, only such a person as the regent has nominated may be elected as vice-regent. The nomination, countersigned by the prime minister, must be conveyed to the National Assembly at the latest by the time at which the joint session to elect the vice-regent begins.

§ 2. The vice-regent is elected by the two houses of the National Assembly in joint session. The joint session must be summoned so as to convene without delay, at the latest on the 8th day from the time when the regent conveys his nomination.

…

§ 3. If the regent has exercised his right of nomination (§ 1, second paragraph), the speaker of the joint session has the regent's statement of nomination read out and orders a vote. The vote is secret.

If the regent nominates a single person, each member of the National Assembly receives a voting paper bearing the words "yes" and "no," and the vote is taken by the voter striking out either the "yes" or the "no" according to his/her intention and placing the voting paper in the urn. If the number of "yes" votes exceeds the total number of "no" votes cast and it exceeds the proportion of two thirds of the members present at the opening of the session, the speaker declares the person nominated to be elected vice-regent. In the contrary case, the election must be considered invalid.

If the regent nominates two or three persons, each member of the National Assembly receives as many voting papers as there are candidates. One voting paper will say yes and the others no; a separate urn must be placed for each candidate, and members vote separately on each nominated person at once, by placing a "yes" or a "no" voting paper in the requisite urn. According to the result of the election, the speaker declares elected as vice-regent the person receiving the plurality of the votes, provided that the number of votes cast exceeds the proportion of two thirds of the members present at the opening of the session.

...[33]

§ 5. If after the opening of the joint session to elect the vice-regent, and confirmation of a quorum—and if the regent exercises his right of nomination, the reading of the regent's recommendation—the National Assembly unmistakably declares its will by acclamation, the speaker will waive the nomination and holding of the election, and declare to be elected vice-regent the one in whom the National Assembly has declared its confidence by acclamation.

...

§ 6. Election of the vice-regent requires confirmation by the regent.

After confirmation by the regent, the vice-regent will swear an oath before the National Assembly—if possible the joint session for the vice-regent's election—and before the regent if the latter wishes to attend the swearing in.

...

Act III/1942 on the Election of István Horthy as Vice-regent
February 20, 1942

The regent of Hungary, in his rescript dated the 15th day of February in the year 1942, expressed a desire that the National Assembly elect a vice-regent according to the terms of Act II/1942 on the vice-regent. The National Assembly held a joint session for this purpose on the 19th day of February in the year 1942. The National Assembly at this session elected as vice-regent *Vitéz* István Horthy of Nagybánya.

The regent of Hungary in a rescript dated on the 19th day of February in the year 1942 informed the National Assembly that he was confirming the election of the vice-regent.

After the regent's confirmation, the vice-regent on the 19th day of February in the year 1942 swore before the National Assembly and in the presence of the regent the oath prescribed in § 6 of Act II/1942.

The National Assembly accordingly enacts the election and swearing in of *Vitéz* István Horthy of Nagybánya as the vice-regent.

Credentials of Edmund Veesenmayer,
Minister Plenipotentiary of the German Reich
March 20, 1944
[Retranslated from Hungarian]

1. The interests of the Reich in Hungary will be followed with attention in future by the minister plenipotentiary in Hungary of the Great German Reich, who bears at the same time the title of envoy.

2. The minister plenipotentiary of the Reich is responsible for all developments in Hungarian politics, and receives his instructions from the Reich minister of foreign affairs. His task is primarily to assist in the formation of a Hungarian government that is committed loyally to preserving allied fidelity under the Tripartite

Agreement until the final victory. The minister plenipotentiary of the Reich will supply guiding advice to this government and represent all the interests of the Reich towards it.

3. The minister plenipotentiary of the Reich shall ensure that the government under his direction conducts the entire public administration of the country—even during the presence of the German forces—with the aim of utilizing all the resources of the country, above all the economic potential, to support the joint war.

4. No civilian bodies may be formed in Hungary without consent from the minister plenipotentiary of the Reich, to which they are subordinate and under whose direction they conduct their activity.

To perform the SS and police tasks in Hungary to be carried out by German forces—primarily in the policing aspects of the Jewish question—there will be attached to the staff of the minister plenipotentiary of the Reich a high-ranking SS and police commander, who will act under the minister's political direction.

5. While German forces remain in Hungary, the commander of these forces will exercise the military prerogatives. The commander will be subordinate to the OKW chief[34] and receive his orders from him.

Military defense of the country's territory and against surprise outside attack is the task of the commander of the forces.

He will support the minister plenipotentiary of the Reich in his political and public administrative tasks, while directly representing the demands of the *Wehrmacht*, particularly in the exploitation of the country for the supply of the German forces.

The minister plenipotentiary of the Reich will carry out the requirements of the *Wehrmacht* in the civilian field.

In the case of delay causing serious danger, the commander of the German forces is also empowered in the civilian field to introduce regulations required for the solution of the military tasks. In this regard he must get in touch as quickly as possible with the minister plenipotentiary of the Reich.

In all matters where the spheres of authority coincide, the minister plenipotentiary of the Reich and the commander of the German forces shall cooperate as closely as possible and coordinate their actions.

6. I appoint as minister plenipotentiary of the Reich and envoy the party member Dr. Edmund Veesenmayer.

Adolf Hitler[35]

Proclamation of Miklós Horthy to the Hungarian Nation
October 15, 1944

When the will of the country placed me at the head of the nation, the main aim of Hungarian foreign policy was to end at least partly the injustices of the peace treaty of Trianon, through [territorial] revision to be obtained by peaceful means. Hopes placed in this field on the work of the League of Nations were not realized.

Nor was Hungary led by a desire to obtain alien territories when the new world crisis appeared. Nor did we have aggressive intentions against the Czech Republic or seek to regain by means of war part of the territories previously lost to it. Likewise, we only marched into the Bácska territory after the collapse of the Yugoslav administration, to protect those of our own blood. With the territories taken from us by Romania in 1918 as well, we only accepted them after a peaceful decision requested by Romania had been taken by the Axis Powers.

Hungary was swept into the war against the Allied Powers by our geographical situation and the German pressure weighing upon us, but we had no power objectives in that regard either, and we did not wish to take a square meter of territory from anybody.

By now there is no doubt in the mind of any sober observer that the German Reich has lost the war. The consequences of this must be drawn by governments responsible for the destiny of their country, for as the great statesman Bismarck said, a people cannot sacrifice itself on the altar of allied fidelity. I must, in the knowledge of my historical responsibility, take every step in the direction of avoiding further superfluous bloodshed. A people that allowed the land inherited from its fathers to become the scene of rearguard battles in slavish defense of alien interests in a lost war would forfeit the respect of world opinion.

I have to conclude with sorrow that the German Reich for its part broke its allied loyalty to us long ago. It has for a long time, against my desire and will, been deploying increasingly an ever greater part of the Hungarian armed forces beyond the borders of the country. And in March this year, the leader of the German Reich called me to Klessheim for talks, precisely because of my pressing for the return of the Hungarian forces, and there informed me that German forces were occupying Hungary, and despite my protest, accomplished this while they detained me abroad. At the same time, the German political police entered the country and arrested many Hungarian citizens, including several members of the legislature, and the minister of the interior of the government of the time, and the prime minister only escaped arrest by seeking refuge in a neutral legation.[36]

On receiving a clear undertaking from the leader of the German Reich that if I appointed a government that enjoyed the confidence of the Germans he would end the violations and restrictions on Hungarian sovereignty, I appointed the Sztójay government. However, the Germans did not keep their promise. Under the protection of the German occupation, the *Gestapo* has used against the Jewish question the well-known measures employed elsewhere in this field, which contravene the requirements of humanity. As the war approached and even crossed the borders of the country, the Germans repeatedly promised the requisite assistance, but they did not keep their word in the promised way or on the promised scale. While evacuating from the country's territory, they plundered it and made it a scene of destruction.

All these actions in contravention of allied loyalty have ultimately been topped by the way in which the agents of the German *Gestapo*, in the midst of the measures taken by the commander of the Budapest corps, Lieutenant General Szilárd Bakay, to maintain domestic order, carried him off one foggy October morning under cover of poor visibility, attacking him treacherously as he got out of his car in front of his home. Then leaflets against the present government were dropped from German planes. I received reliable reports that German politically oriented forces were seeking to gain power for their own people by means of force, while intending to turn the territory of the country into the scene of rearguard actions for the German Reich.

I have decided to defend the honor of the Hungarian nation even against former allies, for instead of giving the military assistance spoken of, they are seeking to rob the Hungarian nation of its greatest treasure, its freedom, its independence. I have therefore informed the representative of the German Reich here that we are concluding a provisional armistice with our enemies,[37] and ending all hostilities against them. Trusting in their sense of justice and with their agreement, I wish to ensure the continuity and peaceful objectives of the future life of our nation. I have therefore given the requisite orders to the commanders of the Hungarian army, and therefore, under the forces' oath and in line with my concurrently issued order of the day, they are obliged to obey their commanders.[38]

I call upon every honest-minded Hungarian to follow the road of sacrifice to the salvation of the Hungarian people.

Notes

1. Novoselitsya, Ukraine.
2. The signatories (in order) are the British, French, Italian and Russian envoys in Bucharest, and the Romanian prime minister.
3. Emperor Charles I, King of Hungary as Charles IV, and Max von Hussarek, Austrian prime minister.
4. *Nemzetgyűlés*.
5. Charles issued a document on November 11, 1918, in his capacity as Emperor, at the Austrians' request, and another two days later, at the Hungarians' request, abdicating from the exercise of his rights as ruler.
6. *Országgyűlés*.
7. *Nemzetgyűlés*.
8. Within Hungary's borders as laid down in the peace treaty, the region beyond the Tisza was under Romanian occupation and southern Baranya County and the Pécs–Komló district under Serbian occupation. The Romanian troops withdrew behind the border in March and the Serbian ones in August, after which supplementary elections could be held.
9. *Nemzetgyűlés*.
10. This was amended by Act XII/1920 on August 19, 1920, to allow the regent to adjourn the legislature for up to 30 days.
11. *Országgyűlés*.
12. *Nemzetgyűlés*.
13. Act XVII/1920 added the following: "In a case of directly threatening danger, however, the regent may order the employment of the army outside the borders of the country without all-ministry responsibility with subsequent approval of the National Assembly to be requested without delay."
14. Act XVII/1920 allowed him to issue a general reprieve; Act XXIII/1933 granted him the old royal rights of adjourning, closing and dissolving the legislature.
15. The terms affecting Hungary's borders are best studied with the help of the maps above. These extracts cover some lesser-known provisions.

16. The rest of Part III Section VI concerns local interpretations and League of Nations decisions on matters in dispute. The stipulations on minorities were presented by the peace conference as a separate text for acceptance by the new states (Czechoslovakia, Yugoslavia and Poland) and Romania.

17. When the successor states (especially Czechoslovakia and Romania) deprived "optants" (those choosing Hungarian citizenship) of their real estate, this article provided the grounds for optant suits for recovery.

18. According to the tables, an infantry regiment might include 414 officers and 10,780 men, a cavalry regiment 259 officers and 5,380 men, and a mixed brigade command and logistical and special troops 198 officers and 530 men.

19. According to the table, there might be 1,150 rifles or carbines, 15 heavy or light machine guns, 2 trench mortars, and 3 field or mountain guns or howitzers per 1,000 men.

20. The Hungarian state cited this provision for not combining the munitions factories. One factor was the fact that they were in private hands and there were no budgetary funds available for building a new state factory.

21. Chapter V of the peace treaty goes on to state that the Hungarian army could possess no armored cars, tanks, warships, aircraft or dirigibles.

22. § 3 was amended by Act XIV/1928 as follows: "The grant of a permit shall be determined, apart from the requirements of loyalty to the nation and moral reliability, by the intellectual capacities of the applicants, while attention is also paid to whether war orphans and the children of those who saw active military service and of state employees, as well as the children of those belonging to the various branches of employment (agriculture, industry, commerce, free professions, etc.) enter higher education in proportion to the numbers and importance of these employments and that the numbers admitted are also divided fairly among the individual municipalities."

23. The persons empowered were István Bethlen and Benito Mussolini.

24. The agreements were signed by representatives of the following states (in French alphabetical order): Belgium, Great Britain and Northern Ireland, Canada, Australia, New Zealand, the Union of South Africa, France, Greece, Hungary, Italy, Japan, Poland, Portugal, Romania, Czechoslovakia and Yugoslavia.

25. *Öncélú.*
26. When the Hungarian Revolution broke out on March 15, 1848, young Pest revolutionaries defied the censors and had their twelve-point demands printed without an official permit. The same pattern was used in 1937 for the demands of the opposition writers making up the March Front.
27. *Törvényhatósági bizottság.*
28. *Községi képviselőtestület.*
29. *Dramaturg.*
30. Werth refers initially to earlier submissions urging agreement with Germany on military cooperation against the Soviet Union, to which he had not received a substantive response from the government.
31. He went on to urge the government to take a position by citing intelligence received by the chief of General Staff that a German attack was due in 9–10 days.
32. Previously, the act makes general provisions about premarital medical examinations, religion, and so on.
33. The act then details the procedure if no candidate gains a majority, or the regent does not exercise his right of nomination, so that no nomination procedure occurs.
34. Chief of the *Oberkommando der Wehrmacht* (High Command of the German Army) at the time was Wilhelm Keitel.
35. Other documents show that Veesenmayer also received more detailed instructions. Among other things, he had to obtain the appointment of Béla Imrédy as prime minister, and cooperate with the commander of the German forces in following up the confinement to barracks by disarming the Hungarian army and transporting it to Germany.
36. The regent's reference is to Miklós Kállay, who received asylum for a time in the Turkish mission, but came under pressure to leave it, fell into German hands, and was transported to a concentration camp.
37. In fact the provisional armistice had already been signed in Moscow by the regent's representatives on October 11.
38. The order of the day failed to reach the commanders due to sabotage by some officers of the General Staff.

CHRONOLOGY

1914

June 28   Serbian student Gavrilo Princip assassinates the Habsburg heir apparent, Francis Ferdinand, and his consort in Sarajevo.

July 28   Austria-Hungary declares war on Serbia, and on August 5 on Russia.

1915

May 23   Italy enters the war on the Entente side.

Oct. 14   Bulgaria joins the war on the side of the Central Powers.

1916

Aug. 17   The Romanian government is promised Dobrudja and the eastern parts of Hungary in the secret Treaty of Bucharest, and agrees in return to enter the war on the Entente side.

Nov. 21   Francis Joseph I, Austrian emperor and Hungarian king, dies. His successor is Charles (I as Emperor of Austria and IV as King of Hungary).

1917

March 12   A revolution in Russia overthrows the Tsarist autocracy. A provisional government forms on March 14.

March 24   Charles IV approaches the French government for a separate peace (the Sixtus Letter).

May 23   Hungarian Prime Minister István Tisza resigns. His successor is Móric Esterházy, followed by Sándor Wekerle.

June 17   Mihály Károlyi and his adherents leave the Independence Party and establish the Independence and '48 Party.

Oct. 20   The Central Powers launch an attack in the Caporetto district in which the Italian army suffers a heavy defeat.

Nov. 7   The provisional government in Petrograd falls. On March 3, 1918, Russia signs a separate peace with the Central Powers and withdraws from the war.

1918

May 7   The Central Powers make a separate peace with Romania in Bucharest.

Sept. 15	French and Serbian forces in the Balkans attack the Central Powers. An armistice is requested by Bulgaria on the 29th and Turkey on the 30th.
Oct. 23–24	The Hungarian National Council is established in Budapest with Mihály Károlyi at its head.
Oct. 24	An Italian offensive assisted by Britain and France is launched at Piavena and breaks all Austro-Hungarian resistance.
Oct. 29	The *sabor* (national assembly) meeting in Zagreb declares Croatia's independence and accession to the new South Slav state (the Serbian–Croatian–Slovenian Kingdom).
Oct. 30	The Slovak National Council meeting at Turócszentmárton (Martin) declares its accession to the Czechoslovak state on October 28.
Oct. 30–31	The Aster Revolution in Budapest succeeds. Archduke Joseph appoints Mihály Károlyi as prime minister.
Nov. 3	Representatives of the Austro-Hungarian Monarchy sign an armistice in Padua.
Nov. 7	A Hungarian government delegation in Belgrade begins armistice negotiations with the Entente commander-in-chief on the Balkan front. On November 13, the Belgrade Convention setting the demarcation line in southern Transylvania and the South Country is signed. On December 15, the Romanians cross the line and occupy northern Transylvania and some of the Partium.
Nov. 8	Czech troops cross the Hungarian border near Nagyszombat (Trnava) and Trencsén (Trenčin).
Nov. 10	Romania announces its reentry into the war and declares war on Germany.
Nov. 13	King Charles IV abdicates.
Nov. 16	The Hungarian National Council declares Hungary a people's republic.
Nov. 24	The Communist Party of Hungary is formed.
Dec. 1–2	The Romanian National Assembly, meeting at Gyulafehérvár (Alba Iulia), announces a union of Transylvania and the Partium with the Romanian Kingdom and promises "full national freedom" to national minorities.
Dec. 6	A Hungarian–Slovak agreement draws a demarcation line on roughly ethnic lines, but this Edvard Beneš, the Czechoslovak foreign minister, rejects. On December 23,

the Hungarian government receives a note showing a demarcation line that accords with the Czech demands.

Dec. 22   The Transylvanian Hungarian Grand Assembly at Kolozsvár (Cluj-Napoca) comes out in favor of a state union between Hungary and Transylvania.

1919

Jan. 11   The National Council invests Mihály Károlyi with the powers of provisional president of the republic. Dénes Berinkey is appointed prime minister.

Jan. 18   The peace conference opens in Paris.

Feb. 6   The People's Act on Allocation of Land to the Farming People is never implemented.

March 20   The Vix Note sets a new demarcation line to the west of the Arad–Nagyvárad–Szatmárnémeti railway line. Having rejected this, President Károlyi and Prime Minister Berinkey resign.

March 21   The merged Hungarian Social Democratic Party and Communist Party of Hungary proclaim a proletarian dictatorship. A Revolutionary Governing Council under Sándor Garbai is formed in the Hungarian Soviet Republic.

April 16   There is a Romanian offensive along the whole eastern front. By April 30, the entire trans-Tisza region is under Romanian occupation.

April 27   The Czechoslovak army crosses the demarcation line, occupies Ózd, Miskolc and Putnok, and enters Subcarpathia.

May 5   A rival government is set up in Arad under Gyula Károlyi, but after the Romanian occupation of the city it moves to Szeged. Later the minister of defense, Rear Admiral Miklós Horthy, sets about organizing an army.

May 9   The northern campaign by the Hungarian Soviet Republic begins. The eastern part of the Uplands is reoccupied and the Polish border reached on June 10. On June 16, a Slovak Soviet Republic is proclaimed at a meeting in Eperjes (Prešov).

June 13   The French prime minister, Georges Clemenceau, sends a note to the government promising to persuade the Romanians to withdraw behind the demarcation line, if Hungary will evacuate the Uplands. This is done, but the Romanians fail to obey the Entente.

July 20	The Hungarian Soviet army attacks the Romanians along the Tisza. The offensive fails. The Romanians enter Budapest on August 4 and then occupy northern Transdanubia as well.
Aug. 1	The Revolutionary Governing Council resigns, giving way to fleeting governments under Gyula Peidl and István Friedrich.
Nov. 14–16	The Romanian troops withdraw from Budapest and retreat behind the Tisza. They evacuate the region beyond the Tisza by March 1920.
Nov. 16	Miklós Horthy enters Budapest at the head of the National Army.
Nov. 24	Károly Huszár forms a government with the blessing of the Allied Powers.

1920

Jan. 16	Albert Apponyi, heading the Hungarian delegation at the Paris Peace Conference, requests plebiscites to decide territorial questions, but the conference rejects this.
Jan. 25–26	The National Assembly elections held in unoccupied territory are won by the National Smallholders' and Agriculturists' Party and the Christian National Unity Party.
March 1	The National Assembly elects Miklós Horthy as regent (head of state) of Hungary. Horthy appoints Sándor Simonyi-Semadam as prime minister on March 15.
June 4	The Peace Treaty of Trianon is signed with Hungary in the Grand Trianon Palace at Versailles.
July 19	Pál Teleki is appointed prime minister.
Aug. 14	A treaty is made between Czechoslovakia and the Kingdom of the Serbs, Croats and Slovenes. This and Czechoslovak–Romanian and Romanian–Yugoslav treaties made on April 23 and June 7, 1921, respectively, create the Little Entente.
Nov. 13	The National Assembly passes István Nagyatádi Szabó's land reform legislation.

1921

March 26–	Charles IV makes his first attempt to regain the throne.
April 5	Teleki resigns as prime minister in the face of protests by neighboring countries.
April 14	István Bethlen forms a government.
Oct. 20	Charles IV makes a further attempt to return, but is beaten back by the regent's troops at Budaörs on October 23 and

exiled by the Allies to Madeira, where he dies on April 1, 1922.

Nov. 6   The National Assembly legislates to dethrone the House of Habsburg-Lorraine.

Dec. 14–16   Two thirds of the votes in a plebiscite in Sopron and its district favor belonging to Hungary.

Dec. 22   The Bethlen–Peyer pact between the government and the Social Democratic Party restricts the latter's operation but legalizes it and allows it to return to politics.

1922

Feb. 2   Bethlen and his supporters join the Smallholders' Party, which takes the name Christian Smallholders', Agriculturalists' and Citizens' Party (usually known as the United Party).

May 28–
June 11   The United Party gains 58 percent of the vote in the second parliamentary elections.

Sept. 18   Hungary is admitted into the League of Nations.

1923

Aug. 2   Several members of Parliament led by Gyula Gömbös secede from the United Party and set up the Racial Protection Party on November 23. Gömbös rejoins the governing party in 1928.

1924

March 5–6   After preparations dating back to 1922, Britain, France and Italy sign a plan for Hungary's financial rehabilitation, including a loan of 250 million crowns from the League of Nations, which begins to be paid out on June 26. Hungary's public finances come under League of Nations supervision until July 1, 1926.

May 21–22   Local elections in Budapest result in left-wing victory.

1926

Dec. 27   A new gold-standard currency, the *pengő*, is introduced.

1927

April 5   A Hungarian–Italian Friendship Treaty is signed.

1929

Oct. 24   The Wall Street Crash precipitates a world depression that lasts until 1933.

1930

Sept. 1   There is a demonstration of 100,000 people in Budapest.

Oct. 12	The Independent Smallholders', Agriculturists' and Citizens' Party (Independent Smallholders) is established in Békés.

1931

Aug. 7	Parliament establishes the Committee of 33 to oversee government spending.
Aug. 24	Gyula Károlyi forms a government.
Sept. 13	Biatorbágy Viaduct is blown up by Szilveszter Matuska as a Vienna express train is crossing, causing 22 fatalities. On September 19, the government orders a state of emergency that is not lifted fully until October 10, 1932.

1932

Oct. 1	Gyula Gömbös forms a government. He launches a 95-point National Plan of Action on October 25.

1933

Jan. 30	Adolf Hitler is appointed chancellor of Germany.
June 17–19	Prime Minister Gömbös pays a visit to Hitler.

1934

Feb. 6	Hungary establishes diplomatic relations with the Soviet Union.
Feb. 21	Hungary and Germany sign a second auxiliary agreement to their commercial treaty, bringing about significant expansion of their economic relations.
March 17	A tripartite Hungarian–Austrian–Italian agreement is signed in Rome.

1935

March 4	Gömbös has the regent dissolve the House of Representatives and seeks to introduce dictatorial rule. Intimidation of opposition voters leads to a big majority for the Gömbös wing of the governing party in general elections on March 31–April 7.

1936

Oct. 12	Kálmán Darányi forms a government after the death of Gömbös on October 6.
Oct. 25	The Berlin–Rome Axis is created by German–Italian agreement.
Nov. 25	Germany and Japan conclude the Anti-Comintern Pact.

1937

March 15	The March Front is established.

1938

March 5	Prime Minister Darányi announces his Győr Program of military-led development.
March 12–13	Germany annexes Austria.
May 14	Béla Imrédy forms a government.
May 25	The Catholic 34th International Eucharistic Congress begins in Budapest.
May 29	The first law on the Jews limits the proportion of religious Jews in the professions and public service to 20 percent. This is reduced to 6–12 percent in the second law on May 5, 1939, which further restricts employment of those of Jewish origin.
Aug. 22	Hungary and the Little Entente conclude an agreement in Bled. Hungary renounces the use of force against its neighbors, and the Little Entente countries acknowledge equal rights to arm themselves.
Sept. 29	The Munich Agreement transfers German-inhabited parts of Czechoslovakia to Germany. Hungary and Czechoslovakia are committed to negotiating on the Hungarian-inhabited areas of the Uplands, with international adjudication if they fail to agree.
Nov. 2	Under the First Vienna Award, Germany and Italy assign most of the Hungarian-inhabited area of the Uplands to Hungary (12,000 sq. km, with 1.1 million inhabitants, 86 percent of whom are Hungarian).

1939

Feb. 16	Pál Teleki forms a government.
Feb. 24	Hungary accedes to the Anti-Comintern Pact. The Soviet Union breaks off diplomatic relations.
March 14	An independent Slovak Republic is proclaimed by Jozef Tiso.
March 15	Germany occupies the rump of the Czech lands. The Hungarian army starts to occupy Subcarpathia (12,000 sq. km, with 600,000 inhabitants, under 7 percent of whom are Hungarian).
Aug. 23	Germany and the Soviet Union sign a treaty of non-aggression.
Sept. 1	Germany attacks Poland; World War II breaks out.
Sept. 17	The Soviet Union attacks Poland.

| Sept. 18 | Hungary opens its borders to Polish refugees. |

1940

Aug. 30	The Second Vienna Award divides Transylvania, giving Hungary 43,000 sq. km, with 2.2 million inhabitants, 51.4 percent of whom are Hungarian.
Sept. 30	A Soviet–Hungarian trade agreement is reached.
Nov. 20	Hungary accedes to the Tripartite Agreement of Germany, Italy and Japan.
Dec. 12	A Hungarian–Yugoslav treaty of non-aggression and eternal friendship is signed in Belgrade.

1941

March 27	The pro-German government in Yugoslavia is ousted in a military coup.
April 3	Prime Minister Pál Teleki commits suicide. László Bárdossy forms a government.
April 6	Germany attacks Yugoslavia.
April 11	Hungary joins in the war on Yugoslavia. It then occupies the Bácska (Bačka), the Baranya Triangle, and the Muraköz (Međimurje) and Muravidék (Pomurje). Hungary gains 11,400 sq. km, with 1 million inhabitants, 37 percent of whom are Hungarian.
June 26	There are air raids on Kassa (Košice), Munkács (Mukachevo) and Rahó (Rakhiv). Prime Minister Bárdossy declares war on the Soviet Union on the following day, and Hungarian troops cross the border.
Oct. 6	There is an anti-war demonstration at the Batthyány Lamp in Budapest.
Dec. 26	The Social Democratic paper *Népszava* publishes an anti-fascist Christmas number.

1942

| March 9 | Miklós Kállay forms a government. |
| April 11 | The march of the Hungarian Second Army to the eastern front begins. |

1943

Jan. 13– Feb. 9	A Soviet offensive on the Don Bend leads to the annihilation of Hungary's Second Army, with some 150,000 men killed, wounded or taken prisoner.
Aug. 23–29	An opposition meeting is held at Balatonszárszó.
Nov. 28– Dec. 1	The Teheran Conference of Stalin, Roosevelt and Churchill decides where to open up a second front against the Axis.

1944

March 19	Hungary is occupied by the German army.
March 22	Döme Sztójay, former envoy in Berlin, forms a government.
March 28	Left-wing, liberal and democratic parties are banned.
May 15	The process of herding the Jews into ghettos and deporting them from the provinces begins.
Aug. 23	Romania changes to the Allied side. The armistice promises it possession of "most of Transylvania."
Aug. 27	Soviet forces cross the Hungarian frontier at that time, at the Ojtoz (Oituz) Pass.
Aug. 29	Colonel General Géza Lakatos forms a government.
Sept. 23	Soviet forces cross the Trianon frontier at Battonya.
Oct. 11	A Hungarian delegation led by Gábor Faragho signs a preliminary armistice in Moscow.
Oct. 15	Miklós Horthy announces the armistice on the radio. On the following day, he appoints Ferenc Szálasi as prime minister, withdraws his statement of the previous day, and resigns as head of state. Szálasi becomes head of state (national leader) on November 4.
Nov. 9	The Liberation Committee of the Hungarian National Uprising is set up with Endre Bajcsy-Zsilinszky as its chairman. Its officials are arrested by the Arrow-Cross on the following day and several of them are executed.
Dec. 2	The Hungarian National Independence Front is set up in Szeged.
Dec. 21	The Provisional National Assembly meets in Debrecen. On the following day, General Béla Miklós forms a Provisional National Government.
Dec. 26	The siege of Budapest begins and continues until February 13, 1945.
Dec. 28	The Provisional National Government declares war on Germany.

1945

Jan. 20	Representatives of the Allied powers and Hungary sign an armistice agreement in Moscow.
Feb. 4–11	The Yalta Conference of Stalin, Roosevelt and Churchill is held.
April 14	Hostilities in Hungary cease.

THE AUTHOR

Mária Ormos (b. 1930)

The author completed her university education in Debrecen and Budapest, in the departments of history, Latin, philosophy, and sociology, and of Hungarian language and literature. She received a teacher's degree in history and Hungarian in 1952, before teaching at Debrecen and Szeged universities until 1957, and joining the staff of the Hungarian Academy of Sciences' Institute of History in 1963. She has done research and given lectures in most European capitals and in the United States and Taiwan. In 1982, she became a full professor of the Janus Pannonius University of Sciences in Pécs, serving as rector from 1984 to 1992. She is at present a professor emeritus and head of the doctoral training program in the 19th and 20th century Hungarian and European history. She was awarded a candidacy (1968) and a doctorate (1980) by the Hungarian Academy of Sciences, of which she became a corresponding member in 1987 and a full academician in 1993. She became chair of the Academy's Department II (philosophy and history) in 2002. She has received Academy, Albert Szent-Györgyi and Széchenyi prizes, along with several other awards and honors. Her research field has been 20th-century European and Hungarian history, especially international systems of relations, the emergence of political systems and theories, and most recently, some aspects of Hungarian intellectual life in the interwar Horthy period.

BIOGRAPHIES OF KEY PERSONALITIES

Ábrahám, Pál (1879–1946)
Hungarian operetta composer and conductor, who achieved success-es in Budapest, Vienna and Berlin. He had to leave Berlin because of Hitler, going first to Vienna then to the USA, but returned to Europe after the war.

Ádám, Lajos (1879–1946)
Hungarian surgeon and university teacher.

Aggteleky, Béla (1890–1977)
Hungarian lieutenant general. He took part in the battles in the Carpathians. Commander of the First Army Corps (1944). He was responsible for the military insurance of the exit from the war. He was arrested on October 15, 1944. He left for Switzerland in 1956.

Alexander I, Karađorđević, King of Yugoslavia (1888–1934)
The first King of the Kingdom of Yugoslavia (1929–1934) and before that King of the Kingdom of Serbs, Croats and Slovenes (1921–1929).

Andrássy, Gyula, Jr., Count (1860–1929)
Hungarian historian and politician. Minister of the interior (1906–1910) and foreign minister of the Austro-Hungarian Monarchy (1918).

Antonescu, Ion Victor (1882–1946)
Prime minister and *conducător* (Leader) of Romania during World War II (1940–1944).

Apponyi, Albert, Count (1846–1933)
Hungarian politician. Member of Parliament and speaker of the Parliament (1901–1903). He headed the Hungarian delegation to the Paris peace talks after World War I. He represented Hungary at the League of Nations (1924–1925).

Apponyi, Geraldine (1915–2002)
Queen of Albania. Her father was the Hungarian Count Gyula Apponyi, and her mother was the American millionaire Gladys Virginia Stewart. Wife of King Zog I. They had to leave the country in 1939, then lived in exile.

Apponyi, György, Count (1898–1970)
Hungarian journalist and politician. Son of Albert Apponyi. MP (1931–1944). He opposed Gömbös's policy. He was arrested by the Gestapo.

Asbóth, Oszkár (1891–1960)
Hungarian aviation engineer, the inventor of the helicopter.

Babits, Mihály (1883–1941)
Hungarian pacifist poet, writer and translator. Editor-in-chief of Nyugat from 1929 until his death.

Bacsó, Béla (1891–1920)
Hungarian writer and journalist. Together with Béla Somogyi, the editor-in-chief of the newspaper Népszava, he was killed by the Ostenburg commando group; their bodies were thrown into the Danube.

Badoglio, Pietro (1871–1956)
Italian soldier and politician. He led the Italian troops into Ethiopia and received the title of Duke of Addis Ababa. He was pessimistic about the chances of Italian success in any war, and resigned in 1940. He was appointed to head the government instead of Mussolini in 1943, and negotiations were opened with the Allies.

Bajcsy-Zsilinszky, Endre (1886–1944)
Hungarian politician. The first racialist right-wing MP, he later moved closer to left-wing trends while preserving his nationalism. During World War II he became the leading figure of the anti-German resistance movement, and was arrested and executed by the Arrow-Cross.

Bakay, Szilárd (1892–1946)
Hungarian lieutenant general. Military attaché in Belgrade and Athens (1933) and Sofia (1934–1939). Commander of the Third Army Corps (1943–1944) and the First Army Corps (1944). One of the key figures of the attempt to exit from the war. He was taken to Mauthausen by the Germans, then executed by the Soviets.

Baky, László (1898–1946)
Hungarian officer, provost and politician. He sympathized with extreme right-wing movements. One of the organizers of the Jewish ghettos and deportations. He was sentenced to death and executed.

Balfour, Arthur James, Earl (1848–1930)
British statesman and prime minister of the United Kingdom from 1902 until 1905. Author of the Balfour Declaration of 1917 that promised a homeland for the Jewish people.

Balla, Aladár (1867–1935)

Hungarian attorney and politician. Minister of the interior (July 12–August 12, 1919). Smallholders' Party MP (1920) and later one of the leaders of the Kossuth Party.

Bandholtz, Harry Hill (1864–1925)

United States army general. The American representative to the Inter-Allied Control Commission for Hungary. He arrived in Budapest to supervise the disengagement of Romanian troops from Hungary, and prevented some Romanian soldiers from removing Transylvanian treasures from the National Museum.

Bánffy, Dániel, Baron (1893–1955)

Transylvanian landowner and right-wing politician. Minister of agriculture in Hungary (1940–1944).

Bánffy, Miklós, Count (1873–1950)

Hungarian writer and politician. Foreign minister in the Bethlen government (1921–1922). He moved to Romania (his family belonged to the greatest Transylvanian nobles) and his aim was to support Hungarian culture there. He took part in an anti-Hitler negotiation in Bucharest in 1943.

Baranyai, Lipót (1894–1970)

Hungarian financial expert. President of the Hungarian National Bank (1938–1943) and member of the Hungarian Academy of Sciences. He was arrested by the Germans in 1944. Representative of the World Bank (1951–1959).

Bárdossy, László (1890–1946)

Hungarian diplomat and politician. Foreign minister, then prime minister (1941–1942). He was sentenced to death and executed.

Bartha, Albert (1877–1960)

Hungarian military officer. Colonel general. Octobrist. Smallholders' Party politician. MP (1945–1947) and minister of defense (1918, 1946–1947). He emigrated in 1948.

Bartha, Károly (1884–1964)

Hungarian military engineer. Minister of defense (1938–1942). He left the country for the West after the end of World War II.

Bartók, Béla Viktor János (1881–1945)

Hungarian composer, pianist and collector of Eastern European and Middle Eastern folk music. He is considered one of the greatest composers of the twentieth century.

Batthyány, Lajos, Count (1807–1849)

Hungarian reform politician. Prime minister of the first independent

Hungarian government in 1848. He was executed by the Habsburg tyrants on October 6, 1849.

Batthyány, Tivadar, Count (1859–1931)

Hungarian politician. Minister of the interior in the Károlyi government. Member of the National Council (1918–1919). He participated in the counter-revolutionary movement of the emigrants in Vienna in 1919, returned to Hungary in 1921, and renewed the Independent Party.

Benárd, Ágost (1880–1968)

Hungarian physician and Christian Democratic politician. One of the leaders of the Society of Awakening Hungarians. Minister of welfare (1920–1921). One of the signatories to the Trianon Peace Treaty. MP of the Party of National Unity (1935–1939).

Benedek, Marcell (1885–1969)

Hungarian literary historian, literary translator and doctor of literary studies (1952). He escaped to Transylvania because of the German occupation, and returned in 1947.

Beneš, Edvard (1884–1948)

Czechoslovak politician. Leader of the country's independence movement. Foreign minister (1918–1935), prime minister (1921–1922), then president (1935–1938, 1945–1948) of Czechoslovakia.

Beniczky, Ödön (1878–1931)

Hungarian politician. Member of the counter-revolutionary committee in Vienna in 1919. Minister of the interior (1919–1920). He published the confession on the Somogyi–Bacsó murder. He committed suicide.

Beregfy, Károly (1888–1946)

Hungarian colonel general. Commander of the General Staff Academy (1939), the Sixth Army Corps (1941), the 3rd Army (1943) and the 1st Army (1944). Minister of defense and chief of the General Staff after the Arrow-Cross takeover. He was executed by the Hungarian People's Court.

Berinkey, Dénes (1871–1948)

Hungarian lawyer, scientist and politician. Minister of justice (1918) and prime minister (1919).

Berthelot, Henri Mathias (1863–1931)

French military officer. Head of the French military mission in Romania after 1916. Commander-in-chief of the Danube Army in Romania. Governor at Metz after World War I and member of the French Supreme War Council.

Bethlen, István, Count (1874–1946)

Great estate owner from Transylvania. A significant political figure of the twentieth-century Hungarian political scene. Prime minister (1921–1931), he consolidated the Horthy regime. He was deported to the Soviet Union by the Red Army.

Boroviczhény, Aladár, Baron (1890–1963)

Hungarian politician. The last chief of cabinet of King Charles IV. Officer in the counter-revolutionary army in 1919–1920. Advisor to the king in his attempt to return. He lived in Austria from 1945.

Böhm, Vilmos (1880–1949)

Hungarian mechanic and politician. Member of the leadership of the MSZDP (1913–1919), minister of defense (1919), member of the Revolutionary Governing Council and commander-in-chief of the Red Army (1919).

Brătianu, Ion I. C. (1864–1927)

Romanian National Liberal Party politician. He was elected president of the party for life in 1909. President of the Council of Ministers (1909–1910, 1914–1919, 1922–1927) and minister of war (1914–1916). Organizer of Greater Romania.

Briand, Aristide (1862–1932)

French politician. Prime minister and minister of several governments (1906–1932).

Brusilov, Aleksey Alekseyevich (1853–1926)

Russian general. He is famous for the "Brusilov breakthrough" on the eastern front in 1916, but the help for the allies cost Russia a million lives. He joined the Soviet army's staff in the war against Poland.

Buchinger, Manó (1875–1953)

Hungarian writer, journalist and Social Democratic politician. He left the leadership of the Social Democratic Party in 1919, emigrated to Vienna in 1920, and returned in 1929. MP of the SDP (1931–1944). MP of the Hungarian Workers' Party until his death.

Budaváry, László (1889–?)

Hungarian right-wing politician. Member of the National Assembly, vice-president of the Society of Awakening Hungarians. Founder of the Hungarian National Party.

Buresch, Karl (1878–1936)

Austrian lawyer and Christian-Social politician. Chancellor of Austria during the First Republic.

Burián, István, Count (1851–1922)
>Hungarian diplomat and politician. Minister of finance (1903–1912, 1916–1918) and foreign minister (1915–1916, 1918).

Chamberlain, Houston Stewart (1855–1927)
>British-born German author of popular scientific books and proponent of a nationalist, pan-Germanic and racist anti-Semitism.

Chamberlain, Arthur Neville (1869–1940)
>British Conservative politician. Minister of health (1923–1929) and prime minister (1937–1940). He signed the Munich Agreement with Hitler in 1938, which allowed Germany to annex the Sudetenland. He entered into a mutual defense pact with Poland and declared war on Germany, but sent only a lightly armed force to Belgium during "The Phony War".

Charles IV (1887–1922)
>King of Hungary and Emperor of Austria as Charles I in 1916–1918.

Chicherin, Georgy Vasilyevich (1872–1936)
>Soviet politician and Marxist revolutionary. People's commissar of foreign affairs in the Soviet government (1918–1930).

Chorin, Ferenc (1879–1964)
>Hungarian factory and mine owner. General manager (1918–1925) then president of the Salgótarján Coalmine Joint-Stock Company. He gave his property to the Germans and left Hungary with the help of the *Gestapo*. He lived in New York.

Chotek, Sophia, Countess (1868–1914)
>Wife of Archduke Franz Ferdinand. Their assassination sparked World War I.

Churchill, Winston Leonard Spencer, Sir (1874–1965)
>English statesman, soldier and author. Prime minister of the United Kingdom during World War II. One of the most important leaders in modern world history.

Ciano, Galeazzo (1903–1944)
>Italian diplomat and politician. Foreign minister (1936–1943).

Clemenceau, Georges Benjamin (1841–1929)
>French politician. Prime minister (1906–1909, 1917–1920). He played an important role in the Paris Peace Conference.

Clerk, George, Sir (1876–1943)
>British diplomat. Special emissary of the Allies to Hungary in 1919.

Curzon, George Nathaniel, Lord (1859–1925)
>British Conservative statesman. Viceroy of India.

Cziráky, József, Count (1883–?)
    Hungarian great landowner and politician. Brother-in-law of Mihály
    Károlyi. Governmental commissioner of Western Hungary. King
    Charles disembarked from his airplane on his land on October 20,
    1921. MP (1922–1944).
Csáky, Imre, Count (1882–1961)
    Hungarian diplomat and politician. Foreign minister (1920). He took
    part in the peace treaties in Brest-Litovsk and Bucharest. Member on
    the Hungarian side at the joint committee to define the borders.
Csáky, István, Count (1894–1941)
    Hungarian diplomat and foreign minister (1938). He took part in the
    Trianon Peace Treaties. He supported the alliance with the Germans.
Csatay, Lajos (1886–1944)
    Hungarian general of the artillery and minister of defense (1943–
    1944). Member of the Red Army (1919). He served on the eastern
    front (1941–1942). He was arrested by the *Gestapo* after the Arrow-
    Cross takeover, and committed suicide with his wife.
Csók, István (1865–1961)
    Hungarian post-impressionist limner. Member of the Nagybánya art
    group. He lived in Budapest, Munich and Paris. His art was broken
    by World War II. His self-portrait is in the Uffizi in Florence.
Dálnoki Miklós, Béla (1890–1948)
    Hungarian politician. Acting prime minister of Hungary (1944–1945).
Darányi, Kálmán (1886–1939)
    Hungarian great landowner and politician. Minister of agriculture
    (1935–1938), prime minister (1936–1938), minister of the interior
    (1937) and speaker of the Parliament (1938–1939).
Darvas, József (1912–1973)
    Hungarian writer and politician. One of the founders of the NPP
    (1939). Minister of construction and minister of public education
    (1951–53). President of the Hungarian Writers' Union (1959–1973).
De Bono, Emilio (1866–1944)
    Italian general during World War I. One of the organizers of the
    Fascist Party in the early 1920s. Marshal of Italy (1935) and minister
    of state (1942). He participated in the Fascist Grand Council of 1943
    and voted against Mussolini. He was executed by the Germans.
Deák, Ferenc (1803–1876)
    Hungarian statesman. Minister of justice (1848). After the defeat of
    the War of Independence he pursued a policy of passive resistance,

and played a major role in negotiations leading to the Compromise of 1867.

Diaz, Armando (1861–1928)
Italian general. Marshal of Italy.

Dohnányi, Ernő (also known as Ernst von Dohnányi) (1877–1960)
Hungarian conductor, composer and pianist. World War II claimed the lives of both of his sons, one in combat, the other executed by the Nazis. He moved to the USA after the war.

Dollfuss, Engelbert (1892–1934)
Austrian conservative statesman. Chancellor for two years from 1932 until his assassination by Nazi agents.

Doyle, Arthur Ignatius Conan, Sir (1859–1930)
Scottish writer, author of the stories of the detective Sherlock Holmes. He also wrote science fiction stories, historical novels, plays and romances, poetry and non-fiction.

Eckhardt, Tibor (1888–1972)
Hungarian lawyer and politician. MP. First secretary of the FKGP (1932–1940).

Eden, Robert Anthony, Earl (1897–1977)
British politician. Foreign secretary (1935–1955) and prime minister of the United Kingdom (1955–1957). His role in the Suez Crisis of 1956 was politically disastrous from a British perspective.

Eichmann, Otto Adolf (1906–1962)
High-ranking Nazi and SS leader. He facilitated and managed the logistics of mass deportation to ghettos and extermination camps. He was captured by Israeli *Mossad* agents in Argentina and hanged for his crimes against humanity and war crimes.

Ernszt, Sándor (1870–1938)
Hungarian papal prelate and leader of the Christian socialist movement in Hungary. Minister of welfare and labor (1930–1931) and minister of public education (1931).

Eskütt, Lajos (1896–1957)
Personal secretary of István Nagyatádi Szabó and one of the secretaries of the Smallholders. Arrested in 1924, he was put into a mental hospital (1938) but released.

Faragho, Gábor (1890–1953)
Hungarian military attaché to Moscow (1940–1941). Signatory to the Moscow preliminary armistice treaty (1944). Minister of public supply in the Provisional National Government.

Féja, Géza (1900–1978)

Hungarian writer, journalist and editor. Organizer of the National Radical Party. He joined the March Front in 1937. He was imprisoned because of his sociological writing. Later he worked for the right-wing *Magyarország*, and was awarded the Attila József Prize (1966).

Franchet d' Espérey, Louis Félix Marie François (1856–1942)

French general during World War I.

Francis Joseph (1830–1916)

Emperor of Austria from 1848, and King of Hungary from 1867, after being crowned with St. Stephen's Crown.

Francis Ferdinand, Archduke (1863–1914)

Archduke of Austria-Este, Prince Imperial of Austria, Prince Royal of Hungary and Bohemia, and heir to the Austro-Hungarian throne from 1896. His assassination in Sarajevo precipitated the Austrian declaration of war that triggered World War I.

Franco Bahamonde, Francisco Paulino Hermenegildo Teódulo (1892–1975)

Commonly known as Generalíssimo Francisco Franco. The ruler and regent of Spain from 1947, and later head of state first of parts of Spain from 1936 and then of all of Spain from 1939 (after the Spanish Civil War) until his death.

Friedrich, István (1883–1951)

Hungarian engineer, manufacturer and politician. Prime minister (1919), minister of defense (1919–1920) and MP (1920s and 1930s). Imprisoned in 1951, he died in prison.

Garami, Ernő (1876–1935)

Hungarian mechanic and politician. Leader of the MSZDP (1898–1919) and minister of trade (1918–1919), he rejected unification with the KMP (1919).

Garbai, Sándor (1879–1947)

Hungarian bricklayer and politician. He accepted the unification of the MSZDP and the KMP (1919). President of the Revolutionary Governing Council during the Hungarian Soviet Republic.

Gárdonyi, Géza (1863–1922)

Hungarian author. His two best-known works are historical novels: *Eclipse of the Crescent Moon* and *Slave of the Huns*.

Gömbös, Gyula (1886–1936)

Hungarian professional soldier and politician. Minister of defense (1929–1932) and prime minister (1932–1936).

Goering (Göring) Hermann Wilhelm (1893–1946)

> German politician and military leader. A leading member of the Nazi Party. Commander of the *Luftwaffe*. He was sentenced to death during the Nuremberg Trials, but committed suicide.

Gratz, Gusztáv (1875–1946)

> Hungarian publicist, minister, writer of economics and history, and associate member of the Hungarian Academy of Sciences (1941). Hungary's ambassador to Vienna and foreign minister in the Teleki government. He participated in the preparation of the second coup for the king. In 1924 he and Jakab Bleyer established the *Volksbildungsverein* (German Public Cultural Association of Hungary).

Herczeg, Ferenc (1863–1954)

> Hungarian writer, journalist, MP (1896), member of the Upper House (1927) and chairman of the Revisionist League (1929).

Hindenburg, Paul von (1847–1934)

> German field marshal and statesman. The last president of Germany before the Third Reich period.

Hitler, Adolf (1889–1945)

> Chancellor, then *Führer* (Leader) of Germany from 1934. Leader of the Nazi Party. Using propaganda and charismatic oratory, he was able to appeal to the economic needs of the lower and middle classes after World War I. He rearmed the military and established a totalitarian and fascist regime. His aggressive foreign policy, aimed at expanding Germany, was the cause of World War II. One of the greatest genocides of human history is connected to his name. He committed suicide with his wife as Berlin fell.

Hóman, Bálint (1885–1951)

> Hungarian historiographer, university teacher, politician and member of the Hungarian Academy of Sciences. Minister of religion and public education (1932–1942). He was sentenced to life imprisonment after the war.

Hoover, Herbert Clark (1874–1964)

> The 31st president of the United States of America (1929–1933). The Great Depression broke out during his presidency.

Horthy, Miklós (1868–1957)

> Hungarian admiral of the Austro-Hungarian Fleet and statesman. Regent of Hungary (1920–1944). From early 1943, he put out various diplomatic feelers concerning Hungary's exit from the war.

Attempts at a separate peace stalled, and a deal was prevented following a coup by the Arrow-Cross. Horthy was taken prisoner by the Germans and then by the Americans. He lived in Portugal until his death.

Huszár, Károly (1882–1941)

Hungarian teacher, journalist and politician. MP (1910) and prime minister (1919–1920). Member of the Upper House.

Illyés, Gyula (1902–1983)

Hungarian poet and novelist. One of the leading *népi* ("populist") authors with left-wing convictions. He worked for *Nyugat* during World War II. An MP after the war, he withdrew from public life after the Stalinist takeover.

Imrédy, Béla (1891–1946)

Hungarian economist and politician. Minister of finance (1932–1935) and prime minister (1938–1939). His pro-German government supported the First and proposed the Second Jewish Law, and limited the right of assembly and the freedom of press. The war tribunal found him guilty of war crimes, and he was executed.

Jány, Gusztáv (1883–1947)

Hungarian colonel general. Commander of the 2nd Hungarian Army in Transylvania and at the River Don. He retired and moved to Germany. He refused to serve under Szálasi, but returned to Hungary to save his fellow officers in 1946. He was sentenced to death and executed. He was rehabilitated in 1993.

Jászi, Oszkár (1875–1957)

Hungarian social scientist, publicist and politician. Ideological leader and practical director of Hungarian bourgeois radicalism. Editor of *Huszadik Század.*

Joseph, Habsburg, Archduke (1872–1963)

Austrian general and politician. He was declared governor after defeating the Hungarian Soviet Republic, but resigned at the demand of the Entente.

József, Attila (1905–1937)

Hungarian poet. He joined the KMP (Communist Party of Hungary) in 1930. He was expelled from the Communist movement and became affiliated to the Social Democrats and liberals. He suffered from mental problems and there is a possibility that he committed suicide.

Kállay, Miklós (1887–1967)

Hungarian landowner and politician. Minister of agriculture (1932–1935), prime minister (1942–1944) and foreign minister (1942–1943). While Hungary was at war against the Soviet Union, he sought separate peace terms from the Allies. He was imprisoned by the Germans and taken to a concentration camp. He emigrated to the USA.

Kandó, Kálmán (1869–1931)

Hungarian engineer, who developed high-voltage three-phase alternating current motors and generators for electric locomotives, and is known as the "father of the electric train."

Károlyi, Gyula, Count (1871–1947)

Hungarian great landowner and politician. Foreign minister (1930–1931) and prime minister (1931–1932).

Károlyi, Mihály, Count (1875–1955)

Hungarian aristocrat and politician of controversial reputation. Prime minister (1918–1919) and temporary president of the Republic. He lived in exile in 1919. A diplomat in 1946–1949, he opposed the Rákosi regime, and emigrated.

Kerensky, Aleksander Fyodorovich (1881–1970)

Russian revolutionary leader, who was instrumental in toppling the Russian monarchy. The second prime minister of the Russian Provisional Government until the October Revolution.

Keresztes-Fischer, Ferenc (1881–1948)

Hungarian politician. Organizer of the nationalist movement in 1919. Minister of the interior (1931–1935, 1938–1944). He personally controlled the political police against the left wing. A representative of the Anglo-Saxon orientation. He was taken to a concentration camp by the *Gestapo*.

Kéthly, Anna (1889–1976)

Hungarian politician. Social Democratic MP (1922–1948). She was expelled from the party because she had opposed the fusion of the two workers' parties. She was imprisoned in 1949 and freed in 1954. President of the Social Democratic Party and minister of state (practically deputy prime minister) during the 1956 Revolution. President of the Hungarian Revolutionary Council (1957).

Klebelsberg, Kunó, Count (1875–1932)

Hungarian minister of the interior (1921–1922) and minister of religion and education (1922–1931). He established Hungarian study centers (each known as a *Collegium Hungaricum*) in Europe.

Kodály, Zoltán (1882–1967)

Hungarian composer, ethnomusicologist, educator, linguist and philosopher. He worked out the so-called "Kodály Method." The *Dances of Marosszék, Dances of Galánta, Missa Brevis* and his opera *Háry János* are among his most well-known works.

Kossuth, Lajos (1802–1894)

Hungarian lawyer and politician. Regent-president of the Kingdom of Hungary in 1849. He was widely honored during his lifetime as a freedom fighter.

Kovács, Béla (1908–1959)

Hungarian Smallholders' Party politician. Member of the second and third governments of Imre Nagy.

Kovács, Imre (1913–1980)

Hungarian writer and National Peasant Party politician. He emigrated before the fusion of the two workers' parties.

Kun, Béla (1886–1938)

Hungarian Communist politician. Founder and leader of the KMP and leader of the Hungarian Soviet Republic as a member of the Revolutionary Governing Council (people's commissar of foreign affairs and defense).

Kunfi, Zsigmond (1879–1929)

Hungarian Social Democratic politician. Member of the National Council (1918), minister of labor and minister of welfare (1918–1919), minister of public education (1919) and people's commissar of public education (1919). He emigrated.

Lakatos, Géza (1890–1967)

Hungarian general in World War II. Prime minister in 1944. His military government stopped the deportation of Hungarian Jews. After the Arrow-Cross takeover he had to resign. He emigrated to Australia.

Lenin, Vladimir Ilych Ulyanov (1870–1924)

Soviet-Russian publicist, professional revolutionary and theoretician. Founder and first leader of the Bolshevik Party and the Soviet state.

Lloyd George, David, Lord (1863–1945)

British politician. Prime minister of the coalition government (1916–1922) and leader of the Liberal Party. He played an important role in the Paris Peace Conference.

Lukács, György (1885–1971)

Hungarian philosopher. Leading ideologist of the MKP and the MDP (1945–1949). Minister of public education of the Imre Nagy government (1956).

Mackensen, Anton Ludwig August von (1849–1945)
German soldier. Field marshal. He commanded with success during
World War I and became one of the German Reich's most prominent
military leaders.

Malinovsky, Rodion Yakovlevich (1898–1967)
Soviet military commander. Minister of defense in the late 1950s and
1960s. He played a key role in World War II, especially in the major
defeat of Nazi Germany in the Battle of Stalingrad, and contributed
to the strengthening of the Soviet Union as a military superpower in
the post-war era.

Marosán, György (1908–1992)
Hungarian politician. First Social Democrat, later Communist, organizer of the fusion of the two workers' parties. He wanted to maintain the Communist dictatorship by means of arms during the 1956
Revolution.

Masaryk, Tomáš Garrigue (1850–1937)
Czech statesman, philosopher and liberal politician. He favored
national independence for the peoples of Austria-Hungary, and
gained international support for his view in Britain between 1914
and 1917, in Russia in 1917 and in the USA in 1918. First president
of Czechoslovakia (1918–1935).

Meskó, Zoltán (1883–1959)
Hungarian politician. Independent Party MP in 1917. Executive
president and parliamentary representative of the Smallholders'
Party. Founder of the first Arrow-Cross party. He was sentenced to
ten years' imprisonment in 1946.

Mihailović, Dragoljub "Draža" (1893–1946)
Serbian general. Leader of the Yugoslav Royal Army during World
War II. After the war he was tried by Communist partisans for col-
laboration, shot and buried in an unmarked grave. President Truman
awarded him the Legion of Merit for rescuing five hundred
American airmen.

Millerand, Étienne Alexandre (1859–1943)
French politician. Minister of commerce (1899), minister of public
works (1909) and minister of war (1912–1915). Prime minister of a
right-center coalition government, then president of France
(1920–1924).

Milotay, István (1883–1963)
Hungarian right-wing politician. Supporter of the *numerus clausus*.
MP (1933–45). He emigrated in late 1944.

Mišić, Živojin (1855–1921)
Serbian Voivod and field marshal. The most successful commander to participate in Serbia's wars between 1876 and 1918.

Molnár, Ferenc (Ferenc Neumann) (1878–1952)
One of the greatest Hungarian dramatists and novelists of the twentieth century, known also as Franz Molnar. He emigrated to the USA to escape the Nazi persecution of Hungarian Jews during World War II. His most important novel is the *Pál utcai fiúk* [The Paul Street Boys] and other novels are *Liliom* and *The Swan*.

Molotov, Vyacheslav Mikhailovich (1890–1986)
Soviet diplomat and politician. A leading figure in the Soviet government from the 1920s to the 1950s. Signatory to the Nazi–Soviet non-aggression (Molotov–Ribbentrop) pact of 1939.

Móra, Ferenc (1879–1934)
Hungarian novelist, journalist and museologist. One of the most important writers and authors in Hungarian literature.

Mussolini, Benito (1883–1945)
Italian politician. Fascist dictator of Italy (1922–1943).

Nagy, Ferenc (1903–1979)
Hungarian Smallholders' Party politician. Prime minister of Hungary (1946–47). He resisted attempts by the Communists to gain complete control, and refused to become a puppet of a Soviet-type state. He resigned because his son was kidnapped, and emigrated to the USA.

Nagyatádi Szabó, István (1863–1924)
Founder of the Hungarian Smallholders' and Peasant Party. Minister on several occasions (1919–1924). His name has become a symbol of the democratic Smallholders' movement.

Neurath, Konstantin Freiherr von (1873–1956)
German diplomat. Foreign minister (1932–1938). Governor of the Protectorate of Bohemia and Moravia (1939–1941).

Nicholas II (Nikolay Aleksandrovich Romanov) (1868–1918)
The last "Emperor and Autocrat of All the Russias" (Tsar of Russia, King of Poland and Grand Duke of Finland) from 1894 until his forced abdication. After the Russian Revolution of 1917, he was executed together with his family. He was canonized by the Russian Orthodox Church.

Nógrádi, Sándor (1894–1971)
Hungarian Communist colonel general and diplomat. He worked for the Communist Youth Internationale and the Comintern in Europe.

Editor of the Hungarian radio broadcasting service in Moscow in 1944. Deputy minister of defense (1948–1956), ambassador to China (1957–1960) and MP (1963–1967).

Pálffy, Fidél, Count (1895–1946)
Supporter of Nazism in Hungary, founding his Hungarian National Socialist Party in 1933. He became an agent of the Reich Security Main Office of Germany. Minister of agriculture during the Szálasi regime. He was hanged for treason.

Pašić, Nikola P. (1845–1926)
Serbian and Yugoslav diplomat and politician. Leader of the Serbian People's Radical Party. Prime minister of Serbia (1891–92, 1904–1918), Prime minister of the later Yugoslavia (1918, 1921–26). He managed to strengthen his small state against the Dual Monarchy, Turkey and Russia.

Pattantyús Ábrahám, Dezső (1875–1977)
Hungarian lawyer and right-wing politician. MP (1906–18, 1947–1948). Prime minister of the second Szeged government (1919). State secretary (1919–1920). He was a hostage in the hands of the Arrow-Cross Party (1944–1945).

Pavelić, Ante (1889–1959)
Leader and founding member of the Croatian national/fascist Ustaše movement in the 1930s. Leader of the Nazi puppet Independent State of Croatia in World War II.

Peidl, Gyula (1873–1943)
Hungarian typesetter and politician. Prime minister in August 1919.

Peyer, Károly (1881–1956)
Hungarian Social Democratic politician. Minister of labor and welfare (1919–1920). His contract with the prime minister (the Bethlen–Peyer pact) allowed the Social Democratic Party to get into Parliament. He was taken to a Nazi concentration camp (1944–1945). He left the country in 1947 because he did not agree to the fusion with the Communist Party.

Pfeffer-Wildenbruch, Karl von (1888–1971)
German military and police officer. Commander of Budapest in 1944–1945. A prisoner of war in the Soviet Union until 1955.

Pichon, Stéphen (1857–1933)
French politician of the Third Republic. Associate of Clemenceau. Foreign minister (1917–1920).

Pius XI, Pope (Ambrogio Damiano Achille Ratti) (1857–1939)
He reigned as Pope from 1922 until his death. His idea was that the Catholic religion must permeate all areas of human life.

Pogány, József (also known as Joseph/John Pepper) (1886–1937)
Hungarian-born Communist. He was accused of taking part in the murder of István Tisza, and fled to Austria, then to the Soviet Union in 1919. He went illegally to the USA in 1922 to work for the Workers' Party there. Returning to the Soviet Union, he became a victim of Stalin.

Princip, Gavrilo (1894–1918)
Bosnian Serb member of the secret society organization, the Black Hand (*Crna Ruka*), who assassinated Archduke Francis Ferdinand and his wife in Sarajevo on June 28, 1914. The Austrian answer led to World War I.

Prohászka, Ottokár (1858–1927)
Hungarian Catholic writer, bishop of Székesfehérvár, representative of Christian Socialism and member of the Hungarian Academy of Sciences.

Prónay, Pál (1874–1946?)
Hungarian military officer. He organized right-wing commandos in 1919 and in 1944, and tortured masses of left-wing people. Leader of the Awakening Hungarians' Association and the Etelköz Alliance. He was elected to the illegal position of Ban of Lajta in 1921. He was taken to the Soviet Union in 1945.

Radnóti, Miklós (Miklós Glatter) (1909–1944)
Hungarian poet of Jewish origin. He identified himself as a Hungarian and converted to Catholicism, but was made to go to Ukraine and Serbia in forced labor service, and could not survive the quick march to Central Hungary. He continued to write poetry until the last days of his life.

Rajk, László (1909–1949)
Hungarian Communist politician. He organized the Hungarian Communists' instruments of power (such as the ÁVH), but fell victim to Rákosi's show trials. Minister of the interior (1946–1948) and foreign minister from 1948 to his death.

Rákosi, Mátyás (1892–1971)
Hungarian politician. He participated in the government of Kun, then fled to the Soviet Union. He returned and was imprisoned in 1924. In 1940, he was sent back to the Soviet Union, in exchange for the

1849 banners captured by the Russian troops. Secretary-general of the Hungarian Communist Party from 1945 to 1956, he developed a cult of personality around himself.

Rathenau, Walther (1867–1922)
German industrialist and politician who became foreign minister in 1922. He was assassinated by two right-wing army officers because of his so-called "Jewish–Communist conspiracy" after the Treaty of Rapallo with the Soviet Union.

Reményi-Schneller, Lajos (1892–1946)
Hungarian financial expert and politician. Minister of finance (1938–1945). He played a great role in subordinating the Hungarian economy to the Nazis' claims. He was sentenced to death and executed.

Révai, József (József Lederer) (1898–1959)
Hungarian Communist politician. He lived in the Soviet Union (1934–1944). Plenipotentiary leader of Hungarian cultural life (1948–1953). Deputy president of the Presidential Council (1953–1958).

Ribbentrop, Ulrich Friedrich Wilhelm Joachim von (1893–1946)
Foreign minister of Germany (1938–1945). He was hanged for war crimes after the Nuremberg Trials.

Roosevelt, Franklin Delano (1882–1945)
The 32nd president of the United States of America (1933–1945). The only US president to serve more than two terms. One of the greatest presidents of the USA.

Rosenberg, Alfred (1893–1946)
German Nazi Party politician. Main author of the key Nazi ideological creeds, including the racial theory, persecution of the Jews and abolition of the Treaty of Versailles. A supporter of neo-paganism. He was sentenced to death and executed after the Nuremberg Trials.

Rubinek, Gyula (1865–1922)
Hungarian writer and politician. MP from 1901. Minister of agriculture (1919–1920), as well as minister of trade in 1920. Honorary president of the Smallholders' Party (1921).

Rubinek, István (1886–1938)
Hungarian lawyer and politician. Founder of the nationalist Széchenyi Alliance. MP (1920–1935).

Salazar, António de Oliveira (1889–1970)
President of the Council of Ministers of Portugal, prime minister and dictator (1932–1968). Founder and leader of the Estado Novo (New State), the right-wing regime of Portugal (1933–197).

Seymour, Charles (1885–1963)
American historian and president of Yale University (1937–1951). Chief of the Austro-Hungarian Division of the American Commission to Negotiate Peace, and the US delegate on the Romanian, Yugoslavian and Czechoslovakian Territorial Commissions in 1919.

Simonyi-Semadam, Sándor (1864–1946)
Hungarian lawyer and politician. Prime minister in 1920. One of the leaders of the Christian National Unification Party, later a Smallholders' Party politician. Governmental commissioner of the Hungarian Mortgage Credit Bank from 1932.

Smuts, Jan Christiaan (1870–1950)
South African and Commonwealth statesman, military leader and philosopher. Prime minister of the Union of South Africa (1919–24, 1939–48). British field marshal in World War I and World War II.

Spann, Othmar (1878–1950)
Conservative Austrian philosopher, sociologist and economist. He held radical anti-liberal and anti-socialist views, yet was imprisoned by the Nazis after the *Anschluss*.

St. Stephen, King (ca. 975–1038)
St. Stephen was the first King of Hungary, the founder of the state.

Stalin, Yosif Vissarionovich Dzhugashvili (1879–1953)
Bolshevik revolutionary of Georgian origin. Secretary-general of the Communist Party of the Soviet Union from 1922 until his death. Dictator of the Soviet Union after Lenin's death. One of the greatest genocides of human history is connected to his name.

Stresemann, Gustav (1878–1929)
German liberal politician and statesman. Chancellor and foreign secretary during the Weimar Republic. He was awarded the Nobel Peace Prize.

Stromfeld, Aurél (1878–1927)
Hungarian military officer. General Staff officer of the Austro-Hungarian Army, military leader of the Hungarian Soviet Republic and chief of staff of the Red Army.

Szálasi, Ferenc (1897–1946)
Hungarian right-wing military officer and politician. Horthy's supporters considered his right-wing views to be dangerous, and he was imprisoned (1937, 1938). With German support, he established the Arrow-Cross Party (1939). On October 15, 1944, he took power in a coup and became Hungary's national leader. He was sentenced to death for war crimes and crimes against humanity.

Szamuely, Tibor (1890–1919)
Hungarian journalist and politician. People's commissar of defense and public education during the Hungarian Soviet Republic. President of the so-called Behind the Front Committees.

Széchenyi, István, Count (1791–1860)
Hungarian statesman. Founder of the Hungarian Academy of Sciences, political writer and minister of transport and public labor (1848). He committed suicide.

Szentgyörgyi, Albert (1893–1986)
Hungarian physiologist and chemist. He was awarded the Nobel Prize for Physiology in 1937. He was also active in the Hungarian resistance during World War II, and entered Hungarian politics after the war.

Szerb, Antal (1901–1945)
Hungarian scholar and writer. One of the major Hungarian literary personalities of the twentieth century.

Szmrecsányi, György (1876–1932)
Hungarian legitimist politician. He left for Vienna during the Hungarian Soviet Republic, and took part in the anti-Bolshevik committee. Deputy president of the National Assembly (1920–1921).

Szombathelyi, Ferenc (Ferenc Knausz) (1887–1946)
Hungarian military officer. General and chief of the General Staff. He was sentenced to life imprisonment by the Hungarian People's Court, but was delivered to Yugoslavia, where he was sentenced to death. He was rehabilitated in 1993.

Sztójay, Döme (1883–1946)
Hungarian soldier and diplomat. Military attaché in Berlin (1925–1933). Ambassador to Germany (1935–1944). Extreme right-wing prime minister and foreign minister in 1944. He was sentenced to death after the war.

Táncsics, Mihály (1799–1884)
Hungarian writer, journalist and politician. He wanted the emancipation of the serfs and the eradication of feudalism. He was imprisoned in 1847. On March 15, 1848, he was rescued by the people of Pest and the revolutionary youth.

Tardieu, André (1876–1945)
Prime minister of France (1929–1930, 1932). Clemenceau's lieutenant during the Paris Peace Conference, and commissioner for Franco-American War Cooperation. Minister of Alsace and Lorraine after the war.

Teleki, Pál, Count (1879–1941)
Hungarian geographer and politician. Prime minister (1920–1921, 1939–1941). He committed suicide.

Tildy, Zoltán (1889–1961)
Hungarian Independent Smallholders' Party politician. Prime minister of Hungary (1945–1946) and president (1946–48). He was forced into hiding after the Nazi takeover. He was held under house arrest until 1956. He became a minister of state during the Revolution. He was imprisoned and released with an amnesty in 1959.

Tisza, István, Count (1861–1918)
Hungarian great estate owner and lawyer. Prime minister (1903–1905, 1913–1917). He was murdered in his home (1918).

Tito, Josip Broz (1892–1980)
Leader of the Second Yugoslavia (1943–1991). He organized the anti-fascist resistance movement, founded the Cominform, and founded and promoted the Non-Aligned Movement.

Tombor, Jenő (1880–1946)
Hungarian military officer and journalist. National Assembly representative (1945) and minister of defense (1945–1946).

Trotsky, Leon (Lev Davidovich Bronstein) (1879–1940)
Ukrainian-born Bolshevik revolutionary and Marxist theorist. Founder and commander of the Red Army. One of the first members of the Politburo. He was expelled from the Communist Party after Stalin's takeover and assassinated in Mexico by a Soviet agent.

Ugron, Gábor (1847–1911)
Hungarian publicist and politician. MP. Minister of the interior (1917–1918).

Uszta, Gyula (b. 1914)
Hungarian army officer and Communist politician. He held various high-ranking army positions, and organized the counter-revolutionary armed forces in Budapest in November 1956.

Vaida-Voevod, Alexandru (1872–1950)
Romanian politician. Supporter and spokesman of the union of Transylvania with the Romanian Old Kingdom. Prime minister of Greater Romania.

Varga, Béla (1903–1995)
Hungarian Roman Catholic priest and Smallholders' Party politician. MP (1939–44, 1945–47) and president of the National Assembly (1946). He emigrated (1947). President of the exiles' Hungarian National Committee.

Vattay, Antal (1891–1966)
Hungarian general. Deputy chief (1939) then chief (1944) of the Military Office of the Regent of Hungary from 1939. Commander of the 1st Cavalry Division and inspector of the Cavalry (1942–1944). He was arrested by the Germans.

Vázsonyi, Vilmos (1868–1926)
Hungarian lawyer and politician. MP (1901) and minister of justice (1917–1918).

Veesenmayer, Edmund (1904–1977)
German economist, diplomat of the Third Reich and high-ranking member of the Nazi Party and the SS. Plenipotentiary commissioner and ambassador of Hitler in Hungary. He was sentenced to 20 years' imprisonment but released in 1951. He took part in the economic recovery of West Germany.

Veres, Péter (1897–1970)
Hungarian left-wing socialist writer of peasant origin. Leading figure in the populist movement between the two World Wars, chairman of the National Peasant Party (1945–49), minister of defense (1947–1948). Chairman of the Writers' Union (1954–56), and was an MP from 1945 until his death.

Veress, László (1908–1980)
Hungarian lawyer and diplomat. Head of the Public Relations Office of the Prime Minister, then head of the Foreign Ministry from 1939. He took part in the Hungarian mission for peace in Ankara in 1943. He went to Istanbul, where he received the conditions of cease-fire from the British.

Villani, Frigyes, Baron (1882–1964)
Hungarian ambassador to Italy (1935–40) and to Albania (1935–39).

Voroshilov, Kliment Yefremovich (1881–1969)
Soviet politician. Marshal of the Soviet Union from 1935. Member of the Central Committee of the Communist Party of the Soviet Union (1921–1961). Chairman of the Military Revolutionary Council (1925–1934). Member of the Politburo (1926–1960) and the State Defense Committee during World War II. President of the Presidium of the Supreme Council of the Soviet Union (1953–1960).

Vörös, János (1891–1968)
Hungarian colonel general. Chief of the General Staff in 1944. He went over to the Red Army after the Arrow-Cross takeover. Minister of defense in 1945. Chief of the General Staff again in 1945–1946. One of the signatories to the armistice agreement in Moscow.

Wallenberg, Raoul Gustav (1912–1947?)

Swedish humanitarian sent to Hungary under diplomatic cover to save Hungarian Jews from the Holocaust (by giving them Swedish passports as Swedish nationals). He was arrested on direct orders from Stalin. He either died of a heart attack or was executed in Moscow.

Werth, Henrik (1881–1952)

General of the Hungarian army, of German descent. Chief of the General Staff of the Hungarian army when the Germans attacked the Soviet Union. Openly pro-German.

Wesselényi, Miklós, Baron (1796–1850)

Hungarian statesman. He became one of the leaders of the liberal movement in the Upper House in 1823. Leader of the Opposition at the Diet of 1834. He was imprisoned, and in prison went blind.

Wilson, (Thomas) Woodrow (1856–1924)

American Democratic politician. President of the United States of America (1913–1921). He entered World War I in 1917. His so-called 14 points prepared for the peace treaties, aiming for justice in peace and for the realization of national self-determination.

Zita of Bourbon-Parma, Queen (1892–1989)

The last Empress-consort of Austria and Queen-consort of Hungary. Commonly referred to as Empress Zita.

Zog I, King (Skander bey III, originally Amet Zogu) (1895–1961)

Albanian politician, prime minister, president, and finally King of Albania.

BIBLIOGRAPHY

Primary sources

Amerikai béketervek a háború utáni Magyarországról. Az Egyesült Államok Külügyminisztériumának titkos iratai 1942–1944 (US Peace Plans for Post-War Hungary. Secret Documents of the US State Department, 1942–1944). Ed. Ignác Romsics. Gödöllő: Typovent, 1992.

Bárdossy László a népbíróság előtt (László Bárdossy before the People's Court). Ed. Pál Pritz. Budapest: Maecenas, 1991.

Diplomáciai iratok Magyarország külpolitikájához 1936–1945 (Diplomatic Records on Hungarian Foreign Policy 1936–1945). Vols. I–V. Ed. Magda Ádám, Lajos Kerekes and Gyula Juhász. Budapest: Akadémiai Kiadó (= AK), 1962–1982.

Documents diplomatiques français sur l'histoire du Bassin des Carpates 1918–1932. Vol. I. Ed. Magda Ádám, György Litván and Mária Ormos. Vol. II. Ed. Magda Ádám, György Litván and Mária Ormos. Vol. III. Ed. Magda Ádám, with Katalin Litván, György Litván, István Majoros and Mária Ormos. Vol IV. Ed. Magda Ádám and Mária Ormos. Budapest: AK, 1993–2002.

"...Fegyvertelen álltak az aknamezőn..." Dokumentumok a munkaszolgálat történetéhez Magyarországon (Unarmed in the Minefield. Documents on the History of the Labor Service in Hungary). Vols. I–II. Ed. Elek Karsai. Budapest: Magyar Izraeliták Országos Képviselete, 1962.

A Forradalmi Kormányzótanács jegyzőkönyvei 1919 (Minutes of the Revolutionary Governing Soviet 1919). Ed. Magda Imre and László Szűcs. Budapest: AK, 1986.

528

Francia diplomáciai iratok a Kárpát-medence történetéről,
1918–1919 (French Diplomatic Records on the History of the
Carpathian Basin, 1918–1919). Ed. Magda Ádám and Mária
Ormos. Budapest: AK, 1999.
Francia diplomáciai iratok a Kárpát-medence történetéről.
Trianon, 1919–1920 (French Diplomatic Records on the
History of the Carpathian Basin. Trianon, 1919–1920). Ed.
Magda Ádám and Mária Ormos. Budapest: AK, 2004.
Gömbös, Gyula. *Válogatott politikai beszédek és írások* (Selected
Political Speeches and Writings). Ed. József Vonyó. Budapest:
Osiris Kiadó, 2004.
Halmosy, Dénes. *Nemzetközi szerződések 1918–1945. A két*
világháború közötti korszak és a második világháború leg-
fontosabb politikai szerződései (International Agreements
1918–1945. Main Political Agreements of the Inter-War Period
and World War II). Budapest: Közgazdasági és Jogi
Könyvkiadó (= KJK), 1966.
Hitler hatvannyolc tárgyalása 1939–1944 (Hitler's 68 Negotiations
1939–1944). Vols. I–II. Intr. and sel. György Ránki. Budapest:
Magvető Könyvkiadó (= MKK), 1983.
Horthy Miklós dokumentumok tükrében (Miklós Horthy in the
Light of Documents). Ed. Éva H. Haraszti. Budapest: Balassi
Kiadó, 1993.
Horthy Miklós titkos iratai (Miklós Horthy's Secret Documents).
Ed. Miklós Szinai and László Szűcs. Budapest: Kossuth
Könyvkiadó (= KKK), 1965.
Károlyi Mihály válogatott írásai (Mihály Károlyi's Selected
Writings). Vols. I–II. Budapest: Gondolat Könyvkiadó (= GKK),
1964.
Karsai, Elek. *A magyar ellenforradalmi rendszer külpolitikája*
1927. január 1–1931. augusztus 24. (Foreign Policy of the
Hungarian Counter-Revolutionary System from January 1,
1927, to August 24, 1931). Budapest: KKK, 1967.

Klebelsberg, Kunó. *Tudomány, kultúra, politika. Gróf Klebelsberg Kunó válogatott beszédei és írásai 1917–1932* (Science, Culture, Politics. Selected Speeches and Writings of Count Kunó Klebelsberg 1917–1932).

Lojkó, Miklós. *British Policy on Hungary 1918–1919.* London: University of London, 1995.

Magyar–brit titkos tárgyalások 1943-ban (Hungarian–British Secret Talks in 1943). Ed. Gyula Juhász. Budapest: KKK, 1978.

A magyar munkásmozgalom történetének válogatott dokumentumai (Selected Documents on the History of the Hungarian Labor Movement). Vols. V–VI/A and B. Budapest: Szikra, 1956/KKK, 1959.

Politikai pártok programjai Magyarországon (Programs of Political Parties in Hungary). Vol. II. 1919–1944. Ed. Jenő Gergely etc. Budapest: KKK, 1991.

Nemes, Dénes, ed. *Az ellenforradalom hatalomrajutása és rémuralma Magyarországon 1919–1921* (The Assumption of Power and the Terror of the Counter-Revolution in Hungary 1919–1921). Budapest: Szikra, 1953.

Nemes, Dénes, and Elek Karsai. *Az ellenforradalmi rendszer gazdasági helyzete és politikája Magyarországon 1924–1926* (The Economic Situation and Policy of the Counter-Revolutionary System in Hungary 1924–1926). Budapest: KKK, 1959.

Nemes, Dénes, and Elek Karsai, eds. *A fasiszta rendszer kiépítése és a népnyomor Magyarországon 1921–1924* (Development of the Fascist System and Destitution in Hungary 1921–1924). Budapest: Szikra, 1956.

Papers and Documents Relating to the Foreign Relations of Hungary. Vols. I–II. Budapest: Royal Hungarian Ministry of Foreign Relations, 1939–1946.

Tilkovszky, Loránt. *Bajcsy-Zsilinszky. Írások tőle és róla* (Bajcsy-Zsilinszky. Writings from and about Him). Budapest: KKK, 1986.

Vádirat a nácizmus ellen (Indictment of Nazism). Vols. I–III. Ed.
Ilona Benoschofsky and Elek Karsai. Budapest: Magyar
Izraeliták Országos Képviselete Kiadása, 1958–1967.

Zsigmond, László, ed. *Magyarország és a második világháború*
(Hungary and World War II). Budapest: KKK, 1961.
*A Wilhelmstrasse és Magyarország. Német diplomáciai iratok
Magyarországról 1933–1944* (Wilhelmstrasse and Hungary.
German Diplomatic Records on Hungary 1933–1944). Comp.
György Ránki *et al.* Budapest: KKK, 1968.

Memoirs, journals, speeches, and correspondence

Andorka Rudolf naplója. A madridi követségtől Mauthausenig
(Rudolf Andorka's Diary. From the Madrid Legation to
Mauthausen). Comp., intr., etc. Zsuzsa Lőrincz. Budapest:
KKK, 1978.

Bandholtz, Harry Hill. *An Undiplomatic Diary by the American
Member of the Inter-Allied Military Mission to Hungary,
1919–1920.* New York: Columbia University Press, 1933.
http://www.hungarian-history.hu/lib/bandh/bandh.pdf.

Barcza, György. *Diplomata emlékeim 1911–1945* (My Diplomatic
Memoirs 1911–1945). Vols. I–II. Budapest: Európa História
(= EH), 1994.

Bethlen István gróf beszédei és írásai (Speeches and Writings of
Count István Bethlen). Vols. I–II. Budapest: Genius, 1933.

Bethlen István emlékirata (István Bethlen's Memoirs). Ed. Ignác
Romsics. Budapest: Zrínyi Katonai Kiadó (= ZKK), 1988.

Borovichény, Aladár. *A király és kormányzója* (The King and His
Governor). Budapest: EH, 1988.

Böhm, Vilmos. *Két forradalom tüzében* (In the Fire of Two
Revolutions). Munich, 1923. Reprinted: Budapest: GKK,
1990.

Demény, Pál. *Rabságaim* (My Imprisonments). Vols. I–II.
Budapest: MKK, 1989.

Garami, Ernő. *Forrongó Magyarország* (Hungary in Uproar). Leipzig and Vienna: Pegazus, 1922.

Gratz, Gusztáv. *A forradalom kora 1918–1920* (Age of Revolutions 1918–1920). Budapest: AK, 1922.

Hennyey, Gusztáv. *Magyarország sorsa Kelet és Nyugat között* (Hungary's Destiny between East and West). Budapest: Európa Könyvkiadó, 1992.

Horthy, Miklós. *Emlékirataim* (My Memoirs). Budapest: EH, 1990.

Hory, András. *Bukaresttől Varsóig* (From Bucharest to Warsaw). Ed. Pál Pritz. Budapest: GKK, 1987.

Jászi, Oszkár. *Magyar kálvária, magyar föltámadás* (Hungarian Calvary, Hungarian Resurrection). Vienna: n. p., 1920.

Juhász Nagy, Sándor. *A magyar októberi forradalom története. A két forradalom értelme, jelentősége és tanulságai* (History of the Hungarian October Revolution. The Sense, Meaning and Lessons of the Two Revolutions). Budapest: Magyar Hírlap Könyvkiadó, 1988.

Julier, Ferenc. *1914–1918. A világháború magyar szemmel* (1914–1918. The World War through Hungarian Eyes). Budapest: Magyar Szemle Társaság, 1933.

Jungerth Arnóthy, Mihály. *Moszkvai napló* (Moscow Diary). Ed. Péter Sipós and László Szűcs. Budapest: ZKK, 1989.

Kádár, Gyula. *A Ludovikától Sopronkőhidáig* (From the Ludovika to Sopronkőhida). Vols. I–II. Budapest: MKK, 1984.

Kállay, Miklós. *Magyarország miniszterelnöke voltam 1942–1944* (I Was Hungary's Prime Minister 1942–1944). Vols. I–II. Budapest: EH, 1991.

Károlyi, Mihály. *Az egész világ ellen* (Against the Whole World). Budapest: GKK, 1956.

Károlyi, Mihály. *Levelezés* (Correspondence). Vols. I–III. Ed. György Litván and Tibor Hajdu. Budapest: AK, 1978–1991.

Kertész, István. *Magyar békeillúziók 1945–1947* (Hungarian Peace Illusions, 1945–1947). Budapest: EH, 1995.

Kornfeld, Móric. *Trianontól Trianonig. Tanulmányok, dokumentok* (From Trianon to Trianon. Studies and Documents). Ed. Ágnes Széchenyi. Budapest: Corvina Kiadó, 2006.

Lakatos, Géza. *Ahogy én láttam* (As I Saw It). Budapest: EH, 1992.

Nagybaczoni Nagy, Vilmos. *Végzetes esztendők 1938–1945* (Fatal Years 1938–1945). Budapest: GKK, 1986.

Náray, Antal. *Visszaemlékezése, 1945* (Memoir, 1945). Budapest: ZAA, 1988.

Páter Zadravetz titkos naplója (Father Zadravetz's Secret Diary). Ed. György Borsányi. Budapest: KKK, 1967.

Prónay, Pál. *A határban a halál kaszál. Fejezetek Prónay Pál feljegyzéseiből* (Death Reaps on the Border. Chapters from the Observations of Pál Prónay). Ed. Ágnes Szabó and Ervin Pamlényi. Budapest: KKK, 1963.

Serédi, Jusztinián. *Feljegyzései 1941–1944* (Observations 1941–1944). Intr. Sándor Orbán and István Vida. Budapest: ZKK, 1990.

Shvoy, Kálmán. *Titkos naplója és emlékirata 1918–1945* (Secret Diary and Memoir 1918–1945). Ed. Mihály Perneki. Budapest: KKK, 1983.

Stomm, Marcel. *Emlékiratok* (Memoirs). Ed. Ferenc Gallyas. Budapest: Magyar Hírlap Könyvek, 1990.

Szombathelyi, Ferenc. *Visszaemlékezései 1945* (Reminiscences 1945). Ed. Péter Gosztonyi. Budapest: ZAA, 1990

Ullein-Reviczky, Antal. *Német háború—orosz béke* (German War—Russian Peace). Ed. László Antal. Budapest: EH, 1993.

Vattay, Antal. *Naplója 1944–1945* (Diary 1944–1945). Budapest: ZAA, 1990.

Comprehensive studies

Hóman, Bálint, and Gyula Szekfű. *Magyar történet* (Hungarian History). Vol. V. Reprint: Budapest: Maecenas, 1990.

Honvári, János. *Magyarország gazdaságtörténete Trianontól a rendszerváltásig* (Economic History of Hungary from Trianon to the Change of System). Budapest: Aula Kiadó, 2005.

Magyarország hadtörténete (Military History of Hungary). Vol. II. Ed. Ervin Liptai. Budapest: ZKK, 1985.

Magyarország története (History of Hungary). Vol. VIII (1919–1945). Ed. György Ránki. 3rd ed. Budapest: AK, 1986.

Magyarország története 1918–1945 (History of Hungary 1918–1945). University textbook. Budapest: Korona Kiadó, n. d.

L. Nagy, Zsuzsa. *Magyarország története 1919–1945* (History of Hungary 1919–1945). University Notes. 2nd ed. Debrecen: Multiplex Média, 1995.

Romsics, Ignác. *Magyarország története a XX. században* (History of Hungary in the 20th Century). Budapest: Osiris Kiadó, 1999.

Studies on subjects referred to in this book

Ablonczy, Balázs. *Teleki Pál* (Pál Teleki). Budapest: Osiris Kiadó, 2005.

Ádám, Magda. *A kisantant (1920–1938)* (The Little Entente 1920–1938). Budapest: KKK, 1981.

Ádám, Magda. *A kisantant és Európa 1920–1929* (The Little Entente and Europe 1920–1929). Budapest: AK, 1989.

Arday, Lajos. *Térkép csata után. Magyarország a brit politikában 1918–1919* (Map after Battle. Hungary in British Politics 1918–1919). Budapest: MKK, 1990.

Beller, Béla. *A magyarországi németek rövid története* (Short History of the Germans in Hungary). Budapest: MKK, 1981.

Berend, T. Iván, and György Ránki. *A magyar gazdaság száz éve* (One Hundred Years of the Hungarian Economy). Budapest: KKK, 1972.

Berend, T. Iván, and György Ránki. *Közép-Kelet-Európa gazdasági fejlődése a 19–20. században* (Economic Development of

Central-Eastern Europe in the 19th and 20th Centuries). Budapest: KJK, 1976.

Berend, T. Iván, and Miklós Szuhay. *A tőkés gazdaság története Magyarországon 1848–1944* (History of the Capitalist Economy in Hungary 1848–1944). Budapest: KJK, 1973.

Borsányi, György. *Kun Béla* (Béla Kun). Budapest: KKK, 1979.

Borsányi, György. *Októbertől márciusig. Polgári demokrácia Magyarországon* (October to March. Bourgeois Democracy in Hungary). Budapest: KKK, 1988.

Braham, Randolf L. *A magyar Holocaust*. Vols. I–II. Budapest/ Wilmington: GKK/Blackbourn Int'l Inc., 1988 (= *The Politics of Genocide: The Holocaust in Hungary*. New York: Columbia University Press, 1981).

Csatári, Dániel. *Forgószélben* (In a Whirlwind). Budapest: AK, 1968.

Diószegi, István. *A hatalmi politika másfél évszázada 1789–1939* (A Century and a Half of Power Politics 1789–1939). Budapest: História/MTA Történettudományi Intézet, 1994.

Dombrády, Lóránd. *Hadsereg és politika Magyarországon 1938– 1944* (Army and Politics in Hungary 1938–1944). Budapest: KKK, 1986.

Dombrády, Lóránd. *A Legfelsőbb Hadúr és hadserege* (The Supreme Commander and His Army). Budapest: ZKK, 1990.

Dombrády, Lóránd, and Sándor Tóth. *A Magyar Királyi Honvédség 1919–1945* (The Royal Hungarian Army 1919–1945). Budapest: ZKK, 1987.

Eördögh, István. *Alle origini dell'espansionismo romeno nella Transilvana ungherese (1916–1920)*. Cosenza: Edizione Periferia, 1992.

Fehér, Ferenc, and Ágnes Heller. *Yalta után* (After Yalta). Budapest: KKK, 1990.

Fejtő, Ferenc. *Rekviem egy hajdanvolt birodalomért. Ausztria-Magyarország szétrombolása* (Requiem for a Former Empire. The Destruction of Austria–Hungary). Budapest: Minerva/

Atlantisz, 1990 (= François Fejto: *Requiem pour un empire defunt: histoire de la destruction de l'Autriche-Hongrie*. Paris: Lieu commun, 1988).

Galántai, József. *Magyarország az első világháborúban 1914–1918* (Hungary in the First World War 1914–1918). Budapest: AK, 1974.

Galántai, József. *A trianoni békekötés 1920* (The Peace Treaty of Trianon 1920). Budapest: GKK, 1990.

Gati, Charles. *Magyarország a Kreml árnyékában* (Hungary in the Kremlin's Shadow). Budapest: Századvég, 1990 (= *Hungary and the Soviet Bloc*. Durham, NC: Duke University Press, 1986).

Gergely, Ferenc. *A magyar cserkészet története 1910–1948* (History of Hungarian Scouting 1910–1948). Budapest: Göncöl Kiadó, 1989.

Gergely, Ferenc, and György Kiss. *Horthy leventei* (Horthy's *Levente* Movement). Budapest: KKK, 1976.

Gergely, Jenő. *A kereszténys zocializmus Magyarországon 1903–1923* (Christian Socialism in Hungary 1903–1923). Budapest: AK, 1977.

Gergely, Jenő. *Gömbös Gyula. Politikai pályakép* (Gyula Gömbös. Political Career). Budapest: Vince Kiadó, 2001.

Gerő, András. *A magyar polgárosodás* (Hungarian Embourgeoisement). Budapest: Atlantisz, 1993.

Glatz, Ferenc. *Nemzeti kultúra—kulturált Nemzet 1867–1987* (National Culture—Cultured Nation 1867–1987). Budapest: KKK, 1988.

Godó, Ágnes. *Magyarok az európai népek antifasiszta harcaiban* (Hungarians in the Anti-Fascist Struggles of the European Peoples). Budapest: Tudományos Ismeretterjesztő Társulat, 1980.

Gosztonyi, Péter. *Légiveszély, Budapest!* (Air Raid Warning, Budapest!). Budapest: Népszava Kiadó, 1989.

Gosztonyi, Péter. *A kormányzó, Horthy Miklós* (Governor Miklós Horthy). Budapest: Téka Könyvkiadó, 1990.

Gosztonyi, Péter. *A magyar honvédség a második világháborúban* (The Hungarian Army in World War II). Budapest: Európa Könyvkiadó, 1992.

Gunszt, Péter. *A paraszti társadalom Magyarorszagon a két világháború között* (Peasant Society in Hungary between the World Wars). Budapest: MTA Történettudományi Intézet, 1987.

Hajdu, Tibor. *Az 1918-as magyarországi polgári demokratikus forradalom* (The 1918 Hungarian Bourgeois Democratic Revolution). Budapest: KKK, 1968.

Hajdu, Tibor. *A Magyarországi Tanácsköztársaság* (The Hungarian Soviet Republic). Budapest: KKK, 1969.

Hajdu, Tibor. *Károlyi Mihály* (Mihály Károlyi). Budapest: KKK, 1978.

Helyünk Európában. Nézetek és koncepciók a 20. századi Magyarországon (Our Place in Europe. Views and Concepts in 20th-Century Hungary). Ed. Éva Ring. Vol. I. Budapest: MKK, 1987.

A History of Hungary. Ed. Peter F. Sugár. Bloomington/Indianapolis: Indiana University Press, 1990, pp. 267–367.

Jelavich, Barbara. *A Balkán története. II. A 20. század.* Budapest: Osiris/2000, 1996 (= History of the Balkans. Vol. 2. Twentieth Century. Cambridge: Cambridge University Press, 1983).

Jeszenszky, Géza. *Az elveszett presztízs* (Lost Prestige). Budapest: Magyar Szemle Alapítvány, 1994.

Juhász, Gyula. *Magyarország külpolitikája 1919–1945* (Hungary's Foreign Policy 1919–1945). Budapest: KKK, 1969.

Juhász, Gyula. *A Teleki kormány külpolitikája 1939–1941* (Foreign Policy of the Teleki Government 1939–1941). Budapest: AK, 1969.

Juhász, Gyula. *Uralkodó eszmék Magyarországon 1939–1944* (Dominant Ideas in Hungary 1939–1944). Budapest: KKK, 1983.

Kardos, József. *A szent-korona tan története 1919–1944* (History of the Doctrine of the Holy Crown 1919–1944). Budapest: Ikva, 1991.

Karsai, Elek: *"Szálasi naplója"*. *A nyilasmozgalom a II. világháború idején* ("Szálasi's Diary." The Arrow-Cross during World War II). Budapest: KKK, 1978.

Katzburg, Nathaniel. *Hungary and the Jews 1920–1943*. Jerusalem: Bar-Ilan University Press, 1981.

Kiútkeresés 1943 (Seeking a Way Out 1943). Ed. Zsuzsa L. Nagy and Kornélia Burucs. Budapest: KKK, 1989.

Kónya, Sándor. *Gömbös kísérlete a totális fasiszta diktatúra megteremtésére* (Gömbös's Attempt to Create Total Fascist Dictatorship). Budapest: AK, 1968.

Korom, Mihály. *Magyarország Ideiglenes Nemzeti Kormánya és a fegyverszünet 1944–1945* (Hungary's Provisional National Government and the Cease-Fire 1944–1945). Budapest: AK, 1981.

Kovács, Endre. *Magyar–lengyel kapcsolatok a két világháború között* (Hungarian–Polish Relations between the Two World Wars). Budapest: AK, 1971.

Lackó, Miklós. *Nyilasok, nemzetiszocialisták 1935–1944* (Arrow-Cross and National Socialists 1935–1944). Budapest: KKK, 1966.

Magyarország és a nagyhatalmak a 20. században. Tanulmányok (Hungary and the Great Powers in the 20th Century. Studies). Ed. Ignác Romsics. Budapest: Teleki László Alapítvány, 1995.

Magyarország miniszterelnökei 1848–1990 (Hungary's Prime Ministers 1848–1990). Ed. Lajos Izsák. Budapest: Cégér Kiadó, 1993.

Nagy, József. *A Nagyatádi-féle földreform 1920–1928* (Nagyatádi's Land Reform 1920–1928). Eger: Bessenyei Kiadó, 1993.

Nagy, Zsuzsa L. *A párizsi békekonferencia és Magyarország 1918–1919* (The Paris Peace Conference and Hungary 1918–1919). Budapest: KKK, 1965.

Nagy, Zsuzsa L. *Bethlen liberális ellenzéke* (Bethlen's Liberal Opposition). Budapest: AK, 1980.

Nagy, Zsuzsa L. *Liberális pártmozgalmak 1931–1945* (Liberal Party Movements 1931–1945). Budapest: AK, 1986.

Ormos, Mária. *Merénylet Marseille-ben* (Outrage in Marseille). 2nd ed. Budapest: KKK, 1984.

Ormos, Mária. *Padovától Trianonig 1918–1920*. Budapest: KKK, 1983–1984 (= *From Padua to the Trianon 1918–1920*. Budapest: AK, 1990).

Ormos, Mária. *Civitas fidelissima. Népszavazás Sopronban 1921* (*Civitas fidelissima*. Plebiscite in Sopron 1921). Győr: Gordiusz Kiadó, 1990.

Ormos, Mária. *"Soha, amíg élek!"* *Az utolsó koronás Habsburg puccskísérletei 1921-ben* ("Never While I'm Alive!" The Last Crowned Habsburg King's Attempts at a Coup in 1921). Pécs: Pannonia Könyvek, 1990.

Ormos, Mária, ed. *Az 1924. évi magyar államkölcsön megszerzése* (Obtaining the 1924 Loan to the Hungarian State). Budapest: AK, 1964.

Ölvedi, Ignác. *Az 1. magyar hadsereg története 1944. január 6-tól október 17-ig* (History of Hungary's First Army January 6–October 17, 1944). Budapest: ZKK, 1989.

Parlamenti képviselőválasztások 1920–1990 (Parliamentary Elections 1920–1990). Ed. György Földes and László Hubay. Budapest: Politikatörténeti Alapítvány, 1994.

Pastor, Peter. "Hungary between Wilson and Lenin. The Hungarian Revolution of 1918–1919 and the Big Three." *East European Quarterly* 20 (1976).

Pölöskei, Ferenc. *Horthy Miklós és hatalmi rendszere 1919–1922* (Miklós Horthy and His System of Power 1919–1922). Budapest: KKK, 1977.

Pölöskei, Ferenc. *A rejtélyes Tisza-gyilkosság* (The Mysterious Tisza Murder). Budapest: Helikon Kiadó, 1988.

Pritz, Pál. *Magyarország külpolitikája Gömbös Gyula miniszterelnöksége idején 1932–1936* (Hungary's Foreign Policy under the Premiership of Gyula Gömbös 1932–1936). Budapest: AK, 1982.

Pritz, Pál. *Magyar diplomácia a két világháború között* (Hungarian Diplomacy between the Two World Wars). Budapest: Magyar Történelmi Társulat, 1995.

Pritz, Pál. *Bárdossy Lajos* (Lajos Bárdossy). Budapest: Elektra Kiadóház, 2001.

Raffay, Ernő. *Trianon titkai, vagy hogyan bántak el országunkkal?* (Secrets of Trianon, or How They Treated This Country). Budapest: Tornado Damenija Kft, 1990.

Ránki, György. *Emlékiratok és valóság Magyarország második világháborús szerepéről* (Memoirs and Reality, on Hungary's Role in World War II). Budapest: KKK, 1964.

Ránki, György. *1944. március 19. Magyarország német megszállása* (March 19, 1944. German Occupation of Hungary). Budapest: KKK, 1978.

Ránki, György. *Mozgásterek, kényszerpályák. Válogatott tanulmányok* (Spaces for Action, Paths of Compulsion. Selected Studies). Budapest: MKK, 1983.

Ránki, György. *A Harmadik Birodalom árnyékában* (In the Shadow of the Third Reich). Budapest: MKK, 1988.

Romsics, Ignác. *Bethlen István. Politikai életrajz* (István Bethlen. Political Biography). Budapest: Magyarságkutató Intézet, 1991.

Romsics, Ignác. *Helyünk és sorsunk a Duna-medencében* (Our Place and Destiny in the Danube Basin). Budapest: Osiris Kiadó, 1996.

Rozsnyói, Ágnes. *A Szálasi-puccs* (The Szálasi Coup). Budapest: KKK, 1977.

Salamon, Konrád. *A Márciusi Front* (The March Front). Budapest: AK, 1980.

Sebestyén, Sándor. *Bajcsy-Zsilinszky Nemzeti Radikális Pártja 1930–1936* (Bajcsy-Zsilinszky's National Radical Party 1930–1936). Budapest: Tankönyvkiadó, 1988.

Sipos, Péter. *Imrédy Béla és a Magyar Megújulás Pártja* (Béla Imrédy and the Party of Hungarian Renewal). Budapest: AK, 1970.

Sipos, Péter. *Legális és illegális munkásmozgalom 1919–1944* (Legal and Illegal Labor Movement 1919–1944). Budapest: GKK, 1988.

Stark, Tamás. *Magyarország második világháborús embervesztesége* (Hungary's Loss of Life in World War II). Budapest: MTA Történettudományi Intézet, 1989.

Stark, Tamás. *Hadak utján. A Magyar Királyi Honvédség a második világháborúban* (On the Path to War. The Royal Hungarian Defense Force in World War II). Budapest: Corvina Kiadó, 1991.

Szábó, Miklós. *Politikai kultúra Magyarországon 1896–1996* (Political Culture in Hungary 1896–1996). Budapest: Atlantisz, 1989.

Szakács, Kálmán. *Kaszáskeresztesek* (Scythe-Cross). Budapest: KKK, 1963.

Szakály, Sándor. *Hadsereg, politika, társadalom* (Army, Politics, Society). Budapest: Lánchíd Kiadó, 1991.

Szekfű, Gyula. *Három nemzedék és ami utána következik* (Three Generations and What Comes Afterwards). Reprint. Budapest: AKV–Maecenas, 1989.

Szita, Szabolcs. *Halálerőd. A munkaszolgálat és a hadimunka történetéhez 1944–1945* (Fortress of Death. History of the Labor Service and War Work 1944–1945). Budapest/Dabas: KKK, 1989.

Szita, Szabolcs. *A Magyar Gyáriparosok Országos Szövetsége. A GyOSz kiépítése és tevékenysége 1902-től 1948-ig* (Hungarian National Federation of Industrials. Structure and Activity 1902–1948). Budapest: MGYOSZ-Könyvek, 1997.

Tar, Imre. *A parasztság társadalmi-termelési viszonyainak átalakulása 1930–1985* (Transformation of the Social/Productive Relations of the Peasantry 1930–1985) Budapest: KKK, 1988.

Tóth, Tibor. *A magyar mezőgazdasági struktúrája az 1930-as években* (Structure of Hungarian Agriculture in the 1930s). Budapest: AK, 1988.

Teleki, Éva. *Nyilasuralom Magyarországon 1944–1945* (Arrow-Cross Rule in Hungary 1944–1945). Budapest: KKK, 1974.

Tilkovszky, Lóránt. *Teleki Pál. Legenda és valóság* (Pál Teleki. Legend and Reality). Budapest: KKK, 1969 (Abridged: *Pál Teleki (1879–1941)*. *A Biographical Sketch*. Budapest: AK, 1974).

Tilkovszky, Lóránt. *Ez volt a Volksbund* (This Was the *Volksbund*). Budapest: KKK, 1978.

Tilkovszky, Lóránt. *Nemzetiség és magyarság* (National Affiliation and Hungarian-ness). Budapest: Ikva, 1994.

Varga, Lajos. *Garami Ernő* (Ernő Garami). Budapest: Napvilág Kiadó, 1996.

Vargyai, Gyula. *A hadsereg politikai funkciói Magyarországon az 1930-as években* (The Political Function of the Army in Hungary in the 1930s). Budapest: AK, 1983.

Vigh, Károly. *Bajcsy-Zsilinszky Endre* (Endre Bajcsy-Zsilinszky). Budapest: Szépirodalmi Könyvek, 1992.

Vigh, Károly. *Ugrás a sötétbe* (Leap in the Dark). Budapest: MKK, 1992.

Zsidókérdés, asszimiláció, antiszemitizmus. Tanulmányok a zsidókérdésről a huszadik századi Magyarországon (Jewish Question, Assimilation, Anti-Semitism. Studies on the Jewish Question in Twentieth-Century Hungary). Ed. Péter Hanák. Budapest: GKK, 1984.

Name Index

Place Index

A = Austria; B = Belgium; BG = Bulgaria; BR = Belarus; CDN = Canada; CH = Switzerland; CZ = Czech Republic; D = Germany; E = Spain; F = France; FIN = Finland; G = Greece; GB = Great Britain; HR = Croatia; I = Italy; IR = Iran; IS = Iceland; J = Japan; M = Macedonia; NL = Netherlands; PL = Poland; PRC = China; RO = Romania; RUS = Russia; SK = Slovakia; SL = Slovenia; SRB = Serbia; TR = Turkey; UA = Ukraine; USA = United States of America; V = Vatican

Ágfalva 100
Ajka 373
Amsterdam (NL) 134
Ankara (TR) 140, 526
Arad (RO) 26, 36, 50, 423, 497
Athens (G) 140, 506
Auschwitz (Oswięcim, PL) 415, 421
Baja 26-27, 99
Balatonszárszó 333, 502
Barcs 26
Battonya 423, 503
Belgrade (SRB) 26-28, 45, 48, 63, 93, 99, 103, 137, 285, 313, 365, 496, 502, 506
Berchtesgaden (D) 294
Berlin (D) 138, 208, 218, 238, 247-249, 262-263, 275, 277, 279, 290, 295, 297, 300, 304, 308-309, 344-345, 349-350, 354, 362, 364, 368, 370, 393-394, 408, 410-411, 413, 479-481, 500, 503, 505, 514, 524
Beszterce (Bistrița, RO) 26
Biatorbágy 223, 500
Bled (HR) 290-292, 501
Brassó (Brașov, RO) 423
Brest-Litovsk (Brest, BR) 11, 13, 45, 511
Bruck (A) 51, 91
Bucharest (RO) 16, 18, 45, 48, 72, 93, 358, 392, 422-423, 452, 492, 495, 507, 511, 532
Buda (part of Budapest) 179, 260, 420, 443, 446-447, 498
Budaörs 68, 102, 262, 313, 498

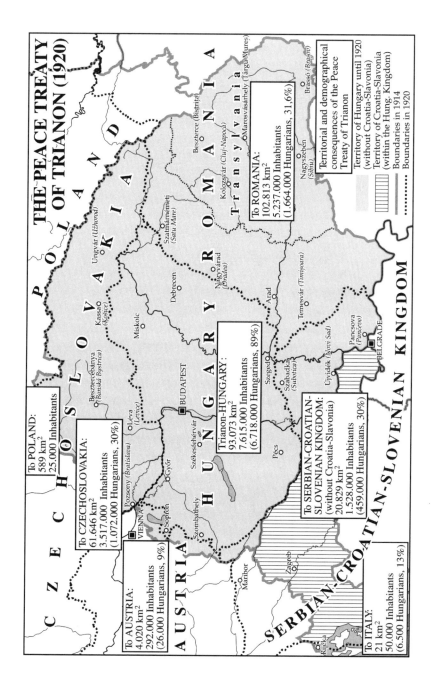

THE PEACE TREATY OF TRIANON (1920)

Territorial and demographical consequences of the Peace Treaty of Trianon

Territory of Hungary until 1920 (without Croatia-Slavonia)

Territory of Croatia-Slavonia (within the Hung. Kingdom)

Boundaries in 1914

Boundaries in 1920

To POLAND:
589 km²
25.000 Inhabitants

To CZECHOSLOVAKIA:
61.646 km²
3.517.000 Inhabitants
(1.072.000 Hungarians, 30%)

To AUSTRIA:
4.020 km²
292.000 Inhabitants
(26.000 Hungarians, 9%)

Trianon-HUNGARY:
93.073 km²
7.615.000 Inhabitants
(6.718.000 Hungarians, 89%)

To ROMANIA:
102.813 km²
5.237.000 Inhabitants
(1.664.000 Hungarians, 31,6%)

To SERBIAN-CROATIAN-SLOVENIAN KINGDOM:
(without Croatia-Slavonia)
20.829 km²
1.528.000 Inhabitants
(459.000 Hungarians, 30%)

To ITALY:
21 km²
50.000 Inhabitants
(6.500 Hungarians, 13%)

POLAND

CZECHOSLOVAKIA

ROMANIA

Transylvania

HUNGARY

AUSTRIA

SERBIAN-CROATIAN-SLOVENIAN KINGDOM

BUDAPEST

VIENNA

BELGRADE

Ungvár (Užhorod)

Szatmárnémeti (Satu Mare)

Beszterce (Bistrița)

Marosvásárhely (Târgu Mureș)

Brassó (Brașov)

Nagyszeben (Sibiu)

Kolozsvár (Cluj-Napoca)

Nagyvárad (Oradea)

Debrecen

Arad

Temesvár (Timișoara)

Kassa (Košice)

Miskolc

Besztercebánya (Banská Bystrica)

Léva (Levice)

Pozsony (Bratislava)

Győr

Székesfehérvár

Sopron

Szombathely

Pécs

Szeged

Szabadka (Subotica)

Újvidék (Novi Sad)

Pancsova (Pančevo)

Zagreb

Maribor

Rijeka (Fiume)

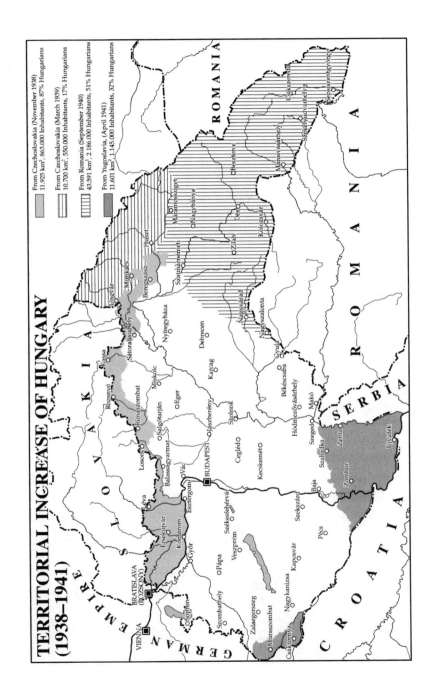

TERRITORIAL INCREASE OF HUNGARY
(1938–1941)

From Czechoslovakia (November 1938)
11,925 km², 863,000 Inhabitants, 87% Hungarians

From Czechoslovakia (March 1939)
10,700 km², 550,000 Inhabitants, 17% Hungarians

From Romania (September 1940)
43,591 km², 2,186,000 Inhabitants, 51% Hungarians

From Yugoslavia, (April 1941)
11,601 km², 1,145,000 Inhabitants, 32% Hungarians

Volumes Published in
"Atlantic Studies on Society in Change"

No. 1   *Tolerance and Movements of Religious Dissent in Eastern Europe.* Edited by Béla K. Király. 1977.

No. 2   *The Habsburg Empire in World War I.* Edited by R. A. Kann. 1978

No. 3   *The Mutual Effects of the Islamic and Judeo-Christian Worlds: The East European Pattern.* Edited by A. Ascher, T. Halasi-Kun, B. K. Király. 1979.

No. 4   *Before Watergate: Problems of Corruption in American Society.* Edited by A. S. Eisenstadt, A. Hoogenboom, H. L. Trefousse. 1979.

No. 5   *East Central European Perceptions of Early America.* Edited by B. K. Király and G. Barány. 1977.

No. 6   *The Hungarian Revolution of 1956 in Retrospect.* Edited by B. K. Király and Paul Jonas. 1978.

No. 7   *Brooklyn U.S.A.: Fourth Largest City in America.* Edited by Rita S. Miller. 1979.

No. 8   *Prime Minister Gyula Andrássy's Influence on Habsburg Foreign Policy.* János Decsy. 1979.

No. 9   *The Great Impeacher: A Political Biography of James M. Ashley.* Robert F. Horowitz. 1979.

No. 10   *Special Topics and Generalizations on the Eighteenth and*
Vol. I*   *Nineteenth Century.* Edited by Béla K. Király and Gunther E. Rothenberg. 1979.

No. 11   *East Central European Society and War in the Pre-*
Vol. II   *Revolutionary 18ᵗʰ Century.* Edited by Gunther E. Rothenberg, Béla K. Király, and Peter F. Sugar. 1982.

* Vols. no. I through XLI refer to the series *War and Society in East Central Europe*

559

No. 27   *Germans in America: Aspects of German-American Relations in the Nineteenth Century.* Edited by Allen McCormick. 1983.

No. 28   *A Question of Empire: Leopold I and the War of Spanish Succession, 1701-1705.* Linda and Marsha Frey. 1983.

No. 29   *The Beginning of Cyrillic Printing — Cracow, 1491. From the Orthodox Past in Poland.* Szczepan K. Zimmer. Edited by Ludwik Krzyżanowski and Irene Nagurski. 1983.

No. 29a   *A Grand Ecole for the Grand Corps: The Recruitment and Training of the French Administration.* Thomas R. Osborne. 1983.

No. 30   *The First War between Socialist States: The Hungarian*
Vol. XI   *Revolution of 1956 and Its Impact.* Edited by Béla K. Király, Barbara Lotze, Nandor Dreisziger. 1984.

No. 31   *The Effects of World War I, The Uprooted: Hungarian*
Vol. XII   *Refugees and Their Impact on Hungary's Domestic Politics.* István Mócsy. 1983.

No. 32   *The Effects of World War I: The Class War after the Great*
Vol. XIII   *War: The Rise of Communist Parties in East Central Europe, 1918-1921.* Edited by Ivo Banac. 1983.

No. 33   *The Crucial Decade: East Central European Society and*
Vol. XIV   *National Defense, 1859-1870.* Edited by Béla K. Király. 1984.

No. 35   *Effects of World War I: War Communism in Hungary, 1919.*
Vol. XVI   György Péteri. 1984.

No. 36   *Insurrections, Wars, and the Eastern Crisis in the 1870s.*
Vol. XVII   Edited by B. K. Király and Gale Stokes. 1985.

No. 37   *East Central European Society and the Balkan Wars, 1912-*
Vol. XVIII *1913.* Edited by B. K. Király and Dimitrije Djordjevic. 1986.

No. 38   *East Central European Society in World War I.* Edited by B.
Vol. XIX   K. Király and N. F. Dreisziger, Assistant Editor Albert A. Nofi. 1985.

No. 39   *Revolutions and Interventions in Hungary and Its Neighbor*
Vol. XX   *States, 1918-1919.* Edited by Peter Pastor. 1988.

562 Volumes

No. 41
Vol. XXII
Essays on East Central European Society and War, 1740-1920. Edited by Stephen Fischer-Galati and Béla K. Király. 1988.

No. 42
Vol. XXIII
East Central European Maritime Commerce and Naval Policies, 1789-1913. Edited by Apostolos E. Vacalopoulos, Constantinos D. Svolopoulos, and Béla K. Király. 1988.

No. 43
Vol. XXIV
Selections, Social Origins, Education and Training of East Central European Officers Corps. Edited by Béla K. Király and Walter Scott Dillard. 1988.

No. 44
Vol. XXV
East Central European War Leaders: Civilian and Military. Edited by Béla K. Király and Albert Nofi. 1988.

No. 46
Germany's International Monetary Policy and the European Monetary System. Hugo Kaufmann. 1985.

No. 47
Iran Since the Revolution—Internal Dynamics, Regional Conflicts and the Superpowers. Edited by Barry M. Rosen. 1985.

No. 48
Vol. XXVII
The Press During the Hungarian Revolution of 1848-1849. Domokos Kosáry. 1986.

No. 49
The Spanish Inquisition and the Inquisitional Mind. Edited by Angel Alcala. 1987.

No. 50
Catholics, the State and the European Radical Right, 1919-1945. Edited by Richard Wolff and Jorg K. Hoensch. 1987.

No. 51
Vol.XXVIII
The Boer War and Military Reforms. Jay Stone and Erwin A. Schmidl. 1987.

No. 52
Baron Joseph Eötvös, A Literary Biography. Steven B. Várdy. 1987.

No. 53
Towards the Renaissance of Puerto Rican Studies: Ethnic and Area Studies in University Education. Maria Sanchez and Antonio M. Stevens. 1987.

No. 54
The Brazilian Diamonds in Contracts, Contraband and Capital. Harry Bernstein. 1987.

No. 55
Christians, Jews and Other Worlds: Patterns of Conflict and Accommodation. Edited by Philip F. Gallagher. 1988.

No. 56
Vol. XXVI
The Fall of the Medieval Kingdom of Hungary: Mohács 1526, Buda 1541. Géza Perjés. 1989.

No. 57   *The Lord Mayor of Lisbon: The Portuguese Tribune of the People and His 24 Guilds.* Harry Bernstein. 1989.

No. 58   *Hungarian Statesmen of Destiny: 1860-1960.* Edited by Paul Bödy. 1989.

No. 59   *For China: The Memoirs of T. G. Li, Former Major General in the Chinese Nationalist Army.* T. G. Li. Written in collaboration with Roman Rome. 1989.

No. 60   *Politics in Hungary: For A Democratic Alternative.* János Kis, with an Introduction by Timothy Garton Ash. 1989.

No. 61   *Hungarian Worker's Councils in 1956.* Edited by Bill Lomax. 1990.

No. 62   *Essays on the Structure and Reform of Centrally Planned Economic Systems.* Paul Jonas. A joint publication with Corvina Kiadó, Budapest. 1990.

No. 63   *Kossuth as a Journalist in England.* Éva H. Haraszti. A joint publication with Akadémiai Kiadó, Budapest. 1990.

No. 64   *From Padua to the Trianon, 1918-1920.* Mária Ormos. A joint publication with Akadémiai Kiadó, Budapest. 1990.

No. 65   *Towns in Medieval Hungary.* Edited by László Gerevich. A joint publication with Akadémiai Kiadó, Budapest. 1990.

No. 66   *The Nationalities Problem in Transylvania, 1867-1940.* Sándor Bíró. 1992.

No. 67   *Hungarian Exiles and the Romanian National Movement, 1849-1867.* Béla Borsi-Kálmán. 1991.

No. 68   *The Hungarian Minority's Situation in Ceausescu's Romania.* Edited by Rudolf Joó and Andrew Ludanyi. 1994.

No. 69   *Democracy, Revolution, Self-Determination. Selected Writings.* István Bibó. Edited by Károly Nagy. 1991.

No. 70   *Trianon and the Protection of Minorities.* József Galántai. A joint publication with Corvina Kiadó, Budapest. 1991.

No. 71   *King Saint Stephen of Hungary.* György Györffy. 1994.

No. 72   *Dynasty, Politics and Culture. Selected Essays.* Robert A. Kann. Edited by Stanley B. Winters. 1991.

No. 73   *Jadwiga of Anjou and the Rise of East Central Europe.* Oscar Halecki. Edited by Thaddeus V. Gromada. A joint publication with the Polish Institute of Arts and Sciences of America, New York. 1991.

No. 74   *Hungarian Economy and Society during World War Two.*
Vol. XXIX Edited by György Lengyel. 1993.

No. 75   *The Life of a Communist Revolutionary, Béla Kun.* György Borsányi. 1993.

No. 76   *Yugoslavia: The Process of Disintegration.* Laslo Sekelj. 1993.

No. 77   *Wartime American Plans for a New Hungary. Documents*
Vol. XXX *from the U.S. Department of State, 1942-1944.* Edited by Ignác Romsics. 1992.

No. 78   *Planning for War against Russia and Serbia. Austro-*
Vol. XXXI *Hungarian and German Military Strategies, 1871-1914.* Graydon A. Tunstall, Jr. 1993.

No. 79   *American Effects on Hungarian Imagination and Political Thought, 1559-1848.* Géza Závodszky. 1995.

No. 80   *Trianon and East Central Europe: Antecedents and*
Vol. XXXII *Repercussions.* Edited by Béla K. Király and László Veszprémy. 1995.

No. 81   *Hungarians and Their Neighbors in Modern Times, 1867-1950.* Edited by Ferenc Glatz. 1995.

No. 82   *István Bethlen: A Great Conservative Statesman of Hungary, 1874-1946.* Ignác Romsics. 1995.

No. 83   *20ᵗʰ Century Hungary and the Great Powers.* Edited
Vol. XXXIII by Ignác Romsics. 1995.

No. 84   *Lawful Revolution in Hungary, 1989-1994.* Edited by Béla K. Király. András Bozóki Associate Editor. 1995.

No. 85   *The Demography of Contemporary Hungarian Society.* Edited by Pál Péter Tóth and Emil Valkovics. 1996.

No. 86   *Budapest, A History from Its Beginnings to 1996.* Edited By András Gerõ and János Poór. 1996.

No. 87   *The Dominant Ideas of the Nineteenth Century and Their Impact on the State.* Volume 1. *Diagnosis.* József Eötvös.

	Translated, edited, annotated and indexed with an introductory essay by D. Mervyn Jones. 1997.
No. 88	*The Dominant Ideas of the Nineteenth Century and Their Impact on the State.* Volume 2. *Remedy.* József Eötvös. Translated, edited, annotated and indexed with an introductory essay by D. Mervyn Jones. 1997.
No. 89	*The Social History of the Hungarian Intelligentsia in the "Long Nineteenth Century," 1825-1914.* János Mazsu. 1997.
No. 90 Vol.XXXIV	*Pax Britannica: Wartime Foreign Office Documents Regarding Plans for a Post Bellum East Central Europe.* Edited by András D. Bán. 1997.
No. 91	*National Identity in Contemporary Hungary.* György Csepeli. 1997.
No. 92	*The Hungarian Parliament, 1867-1918: A Mirage of Power.* András Gerõ. 1997.
No. 93 Vol. XXXV	*The Hungarian Revolution and War of Independence, 1848-1849. A Military History.* Edited by Gábor Bona. 1999.
No. 94	*Academia and State Socialism: Essays on the Political History of Academic Life in Post-1945 Hungary and East Central Europe.* György Péteri. 1998.
No. 95 Vol.XXXVI	*Through the Prism of the Habsburg Monarchy: Hungary in American Diplomacy and Public Opinion during World War I.* Tibor Glant. 1998.
No. 96	*Appeal of Sovereignty in Hungary, Austria and Russia.* Edited by Csaba Gombár, Elemér Hankiss, László Lengyel and Györgyi Várnai. 1997.
No. 97	*Geopolitics in the Danube Region. Hungarian Reconciliation Efforts, 1848-1998.* Edited by Ignác Romsics and Béla K. Király. 1998.
No. 98	*Hungarian Agrarian Society from the Emancipation of Serfs (1848) to Re-privatization of Land (1998).* Edited by Péter Gunst. 1999.
No. 99	*"The Jewish Question" in Europe. The Case of Hungary.* Tamás Ungvári. 2000.
No. 100	*Soviet Military Intervention in Hungary, 1956.* Edited by Jenõ Györkei and Miklós Horváth. 1999.

No. 101   *Jewish Budapest.* Edited by Géza Komoróczy. 1999.

No. 102   *Evolution of the Hungarian Economy, 1848-1998.* Vol. I. *One-and-a-Half Centuries of Semi-Successful Modernization, 1848-1989.* Edited by Iván T. Berend and Tamás Csató. 2001.

No. 103   *Evolution of the Hungarian Economy, 1848-1998.* Vol. II. *Paying the Bill for Goulash-Communism.* János Kornai. 2000.

No. 104   *Evolution of the Hungarian Economy, 1848-2000.* Vol. III. *Hungary: from Transition to Integration.* Edited by György Csáki and Gábor Karsai. 2001.

No. 105   *From Habsburg Agent to Victorian Scholar: G. G. Zerffi (1820-1892).* Tibor Frank. 2000.

No. 106   *A History of Transylvania from the Beginning to 1919.* Vol. I. Edited by Zoltán Szász and Béla Köpeczi. 2001.

No. 107   *A History of Transylvania from the Beginning to 1919.* Vol. II. Edited by Zoltán Szász and Béla Köpeczi. 2001.

No. 108   *A History of Transylvania from the Beginning to 1919.* Vol. III. Edited by Zoltán Szász and Béla Köpeczi. 2002.

No. 109   *Hungary: Governments and Politics, 1848–2000.* Edited by Mária Ormos and Béla K. Király. 2001.

No. 110   *Hungarians in the Voivodina, 1918–1947.* Enikõ A. Sajti. 2003.

No. 111   *Hungarian Arts and Sciences, 1848–2000.* Edited by László Somlyódy and Nóra Somlyódy. 2003.

No. 112   *Hungary and International Politics in 1848–1849.* Domokos Kosáry. 2003.

No. 113   *Social History of Hungary from the Reform Era to the End of the Twentieth Century.* Edited by Gábor Gyáni, György Kövér and Tibor Valuch. 2003.

No. 114   *A Millennium of Hungarian Military History.* Edited by
Vol.XXXVII László Veszprémy and Béla K. Király. 2002.

No. 115   *Hungarian Relics. A History of the Battle Banners of the 1848-49 Hungarian Revolution and War of Independence.* Jenõ Györkei and Györgyi Cs. Kottra. 2000.

No. 116 *From Totalitarian to Democratic Hungary. Evolution and Transformation, 1990-2000.* Edited by Mária Schmidt and László Gy. Tóth. 2000.

No. 117 *A History of Eastern Europe since the Middle Ages.* Emil Niederhauser. 2003.

No. 118 *The Ideas of the Hungarian Revolution, Suppressed and Victorious, 1956–1999.* Edited by Lee W. Congdon and Béla K. Király. 2002.

No. 119 *The Emancipation of the Serfs in Eastern Europe.* Emil Niederhauser. 2004.

No. 120 *Art of Survival. Hungarian National Defense and Society in Modern Times.* Béla K. Király. Edited by Piroska Balogh and Tamás Vitek. 2003.

No. 121 *Army and Politics in Hungary, 1938–1945.* Lóránd Dombrády.
Vol.XXXVIII Edited by Gyula Rázsó. 2005.

No. 122 *Hungary and the Hungarian Minorities (Trends in the Past and in Our Time).* Edited by László Szarka. 2004.

No. 123 *Roma of Hungary.* Edited by István Kemény. 2005.

No. 124 *National and Ethnic Minorities in Hungary, 1920–2001.* Edited by Ágnes Tóth. 2005.

No. 126 *The Occupation of Bosnia and Herzegovina in 1878.* László
Vol.XXXIX Bencze. 2005.

No. 127 *Wars, Revolutions and Regime Changes in Hungary, 1912–2004. Reminiscences of an Eyewitness.* Béla K. Király. Edited by Piroska Balogh, Andrea T. Kulcsár and Tamás Vitek. 2005.

No. 128 *1956: The Hungarian Revolution and War for Independence.*
Vol.XL Edited by Lee W. Congdon, Béla K. Király and Károly Nagy. 2006.

No. 129 *The History of the Hungarian Military Higher Education*
Vol. XLI *1947–1956.* Miklós M. Szabó. 2006.

No. 133 *Hungary in the Age of the Two World Wars, 1914–1945.* Mária Ormos. 2007.

No. 135 *From Dictatorship to Democracy. The Birth of the Third Hungarian Republic, 1988–2001.* Ignác Romsics. 2007.